Recommended

COUNTRY INNS®

THE SOUTH

Alabama / Arkansas / Florida / Georgia / Kentucky / Louisiana

Mississippi / North Carolina / South Carolina / Tennessee

Seventh Edition

by Carol and Dan Thalimer

illustrated by Duane Perreault

The
Globe
Pequot
Press

OLD SAYBROOK, CONNECTICUT

To Sara Pitzer,
who laid the groundwork

ISBN 0-7627-0299-0
ISSN 1078-5493

Cover photo: (IMA) Akio Inoue/Photonica
Cover and text design: Nancy Freeborn/Freeborn Design

Manufactured in the United States of America
Seventh Edition/First Printing

Contents

About the Authors

CAROL and DAN THALIMER have been associated with the travel industry for seventeen years, and for seven of them they owned travel agencies. During those seventeen years they've inspected dozens of cruise ships and hundreds of hotels, inns, and bed-and-breakfasts and reported on them for travel agent publications and guides such as *Travel Agent Magazine* and *ABC Star Service*. For the past twelve years they have written about travel for fifty magazines and newspapers and for guidebook publishers. They are the authors of *Quick Escapes from Atlanta, Fun with the Family: Georgia,* and *Romantic Days and Nights in Atlanta,* all from The Globe Pequot Press. Their next book for Globe Pequot is *Recommended Bed & Breakfasts: The South.*

Introduction

ince the first edition of this book was published in 1987, it has been called *Recommended Country Inns* and has included urban inns as well as rural bed-and-breakfasts. Some definitions are in order. What's an inn and what's a bed-and-breakfast? In general, we think of an inn as having a restaurant, other amenities such as sports facilities, and somewhere between ten and one hundred rooms, with the vast majority having between twenty-five and fifty rooms. A stay there may or may not include breakfast in the overnight rate. We generally think of a bed-and-breakfast as having ten or fewer rooms and no restaurant. Naturally, it usually does include breakfast in your stay. Unfortunately, every establishment does not fit neatly into either of these categories, so we've devised a third classification: B&B Inn. This describes a property that may be small but has a restaurant or a property that's large but doesn't have a breakfast.

The text for each entry in this book will identify the establishment as an inn or B&B inn. In cases where a property doesn't exactly fit these categories, we've gone with whichever classification we think best describes the hostelry. In a few cases, you'll find establishments that clearly fit the bed-and-breakfast definition. We've kept them in this book to give some states adequate coverage. You'll also find a few inns with more than one hundred rooms: we've included them because we think they have the intimate appeal of a smaller property. If you miss some of your favorites in this edition, it's probably not because they're closed but because we've moved them to a new companion book, *Recommended Bed & Breakfasts: The South,* also published by The Globe Pequot Press.

There are other changes to this new edition: In each chapter some of the inns are designated as a Top Pick, and these outstanding properties have a more thorough description than the others. Sprinkled throughout each chapter you'll also find an amusing anecdote; a recipe; more information about an inn, city, or region; or attractions you shouldn't miss.

SETTING THE STANDARDS

The inspection and requirements an inn must meet before such guides accept them are rigorous and standardized. It means the bathrooms of such places will be reliably clean and the toilet paper folded into a triangle. An escape from standardization, however, is what drove some of us into searching for inns in the first place. As a traveler, one of the main ways you can keep a wave of sameness from overtaking the inn world too is by letting innkeepers know specifically what you like about their facilities and what doesn't matter. If you truly want the most expensive little bottles of shampoo and hand lotion (known as "amenities" in the hospitality business), say so. If you think they're beside the point, say that, too. One of the best inns in the South will never make it into a standardized guide. In each of its bathrooms you'll find a full-sized bar of Ivory soap. Period. No little baskets and bottles. The issue here isn't whether these things are good or bad but whether they matter to you or not. You must speak up or the formal check-sheet of a guide rating will decide for you.

Something else you are bound to notice: The cost of staying at inns has gone up. This is not a result of greed on the part of the innkeepers; it simply reflects an increase in the cost of maintaining a nice inn. If we want private baths as well as pitchers of wildflowers on our breakfast tables, we have to expect to pay for them. If we want Ritz-quality linens as well as muffins made by hand in small batches from old family recipes, we have to expect to help bear the cost.

That's why you can now stay in most motel chains for a lot less than it costs to stay at most inns. The price of a motel is right, but of course the individuality and charm of small inns is missing. Sometimes you still want something special, more personal; when you wake up in the morning you don't want to struggle to remember where you are. That's where inns come in.

As you travel, you are bound to find some wonderful inns that are not in this guide. That's not because we're discriminating against them; it's either because we haven't been able to visit yet or because we don't know them. If you find a must-not-miss inn, let us know. We always follow up on readers' recommendations and have found some of our favorite inns that way.

Sometimes, in spite of our best efforts to choose only very stable inns for this book, an inn changes, declines in quality, and disappoints a reader. We hope it won't happen to you, but if it does, let us know about that, too.

Your comments and questions are invaluable in guiding our travels.

—Carol and Dan Thalimer

How to Use This Inn Guide

*W*orking on the theory that most of us know our alphabet better than our geography, we have arranged the listings in this book alphabetically. The ten Southern states are listed in alphabetical order, as are the towns within each state and the inns (by name) within each town. The maps at the beginning of each chapter show you where the inns are, geographically.

CAVEATS

Rates: Often they are complicated, and they change. We have tried to indicate general ranges here, but you should always discuss rates when you make reservations. They may have gone up, or, as it happens, you may qualify for a discount that you don't know about.

Forms of payment: Innkeepers love cash. Every inn in this book will gleefully accept your folding money or traveler's checks. These days most inns accept Visa and MasterCard, as well as personal checks. Some accept other credit cards, too. We have mentioned under "Rates" if an inn does not accept credit cards or personal checks; nevertheless, when you are making your reservations, it is always a good idea to ask because, as with everything else, these things change, sometimes without notice.

Children: Life used to be so simple. An inn could specify whether children were accepted or not and could even specify what ages were appropriate to the inn. A couple of legal discrimination-against-children battles have changed that. Therefore, in these guides we usually mention children only when an inn welcomes them especially. That doesn't change the fact that some inns are not suited to small children. Some have priceless fragile antiques that could be destroyed by one toddler's misstep; others have lofts, balconies, mountaintop locations, and other features that make the places downright dangerous for children. Moreover, some inns don't have cribs or extra beds to accommodate a child in a room with adults. Don't ever just show up with a child at an inn. It's simply not fair to you or the child or the innkeeper. Talk it over when you call for reservations.

Pets: In the South few inns accept pets. In some cases, it may be because the long warm season and frequent humidity are as pleasing to fleas as they are to sunbathers. More likely, prohibiting pets is a local health regulation, or the owners aren't prepared to have strange pets among their priceless antiques and Oriental rugs. In smaller properties that are actually in the owner's home, there may be family pets. Local laws may or may not restrict them from the kitchen and/or guest areas, so if you are extremely allergic to pets, be sure to check whether there are any in residence. Assume that pets are not accepted unless otherwise noted.

Smoking and Fireplaces: In response to the public furor over smoking and second-hand smoke, more and more places, including large properties, have adopted a "No smoking indoors" policy as a matter of course. In addition, many insurance companies have genuine concerns about fire hazards in fine old frame homes and historic buildings and refuse to grant insurance if smoking is allowed or if wood-burning fireplaces are used. Therefore it is best to assume that in all but the largest properties, smoking will be permitted only outdoors. Larger properties, which are really small hotels, may offer smoking and nonsmoking rooms and permit smoking in the bar. If smoking—its presence or absence—is important to you, ask about it when you make reservations. Smoking policies are definitely in a state of flux, so what we've indicated here may not be the policy by the time you decide to visit.

Many older properties have drop-dead gorgeous fireplaces but don't use them at all for insurance reasons. We've tried to indicate those as "decorative fireplaces." We also indicate the presence of gas-log fireplaces, some with an electric switch starter, as well as the few wood-burning fireplaces that are available. Likewise, if a working fireplace is important to setting the scene for a romantic or just-plain relaxing getaway, be sure to ask. In fact, although many inns have at least one guest room fireplace, very few have a fireplace in every guest room, so it's very important to you to let the innkeeper know that you want one before he/she assigns you a room.

Wheelchair access: Increasingly, inns are finding ways to accommodate wheelchairs, but in some old buildings what they are able to do is limited. Discuss your particular needs with the innkeeper.

Air conditioning, television, and *telephones:* Most inns in the South are air-conditioned these days. The only ones that don't have air conditioning are those at high altitude, where you sleep under blankets even in July and are more apt to be looking for a heater than a cooler. As for television and telephones, there's absolutely no consistency. Some inns have one or the other, some both, some neither. We've listed those facts about each inn in the category "Rooms" in the basic information.

Business travel: Increasingly, business travelers are staying at inns instead of at hotels and motels. To attract corporate business some inns are adding such features as fax and copy service, in-room telephones, and desks. We have noted such features in the basic information following each inn profile. Since the needs for each business traveler differ, we urge you to ask about any features you need. Often an inn can supply them even if they are not advertised.

Booze: One of the most charming features of many small properties has often been the late afternoon/early evening wine-and-cheese reception where you can get to know the innkeepers and your fellow guests. Liquor laws are becoming tougher and tougher on the ability to serve liquor (even for free) without an expensive or impossible-to-get liquor license; insurance liability is causing further restrictions. Inns that have offered this amenity in the past may have had to exchange the wine for something nonalcoholic.

The laws about serving alcohol in the South vary from state to state and from county to county within the states. You can drive the better part of a day in some states—North Carolina, Kentucky, and Arkansas especially—and never get out of dry counties. Some states, such as South Carolina, sell no alcohol on Sunday, except in "open" tourist areas. Others, like North Carolina, don't sell alcoholic beverages until after 1:00 p.m. Some inns, in such states as Tennessee, are in areas that forbid the sale of liquor by the drink but allow the sale of bottled liquor, even though they are in dry counties. We have tried to indicate what to expect at each inn, but if an evening cocktail or wine with dinner is important to you, we suggest that you travel with your own supply. Make sure that you understand the inn's policy before taking alcoholic beverages into any public area. In the South, we use the phrase "brown bagging" to mean bringing spirits of your own into a public place like a restaurant.

Reservations: Make them. You go to inns for personal attention and the feeling of being a special guest. Your responsibility is much the same as it would be if you were going to visit friends. You don't show up without warning. Many bed-and-breakfast inns are in a person's home and there may be no extra staff. If you aren't expected, there may be no one home.

Shared baths and nonattached baths: Shared baths are more common in small bed-and-breakfasts than in inns and B&B inns. We've tried to indicate properties that have any shared baths. Some make a policy of renting only one of the rooms that share a bath at a time unless it would be shared by a family or adults traveling together so that in effect you do have a private bath. In a few cases at older properties, you may have to go out in the hall to get to a private or shared bath, so some inns provide bathrobes. Unless you're absolutely sure that the inn provides robes, if you're likely to be sharing a bath or having to go out in the hall, it's always a good idea to travel with robes.

Special functions: Many properties are used for other functions, such as luncheons, weddings, corporate meetings, and so forth. Some have restaurants and shops, so the public may be wandering through as well. The smaller the property, the more disruptive these other activities may be, so you may want to ask about what else may be going on.

Breakfast: Breakfast can range from true continental (a roll, juice, and coffee) to a vast plantation breakfast that includes enough food for your entire day's sustenance. We've tried to indicate what type of breakfast to expect, but the morning meal may depend on the whims of the chef. Some inns will try to accommodate any special dietary restrictions if given advance notice.

Feedback: If you have any particularly good or not-so-good experiences when visiting any of these properties, we'd like to know about them before we do our next update. We're also interested in suggestions for wonderful inns that aren't included so that we can visit them before the next edition. Please drop a note to the publisher and it will be forwarded to us.

Disclaimer: When studying this guide, please keep in mind that because of the long research, writing, and publishing time involved, some of these inns may no longer be in business. In addition, features and policies at other properties may have changed drastically for the better or worse. This guide is simply meant to give you some ideas about inns you might want to investigate further.

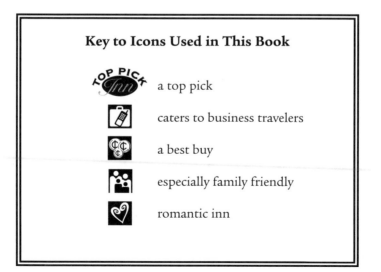

Key to Icons Used in This Book

a top pick

caters to business travelers

a best buy

especially family friendly

romantic inn

Recommended

COUNTRY INNS®

THE SOUTH

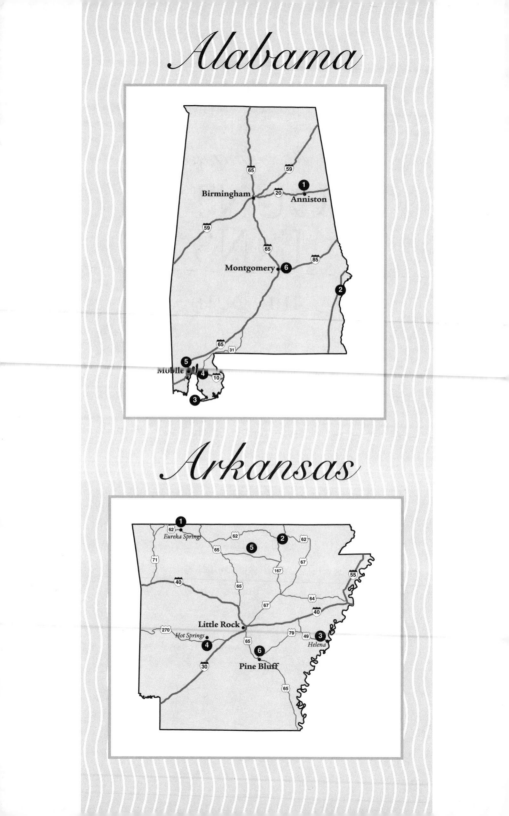

Alabama

Numbers on map refer to towns numbered below.

Arkansas

Numbers on map refer to towns numbered below.

* A Top Pick Inn

The Victoria
Anniston, Alabama 36201

INNKEEPERS: Beth and Fain Casey

ADDRESS/TELEPHONE: 1604 Quintard Avenue (mailing address: P.O. Box 2213); (256) 236–0503 or (800) 260–8781; fax (256) 236–1138

E-MAIL: victoria@thevictoria.com or TheVic97@aol.com

WEB SITE: www.thevictoria.com

ROOMS: 3 suites in main house, 56 rooms in adjacent hotel, 1 guest house; all with private bath, telephone, and cable television, some with whirlpool, some with refrigerator.

RATES: $69 to $79 hotel, double. Single $10 less. Suites $129 to $169. Inquire about guest house rates. Continental breakfast Monday through Saturday, full breakfast Sunday. Two rooms fully equipped for handicapped. No-smoking rooms available.

OPEN: Year-round.

FACILITIES AND ACTIVITIES: Full cocktail service, dining room serves dinner Monday through Saturday for guests and the public by reservation; swimming pool. Nearby: Anniston Museum of Natural History, antiques shops, Cheaha State Park, and Silver Lakes Golf Course on the Robert Trent Jones Trail.

*W*hen you need the kind of escape that makes the real world seem far away and unimportant, try The Victoria, an inn property that fills almost an entire square block in Anniston. The heart of the inn is the rejuvenated 1888 mansion that was once home to several important families in Anniston. But this is not just an old home that's been "fixed up." An architect, some developers, and a general contractor collaborated to preserve the existing structure and add additional spaces for outdoor activities and lodging.

The original house, with its turrets and towers, fairly gleams in the sun. Inside, on the first floor, are dining spaces, a piano lounge, and a glassed-in veranda. In one of many nice touches, the piano lounge is in what was originally the music room of a musically inclined resident toward the end of The Victoria's days as a private home. These rooms are furnished and decorated with parquet floors, elaborate draperies, carved mantels and crystal chandeliers in a style appropriate to the exterior of the building. The food fits the mood, too.

The Victoria's meals keep earning raves. The continental-style cuisine features subtle sauces—nothing swims in excesses of goo here—and uses lots of fresh vegetables and fruits in imaginative ways. The inn has a good wine list and staff knowledgeable enough to help you make appropriate choices.

Although there are three luxury suites furnished with antiques on the third floor of the old house, most of the inn's rooms are in a new hotel building that was designed to blend in with the older structures. Unlike hotels, however, the rooms in this addition are all decorated differently, featuring mostly cool, light colors and comfortable furnishings of pine, wicker, glass, and brass.

We were personally taken with the staff, all of whom struck us as being enthusiastic and unusually professional in demeanor. The entire staff seems to be thoroughly versed in the history of the inn, interesting things to do and see in the area, and simple directions for getting around.

Given the extent of the landscaped grounds, the swimming pool, and the patios on the property, you could enjoy a complete escape and not go anywhere else at all.

HOW TO GET THERE: From I-20, take the Oxford–Anniston exit 185, go north on Highway 21/431 (Quintard Avenue) for 4 miles. The Victoria is on the left side of Quintard.

Kendall Manor Inn and Bed and Breakfast

Eufaula, Alabama 36027

INNKEEPERS: Barbara and Tim Lubsen

ADDRESS/TELEPHONE: 534 West Broad Street; (334) 687–8847; fax: (334) 616–0678

E-MAIL: kmanorinn@aol.com

WEB SITE: www.bbonline.com/al/kendallmanor/

ROOMS: 6; all with private baths.

RATES: $84 to $109; includes full breakfast, welcome beverage, afternoon tea, fresh flowers, a sweet with turndown service. No smoking inn. Children older than age fourteen.

OPEN: All year.

FACILITIES AND ACTIVITIES: Upstairs and downstairs porches, sunny private deck. Dinner served by reservation at additional charge. Nearby: Seth Lore and Irwinton Historic District—the state of Alabama's most extensive collection of Italianate architecture; numerous water sports on Lake Eufaula, called the Big Bass Capital of the World; Eufaula National Wildlife Refuge, Tom Mann's Fish World (one of the most unusual attractions you'll ever visit), Callaway Gardens, Auburn University, U.S. Army Aviation Museum, Farley Nuclear Visitor's Center, Providence Canyon; deer and small-game hunting, hiking, bicycling, golf, nature trails. The Eufaula Pilgrimage and Antiques Show each April draws thousands of visitors, as does the autumn Indian Summer Festival, which celebrates the area's Native American culture.

BUSINESS TRAVEL: Ideal for small meetings and retreats.

*K*endall Manor, a National Register of Historic Places treasure, is the quintessential wedding-cake Victorian, built in the 1860s when cotton was king. An architectural masterpiece in the Italianate style, the majestic two stories are festooned with columns and porches. The mansion is crowned with a graceful towering belvedere, a tall addition to a house that was put there not for its striking good looks but to let hot air escape from the house. Do yourself a favor and make the climb to the belvedere tower. From its tall windows, 75 feet above the street, you can see for miles in every direction.

Despite the breathtaking view, Kendall Manor's belvedere is special in another way. Over the more than one hundred years since the house was built, guests have gathered in the belvedere to see the view and enjoy the cool breezes. They've left behind graffiti—names, salutations, and anecdotes. These have never been scrubbed off or painted over. In fact, *graffiti* is not a dirty word here. As guests, you'll even be invited to leave your own mark by adding your remarks to the collection. Inns, more likely than not, have guests books in which guests are encouraged to leave comments. This is the only one we know of where you're induced to leave a permanent record of your visit directly on the house.

Eufaula is one of the most beautiful towns in the South, with a collection of more than 700 preserved and restored historic buildings. We've always thought Kendall Manor was the most beautiful structure in town, indeed perhaps in the South, and were overjoyed when it opened its doors as an inn. Named one of the Top Fifty All-American Getaways by *Condé Nast Traveler,* the inn offers a  warm welcome and the gracious ambience of the Old South as well as exquisite accommodations, delicious food, and exceptional attention to detail. Public rooms and guest chambers showcase 16-foot ceilings, gold-leaf cornices, Italian-marble fireplaces, and ruby-colored glass windows and are opulently decorated in the lavish Victorian style with antiques, period reproductions, and ornate fabrics. Large, light, and airy, with high ceilings and numerous windows, guest rooms blend history with modern amenities and personal touches. Each individually decorated, in addition to king- or queen-size beds the well-appointed rooms feature cozy sitting areas and spacious baths.

After an exceptional night's sleep in your romantic bed chamber, you might be tempted to lie in bed indefinitely. The wafting aromas of homemade breads and muffins and a special blend of freshly ground coffee will draw you out of bed and down to a delicious full breakfast, which might include an entree such as Eggs Kendall, orange French toast with berry sauce, or gingerbread pancakes accompanied by coffee, tea, fruits, and juices.

To make your Kendall Manor experience even more special, arrange ahead of time to have a romantic, multicourse gourmet dinner for two served by candlelight in the Manor Dining Room or in front of the fireplace in the Original Kendall Dining Room. After a stay here, it will be difficult to reenter the twentieth century.

HOW TO GET THERE: Follow U.S. 431 to Eufaula; at Broad Street turn west. The inn is in the third block on your right.

You Say Tom Ato, I Say Tomahto You Say Cupola, I Say Belvedere

What we twentieth-century folks might think of as a purely decorative addition perched on the roof of a historic house, barn, or other structure was really an early method of air-conditioning. Heat rises, which is why old houses had high ceilings on every floor—so that the heat would rise above the height of the people. By the time the heat collected on the upper floors or in attics, however, the temperature could be unbearable. An opening in the roof would allow some of the heat to escape.

But how to put an opening in the roof without letting in the elements? Little covered rooms with windows all around that could be raised during hot weather solved the problem. If the additions are square, they're called belvederes; if they're domed shaped and on a round base, they're called cupolas. Of course, the more opulent the house, the larger and fancier the belvedere or cupola was likely to be. Although most belvederes and cupolas were simply big enough to do the job, others—such as the one at Kendall Manor—are large enough to hold a roomful of furniture and people. During cold weather, the belvedere was probably the warmest place in the house, so a room big enough to be furnished as a sitting room was a very comfortable place to be. As an added benefit, the belvedere provided wonderful views.

Bay Breeze Guest House
Fairhope, Alabama 36533

INNKEEPERS: Bill and Becky Jones

ADDRESS/TELEPHONE: 742 South Mobile Street (mailing address: P.O. Box 526); (334) 928–8976; fax (334) 928–0360

WEB SITE: www.bbonline.com/al/

ROOMS: 3 in main house, plus 2 cottage suites; all with private bath and television, cottage suites with telephone, small kitchen, and wheelchair access. No smoking inn.

RATES: $95, single or double; $105, suites; full breakfast in main house; breakfast extra for cottage suites. $15 each additional person in suites.

OPEN: Year-round.

FACILITIES AND ACTIVITIES: Private pier, decks, and beach on Mobile Bay. Nearby: walking distance to downtown historic Fairhope, restaurants, and shops.

BUSINESS TRAVEL: Suites have telephone and excellent light and work area; fax available.

Becky Jones once wrote a letter saying that some of her guests thought Bay Breeze Guest House deserved to be included in this guide. "We are very special, too," Becky wrote. So we went to see. The inn, the location, and the Joneses are, indeed, special.

This B&B inn sits on a three-acre site right on the shores of Mobile Bay. The grounds are filled with mature shrubs and trees that give you a feeling of being in the woods. The stucco building was built in the 1930s and has been variously remodeled and enlarged over the years to accommodate the family's changing needs. It works beautifully as an inn.

The entire downstairs—a sitting room with fireplace, glassed-porch bay room, living room, and kitchen—is devoted to guests. (The Joneses have private quarters upstairs.) Most of the furnishings in the main house are family heirlooms going back as far as five generations. The mix of wicker, stained glass, and hooked and Oriental rugs produces a homey feel no designer could duplicate. "And everything has a story," Becky says.

The cottage suites are newer. They have pickled, white pine walls, old brick floors, vaulted ceilings, and lots of generously sized windows. One of these cottages is well equipped for the handicapped, with wide spaces to accommodate a wheelchair, grab bars in the proper places in the bathrooms, and flexible shower wands. The cottages are decorated with just the right combination of antiques, Oriental rugs, new sofas, and good beds. You feel comfortable but not overwhelmed with stuff. Becky has been careful to keep the suites light and spacious.

As a hostess, she knows how to find out what you like and provides it without apparent effort: a special jelly, a particular bread or coffee or drink. And if you come back again, she'll remember what you liked and have it ready for you.

HOW TO GET THERE: From I-10, take U.S. Highway 98 toward Fairhope and exit right onto Scenic/Alternate Highway 98 at the WELCOME TO FAIRHOPE sign. At the third traffic light, turn right onto Magnolia Avenue. Go 4 blocks and turn left on South Mobile Street at the municipal pier. Bay Breeze Guest House is about a mile farther, on the right.

The Beach House
Bed and Breakfast 💙
Gulf Shores, Alabama 36542

INNKEEPERS: Carol and Russell Shackelford

ADDRESS/TELEPHONE: 9218 Dacus Lane; (334) 540-7039 or (800) 659-6004

WEB SITE: www.bbchannel.com

ROOMS: 5; all with private bath.

RATES: Peak Season (Friday before Mother's Day to Thursday after Labor Day), Long Weekend Plan or Short Week Plan $500 to $695, Full Week Plan $1,000 to $1,390; Off Season (Friday after Labor Day to Thursday before Mother's Day), Long Weekend or Short Week Plans $450 to $585, Full Week $900 to $1,170 (which means the seventh night is free). Rates are double occupancy and include breakfast, snacks, beverages, afternoon wine and cheese; credit cards are not accepted; single deduct $25.

OPEN: Eleven months (usually closed from mid-December to mid-January, but dates change, so be sure to ask).

FACILITIES AND ACTIVITIES: Use of the living room, kitchen, porches, and hot tub. Smoking outside only. Nearby: Historic Fort Morgan and Mobile Bay are only a few miles to the west; the towns of Gulf Shores, Orange Beach, and Foley with shopping, restaurants, amusement parks, museums, theaters are only a few miles to the east. Take the auto ferry across the bay to Dauphin Island, Bellingrath Gardens, or the casinos of Biloxi. A variety of golf courses include the nationally ranked Kiva Dunes. Also bicycling, boating, fishing, hiking, horseback riding, sailing, and tennis nearby.

BUSINESS TRAVEL: Thirty-five miles from Mobile, 33 miles from Pensacola; suitable for very small meetings.

*F*or us, there is no better place to be rejuvenated than at the beach. So there's nothing we love better than a beach getaway, and when we go we want to stay right at the water's edge so that all we have to do is step outside our door to swim, sun, take long walks, or search for shells. Even when we're in our room, we want to be able to open the doors and windows to see the waves crashing, hear the soothing sounds of the sea, and watch the vivid displays of color as the sun rises or sets. The problem has always been finding just the right accommodations.

Luckily we've found the perfect solution to our dilemma. The delightful Beach House Bed and Breakfast, a B&B inn near Gulf Shores on the Alabama Gulf Coast, fulfills our every requirement and desire—even things we hadn't previously realized we wanted. Owners Carol and Russell Shackelford provide an intimate, friendly atmosphere with lots of amenities to spoil you outrageously—and they do all the work. Their philosophy is to balance "leaving you alone" with "taking care of you." The biggest decision you'll have to make is whether to relax in one of the hammocks, soak in the hot tub, go to the beach, or leave the property for sight-seeing, shopping, or dinner.

Perched on high dunes directly on the shores of the Gulf of Mexico, the rambling, three-story Beach House sits on the last lot before the Bon Secour National Wildlife Refuge, which guarantees that the vast stretch of dune-backed beach next door will never be developed. This provides you with solitude when you want it. Although the house is only five years old, the tin-roofed exterior is reminiscent of the grand beach houses built early in this century. A huge screened porch wraps around the front of the first floor. This is a perfect place to get out of the sun and get to know your hosts and fellow guests. Outdoor stairs lead to the hot tub deck, where you can soak away your tensions—a particularly popular place to go at night to enjoy the canopy of stars. A smaller second floor screened porch is another popular retreat. Wicker seating, hammocks, and hanging chairs provide numerous choices for unwinding.

Inside, the Beach House is filled with modern amenities. Ample use is made of pine, ceramic tile, and beaded board. Round timbers rise through all floors of the house like the masts of old sailing ships. The living room/kitchen is a large open room with a wall of windows looking out onto the Gulf. Comfortable seating invites guests to settle in, and a large library table is a great place to play games or put together a puzzle. In the kitchen area a guest refrigerator is stocked with lemonade, juices, and soft drinks, and there's an icemaker and coffeemaker as well whenever the craving for a little something strikes. Bookcases in the living room and up the stairways on all three floors are laden with books and magazines on every subject. What you happily won't see are televisions and telephones. In fact, the Shackelfords advertise their home as a "no phone, no TV, no shoes zone." Instead they provide kites and floats, beach chairs, and even flip-flops. (If you absolutely can't live without television, you can request to have one put in your room.)

All five luxurious guest rooms have their own distinct personality, indicated by their names: Nags Head, Cape May, Key West, Cumberland Island, and West Indies. All boast fabulous views, pine floors, Oriental rugs, and ceiling fans (air-conditioning is used in particularly hot weather). Private baths are large; some have tub/showers, others have huge walk-in showers, but all are amply supplied with plush towels and bathrobes. Beds are king- or queen-size and feature premium mattresses topped with plump feather beds and use down pillows and luxury linens. With all the reading that goes on in the house, the Shackelfords have thoughtfully provided bedside tables and reading lamps on both sides of the bed—a big plus to our twosome. Two of the rooms open onto the second-floor porch. The two suite-size rooms on the third floor feature seating areas and private Jacuzzis; one has a private deck.

Upon afternoon arrival, you'll be treated to freshly baked goods, assorted spreads, and a beverage. Cool drinks, fruit, and snacks are available all afternoon, followed by wine and cheese in the late afternoon. In the morning you'll awake to freshly brewed imported coffee and chilled juice followed by a hearty breakfast casserole and delicious side items.

Firmly believing that a one-night stay simply isn't sufficient in which to unwind and get all the benefits of the ocean, beach, and fresh salt air—as well as the inn itself—the Shackelfords require a minimum three-night stay. Choose a Friday to Monday long-weekend plan, a Monday through Thursday short week, or a full week. Some folks even go all out and choose the week-and-a-half plan by combining a full week with either the long weekend or short week stay. We'd consider that heaven.

HOW TO GET THERE: From I-10 (exit 44), follow Alabama Route 59 south to Gulf Shores. At the fourth traffic light after the bridge over the Intracoastal Waterway, turn right (west) on Route 180 (Fort Morgan Parkway). Continue approximately 11 miles. When you see the Meyer Real Estate office on the left, continue approximately 7/10 mile and turn left on the Veterans Road. Take the second left, onto Dacus Lane. At the end of Dacus Lane, The Beach House is on the right, atop the dunes.

Malaga Inn
Mobile, Alabama 36602

INNKEEPER: Julie Beem

ADDRESS/TELEPHONE: 359 Church Street; (205) 438-4701 or (800) 235-1586; fax (205) 438-4701 *123

ROOMS: 40; all with private bath, television, and telephone; some with refrigerator. Some with wheelchair access. No-smoking rooms available.

RATES: $69 to $79 rooms; $135 suites; includes coffee and daily newspaper; all meals extra.

OPEN: Year-round.

FACILITIES AND ACTIVITIES: Restaurant, cocktail lounge, swimming pool. Nearby: located in historic district of downtown Mobile; within walking distance of the Museum of the City of Mobile, Mobile Civic Auditorium, Conde-Charlotte House Museum; Oakleigh Period House Museum, The Cox-Deasy House, The Minnie Mitchell Archives, The

Fine Arts Museum of the South, Fort Conde Military Museum; short drive to Bellingrath Gardens and Home and USS *Alabama* Battleship Memorial Park.

*A*lthough Malaga looks pretty much like a hotel now, it started out as two three-story town houses built in 1862 by two brothers-in-law. Had the outcome of the Civil War been different, they might still stand as two town houses. Instead, the two homes have been restored, beginning in 1968 with a patio and garden and space for new accommodations between them.

Twenty of the guest rooms are in the restored homes. Some of these still have the original wallpaper and hardwood floors. One has the remains of a fine marble fireplace. The rooms are furnished comfortably with both traditional furniture and some good antiques. The other twenty rooms, in the newer addition, are more elaborate but perhaps less interesting because they have less history. Many of the rooms overlook the court-

yard, a pretty, spacious, tiled area with a fountain and lots of plants.

The inn's restaurant, Mayme's, serves contemporary cuisine with French overtones, for instance, seared tuna *au poivre* with roasted garlic cream sauce, roasted rack of lamb with rosemary, and risotto-stuffed quail with apricot sauce.

With forty rooms, you can't expect highly personal, hold-hands-around-the-table treatment, but the inn's staff is very friendly and helpful in the tradition of old Southern gentility.

HOW TO GET THERE: Traveling east on I–10, take the Canal Street exit. Cross Canal to Jackson Street and follow it to Church. Turn left on Church. Traveling west on I–10, take the Government Street exit from Bayway through the Bankhead Tunnel. Follow Government Street to Claiborne, turn left, go to Church Street, and turn left again. From I–65 take I–10 east and follow the directions for traveling east on I–10. You will come to the inn almost immediately.

Red Bluff Cottage
Montgomery, Alabama 36104

INNKEEPERS: Anne and Mark Waldo

ADDRESS/TELEPHONE: 551 Clay Street (mailing address: P.O. Box 1026); (334) 264–0056 or (888) 551–2529; fax (334) 263–3054

WEB SITE: www.bbonline.com/al/redbluff

E-MAIL: RedBlufBnB@aol.com

ROOMS: 4, plus 1 children's room; all but children's room with private bath. No smoking inn.

RATES: $65, single; $75, double; full breakfast. Inquire about special arrangements for children. No credit cards.

OPEN: Year-round.

FACILITIES AND ACTIVITIES: Guest refrigerator and coffeemaker, children's fenced-in play yard, gazebo. Nearby: restaurants, Alabama State Capitol, historic sites, Jasmine Hill Gardens, Montgomery Museum of Fine Arts, Alabama Shakespeare Festival Theatre.

*R*ed Bluff Cottage is a new building, built especially as a B&B inn in 1987. The guest rooms are all on the ground floor, with the kitchen, dining room, living room, den, and music room on the second floor, which makes the guest rooms quiet and the public rooms exceptionally light and airy, looking out over the yard and gardens.

The flower gardens are an important part of Red Bluff Cottage; guest rooms are filled with fresh flowers, and seasonal blooms adorn the breakfast table. Anne has been a passionate gardener for years, an especially rewarding activity in Montgomery's climate, where it's moist and warm most of the year. When I visited, her border, full of intertwined patches of pink, white, yellow, and blue, looked like Monet's garden.

The Waldos' personal passions influence the look of the rooms inside the inn as well. In the music room, a harpsichord, a piano, and a recorder testify to the talent in the family—no guarantee that you'll hear a little concert during your stay, but it does happen.

In the guest rooms, you see furniture that's been in the family for years: the bed Anne slept in as a child, her Grandmother Sims's little rocker, and an old leather trunk from Mark's great-aunt in Wisconsin, which contained invitations to firemen's balls dated 1850.

But artifacts of family past don't mean much unless you enjoy the present family. Every time we see them, we find something more to talk about. They're simply nice people to know.

Mark was the rector of an Episcopal parish in Montgomery for almost thirty years. During these years, the Waldos raised six children, all of whom keep in touch regularly. They have funny tales of those tumultuous times, including one about driving away from a rest stop in the van one vacation and not noticing that a child had been left behind until a routine "count-off" revealed that number three was missing.

Spa Wafers: Sweet Memories of Eureka Springs

SpaWafers began as a tasty European treat at luxurious Old World health spas in 1856. Spa visitors looked forward to nibbling on the delicacies while enjoying lively conversation and the fragrance of the sweet delicious wafers filling the air. The crispy wafers were much loved by such historical notables as Edward VII and composer Johann Strauss. It was only natural that when Eureka Springs became a popular spa resort in this country that visitors would want the wafers to enhance their experience. The only American producer of these international gourmet treats is Eureka Springs' Forest Hills Restaurant, which conforms to the strictest European standards and uses a specially designed oven it had shipped from Europe.

Created in creamy chocolate and vanilla hazelnut flavors, each wafer is embossed with a special design unique to Eureka Springs. Each colorful box contains six original sweet and crispy wafers. Naturally when you visit Eureka Springs you'll want to take home several boxes for yourself and for gifts. When you run out, you can order more by logging on to www.SpaWafers.com.

After Mark's retirement, the Waldos became innkeepers because they wanted to keep new people coming into their lives. How can Mark and Anne fail? People who love flowers and books and music and can raise six kids and still be enthusiastic about taking in more of the human race must be genetically inclined to be innkeepers.

HOW TO GET THERE: Take exit 172 off I-65. Go toward downtown (east) on Herron Street 1 block. Turn left on Hanrick Street. Parking is on the right off Hanrick by the inn's rear entrance.

Heartstone Inn and Cottages ♥
Eureka Springs, Arkansas 72632

INNKEEPERS: Iris and Bill Simantel

ADDRESS/TELEPHONE: 35 Kingshighway; (501) 253-8916 or (800) 494-4921; fax (501) 253-6821

E-MAIL: billiris@ipa.net

ROOMS: 10, plus 2 suites and 2 cottages; all with private bath.

RATES: $68 to $125, single or double; includes full breakfast. Inquire about winter discounts.

OPEN: Year-round, except January through February.

FACILITIES AND ACTIVITIES: Gift shop, massage/reflexology therapist available by appointment. Located in the historic district, within walking distance of downtown Eureka Springs tourist activities; golf privileges at private course. Nearby: restaurants.

*T*he Heartstone Inn gets its name from a large, flat, vaguely heart-shaped stone that the Simantels found on the property. They play with the heart theme, using the phrase "Lose your heart in the Ozarks" and a heart-shaped logo in their brochure. The doors have heart-shaped welcome signs. The stone that justifies it all rests in the front garden, surrounded by flowers.

As far as we're concerned, the Simantels have such heart they could use the theme even without the stone.

They came to the Ozarks from Chicago to become innkeepers. They love Eureka Springs. They love their inn. They love their guests.

The B&B inn is pretty. It's an Edwardian house, painted pink, with a white picket fence and lots of bright pink geraniums and roses all around.

Most of the rooms are furnished with elegant antiques, though a couple are done in country style. One of the newer touches is an especially elegant Jacuzzi suite. The fairly steady addition of such outdoor niceties as decks and a gazebo means there are always glorious places for special gatherings such as weddings.

But we think the attractiveness of the inn comes not so much from its pretty artifacts as from what those things reflect of Iris and Bill. For example, in the dining room is a Pennsylvania Dutch hex sign in which tulips and hearts make up the pattern. Iris said that the sign stands for everything they believe in and explained the symbols for faith, hope, charity, love of God, and smooth sailing. Then she kept the moment from getting too solemn by pointing to a print of yellow irises on the other wall. She said, "That's so I remember who I am in the morning."

In the living room, she keeps a collection of ceramic English cottages and ceramic pieces decorated with pictures of cottages. She says that it's how she keeps in touch with the fact that she's English in spite of having lived in Chicago. This pottery, English Torquay, is very expensive and hard to find. The collection has attracted a lot of publicity lately. Another way she "keeps in touch" is with "pilgrimages" back to England, so you always find touches of the Brit on the Heartstone scene.

The Simantels have been enjoying a good bit of "discovery," applause from magazines and newspapers and other innkeepers for doing such a good job. The praise, Iris says, has not gone to their heads. They are still keeping their prices moderate because they don't want to attract snobs who go to places only because they are expensive. Not that Bill and Iris could be snobs if they wanted to. That Simantel humor bubbles too close to the surface. In fact, Iris says there are lots of new jokes between them but some, she thinks, may not be suitable for print.

When Iris was talking about the elaborate breakfasts they serve, she said that guests feel pampered by breakfasts including strawberry blintzes, coffeecake, and several kinds of fruit. And, of course, it's served not with a mere smile but with giggles and grins.

HOW TO GET THERE: From the west, take the first 62B exit off Route 62. From the east, take the second 62B exit. Follow 62B through town until it becomes Kingshighway.

The Olde Stonehouse B&B Inn
Hardy, Arkansas 72542

INNKEEPER: Peggy Volland

ADDRESS/TELEPHONE: 51 Main Street; (870) 856–2983 or (800) 514–2983; fax (870) 856–4036

E-MAIL: oldstonehouse@centuryinter.net

ROOMS: 6 in stone house, 2 two-room suites in cottage; all with private bath; suites with television; telephone available on request. No smoking inn.

RATES: $69 to $100, double; includes full breakfast and evening desserts with beverages.

OPEN: Year-round.

FACILITIES AND ACTIVITIES: Player piano, organ, musical instrument collection, bicycles, across the street from the Spring River.

NEARBY: restaurants, shopping; swimming and sunbathing at Spring River Beach; 1 mile to Cherokee Village golf, horseback riding, and marina boat rentals. Vintage car museum, Veterans Museum, Country Music Theater.

BUSINESS TRAVEL: Fax, copy machine, dataports, corporate rates.

This B&B inn occupies two very different buildings. The main house is stone, built in 1928, and has in its common area a wonderful fireplace made with local rocks containing everything from fossils to pieces of Arkansas diamonds and remnants of Native American artifacts. The Shaver Cottage is older, built in 1905, and is a simple frame building that looks as if it belongs somewhere on the prairie.

These are the kinds of accommodations that don't demand anything except your relaxation. You don't have to move cautiously around delicate fine antiques, you can just appreciate being surrounded by things that are older and were meant to be used. For example, Aunt Jenny's Room, in the main house, has a cathedral ceiling, a white iron bed with a quilt, and the original claw-foot tub in the bath. The furnishings are feminine without being fragile.

Grandpa Sam's and Uncle Buster's have more masculine decor. One big old window of etched glass depicts a voluptuous nude woman. Now, this ain't exactly the stuff of the prairie!

For that matter, neither are the rockers built for two on the front porch of the stone house. The point here is that nothing is constrained by what history "ought to be," and everything is interesting.

Peggy is active in local preservation and historic activities. She understands the town's history—it's always been a resort town, about two and one half hours from both Memphis and Springfield—and she knows the stories of all the buildings on the property.

She also understands our eating habits these days and offers breakfasts that let you be as "good" or as "bad" as you wish. Choose fresh fruit and homemade granola with yogurt or a baked apple pancake with turkey sausage, for instance. Come to think of it, turkey sausage isn't all that bad. This lady's smart.

She suggests that although the inn is equipped for business travelers, it's great for the rest of us who just want to unwind, too. One weekend of each month, October through May, is a Murder Mystery Weekend. They offer Romance, Golf, and Fly Fishing packages, too.

HOW TO GET THERE: Highway 62/63/412 runs directly through Hardy; in town it becomes Main Street. The inn is at 51 Main Street.

Edwardian Inn
Helena, Arkansas 72342

INNKEEPERS: Olive Ellis and Anna Steele

ADDRESS/TELEPHONE: 317 Biscoe; (870) 338–9155; fax (870) 572–9105

WEB SITE: www.bbonline.com/ar/

ROOMS: 12, including 4 on ground floor; all with private bath; 1 with wheelchair access.

RATES: $50 to $75, single or double; includes full breakfast.

OPEN: Year-round.

FACILITIES AND ACTIVITIES: Conference room. Nearby: restaurants, antiques shops, Delta Cultural Center, Mississippi Riverfront Park; St. Francis National Forest with two lakes for hiking, fishing, and swimming.

BUSINESS TRAVEL: Located in downtown Helena. Rooms with direct-dial phone with computer capabilities, good work space or desk, excellent lighting. Card tables and fax available.

*A*very rich man built the Edwardian Inn for his family home in 1904. And even though he went broke, lost it, and a lot of bad things happened to it over the years, it is perfectly obvious (now that the restoration is done) that it is a fabulously expensive building and a wonderful B&B inn.

Everyone notices the woodwork first. The first floor is something called *wood carpeting.* It was parqueted in Germany from strips not more than 1 inch wide, mounted on canvas, and shipped to Helena in rolls. The wainscoting on the walls is elaborately carved. Barleytwist balusters adorn the banister of the oak stairway.

The rooms are correspondingly lovely, with high ceilings and outstanding period antiques. Many businesspeople stay here regularly because each room has a comfortable modern bath, lots of space, and places to open up a briefcase, spread out papers, or even set up a portable computer, existing in surprising harmony with the fine old furnishings and restored mantels, mirrors, and candelabra.

Although the entire setting is more expensive than most of us are accustomed to at home, the sociability of the innkeepers and the quiet good taste of the decor make it all feel very comfortable—an easy place to be.

There is a second-floor sitting room in addition to the downstairs common rooms. And, even though the inn is right downtown, you can watch racoons, birds, and squirrels playing right outside the window.

In the morning, guests have homemade rolls, whatever fruit is fresh in season, and coffee in the sunny little latticed breakfast room. The innkeepers take pride in serving breakfasts that are not ordinary and in adding special touches, such as using real cloth napkins.

HOW TO GET THERE: Take 49B into Helena and follow it up a hill directly to the inn, which is painted deep yellow.

Stillmeadow Farm
Hot Springs, Arkansas 71913

INNKEEPERS: Jody and Gene Sparling

ADDRESS/TELEPHONE: 111 Stillmeadow Lane; (501) 525–9994

ROOMS: 4; 2 with private bath; 2 can be rented as a suite; Honeymoon Cottage. No smoking inn.

RATES: $70 to $85, double; Cottage, $90 double; includes full breakfast.

OPEN: Year-round.

FACILITIES AND ACTIVITIES: Antiques shop, hiking trails, herb garden, stocked fishing pond with wild ducks; Mountain Brook Stables, Inc., on premises. Nearby: restaurants, Hot Springs bathhouses, Hot Springs National Park and lakes Catherine, Hamilton, and Ouachita.

We have to start with the obvious question: What's a reproduction 1740 post-and-beam saltbox furnished with early country antiques doing in Arkansas? Simple. Jody and Gene are not homesick New Englanders; they're natives of Arkansas who happen to like saltboxes and country antiques.

They're neat people who decided to get away from the pressures of working in the nine-to-five world. They make their living now with the B&B inn and by selling antiques in their adjacent shop.

The inn is a delight to be in. It is filled with sturdy, comfortable antiques. The four-poster bed in the room was covered with a crocheted white bedspread. An old painted blanket chest stood as a bedside table.

Downstairs, Jody and Gene have set aside a parlor especially for guests, where you can have a fire in the fireplace when the weather's right.

At breakfast they share another sitting and dining area that has a table at a big window looking out over the woods and meadows. It's all true New England, with herbs hanging to dry and a braided rug in front of another brick fireplace. Jody has acquired some good old wooden kitchenware, pottery, and baskets. After breakfast we talked around the table for a long time, then moved to the couch in front of the fireplace for a long time more.

There was much to talk about. Jody is expanding her herb garden. Gene knows detailed history of the Hot Springs thermal baths. Their son just bought his very own backhoe. A guest in her nineties who had been there to look around carried two canes—one for walking and one with a handle so heavy that it seemed it must be for defense. Oh, and Jody and Gene hoped that darned woodpecker hadn't awakened anyone trying to take out his own reflection in the bedroom window.

We traded recipes and kid stories and what-it-used-to-be-like-to-work-in-the-real-world stories. We talked about several good restaurants nearby and

how surprisingly good the Moo Shu Pork is at the Hunan, given that Chinese food isn't overly appreciated in the South. Probably we'd all still be talking if we hadn't had so many other things we needed to do.

A young couple on a fishing trip, who shared a lot of the talk with us, must have felt as fully at home as we did because Gene noticed that they had made their bed before leaving. Even though the bed still had to be stripped for clean sheets, it seemed like a special gesture. Gene grinned and looked sentimental when he saw it. "Will you look at that? Just look at that. Now isn't that something, though?" he said.

HOW TO GET THERE: The inn is 5 miles south of Hot Springs, off State Highway 7. From Highway 7, go east on Highway 290 about 1½ miles to the STILLMEADOW FARM sign. Follow the signs down the drive another ½ mile to the inn. Jody will send a map when you make a reservation.

Williams House
Bed & Breakfast Inn ♥

Hot Springs National Park, Arkansas 71901

INNKEEPERS: Karen and David Wiseman

ADDRESS/TELEPHONE: 420 Quapaw; (501) 624–4275 or
(800) 756–4635

WEB SITE: www.bbonline.com/ar/williamshouse/

E-MAIL: willmbnb@ipa.net

ROOMS: 4, plus 2 suites, 1 suite has two bedrooms; all with private bath
and cable TV. No smoking inn. Children older than twelve welcome.

RATES: $75 to $112, single or double; additional $20 for third and
fourth guest in two-bedroom suite. Ask about midweek and corporate
rates; includes full breakfast.

OPEN: Year-round. Sometimes closed in January, depending on weather.

FACILITIES AND ACTIVITIES: Nearby: restaurants, art galleries, national
park hiking trails, Hot Springs thermal baths, Oaklawn Park Race
Track, three lakes for boating, fishing, and swimming, golf.

BUSINESS TRAVEL: Fax available. Upstairs common area suited to computer setup. Corporate rates.

Many innkeepers say that guests want good beds and good breakfasts and that their inns are popular because they provide cus-
tom-made beds and excellent food. While all of this is true at the
Williams House, we think there is more to it than that.

Start with the building. You won't find many Victorian brownstones in
Hot Springs. The doctor who built it in 1889 had the stone hauled in. In the
ensuing years, it's been through some hard times, but the Wisemans have
refurbished it well. You can't help being impressed by the turret and tower with
notched battlements on the outside, the wraparound upstairs and downstairs
verandas, and the lovely woodwork and the black marble fireplace inside.

Guests will enjoy the charm and elegance of the 6,500-square-foot inn
with seven guest rooms and suites—five in the main house and two in the
carriage house and each furnished differently with antiques. Located in the
main house, two particularly popular rooms are the rounded Parlor Suite
and West Chamber. Both feature queen-size beds, separate sitting parlors,
and cable television. Romantics love the big claw-foot tub in the Carriage
Suite or the china tub for two in the Guest Chamber.

But to us, the real attraction is the innkeepers. Take David's penchant for refurbishing and fixing things. Just about all the work around the house is done by David and Karen, and with an older home there is plenty to keep them busy. However, it is evident that David really enjoys getting in and fixing things. Just ask him about the work they've done since they took over the inn in 1996—the woodwork that has been stripped and restored, the old carpets that were torn up to reveal magnificent hardwood floors, Karen's marvelous flea market finds that now add so much to the decor, and even the addition of a general store in the cottage that contains items they have found, refurbished, and now offer for sale at very reasonable prices.

In the kitchen, Karen does most of the cooking—preparing an array of mouthwatering dishes such as her stuffed croissants, blueberry-filled French toast, hash-brown omelette and different quiches. However David shows that he hasn't completely lost his touch with the baking industry by preparing his bran muffins while pitching in as head waiter and busboy.

Karen and David's almost-instinctive sharing of the myriad duties involved in running a successful inn—while always being ready to answer guests' questions, imparting their significant knowledge of the area, and in general being "super hosts"—make them perfect examples of what it takes to be effective innkeepers.

Another nice extra is a sheet for guests entitled "How a Thermal Bath Is Taken in Hot Springs National Park." It tells you exactly what happens. In addition, the Wisemans keep ice and jugs of mineral-spring water in a refrigerator at the bottom of the stairs outside the kitchen so that you can sip the waters even if you don't go to the baths. If you like a little more fire in your water, they offer complimentary wine, as well.

HOW TO GET THERE: From the north on I–40, take Route 7 and follow it into Hot Springs. This is a drive of about two hours, longer than it looks on the map, because the road winds through mountains. In Hot Springs turn right off Route 7 onto Orange Street. Go 3 blocks to the corner of Orange and Quapaw, where you will find the inn. From the south on I–30, take Route 7 for 22 miles into Hot Springs and stay on 7 until you come to Orange. Turn left onto Orange and go to Quapaw.

Wildflower Bed and Breakfast
Mountain View, Arkansas 72560

INNKEEPER: Lou Anne Rhodes

ADDRESS/TELEPHONE: Court Square (mailing address: P.O. Box 72); (870) 269–4383 or (800) 591–4879

ROOMS: 9; 7 with private bath; 1 is a three-room suite with kitchenette, living room, and sleeping loft.

RATES: $46 to $68, double; single $5 less; includes full breakfast buffet.

OPEN: Year-round.

FACILITIES AND ACTIVITIES: Located on historic Court Square—where folk musicians gather informally to pick with one another. Nearby: restaurants, Blanchard Springs Caverns, Ozark Folk Center, swimming in Sylamore Creek, many mountain-music programs.

*T*his B&B inn has been listed in earlier editions as Commercial Hotel. That had been its name since 1918, when it was built to accommodate commercial travelers. After running it under that name for more than a decade, the former owners, the Budys, decided that the name didn't really reflect the kind of inn they were running—hence the change. But changing the name won't eclipse the spirit of the old place. An unusual diary is kept at the Wildflower. It contains entries from people who stayed at the inn when it was the Commercial Hotel.

One entry reads, "Vera and Laren Waggoner honeymooned here January 1, 1920." Another man wrote that he boarded here in 1929 for $5 per month, with meals. And a woman wrote that it was nice to see the lobby clean and white—she remembered that it always used to be thick with cigar and cigarette smoke.

The entries are accumulating—from a traveling salesman who stayed here regularly during World War I, from vacationers who stopped only a few times but always loved the place, and from people who stayed here for one reason or another as children and have not been back until now.

The inn they are remembering isn't elaborate now. Never was. Never presumed to be. When the Budys took it over, it was a battered old boarding-house, like a fat lady in a tight corset, structurally sound but sagging at the edges. In restoring it and returning it to operation as an inn, they added such niceties (or should I say necessities?) as central air-conditioning and heat, lots of nice pale-blue carpeting, and good clean paint. They kept the original furniture and iron beds. Today they're antiques.

You'll find an antique claw-foot bathtub in one of the private baths upstairs; the others have showers. The two rooms sharing a bath have an always-clean hall bathroom with a modern shower.

We haven't mentioned the inn's most unusual feature yet. How would you like to have your own group of folk musicians that get together most nights on your front porch to do a little pickin'? Lou Anne just loves it.

Mountain View is the "folk music capital of the world." One of the town traditions is for musicians to gather each night and play together. The big wraparound porch at Wildflower has become their favorite place to gather. One group likes the inn so much that it has changed its name to the Wild-flower String Band. As long as the weather doesn't get too cold, this is where they can be heard most any night. If you like folk music, here's a great way to have a wonderful weekend and be entertained at the same time.

HOW TO GET THERE: From the east, follow Highway 9, 5, and 14 to where it becomes Highway 5 and 14 (Main Street). Go to Court Square and turn right. From the west, Highway 66 goes into Mountain View directly to the square. From the north, Highway 9 goes to the square. The hotel is on the corner across from the square.

Margland Bed and Breakfast Inns
Pine Bluff, Arkansas 71601

INNKEEPER: Wanda Bateman

ADDRESS/TELEPHONE: 703 West Second Avenue; (870) 536–6000 or (800) 545–5383; fax (870) 536–7941

ROOMS: 22; all with private bath, cable television, and telephone, 8 with whirlpool tubs. Margland Two is equipped for handicapped access with elevator and ramp. Smoking in designated areas.

RATES: $85 to $105, double; includes extended continental breakfast.

OPEN: Year-round.

FACILITIES AND ACTIVITIES: Exercise room, swimming pool. Nearby: restaurants; murals on Main Street showing Pine Bluff history; Marks' Mills Battle Site, Martha Mitchell Home, Pine Bluff/Jefferson County Historical Museum, Pine Bluff Regional Park, Pioneer Village, Arkansas Railroad Museum. Forty-five minute drive from Little Rock Regional Airport.

BUSINESS TRAVEL: Fax and copier available; good light and workspace in rooms; discounts.

*M*argland comprises four turn-of-the-century homes clustered in a residential area of Pine Bluff. Each of the homes has its own personality, and when you first see them you don't think of public lodgings at all, because they are treated so much like other homes in the neighborhood, with window boxes, fenced lawns, chairs on the porch, lace curtains at the windows, and crape myrtle growing along the street. The houses are called Margland One, Two, Three, and Four. In all four, the rooms are designed with obvious attention to detail. Guests have a choice of rooms decorated in a variety of styles— French, Victorian, Country, for instance. Many of the furnishings are fine antiques and interesting collections cover many surfaces in the houses. Three suites have loft bedrooms to which you ascend via a spiral staircase.

Outside, the yards for each of the four houses open to each other, giving a strong sense of relationship among the buildings, and there are sitting spaces under the trees in the landscaped gardens, beautifully delineated with terraces of old brick salvaged from the properties during renovations. The innkeeper, Wanda Bateman, says, "We don't throw anything away."

A gazebo behind Margland Two is a nice sitting area, and in good weather it's delightful to take your breakfast in the garden outside Margland One, although service is available also in the formal dining room. They call breakfast at Margland "extended continental," and it is often extended quite a bit, especially in response to guests' special requests. One guest, Wanda recalls, asked for pancakes and later assured her that eating them had been "a religious experience."

At Margland Three, the kidney-shaped swimming pool, which serves all four homes, is also set off with a wall of old brick and a slate-paved sunning area that integrates the pool into the landscape rather than having it seem unrelated to the property, as swimming pools sometimes do.

HOW TO GET THERE: From U.S. Highway 65 at Lake Pine Bluff take Cherry Street to West Second Avenue. Turn left. The inns are in the fourth block. You will receive a map when you make reservations.

Select List of Other Alabama and Arkansas Inns

Alabama

Lakepoint Resort

AL 431 North
Eufaula, AL 36072
(334) 687–8011 or (800) 544–5253

Rustic lodge; 101 rooms and suites, 22 cottages, some with fireplace; restaurant, pool, golf, tennis, lake, marina.

DeSoto State Park Lodge

Route 1, Box 205
Fort Payne, AL 35967
(256) 845–5380 or (800) 568–8840

Rustic lodge; 25 rooms, 22 cottages, some with fireplace; restaurant, pool, tennis.

Lake Guntersville State Park Lodge

1155 Lodge Drive
Guntersville, AL 35976
(256) 571–5440

Rustic lodge; 100 rooms and suites, 35 cottages, some with fireplace; two restaurants, pool, golf.

Mentone Inn B&B

P.O. Box
Mentone, AL 35984
(256) 634-4836 or (800) 455-7470

Historic 1920s mountain hotel; 12 rooms; restaurant; full breakfast.

Joe Wheeler State Park Lodge

U.S. 72
Rogersville, AL 35652
(256) 247-5461

Rustic lodge; 75 rooms and suites; restaurant, pool, golf.

Twin Pines Resort and Conference Center

1200 Twin Pines Road
Sterett, AL 35147
(205) 672-7575

Rustic; 46 rooms and suites, some with fireplace; restaurant.

Arkansas

5 Ojo Inn B&B

5 Ojo Street
Eureka Springs, AR 72632
(501) 253-6734 or (800) 656-6734

Turn-of-the-century Victorian with wraparound porch; 10 rooms, some with fireplace and/or whirlpool.

The Anderson House Inn

201 East Main
Heber Springs, AR 72543
(501) 362-5266 or (800) 264-5279

Williamsburg-style inn with turn-of-the-century appeal; 16 rooms; full breakfast; cooking school and murder mystery weekends.

Foxglove B&B

229 Beech Street
Helena, AR 72342
(870) 338-9391 or (800) 863-1926

Beautiful Victorian with wraparound porch overlooking Helena and the Mississippi River; 10 rooms, some with whirlpool tub.

Inn at the Mill

P.O. Box 409
Johnson, AR 72741
(501) 521-8091 or (800) CLARION

1835 mill; 48 rooms, some with whirlpool bath; restaurant, bar.

The Inn at Mountain View

307 Washington
Mountain View, AR 72560
(870) 269-4200 or (800) 535-1301

Rustic Victorian; 10 rooms; country breakfast; murder mystery weekends.

Magnolia Gardens Inn

500 North Main
Springdale, AR 72764
(501) 756-5744 or (800) 756-5744

1880s Victorian; 10 rooms; ten acres of gardens and paths, outdoor hot tub; full plantation breakfast.

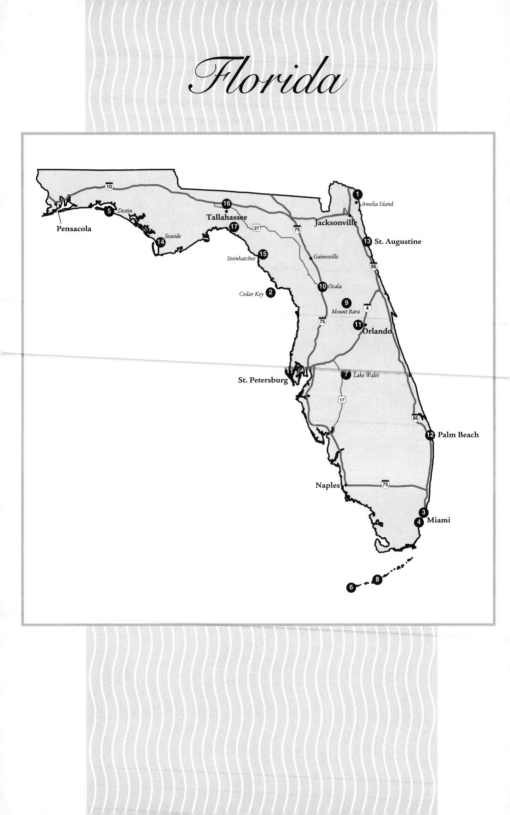

Florida

Florida

Numbers on map refer to towns numbered below.

* A Top Pick Inn

Elizabeth Pointe Lodge
Amelia Island, Florida 32034

INNKEEPERS: David and Susan Caples

ADDRESS/TELEPHONE: 98 South Fletcher Avenue; (904) 277–4851, fax (904) 277–6500 or (800) 772–3359

WEB SITE: www.bbonline/fl

E-MAIL: Eliz.pt@worldnet.att.net

ROOMS: 25; all with private bath and oversized marble tub, telephone, and television, some with Jacuzzi. Wheelchair accessible. No smoking in guest rooms.

RATES: $115 to $225 double; single $15 less; full breakfast and morning newspaper. $20 additional person in room. Children five and under free. Some rooms can be combined to form suites; inquire about rates.

OPEN: Year-round.

FACILITIES AND ACTIVITIES: Light lunches, dinners, and snacks. Full beach privileges, bicycles, twenty-four-hour room service. Nearby: restaurants, tennis, golf, horseback riding, boating, deep-sea fishing; a short drive to Fernandina Seaport.

BUSINESS TRAVEL: Located thirty minutes from Jacksonville. Telephone in room; fax, telecommunications, audiovisual equipment, copy machine, and secretarial services available; conference room. Special packages for small conferences and retreats.

*T*his is a new inn built in the 1890s Nantucket shingle style. It has guest rooms furnished with a nautical theme, common areas furnished with antiques, a great stone fireplace, 13 miles of quiet, uncrowded Atlantic Ocean beaches, and a highly personable staff. Dunes separate the house and the beach.

The Capleses have managed to give the inn interesting nooks and crannies . . . and a feeling that the building has always been right where it is. The guest rooms have a nautical feel but are much more spacious than you'd find in anything that floats. For example, one of the rooms with large windows facing the sunset has hardwood floors brightened with pastel area rugs, a mahogany armoire containing hanging space, drawers, the television, and a full mirror. The bed is a bright green, pencil-post reproduction with a pastel comforter in the star pattern. A white-wicker rocker and live plants make the space cheery, while nautical photos and a porthole window to one side of the bed continue the nautical theme.

If you come here for a low-key vacation, you can do all the beach things most folks like, or you can read on the porch, out of the sun. You can sit by the fireplace, surrounded by books, handmade quilts, and antiques, or you can get physical with golf, tennis, boating, and fishing. Whatever you want can be arranged with little effort on your part right from the inn.

Unlike many inns, this one works well with children. Shelves with kids' books and toys are placed low to be reached easily.

If you let yourself relax, you might end up doing some kidlike things yourself—drinking lemonade, learning to make fishnets by hand, or searching for sand crabs with a flashlight on the beach at night.

They have added twenty-four-hour, light-fare room service and evening turndown service (on request), so whenever you feel the need for a snack you don't need to leave the lodge.

HOW TO GET THERE: From I-95, take the Amelia Island/Fernandina Beach/Route A1A exit just inside the Florida border, near Georgia. Go east on A1A for 15 miles—you will cross the bridge onto the island. Continue on Route A1A to the fifth stoplight and the intersection with Centre Street. Turn right on Atlantic Avenue, and go east 2 miles to the second red light. Turn right on Fletcher. The inn is on the left.

The Fairbanks House
Amelia Island, Florida 32034

INNKEEPERS: Bill and Theresa Hamilton

ADDRESS/TELEPHONE: 227 South Seventh Street; (904) 227-0500 or (888) 891-9882; fax (904) 277-3103

WEB SITE: www.fairbanks.com

E-MAIL: fairbanks@net-magic.net

ROOMS: 10; all with private bath and cable television; some with Jacuzzi; tower suite with kitchen; 3 cottages with kitchen; some with wheelchair access. No smoking inn.

RATES: $125 to $225, double or single; includes full breakfast and evening social hour. Two-night minimum nonholiday weekends, three-night minimum holiday weekends.

OPEN: Year-round.

FACILITIES AND ACTIVITIES: Swimming pool, bicycles. Nearby: walking distance to historic downtown, restaurants, shopping; short drive to marina, beach, horseback riding.

A trip to the beach usually means sand in your shoes, salt in your hair, sunburn on your nose, and a room or two in a touristy condo—unless you visit Amelia Island, which is bustin' out all over with small inns in restored old buildings. The Fairbanks, opened in 1994, is one of the best.

This B&B inn is housed in a restored 1885 Italianate Victorian with all the trimmings of that era: a 15-foot square tower, dormers, bay windows, gables, chimneys, and romantic balustraded balconies. Built by the Confederate veteran Major George Rainsford Fairbanks, the house was once known as "Fairbanks Folly." Local lore isn't quite clear on whether the house earned its name because it was such a wedding-cake-pretty place or because it was supposed to be a surprise for his wife, who, possibly, didn't like surprises. In renovating the house, the former owners, the Smelkers, tried to be faithful to its original style and decorate and furnish it appropriately.

The quality inside matches the exterior: 12-foot-high ceilings, fancy moldings, heart-of-pine floors, and dramatic colors. The living spaces are filled with crystal chandeliers, Eastlake and French antiques, and Oriental rugs. And there's an upstairs luxury suite in the tower that makes you willing to be the crazy aunt who's been kept there for years.

In a setting this formal you might expect to feel formal yourself, but you don't. That has a lot to do with the tastefulness of the arrangements—furniture isn't crowded into spaces too small for it, and surfaces are not cluttered with too many knickknacks.

Bill and Theresa Hamilton are new innkeepers who have added a few special touches to make their guests' stays even more memorable. They now offer Romantic and Mystery weekends that include one or two delectable dinners served on-property, depending on how long you plan to stay.

Gourmet breakfasts served on fine china are pull-out-all-the-stops affairs, including such exotic choices as apple-pecan crepes with bourbon sauce and amaretto applesauce. On the other hand, you can also arrange ahead of time for breakfasts accommodating dietary restrictions.

The house sits on an acre of land, which allows plenty of space for a swimming pool, a spacious brick courtyard, and lots of blooming plants. Also on the grounds, three cottages with kitchen, living and dining rooms and done in white wicker and floral prints, provide extra seclusion and privacy.

HOW TO GET THERE: From I-95 take exit 129 onto A1A. Follow A1A onto the island and turn left on Cedar Street. The inn is at the corner of Cedar and Seventh Streets.

Florida House Inn
Amelia Island, Florida 32034

INNKEEPERS: Bob and Karen Warner and Janine Rowe

ADDRESS/TELEPHONE: 20 and 22 South Third Street; (904) 261–3300 or (800) 258–3301; fax (904) 277–3831

WEB SITE: www.floridahouse.com

E-MAIL: flahseinn@net-magic.net

ROOMS: 11; all with private bath; some with shower only, some with tub/shower, some with whirlpool and separate shower; some rooms open onto one of the porches; some rooms have a fireplace; all with television, telephone, clock radio. Bedding ranges from twin to king-size beds.

RATES: $70 to $150, double occupancy; includes full breakfast and free newspaper. Additional guests in the room are charged $10. During the week in the off-season, October through January, stay two nights and get a third night free (does not include stays that include a Friday or Saturday).

OPEN: Year-round.

FACILITIES AND ACTIVITIES: Pub, restaurant, guest laundry facilities, concierge. Smoking is permitted only in outdoor areas and the pub. Nearby: beaches, horseback riding on the beach from Sea Horse Stables,

Fort Clinch State Park, diving, snorkeling, nature preserves and trails, bicycling and jogging trails, boating, fishing, golf course, hiking, tennis, museums, galleries, shopping, theater.

BUSINESS TRAVEL: Business center with secretarial services, fax, and copier; meeting and banquet facilities.

*T*his fine old inn is located behind a whitewashed picket fence in the heart of the historic district of Fernandina Beach on popular Amelia Island. The charming frame building—graced with smatterings of gingerbread, long windows flanked by shutters, and delightful full-length, first- and second-story verandas with ornate porch railings both front and back—has been welcoming lodgers for more than 140 years. Listed on the National Register of Historic Places and featured in *Best Places to Stay in Florida*, this quaint inn is located in an 1857 building, which originally opened as an inn serving passengers on the Florida Railroad, making it the oldest lodging property in the state. During the town's bustling nineteenth-century heyday, when fortunes were made in shipping, lumber, and the railroad, such luminaries as General Ulysses S. Grant and Jose Marti enjoyed the genteel hospitality of the hotel; others such as Rockefellers and Carnegies dined there frequently.

We were pleased to find out that although the original hotel had twenty-five small rooms and no indoor plumbing, the current reincarnation of the inn offers every modern comfort and convenience without sacrificing the historic character. Today the space is divided into only fourteen spacious and comfortable bedrooms and one suite, all featuring private baths. Ten rooms boast working fireplaces, two feature old-fashioned claw-foot tubs, and six offer whirlpool tubs. Furnished with antiques and period reproductions and decorated with quilts and handmade rugs, the cheery rooms feature romantic four-poster beds or quaint iron beds, a telephone, and a television.

Common areas where guests can mingle and get to know one another or find a private place to read a good book include the elegant formal parlor, the vast courtyard, or the clubby pub with its fireplace. Our favorite place to while away some time and catch the gentle breezes is the brick-paved courtyard shaded by the sprawling branches of one gigantic 200-year-old live oak tree or one of the rear porches overlooking the courtyard.

In addition to a full hot breakfast served to guests each morning, the inn also offers a full-service restaurant featuring boardinghouse–style dining. Lunch—which costs only $6.98 for fried chicken, another meat entree, four or five vegetables, biscuits, cornbread, dessert, and iced tea—is served Monday through Saturday. Sunday brunch ($8.98) features egg dishes, grits, home-fried potatoes, sausage gravy, fried chicken, ham, vegetables, fresh fruit, breads, desserts, and tea. Dinner ($11.98) includes all the lunch items and more and is served Tuesday through Saturday. Large tables seat twelve, so you get to know your fellow guests and other visitors to Amelia Island.

The inn's location is ideal for exploring the historic 30-square-block Victorian seaport village and the harbor area, which first lured swashbuckling pirates to the island, and the shrimp docks. The wide, spectacular Atlantic beaches are less than 2 miles away.

HOW TO GET THERE: From I–95 take exit 129 and travel east on A1A over the large bridge that leads to Amelia Island. A1A becomes Eighth Street. When the divided four-lane roads becomes three lanes with a center turn lane, continue to the third traffic light, which is the intersection of Atlantic and Centre Streets. Turn left and go 2 blocks, passing the large courthouse. Turn left onto Third Street. The inn is ½ block on the left. Look for the fluttering flags depicting the various governments under which Amelia Island has served.

Island Hotel
Cedar Key, Florida 32625

INNKEEPERS: Tony and Dawn Cousins

ADDRESS/TELEPHONE: 373 Second Street; (352) 543–5111 or (800) 432–4640; fax (352) 543–6949

WEB SITE: www.islandhotel-cedarkey.com.

E-MAIL: info@islandhotel-cedarkey.com.

ROOMS: 13; 11 with private bath, some with a claw-foot tub; double or queen-size beds; all rooms are air-conditioned, some also have ceiling fans; no in-room telephones or television. The hotel has limited suitability for children, so ask about bringing yours. Smoking is restricted to the bar and outdoor areas.

RATES: $75 to $110, single or double occupancy; additional occupancy $20 per person; includes breakfast. Minimum stays during special events.

OPEN: Year-round.

FACILITIES AND ACTIVITIES: Gourmet restaurant, King Neptune Bar, wraparound porch. Nearby: beach, fishing, boating, antiques and other shopping.

*A*pre–Civil War structure built in 1859 from seashell tabby with oak supports, the Island Hotel has withstood hurricanes and other natural and man-caused disasters for almost 150 years. Rustic and authentic, the venerable inn is listed on the National Register of Historic Places.

Noted for its muraled walls of Cedar Key scenes and one of King Neptune painted in 1948, nostalgic ceiling fans, French doors opening onto the wide wraparound second-story porch—the later addition of which gives the structure a gingerbready Jamaican appearance—and the cozy King Neptune lounge bar, the Island Hotel is a perfect place to kick back and relax. Sit in a rocker to watch the sun set on the Gulf, or relax in the upstairs or downstairs hotel lobby (downstairs has a grand piano) where you can get to know your fellow guests and dine on gourmet seafood, especially Cedar Key specialties.

Your hosts are Tony and Dawn Cousins, two transplanted Brits whose laid-back personalities are a terrific match for this grand old property with a character all its own.

The thirteen individually decorated guest rooms in the old inn and the annex are simple but attractive—many with double or queen-size iron beds romantically draped with mosquito netting (for atmosphere, not necessity). Those in the main building retain the charm of hand-cut walls and floors, while those in the annex feature tile floors. Eleven rooms have private bathrooms—some with claw-foot tubs (bubble bath provided), others with showers or tub/shower combinations.

Although we always swear that we're going to eat lightly while we're on vacation, what can you do when the dining room is legendary. Chef Kim Cash's culinary skills are generally believed to be unsurpassed on the island. You'll get the day off to a good start with an ample breakfast, included in the overnight rate, which can be served in the dining room or on the screened porch. This delightful meal includes fresh brewed coffee served in a French press, juice, toasted homemade poppy-seed bread, and a house specialty entree. On weekends special gourmet breakfasts are available at an additional price.

Don't limit your culinary experiences at the Island Hotel to breakfast, though. At dinner, Chef Kim's crab bisque is a specialty. Among other specialties you should try are *Escargot à la Jahn* (named for a former longtime chef), the Island Hotel Original Heart of Palm Salad, developed by former owner Bessie Gibbs during the forties, a dozen or more seafood dishes from fish in parchment paper to Cedar Key soft-shell crabs, stone crab claws, and oysters—all in season. Enjoy your meal in the casually elegant dining room or on the screened porch.

If you're looking for a place where you can totally relax, which has 140-plus years of history, and features a gourmet kitchen, pack your bags and head for Cedar Key and the Island Hotel.

HOW TO GET THERE: Cedar Key is 58 miles southwest of Gainesville at the end of FL 24. At the stop sign, turn left onto Second Street. The inn is 3 blocks on the left.

Island Hotel

It's not surprising that an inn that has survived 140 years of eventful history would have many interesting stories to tell. The crotchety old building, which has survived innumerable hurricanes, floods, storms, and even fires, contracts and expands with the seasons and moans and groans like an elderly person with aches and pains.

What began as Parson's and Hale's General Store had its purpose interrupted during the Civil War when Union troops, who occupied Cedar Key because it was a strategic port, torched almost the entire town. It is believed that the store was spared because it served as a barracks and warehouse for the Yankees. During its long history, offices of the Customs House and the Cedar Key Post Office were also located in the store, and it's even believed that for a short while the building was occupied by a brothel before becoming a hotel.

One of the most fascinating stories about the hotel involves a former long-time owner—Loyal "Gibby" Gibbs and his wife, Bessie. Unfortunately, Gibby died in 1962 and it's reported that Bessie had to store his ashes behind the bar until the tide changed so that she could scatter his remains at sea. When some locals found this somewhat tasteless, Bessie is said to have retorted, "Why not. That's where he was happiest!"

During the seventies, Jimmy Buffet was a frequent visitor and held many an impromptu concert in the Neptune Bar. He mentions Cedar Key in his song "Incommunicado."

Mayfair House Hotel 🖤 📱
Coconut Grove, Florida 33133

INNKEEPER: Amauri Biedra, general manager

ADDRESS/TELEPHONE: 3000 Florida Avenue; (305) 441–0000 or (800) 433–4555; fax (305) 447–9173

WEB SITE: www.hotelguide.net/data/h100696.htm (By the time this book goes to press, you'll be able to check out a new site: mayfairhousehotel.com.)

E-MAIL: coryf@bellsouth.net.

ROOMS: 179 suites; all with private bath, hair dryer, cable television with VCR, central stereo system, telephone, minibar, indoor or outdoor Jacuzzi.

RATES: $199 to $269 for standard suites; $249 to $279 for executive suites, double occupancy; children twelve years of age or younger may stay in an adults' guest room at no additional charge. Extra charges apply for older children and adults staying in the room. Ask about Weekend Break rates, which are applicable for stays of two nights or more between Friday and Sunday inclusive and include breakfast and added value benefits such as complimentary use of sports and leisure facilities.

OPEN: Year-round.

FACILITIES AND ACTIVITIES: Room service, valet parking, concierge, fitness center, pool, spa, restaurant, champagne bar, laundry service, car rental, facilities for the disabled. Nearby: restaurants, movie theaters, boutique shopping, Key Biscayne beaches, Viscaya Museum, University of Miami.

BUSINESS TRAVEL: Ten miles from downtown Miami, 15 miles from the Miami airport; eight meeting rooms; business-friendly rooms have dataport phones, fax facilities, and desks that are big enough on which to do some real work.

*L*ocated in the quaint shopping district of Coconut Grove across the street from the exciting Cocowalk, this superior, first-class, five-story inn comes as a surprise. Above the first floor of shops, an ivy-covered structure rises. It isn't immediately apparent whether it's a parking deck, an office building, a department store, or hotel. You'll be well rewarded by finding out what's inside. Awarded four stars and four diamonds by the major hotel rating services, the all-suite Mayfair House Hotel offers unsurpassed service in exquisite surroundings. Beautifully appointed, the mahogany-furnished suites boast either a Japanese spa tub nestled on a private veranda hidden behind the ivy or an indoor marble Roman tub Jacuzzi.

American contemporary cuisine is served in the exquisite white-linen restaurant, where seafood is a specialty. Begin your epicurean feast with an appetizer such as Chardonnay-steamed white clams, garlic-grilled squid, or pan-fried lump crabcakes, then move on to an entree such as Florida snapper, grilled veal steak, grilled tenderloin of Sterling beef, or rosemary-roasted rack of lamb—but save room for the specialty desserts of the day.

The well-trained, friendly staff of helpful professionals, who help impart the feeling of an upscale inn, are always ready to give you directions to the many sights in the area, other places to eat, the best nightspots, or the quietest beach.

HOW TO GET THERE: I–95 becomes U.S. 1, which you will take south to Unity Boulevard. Continue south to Tigertail Avenue, turn right and go to May Street. Turn left on May and go 1 block to Florida Avenue. Turn right on Florida; the hotel is on your right.

Hotel Place St. Michel
Coral Gables, Florida 33134

INNKEEPER: Christian Horsley, manager

ADDRESS/TELEPHONE: 162 Alcazar Avenue; (305) 444–1666 or (800) 848–HOTEL; fax (305) 529–0074

WEB SITE: www.hotelplacestmichel.com

ROOMS: 27, including five junior suites; all with private bath and antiques.

RATES: $125 to $165 for rooms, $160 to $200 for suites, depending on season, includes continental breakfast, fruit on arrival, and morning newspaper.

OPEN: Year-round.

FACILITIES AND ACTIVITIES: Restaurant St. Michel, piano bar, French deli. Nearby: sight-seeing, shopping, fine dining, and nightlife in Coral Gables, Coconut Grove, Miami, and Miami Beach.

The friendly folks at this exquisite boutique hotel are fond of saying, "If you can't get to Paris or Provence this year, just book yourself into the Hotel Place St. Michel instead." Actually, your first impression will be that of the Spanish countryside. Built in 1926, the hotel had to adhere to the Spanish/Mediterranean–style architecture decreed by the city of Coral Gables at that time. Not at all ostentatious looking, the entrance to the hotel is almost as homey and welcoming as someone's residence. Shielded by an awning traced in tiny lights, the stylized double front doors sit under an ivy-entwined window with a quaint wrought-iron balcony.

Inside, things take on a grander, but not overpowering, air. A barrel-vaulted ceiling accented with ornate plaster looms over a checkerboard floor. Filled with English and French antiques as well as fresh flowers and lush greenery, accompanied by exceptional service and a friendly atmosphere, the inn exudes elegance and charm.

Dan's favorite attraction is the 1926 Otis manual elevator, which is still in use. The hotel staff is happy to operate this slice of the past for you— this is definitely *not* a self-service elevator.

The cozy mahogany-paneled Stuart's Bar and Lounge is a popular piano bar and gathering place, where complimentary hors d'oeuvres accompanied by live piano entertainment are offered in the late afternoon. Performances on another grand piano set the romantic dinner mood in the elegant Restaurant St. Michel, where many a proposal has been offered. The award-winning restaurant, lauded for its French/continental cuisine, also serves breakfast and lunch. Charcuterie St. Michel is a French deli offering takeout.

Spacious guest rooms and junior suites feature French antiques and period reproductions as well as opulent floral fabrics in the bed coverings and window treatments. It is next to impossible to describe these wonderful accommodations adequately because each has such a distinct personality and furnishings. Junior suites include a spacious seating area.

The attentive staff sets the tone for this elegant small hotel that takes us back to the past when gentility and charm were the rule. If this type of ambience turns you on, as it does us, give this hidden jewel a try.

HOW TO GET THERE: Take I-95 to FL 836 and go west. Turn south on South Le Jeune Road and continue to Alcazar, where you will turn left (east). The inn is on the right.

Henderson Park Inn
Destin, Florida 32541

INNKEEPER: Susie Nunnelly

ADDRESS/TELEPHONE: 2700 Scenic Highway 98E; (850) 837-4853 or (800) 336-4853

WEB SITE: www.hendersonparkinn.com

E-MAIL: admin@abbott-resorts.com (This is the management company; there is no e-mail direct to the inn.)

ROOMS: 35; all with private baths, refrigerator, icemaker, coffeemaker, microwave, telephone, cable TV, in-room safe, bathrobes, and evening turndown service.

RATES: $109 to $239 in high season (summer), includes breakfast and a late afternoon cocktail hour around the gulfside gazebo; reduced rates fall through spring.

OPEN: Year-round.

FACILITIES AND ACTIVITIES: The Veranda Restaurant; heated pool in season; complimentary beach chairs, umbrellas, and beach towel service in season; sundeck area, beach gazebo, and barbecue grills. Nearby: championship golf courses, charter deep-sea fishing boats, shopping, several state parks, Indian Temple Mound and Museum, U.S. Air Force Armament Museum, Focus Center children's Museum, zoo, Gulfarium.

BUSINESS TRAVEL: Dedicated meeting facility can accommodate up to fifty persons with audiovisual equipment and complete food and beverage service; also business center with fax, computer, and modem lines.

*T*his is our kind of place: where we can sit on the beach with a good book to our heart's content; take a refreshing dip in the Gulf if we get too hot; retreat to one of the old-fashioned porch swings on the veranda when we've had enough sun; take long, long walks on the powder-soft beach; or enjoy the caress of soft breezes, the lulling sound of crashing waves, the brilliant colors of sunrise or sunset, or the sparkle of moonlight reflecting off the Gulf waters from our patio or balcony. Only when we've unwound completely would we leave this inn for shopping or sight-seeing.

Built only six years ago, but resembling a stately old New England shingle-style inn with full-length verandas on the first and second floors, the Henderson Park Inn is beachfront on one of the most beautiful soft white-sand beaches on the Gulf

of Mexico. As if it needed any added attractions, the inn is located on the eastern boundary of Henderson Beach State Park, ensuring an undeveloped mile-long stretch of beach beyond the inn in perpetuity. Although we usually prefer historic properties, this thoroughly modern inn is so well done, we completely forgive it its lack of age. Combining the best of beachside charm and elegance with all the modern comforts and conveniences, the inn and its surroundings are the perfect antidote to the hectic everyday world.

Evoking a nostalgic ambience, lavish guest rooms are furnished with Victorian-era reproductions and accented with luxuriant fabrics for the bed coverings and window treatments as well as Impressionist art. Graceful and romantic bed chambers, many of which sport high ceilings and feature a king- or queen-size four-poster, canopied, or iron beds draped with fine linens. All rooms offer a private bath, most with a whirlpool tub, as well as a small refrigerator, icemaker, coffeemaker, microwave, telephone, cable television, in-room safe, bathrobes, and patio or private balcony. Some extra-special accommodations boast a fireplace as well.

You'll enjoy fine seafood specialties and eclectic continental cuisine in the inn's aptly named Veranda Restaurant, where you can choose a table by a wall of windows overlooking the beach and the Gulf or dine out on the veranda itself. The delightful dining room is where you will enjoy your complimentary breakfast and where you can sample from the lunch buffet or share an elegant, romantic candlelight dinner with your loved one. Cocktails are served and there is an impressive wine list. In season, you don't even have to leave the beach and get dressed for lunch; beachside menu service is offered.

Holiday Inn La Concha
Key West, Florida 33040

INNKEEPER: Robert Layman

ADDRESS/TELEPHONE: 430 Duval Street; (305) 296-2991 or (800) 745-2191; fax (305) 294-3283

WEB SITE: www.keywest.com/laconcha.html

ROOMS: 160 rooms and suites; all with private bath, telephone, and television.

RATES: The basic rate is $220 to $275, double occupancy, but rates vary greatly for special-events weekends, which go as high as $400 per night. Rumor has it that the rate for December 31, 1999, will be $600. Suites begin at $325.

OPEN: Year-round.

FACILITIES AND ACTIVITIES: Celebrities Restaurant, cocktail lounge, outdoor pool, two gift shops, bicycle and scooter rental, concierge; Old Town Trolley stops at the front door. Nearby: Mallory Square, Havana Docks, Mel Fisher Museum, Audubon House, Hemingway House, Key West Lighthouse, shopping, casual and fine dining, nightspots.

BUSINESS TRAVEL: Ideal for meetings and corporate retreats.

*I*t's been said that Duval Street is to Key West what Bourbon Street is to New Orleans, and it's certainly true, even if a somewhat toned-down version. On our first trip to Key West we wanted to be in the center of all the action, so what could be more ideal than a stay at the then newly restored La Concha on Duval Street, the main drag? We had a wonderful trip and fell in love with this quaint old downtown property located in the heart of one of this country's most famous party towns. Don't be put off by the fact that it is a Holiday Inn, this is a genuine historic and intimate inn, which stands on its own merits.

Built in 1925, the charming six-story hotel has admirably stood the test of time. In its original heyday, the La Concha hosted such luminaries as royalty, presidents, and Pulitzer prize winners. Today the National Register inn's award-winning restoration echoes the grandeur of days past while providing all the modern comforts and conveniences. We particularly admire the original Art Deco fixtures and designs, the seclusion of the multilevel tropical pool terrace and its gazebo, and The Top rooftop bar, where we can get an uncrowded, unobstructed view of Key West's spectacular sunsets as well as a bird's-eye view of the quaint town.

Casual guest rooms, which have private baths, are authentically furnished in the style of the twenties. Most overlook the pool or Duval Street. Just a hint: Depending on your age and lifestyle and the time you like to turn in, you'll either love or loathe rooms on the Duval Street side, which are subject to the noisy action of crowds out on the streets until the wee hours of the morning.

HOW TO GET THERE: Take U.S. 1 to Whitehead Street. Turn right and proceed to Eaton Street, where you will turn right. Go 1 block to Duval Street and turn left. The hotel is on the right.

The Marquesa Hotel
Key West, Florida 33040

INNKEEPER: Carol Whitman, manager

ADDRESS/TELEPHONE: 600 Fleming Street; (305) 292–1919 or (800) 869–4631; fax: (305) 294–2121

WEB SITE: www.marquesa.com.

ROOMS: 27, plus 9 nine junior suites; all with private bath, king- or queen-size beds, ceiling fan, central air, television, telephone, hair dryer, and safe; some have private porch, sitting area, and robes.

RATES: Rates depend on the season and whether midweek or weekend; $135 to $195 for rooms, $205 to $290 for junior suites, includes breakfast. Higher rates and minimum stays may apply for special events and holidays.

OPEN: Year-round.

FACILITIES AND ACTIVITIES: Restaurant, two swimming pools, twenty-four-hour concierge.

BUSINESS TRAVEL: Guest room phones have a dataport plug-in; corporate rate Sunday through Thursday for business travelers who have stayed at the inn four or more times.

After a hard day of getting to Key West, whether by car or by plane, the welcome glass of wine is just what the doctor ordered and a prelude to the kind of pampering you'll get at the Marquesa. Hotel manager Carol Whitman and her staff are dedicated to making your stay memorable. The atmosphere is casual and friendly, a Key West norm, but taken to new heights at this exquisite inn.

A compound of four historic buildings set around a lush interior garden, the longtime four-diamond Marquesa offers a luxurious, quiet retreat for those wanting pampering and privacy. One of the Southeast's finest small hotels, the Marquesa was transformed from an 1884 conch house to its present incarnation of beautiful rooms and suites with marble baths and numerous amenities.

Immaculate, light, and airy, the sumptuous guest chambers are filled with all the amenities that make you feel at home. All guest rooms feature a private marble bath, central air-conditioning, remote-control television, telephone, hair dryer, personal safe, and Caswell-Massey toiletries. Standard rooms, which are anything but standard in our opinion, feature a queen-size bed; junior suites boast a king-size bed, a private porch with lounge chairs and a breakfast table, a living room grouping, and bathrobes. Evening turndown service for all rooms culminates with a Godiva chocolate on your pillow.

Your breakfast is served from Cafe Marquesa and you can choose the decadent luxury of having it brought to your room or the delights of eating in the pool and courtyard area, where your meal will be accompanied by the soft sounds of rustling palms, the sparkling fountain, and a trickling waterfall. The white-linen Cafe Marquesa, which is renowned in Key West and south Florida, serves cuisine of the Americas—foods from North, South, and Central America. Feast on specialties such as grilled meats; fresh local seafood such as pecan-crusted grouper, spicy Caribbean prawns, and grilled yellowtail tuna; as well as inventive vegetable dishes and fresh-baked breads and desserts. You can watch these masterpieces being created in the theater-kitchen behind a *trompe l'oeil* wall of a kitchen scene. The cafe is open for dinner seven nights a week and is so popular that reservations are strongly suggested.

The Marquesa's location is ideal for exploring historic Key West—just 1 block from Duval Street and 4 blocks from Mallory Square and the Gulf of Mexico. Almost the entire area can be explored on foot.

HOW TO GET THERE: As you drive into Key West, bear right following U.S. 1. As it narrows it becomes Truman Avenue. Continue to Duval Street. Turn right and follow Duval to Fleming Street. Turn right and the hotel is on the left.

Pier House Resort and Caribbean Spa
Key West, Florida 33040

INNKEEPER: Joy Smatt, general manager

ADDRESS/TELEPHONE: One Duval Street; (305) 296–4600 or (800) 327–8340; fax (305) 296–9085

WEB SITE: www.pierhouse.com

E-MAIL: info@pierhouse.com

ROOMS: 128, plus 14 suites; all with private bath and an ocean, pool, or garden view as well as a private balcony or terrace, television, VCR, telephone, clock radio, hair dryer; some with patio or balcony; bathrobes in suites and spa rooms.

RATES: (Rates given are dependent on season: Low season is April 12 through December 25; high season is December 25 through April 12. The low season rate is given first.) $195 to $275 for standard room; $250 to $335 for garden courtyard rooms, $300 to $400 for Caribbean Spa rooms, and $350 to $450 for harbor-front rooms. Suites range from $325 to $1,200 during low season and $450 to $1,400 during high season. Several packages are also available: Honeymoon Hideaway $735 to $975, Stress Breaker Plus $659 to $885. Rates are for single or double occupancy. Add $35 for extra guests in the room. Special events require a minimum stay and must be prepaid in full. Spa services range in price from $10 to $125, and packages are available.

OPEN: Year-round.

FACILITIES AND ACTIVITIES: Caribbean spa, Pier House Restaurant and Wine Gallery Piano Bar, Harbour View Cafe, Pier House Market Bistro, Chart Room Bar, Havana Docks Sunset Deck, pool with whirlpool, private beach, topless beach. Nearby: Mallory Square, Key West Aquarium, Mel Fisher Museum, Audubon House, Hemingway House, Key West Lighthouse, shopping, dining, nightspots.

BUSINESS TRAVEL: Located 150 miles south of Miami; dedicated conference center with banquet and classroom settings can handle groups up to 175; audiovisual equipment, food and beverage service including beach barbecues, private island parties, or private sunset cruises.

We've always loved the carefree, laid-back paradise of Key West—a longtime favorite refuge of preachers, poets, pirates, and presidents—and to us it's been the ultimate, secluded warm-weather getaway while still on U.S. soil. After several trips and experimenting with different hotels and bed-and-breakfasts, we discovered the Pier House and decided we'd died and gone to heaven. Located in the heart of Old Town overlooking the Gulf of Mexico, the intimate resort is just steps away from the hustle and bustle of Duval Street, Mallory Square, and the Havana Docks—the traditional spot where everyone in Key West gathers to watch the spectacular sunset each evening—but still remains a little world unto itself.

Almost hidden by exotic tropical foliage and flowers, the resort boasts a variety of rooming arrangements, a private white-sand beach, a spa, nightly live entertainment at several lounges, and exquisite cuisine at formal and informal restaurants. We love the ambience of a fine small hotel with a well-trained professional staff ready to cater to our every need.

On this particular trip, we'd decided that some ultimate pampering and indulgence were in order, so we picked the Pier House for its spa and stayed in one of the spacious spa rooms. All the rooms at the resort are graciously elegant, but these bright and breezy upscale spa accommodations feature hardwood floors, California king-size beds, vibrant Florida fabrics and colors, whirlpool tubs, and VCR and CD player in addition to the television available in all rooms.

Among the spa services of which we availed ourselves, the aptly named Caribbean Coma was the preeminent relaxation. First the hands and feet are dipped into warm paraffin. Then the rest of the body is massaged using ele-

ments from various massage techniques. When the paraffin is removed, the feet are massaged with reflexology. The treatment is brought to an end with more soothing massage of the neck, head, and face. You'll hate for it to be over. Other spa services range from loofah salt glow, to dozens of facials, to hair and nail care. You can have your body composition analyzed, but why would you want to know that while you're in an area so renowned for its food and drink? And, although we didn't want to work that hard, there are fitness classes and you can even arrange for a personal trainer. Instead we spent time on the beach watching the shrimp boats and pleasure craft plying the channel.

You'll want to savor at least one innovative, elegantly prepared American-Caribbean dinner either indoors or out at the celebrated, four-diamond Pier House Restaurant, which is built out over the water. The number-one dining destination for scores of locals and tourists alike, the restaurant has served the likes of Tennessee Williams, Truman Capote, and Peter Fonda. Dine on stone crab claws and yellowtail while swilling sinful libations and listening to live piano entertainment. The Sunday brunch is legendary. For other meals during your stay, satisfy your appetite with casual beachside snacks at DJ's Sand Bar, light delights at the Harbour View Cafe, and creative deli fare at the Market Bistro, which has a casual setting overlooking bustling Old Town. Also enjoy the live musicians at the Beach Club Bar, join the sing-along in the Wine Gallery and Piano Bar, or drop in to the offbeat Chart Room Bar, where you can get the true flavor of old Key West. Of course, the place to be at sunset is atop the Havana Docks Sunset Deck, where you can enjoy live music, a raw bar, and spectacular views.

And when you can drag yourself away from the resort, all the enticements of Key West are just steps away from your door.

HOW TO GET THERE: Key West is located on the southernmost tip of Florida, approximately 150 miles south of Miami via U.S. 1 and 90 miles north of Cuba. There is frequent air service daily from Miami, Tampa, Ft. Lauderdale, and Orlando. Follow the signs to the business district and stay to the right. Follow North Roosevelt Boulevard, which turns into Truman Avenue and continue to Duval Street. Turn right and continue Duval to its end at the waterfront. The Pier House is on your right.

Chalet Suzanne
Lake Wales, Florida 33859

INNKEEPERS: Carl and Vita Hinshaw

ADDRESS/TELEPHONE: U.S. Highway 27 (mailing address: 3800 Chalet Suzanne Drive); (914) 676–6011; for reservations, (800) 433–6011; fax (941) 676–1814

WEB SITE: www.chaletsuzanne.com

E-MAIL: infa@chaletsuzanne.com

ROOMS: 30; all with private bath, television, and telephone, 5 with Jacuzzi.

RATES: $135 to $195, single or double; includes full breakfast. Pets $20 extra.

OPEN: Year-round.

FACILITIES AND ACTIVITIES: Lunch, dinner, wheelchair access to dining room; restaurant closed Monday. Cocktail lounge, wine cellar open for sampling, gift shop, antiques shop, ceramics studio, swimming pool, lake, soup cannery, airstrip. Nearby: golf, tennis, fishing, Cypress Gardens, Bok Tower Gardens.

BUSINESS TRAVEL: Conference facilities; access to fax; telephone in room.

Chalet Suzanne releases a photograph for publicity along with this caption: "Through wrought-iron gates one can view the unlikely hodgepodge of towers, turrets, and gables that ramble in all directions." Well, yeah, that too.

Everyone who writes about this inn falters under the burden of trying to describe what they've seen—a collection of whimsical, odd buildings assembled over a number of years by Carl Hinshaw's mother, who got into innkeeping and the restaurant business trying to keep body and soul together after being widowed during the Great Depression. We've seen the words "Camelot," "phantasmagoria," "fairy tale," "magical," in the reviews of writers trying to capture the mood of the place. Any and all will do. Staying here is a great giggle for anyone who doesn't like too many straight lines, who enjoys walks and walls that tilt, and who appreciates the kind of humor represented by a potted geranium atop the ice machine.

We enjoy the Orchid Room, a roughly octagonal space where sherry and fruit were set out on a small table between two comfortable chairs. Live plants and fresh flowers are scattered throughout the room and its bath, and the furniture was painted various shades of aqua, cream, and deep orchid. The bath has been updated and features a whirlpool jet tub and new tile.

Chalet Suzanne is famous for its award-winning restaurant, in which the tables are all set with different kinds of china, silver, and glasses collected by the Hinshaws over years of travel. Carl's Romaine soup, Vita's broiled grapefruit garnished with chicken livers, and the shrimp curry are all much-extolled selections, so we tried them all with a nice house wine dispensed in generous servings. We enjoyed everything, including being served by waitresses in costumes that looked Swiss in the Swiss dining room, where European stained-glass windows provide a focal point.

A waitress told us that Carl Hinshaw's soups—which have become so popular that he started a cannery on the premises for people who want to take soup home—have made it to the better gourmet shops and even to the moon with the Apollo astronauts—not necessarily in that order.

So there you are, in a wacky, unreal environment, eating multi-star-winning food that must be famous by now on the moon, served by waitresses dressed like Snow White, and you're sleeping in a room that looks as though it came out of a Seven-Dwarfs coloring book . . . how are you going to describe it? You're not—so simply enjoy.

HOW TO GET THERE: Chalet Suzanne is 4 miles north of Lake Wales on Chalet Suzanne Road, which turns off Highway 27. Signs clearly mark the turns.

Little Palm Island 💚
Little Torch Key, Florida 33042

INNKEEPERS: Ben Woodson, owner; Paul Royall, director

ADDRESS/TELEPHONE: 28500 Overseas Highway; (305) 872–2524, (800) 343–8567, or (800) 3–GET–LOST; fax (305) 872–4843

WEB SITE: www.littlepalmisland.com

E-MAIL: littlepalm@relaischateaux.fr

ROOMS: 30 suites; all with private bath with Jacuzzi, private sundeck, ceiling fan, air-conditioning, coffeemaker, wet bar/minibar, outdoor shower.

RATES: $350 to $850 per couple per night, depending on the season, includes launch service to and from the island, daily newspaper, and use of swimming pool, sauna, exercise room, kayaks and canoes, windsurfers and instruction, Hobie day sailers, snorkel and fishing gear, beach lounges, towels, and floats. Suites will sleep four adults, additional persons, $100 per night. Full American dining plan is available for $140 per person per day; modified American plan $125 per person per day. Holiday meals may be subject to a meal plan surcharge.

OPEN: Year-round.

FACILITIES AND ACTIVITIES: Sauna, Jacuzzi, spa, beauty salon, water sports, fishing tournaments, scuba diving and certification, snorkeling, cruises aboard the *First Lady*—a Columbia 42-foot yacht—sailing courses and certification, deep-sea fishing charters, backcountry and flats fishing, pontoon boat rental, natural history backcountry ecotours.

BUSINESS TRAVEL: Ideal for small corporate meetings and retreats.

*D*oes Bali Hai exist? Do we have to travel to the South Pacific or deep into the Caribbean to find and enjoy complete relaxation amid unspoiled natural tropical surroundings? The answers to these questions are yes and no. You can find your very own private Bali Hai paradise at Little Palm Island, just off the Florida Keys.

A mere five-acre private island located 3 miles offshore Little Torch Key midway down the Keys, the island's location at the entrance to Newfound Harbor and its fast-running tides created a white sandy beach and deepwater dockage sure to please any adventurer.

This idyllic refuge was once visited by President and Mrs. Truman, John Foster Dulles, Admiral Bull Halsey, and other luminaries. *PT-109,* the story of John F. Kennedy's war exploits starring Cliff Robertson, was filmed here in 1962. It was only during the filming that the state of Florida ran electricity and water to the island. In 1986 a magnificent exclusive hideaway resort akin to the Rock Resorts at St. John's and Little Dix Bay in the Caribbean was born, and this is where you can truly get away from it all. In fact, the island is accessible only by boat.

Within the lush grounds of the Jamaican coconut palm–ringed island are flamboyant bougainvillea, oleander, hibiscus, and other vibrant tropical blooms. Scattered among this profuse vegetation, and very subdued in contrast, are fourteen thatched-roof villas on stilts—like charming treehouses. Designed for seclusion, each villa houses two luxurious ocean-view suites. The interior of each features a sitting room and bedroom decorated and furnished as a tropical retreat with bold, bright colors, plantation shutters, and ceiling fans and a luxurious bath with a Jacuzzi. You'll love the romantic mosquito netting draped over the bed. Although the villas are air-conditioned, with an average year-round temperature of 76.8 degrees, you'll prefer to enjoy the fresh air and natural breezes.

Our idea of a really strenuous day is breakfast on our deck, then spending some time on the pristine white beach with a good book, followed by a dip in the aquamarine Gulf waters or the lagoon-style freshwater pool with its tinkling waterfall, followed by a nap in a hammock strung between two palms, punctuated by a snack or a cool drink, and finally ending the day sitting on our private veranda sipping a frosty cocktail while contemplating the sunset—all the while serenaded by colorful birds and fanned by ocean breezes. Ah, it's all so exotic and seductive. Another day, maybe, we'll have a massage in the massage treehouse, where fresh breezes and birdsong blow through the windows or avail ourselves of some spa services.

An alternative activity might be standing on the main dock looking west to Loggerhead Key, where 2,000 Rhesus monkeys live, or waiting quietly in the evening to see the endangered Key deer feeding on the hibiscus and the herbs in the kitchen garden. During the day, watch the wading birds such as the roseate spoonbill.

An Affair with
the Lady Bess

Although totally decadent, this is not a clandestine affair. Rather it's one you'll engage in with your spouse or significant other and maybe another couple or family members, because the *Lady Bess* is actually a luxurious, private 42-foot motor yacht with a captain and crew to pamper you and a chef to captivate your taste buds. You'll travel slowly through the pristine aquamarine waters surrounding the Florida Keys, availing yourselves of as many or as few water sports and other activities as your heart desires.

This romantic adventure begins with limousine pickup at the Key West airport. As soon as you board the *Lady Bess* and settle in, you can explore the classic yacht that's fitted out with rich teakwood decks, an elegantly appointed salon with an entertainment center, an afterdeck with a wet bar, a cockpit with two fighting chairs for serious deep-sea fishermen, and two large staterooms. Then, while you watch the flaming sunset, you'll be treated to cocktails and appetizers prepared by your gourmet chef. Later the chef will treat you to his culinary magic with dinner under the stars. At the end of an idyllic day, the sea will gently rock you to sleep off the uninhabited island of Boca Grande.

In the days that follow, do nothing—or fish, explore the mangroves in a dinghy or kayak, go ashore at a secluded beach for a picnic, or snorkel or scuba dive at Looe Key reef. If you catch a snapper or grouper, the chef will prepare it for you. Spend one day and two nights anchored at Little Palm Island, where you can enjoy the resort's amenities: the pool, beach, spa, shop, and dining room presided over by Chef Michel Reymond.

All good things must come to an end, so you'll be returned to the mainland by launch and transported to the Key West Airport by limousine. This all-inclusive package provides four days and nights aboard the *Lady Bess*, all meals while onboard or at Little Palm Island, and all activities while aboard. The itinerary is flexible and can be adapted to your desires. Rates, including tax and gratuity, range from $5,600 August through November; $6,600 December, January, and May through July; and $7,600 February through April.

For those who are more active, there's plenty to do. They can snorkel or dive to explore Looe Key reef where the HMS *Looe* sank in 1744 after hitting the reef—one of the prettiest in the world. Looe Key National Marine Sanctuary is rated as one of the top-ten reefs in the world and is the only living reef in North America. Scuba and sailing certification courses are offered, as are fishing charters and pontoon boat rentals. Environmentalists will appreciate a visit to bird rookeries and wilderness sanctuaries in the backcountry of the Great White Heron National Wildlife Refuge.

The only problem we experience with all this inactivity is the calories that don't get burned off from the award-winning French cuisine accented with Caribbean flavors. Meals are served in the spacious airy dining room on the terrace or, more romantic to us, right on the beach. Chef Michel creates a six-course gourmet feast each Thursday and is renowned for his Sunday brunch and holiday offerings. Because the island is so close to the mainland, folks come over by boat to dine at Little Palm Island (by reservation only). Every night reveals a new delicacy to savor such as lobster and stone crab soup, smoked salmon parfait with Belgian endive and green apple, Chef Michel's signature rack of lamb, or duck breast—all culminated by a mouthwatering dessert such as coconut cream–filled chocolate ravioli with praline sauce.

Is it any surprise that Little Palm Island has been named one of the twelve most romantic hotels in the country? Come find out for yourself.

HOW TO GET THERE: Take U.S. 1 from Miami through the Keys to Little Torch Key, then the ferry to Little Palm Island.

Lakeside Inn
Mount Dora, Florida 32757

INNKEEPER: James Barggren, general manager

ADDRESS/TELEPHONE: 100 North Alexander Street; (352) 383–4101 or (800) 556–5016; fax (352) 735–2642

WEB SITE: lakeside-inn.com.

E-MAIL: Via Web site.

ROOMS: 88 rooms and suites; all with private bath, cable television, telephone; smoking and nonsmoking rooms available; limited access for the disabled.

RATES: There are three seasons: January 1 through May 15, May 16 through September 30, and October 1 through December 31. On top of that, there are selected weekends when price is affected. Lakefront rooms and suites cost more than others. In general, weekday rates range from $90 to $165 and weekend and holiday rates from $120 to $215, single or double occupancy; includes continental breakfast. An occupancy charge of $10 per person is levied for additional persons in the room. The Romantic Rendevouz (high season, $359) and Sweetheart Season (low season, $299) packages are for Friday and Saturday night stays and include dinner one night with a bottle of house wine and champagne, fruits, and cheeses the second night. The Great Gatsby package ($269) is for a midweek stay and includes dinner one night and a bottle of house wine.

OPEN: Year-round.

FACILITIES AND ACTIVITIES: The Beauclaire dining room restaurant, Tremain's Lounge, room service, Olympic-size pool and towel service, tennis courts, croquet; Mount Dora trolley stops at the inn; variety of boat rentals by the hour or day, carriage rides; live entertainment midweek through the weekend. Nearby: antiques shopping, golf, Ice House Theater, concerts, exhibitions at the Mount Dora Center for the Arts, Royellou Museum, Gilbert Park, Palm Island Park, House of Presidents wax museum, Lakeridge Winery, Yalaha Bakery, horseback riding in Ocala National Forest.

BUSINESS TRAVEL: Twenty-five miles north of Orlando; five meeting rooms and lobby can accommodate up to 125 for small meetings and retreats.

Follow the quiet lane lined with lampposts to the shores of central Florida's Lake Dora and go back in time to the Lakeside Inn of yesteryear. Beginning with a modest ten rooms in 1883, the original inn was expanded over many years until it reached its current size of eighty-eight rooms in the early 1930s. In fact, it was Calvin Coolidge, having just completed his term in the presidency, who dedicated the Gable and Terrace wings and then decided he liked the inn so much he stayed all winter. The 1920s, the Gatsby era, saw the inn's heyday. It is the ambience, traditions, and hospitality of the 1920s and 1930s that today's proprietors strive to evoke in this English country–style refuge. Permeated with history and infused with romance, this venerable hostelry has been a perennial favorite as a winter haven for all kinds of travelers.

We think it's a little bit of heaven to step onto the sweeping verandas cooled by paddle fans and comfortably furnished with colonial rockers, from which you can watch the stirring sunsets over the lake. In less-than-perfect weather, it's fun to gather in the ballroom-size lobby for fireside chats, games, and tea dances. Evenings are the time to enjoy vibrant conversation and vintage music in Tremaine's Lounge. Almost any time of day is perfect to dine on epicurean delights in The Beauclaire, the award-winning restaurant. Continental breakfast is included in the room rate, but you can also order more substantial breakfast items a la carte; a sumptuous brunch is served on Sunday. Light lunch items are served Monday through Saturday. Reservations are strongly recommended for dinner in The Beauclaire.

Deluxe guest rooms are sure to please whether they have two twin beds, one or two doubles, or a king-size bed. Our only complaint about the spacious, well-proportioned and well-equipped guest chambers is the overuse (in our opinion) of multiple floral patterns in the wallpaper, bed coverings, and window treatments. Parlor rooms boast a similar deluxe guest room with an additional connecting room, which serves as a cozy parlor. In most cases the parlor has a sofa bed to accommodate children or additional travelers. Naturally, the most sought-after rooms are the lakefront ones with their magnificent views. One in particular boasts a private balcony with rocking chairs.

For the sports enthusiast, the pool is open year-round and there are two lighted tennis courts, a croquet lawn, and boat rentals. The inn serves as the base for the Mount Dora annual sailing regatta, the oldest in the state. Angling for bass and catfish is a longtime tradition. Bird-watching is just as popular as it was when the inn was founded, but as far as we know, intrepid guests don't go out into the wilderness anymore with a pronged stick to hunt for snakes.

HOW TO GET THERE: Take U.S. 441 to FL 46, exit west to FL 500A west. Follow FL 500A west (it becomes Highland Avenue). Turn left onto Fifth Avenue, then left on Alexander Street. The inn is at 100 North Alexander.

Seven Sisters Inn
Ocala, Florida 34471

INNKEEPERS: Bonnie Morehardt and Ken Oden

ADDRESS/TELEPHONE: 820 Southeast Fort King Street;
(352) 867–1170; fax (352) 867–5266

WEB SITE: www.7sistersinn.com

E-MAIL: sistersinn@aol.com

ROOMS: 8; all with private bath; 3 with fireplace; 1 on first floor with
wheelchair access and equipped for handicapped. No smoking inn.

RATES: $115 to $185, depending on season, single or double; includes
full breakfast and five-course gourmet dinner. Inquire about senior and
military rates.

OPEN: Year-round.

FACILITIES AND ACTIVITIES: Club room, smoking porches, bicycles.
Nearby: walking distance to restaurants, historic downtown, antiques
and gift shops; short drive to Silver Springs Park, Appleton Art
Museum.

BUSINESS TRAVEL: Scott Room has desk with private phone and
computer setup; corporate rates.

"*B*eing an innkeeper is like having 1,800 of your best friends visit
you each year," Ken said. His comment sets the tone at this inn.
Ken is an airline pilot and accustomed to meeting lots of people.
"It's a great way to stay in the hospitality business," his wife, Bonnie, said.
Well, she's a pilot, too, and for a while decided that the innkeeping business
was more stable than flying. She put all her energy into the inn in what Ken
calls a "damn the torpedos" mode. Practically everything pretty you see is a
project of Bonnie's, from the lacy, yellow, Monet-like breakfast room to the
beautifully conceived and executed decor of the guest rooms. However, the
air is a temptress that cannot be denied, and Bonnie is flying again.

The Seven Sisters Inn started as a family home in 1888. The rooms on the
upper two floors are named for the seven sisters of the woman who renovated
the building in 1985. The decor of each room reflects the interests of each of
the sisters, and you'll find a picture of each sister somewhere in her room. The
downstairs room that is equipped for the handicapped people really works
because a member of the family who lived here was handicapped.

More of Bonnie's formidable energy and creativity go into special weekends, ranging from slick murder mysteries to scavenger hunts and chocolate

extravaganzas. The inn often has wine-tasting weekends, cooking classes, Friday-night bistros, and theater packages, too.

Bonnie is proud of her special breakfasts. She likes to serve unusual juices such as pear nectar, followed by fresh fruit and cream and specialties such as blueberry French toast. Bonnie started as a flight attendant and worked to earn her pilot's license because, as she put it, "I decided I'd rather drink coffee than serve it." Come to think of it, the day I visited, Ken was pouring the coffee.

When it originally opened, Seven Sisters Inn occasionally served candlelight dinners for small groups and dinner buffets for some of the special weekends. However, bowing to demand they are now deep into the dinner trade. Their new rates now include a five-course gourmet dinner in addition to their sumptious breakfast. A pure B&B rate is also available for those who insist on going elsewhere for dinner.

HOW TO GET THERE: From I-75, take exit 69 onto State Road 40, which becomes Silver Springs Boulevard downtown. Turn right at Southeast Ninth Avenue and right again in the next block at Southeast Fort King Street.

The Courtyard at Lake Lucerne
Orlando, Florida 32801

INNKEEPER: Eleanor Meiner

ADDRESS/TELEPHONE: 211 North Lucerne Circle East; (407) 648-5188 or (800) 444-5289; fax (407) 246-1368

WEB SITE: www.travelbase.com/destinations/orlando/lake-lucerne

E-MAIL: lucerne@travelbase.com

ROOMS: 24 in three buildings; all with private bath, television, and telephone; some with steam shower and oversized whirlpool tub; some with small kitchen. No smoking building.

RATES: $89 to $165, single or double; includes continental buffet breakfast and wine.

FACILITIES AND ACTIVITIES: Courtyard gardens, reception areas. Nearby: Lake Cherokee Historic District trail begins here; walking distance to restaurants and downtown Orlando; health club facilities, golf and tennis can be arranged; sailing on Lake Eola; twenty-minute drive to Walt Disney World, Splendid China, and other regional theme attractions.

BUSINESS TRAVEL: Located five minutes from business district. Telephone and good work space in room; fax, copy machine, and computer setup available; conference facilities; corporate rates.

*T*his B&B inn comprises three separate historic buildings from three distinct eras grouped around a 20,000-square-foot semitropical garden. The Norment-Parry, Orlando's oldest house, is Victorian; the Wellborn is an excellent example of Art Deco architecture and decor; the I. W. Phillips House is an antebellum-style manor house furnished in Edwardian and Eastlake antiques. The Norment-Parry stands on its original location; the other two buildings were moved to the site. If you look at the whole place at once you are simply overwhelmed with color, design, and antiques.

Since most of the rooms look onto the garden, let's start there. Orlando is a good place to grow tropicals, anyhow. What Eleanor Meiner's daughter-in-law, Paula, has done with this garden enchants you. The lines are curved rather than straight and stiff, the walks are old brick for a softer appearance, and the plants are an astonishing collection of azaleas, bird of paradise, heliconia, bougainvillea, ginger, banana trees, 80-foot camphor trees, and scores of other plants, familiar and rare.

You find more vivid colors in the guest rooms. For example, in the Norment-Parry, each of the six guest rooms, four of which have sitting rooms, has been decorated by a different architect, artist, or designer.

The jazzy Art Deco decor of the Wellborn gives the impression that a well-to-do family of the time has simply stepped out for the day. One of the honeymoon suites is in this house.

And the I. W. Phillips house is furnished in Belle Epoque style. French doors open out to verandas overlooking the garden. These are luxury rooms with double tubs and, in one, a steam room and whirlpool.

A conference room at the rear of the I. W. Phillips house opens from the downstairs reception room through pocketed mirror French doors.

For all the glamour, the staff are pleasant, unpretentious, and very helpful. Once you get your senses calmed down and can appreciate one thing at a time, this is an easy place to be.

HOW TO GET THERE: From I–4 going east, take the Anderson exit. At the stop light at the top of the ramp, turn right. Go three lights and turn right onto Delaney Avenue. Take the first right onto Lucerne Circle North. Going west on I–4, take the Anderson Street exit, go four lights, turn right onto Delaney, and almost immediately take the first right onto Lucerne Circle North.

Palm Beach Historic Inn
Palm Beach, Florida 33480

INNKEEPERS: Chris Rohman

ADDRESS/TELEPHONE: 365 South County Road; (561) 832–4009; fax: (561) 832–6255

WEB SITE: www.palmbeachhistoricinn.com

E-MAIL: info@palmbeachhistoricinn.com

ROOMS: 9, plus 4 suites, all with private bath, refrigerator, cable television, telephone, and robes.

RATES: $75 to $125 in low season (May 8 through December 15), $150 to $225 the rest of the year; single or double occupancy, includes deluxe continental breakfast and morning newspaper.

OPEN: Year-round.

FACILITIES AND ACTIVITIES: Nearby: 1 block to the beach, 2 blocks to Worth Avenue; casual and gourmet dining, art galleries, antiques shops, specialty boutiques, golf, tennis, horseback riding, polo, croquet, jai alai, greyhound racing, performing arts, cruise ships, museums, zoo, planetarium, botanical gardens, water sports.

We admit it—we were starstruck by the glitz and glamor and rarified atmosphere of enchanting, tropical Palm Beach, especially the Henry Morrison Flagler Museum and the tony boutiques and galleries on Worth Avenue. Just about everything there might be way, way out of our price range, but it's oh so much fun to look. And never have we seen such a concentration of shiny Rolls Royces.

The good news is, you don't have to be a multimillionaire to stay in Palm Beach. Although there are plenty of hotels with astronomical prices, there is a secret little historic gem of a B&B inn where you can stay in luxury on a regular person's salary.

Located in a landmark Moorish-style building with numerous arches and a red tile roof, the inn has been carefully restored to preserve its structural integrity and refined elegance, while adding every modern convenience.

The look and feel of an intimate European parlor characterize the lobby. Spacious, high-ceilinged guest rooms are tastefully appointed with antiques and reproductions as well as opulent bed coverings and elegant window treatments. Beds, many of which are romantic four-posters, testers, or half-testers, range in size from doubles to kings. Several particularly spacious bed chambers and two-room suites feature a trundle bed, additional twin beds, and/or a sofa bed to accommodate additional travelers in your party making them ideal for families or friends traveling together.

You'll get your day off to a good start with a sumptuous continental-plus breakfast served in your room and accompanied by the morning newspaper. Through careful attention to every service detail, the staff has your utmost comfort in mind. You'll feel like royalty when you stay at the Palm Beach Historic Inn.

HOW TO GET THERE: From I–95 exit at 52A Okeechobee Boulevard. From the Florida Turnpike exit at 99 West Palm Beach. Drive east on Okeechobee Boulevard, cross over the bridge to Palm Beach onto Royal Palm Way. Turn right onto A1A and drive south to 365 South County Road. The inn is opposite the historic city hall.

Kenwood
St. Augustine, Florida 32084

INNKEEPERS: Mark, Kerrianne, and Caitlin Constant

ADDRESS/TELEPHONE: 38 Marine Street; (904) 824–2116; fax (904) 824–1689

WEB SITE: www.oldcity.com/kenwood

E-MAIL: kenwood@travelbase.com

ROOMS: 10, plus 3 two-room suites and 1 three-room suite; all with private bath. No smoking inn.

RATES: $85; includes continental breakfast. Two-night minimum on weekends.

OPEN: Year-round.

FACILITIES AND ACTIVITIES: Swimming pool. Nearby: restaurants, St. Augustine historic sites and tourist activities, short drive to ocean beaches.

*K*enwood gets better and better. The story of this B&B inn is interesting. A number of years ago the building languished as a dilapidated boardinghouse. It was purchased by owners whose specialty was renovation, and they set about restoring it to soundness and safety, named it Kenwood, and started modest operations as an inn. When they went on to their next project, the new owners continued improving the property and ran Kenwood in their own laid-back style until health problems eventually forced them to give it up.

Then the Constant family entered the scene. Mark and Kerrianne were innkeepers in New England who, like so many visitors, got the St. Augustine I-wanna-stay bug. Caitlin, their daughter, was too young to do much innkeeping in New England, but she's rapidly growing into it all in St. Augustine. Kenwood is definitely a family project now.

The Constants are adding even more improvements at Kenwood. They've redone the courtyard and gardens to include a great variety of tropical plants and lots of colorful blooms. The swimming pool sits in the newly landscaped area like a summertime jewel.

Mark and Kerrianne brought many of their favorite antiques from New England and have mixed these antiques with comfortable couches and chairs in cool greens, creams, and rose. We especially like the way they've arranged furniture into several groupings so that people can gather in any one of several places at any time. It is not unusual to find three different, animated conversations going on.

We had a lot of conversation at breakfast, too, inspired mostly by Kerrianne's unusual offerings. We got into much "What do you think this is?" and "Oh, taste this, it's marvelous" as we nibbled our way through several generous trays full of goodies.

When we weren't talking about food, we were asking Kerrianne questions about her family in New York, and, this sounds awful, we were cracking up at how she could turn what should have been disastrous episodes into funny stories. It tells you something about Kerri's style that she did all this casually dressed.

Mark's approach is relaxed, too. We kept trying to move from the entrance to a far corner of the living room without walking on an especially lovely, pale Oriental carpet. Mark kept laughing at us and saying that in New Hampshire everyone walked over it with slush on their boots.

HOW TO GET THERE: From I-95 south exit to Route 16 east. At the end of Route 16, turn right onto San Marco Boulevard. After the fifth set of lights, bear right at immediate fork onto Marine Street. The inn is 2 blocks on the right. From I-95 north take exit 94 to Route 207. At the end of Route 207, turn left onto Route 1 North. At the first set of lights, turn right onto King Street. At the end of King Street, turn right and bear right at immediate fork onto Marine Street. The inn is 2 blocks on the right. Parking is on Marine Street and in a private lot 1 block from the inn.

St. Francis Inn 💙
St. Augustine, Florida 32084

INNKEEPER: Joe Finnegan

ADDRESS/TELEPHONE: 279 St. George Street; (904) 824–6068 or (800) 824–6062; fax (904) 810–5523

WEB SITE: www.stfrancisinn.com.

E-MAIL: innceased@aug.com

ROOMS: 11 rooms and suites, two-bedroom cottage, three-bedroom cottage for groups only; all with private bath, telephone, cable television, queen- or king-size bed; some with electric fireplace, kitchenette, whirlpool tub, sleeper sofa.

RATES: $70 to $130 weekdays; $89 to $179 weekends, holidays, or special events for double occupancy, includes full breakfast, evening social hour, use of bicycles, and admission to The Oldest House. Add $12 for each additional person.

OPEN: Year-round.

FACILITIES AND ACTIVITIES: Swimming pool, courtyards, gardens. Nearby: historic St. Augustine, Castillo de San Marcos, restaurants, museums, galleries, antiques shopping, boutiques, narrated trolley or horse-and-buggy tours, water sports, beaches, St. Augustine Lighthouse.

BUSINESS TRAVEL: Three-bedroom house for groups; three conference areas; audiovisual equipment; Internet access; fax, copier, and secretarial services; complete food and beverage service.

When we visited St. Augustine for the first time, we instantly fell in love with the restored old Spanish town, as almost everyone does who even passes through this country's oldest continuously inhabited city. With the exception of a few cheesy tourist traps, what's not to love? There are ancient (by New World standards) Spanish-influenced homes, churches, commercial buildings, and a fort as well as narrow, old brick-paved streets, charming restaurants, museums, galleries, and shops— all topped off by near perfect weather. There's even a beach nearby. Unfortunately, we were passing through and could spend only a day. One short look, however, and we knew we'd be back to stay much longer. So before we left we checked out a few B&Bs and inns so that we'd know where we wanted to stay the next time. Our choice was the St. Francis Inn.

Although St. Augustine has many charming Victorian-era B&Bs, what could be more natural in America's oldest city than to stay in its oldest lodging, now a B&B inn? Located in St. Augustine Antigua, the restored historic district, the structure in which the St. Francis Inn is housed was originally constructed in 1791 by Señor Gaspar Garcia. You might think the Spanish colonial–style inn was constructed using stucco over frame, but it is actually made from native coquina limestone, a quarried stone of compressed shells. As might be expected from a structure so old, the building has many eccentricities. For example, there are no right angles in the building because Señor Garcia's land at the junction of two drunken streets forced him to construct his house as a trapezoid rather than a rectangle.

Step through the wrought-iron fence and under the romantic archway into one of the inn's serene courtyards filled with lush banana trees, flaming bougainvillea, fragrant jasmine, and other exotic flora to experience old St. Augustine coupled with all the modern amenities discriminating travelers of the end of the twentieth century have come to expect. You'll literally feel all your cares slip away.

Public spaces and bed chambers are tastefully furnished—but not overdone—with simple antiques, tropical art, and Oriental carpets. Exposed ceiling beams, arched doorways and windows, fireplaces with ornate mantel pieces that were added later, and rough plaster walls characterize the public spaces.

Each bed chamber has its own distinct, old-fashioned personality. Rooms might be highlighted by stained-glass windows, a hammered-tin ceiling, a private balcony, or a claw-foot tub. Most feature queen-size beds, a ceiling fan, and an electric fireplace. Several boast a single- or double-size whirlpool tub. Two suites deserve special mention: Elizabeth's Suite features two rooms overlooking St. Francis Park, a fireplace in the bedroom, a double whirlpool tub, and a kitchenette. The Garcia Suite includes the same amenities, as well as a king-size bed. Located in the former cookhouse and slave quarters, the Cottage, which easily sleeps four, has two bedrooms and two baths.

Plan several leisurely days in St. Augustine so that you can indulge in short days of sight-seeing and long respites at the inn. In addition to the early-evening social hour with a wide variety of tasty treats, you'll want to relax in or around the pool and end your day (spring through fall) with warm breezes and the lilting notes of music performed in the candlelit courtyard. Sweet dreams are guaranteed.

HOW TO GET THERE: From the Visitor Information Center and Castillo de San Marcos, follow South Castillo Drive, which merges into Avenida Menendez. Follow it south to St. Francis Street and turn right. Go 3 blocks to St. Georges Street (you'll have passed The Oldest House in the second block). The inn is on the corner.

Josephine's French Country Inn
Seaside, Florida 32459

INNKEEPERS: Bruce and Judy Albert

ADDRESS/TELEPHONE: 101 Seaside Avenue; (850) 231–1940 or (800) 848–1840; fax (850) 321–2446

WEB SITE: www.josephinesfl.com.

E-MAIL: josephine@josephinefl.com.

ROOMS: 9, all with private bath, television, VCR, microwave, coffeemaker, refrigerator, and wet bar; 7 have a fireplace; rooms offer double, queen-, or king-size beds; suites feature a full kitchen.

RATES: $130 to $190 for rooms, $195 to $215 for suites, includes breakfast.

OPEN: Year-round.

FACILITIES AND ACTIVITIES: Restaurant. Nearby: art galleries, specialty shops, weekend entertainment, beach and water sports.

BUSINESS TRAVEL: Ask about business rates.

*I*f we hadn't known better ahead of time, we'd have been convinced that the stately Georgian-style mansion with the six soaring pillars across the front was an authentic plantation home. But we were in Seaside, Florida—one of this country's premier experimental planned communities and, in our opinion, an unqualified success. This captivating beach community, which you might recognize from the movie *The Truman Show,* is internationally recognized for its excellence in architectural design. Both *Life* and *Newsweek* magazines have called the small town's beautiful stretch of Gulf of Mexico beach the number-one beach in America.

Located in the heart of this paradise, the elegant, upscale, intimate inn is surrounded by storybook cottages and picture-perfect shops and galleries. Named one of the top inns in the country by *Country Inns* magazine, Josephine's is owned and operated by the Albert family, who offer you all the comforts of home with amenities you expect of a premier hotel.

Innkeepers Bruce and Judy Albert are people after our own hearts. The first time we talked to them we got into a philosophical discussion about whether they should keep telephones in the rooms. We all agreed that a phone in the room at such a wonderful destination is not only out of place, but just plain wrong—so the phones are out.

Each pleasant, light and airy guest room, named for an infamous character in French history, has unique charm accented by antiques, Battenburg lace, other fine fabrics, and decorative accents. Realizing that vacationers don't always want to go out for meals, the Alberts have equipped each room with a microwave, coffeemaker, and small refrigerator. On the occasional inclement day or late in the evening, you might enjoy the television and VCR, but we don't think you'll feel the need for them. You're more likely to want to while away the hours with a good book on one of the sprawling rocker-filled porches or in one of the common rooms.

You'll wake up with a smile, eager to start the day with a complimentary heart-healthy breakfast buffet of fruits, cereals, yogurts, and signature breads along with a gourmet entree prepared by Bruce, which changes daily.

After a busy day or one spent doing absolutely nothing, enjoy four-star cuisine in the dining room where romantic candlelight embellishes the richness of mahogany and fine antiques. Your hardest decision of the day might be making a choice from the world-class crab cakes or other seafood dishes, rack of lamb, or filet mignon. Signature dishes are adorned with scented herbs and edible flowers from the Alberts' nearby farm.

HOW TO GET THERE: From U.S. 98 take FL 395 south to FL 30A and turn west to Seaside. Follow the signs to the inn.

Steinhatchee Landing Resort 🖤 🏨
Steinhatchee, Florida 32359

INNKEEPERS: Dean and Loretta Fowler

ADDRESS/TELEPHONE: P.O. Box 789 (Highway 51 North); (352) 498–3513 or (800) 584-1709; fax (352) 498–2346

WEB SITE: www. steinhatcheelanding.com

E-MAIL: SLI@Dixie.4ez.com

ROOMS: 20 cottages with one to three bedrooms; all centrally heated and cooled and with one or more private baths, fully equipped kitchen with dishwasher, coffemaker, microwave, laundry, telephone, TV, VCR, stereo system, barbecue grill, picnic table; some with fireplaces or woodstoves; some with whirlpool baths; some handicapped accessible.

RATES: June 1 to September 10, $135 for a one-bedroom cottage to $280 for a three-bedroom cottage; September 11 to May 30, $120 to $245; slightly higher on holiday weekends when there is a three-night minimum. During June, Florida residents can book one-bedroom units for $500 per week and two-bedroom units for $700; July and August are the busiest months; includes complimentary use of most recreational facilities; meals extra. Ask about honeymoon and other packages, which include flowers, candles, fruit, champagne, breakfast, and dinner. One package includes the wedding and many extras.

OPEN: Year-round.

FACILITIES AND ACTIVITIES: Riverside swimming pool and hot tub, archery range, outdoor barbecue area, basketball, volleyball, badminton, jogging and nature trails, shuffleboard, bicycles, canoeing, horseback riding, kiddie playground, fishing, tennis, horseshoes, fitness, club, boat docks, and pontoon boat (horseback riding, pontoon boat, and fitness club are extra). Corral facilities for those who bring their own horse. Nearby: picturesque fishing village of Steinhatchee, Econfina River State Park, Wakulla Springs State Park, Manatee Springs, Weeki Wachee Springs, Silver Springs, High Springs, High Springs Station Museum, Poe Springs Park, Blue Springs, St. Marks Wildlife Refuge, Suwanee River, Stephen Foster Cultural Center, Forest Capital State Museum, area historical museums, Horseshoe Beach, Keaton Beach, antiques shopping.

BUSINESS TRAVEL: Seventy miles from Gainesville, 90 miles from Tallahassee; ideal for small business retreats; audiovisual equipment, food service.

One waggish travel writer called Steinhatchee Landing Resort "Dean's World"—and with very good reason. First of all, the charming resort village, dedicated to the spirit and romance of the Old Florida—the one that existed long before the famous mouse invaded the state—is the brainchild and baby of Dean Fowler, an early-retired entrepreneur and business executive. In the second place, Dean is not a hands-off owner. You'll see him everywhere, usually accompanied by his dog, Justin, checking on everything and chatting with his guests. Dean says, "I think of this place as a summer camp for adults and children." His recipe for a great vacation here is "a splash of water, a cup of nature, and lots of fun." This is indeed a place where we ignored our watches and traded our car for walking or bicycling around the compound, where we sat on our deck or screened porch to listen to the chirping birds and the barest ripple of the river while we watched the brilliant sunset or counted the stars in the startlingly clear inky sky, where time truly did seem to stand still. In no time at all our blood pressure lowered, our nerves were calmed, and our cares and woes faded.

Sitting on thirty-five acres on the banks of the placid, coffee-colored Steinhatchee River, just 3 miles from the Gulf of Mexico, the restful retreat contains twenty wood-frame, earth-tone, tin-roofed, two-story cottages set under the canopy of shade provided by the ancient live oaks and nine other varieties of oak as well as palms, cedars, magnolias, and cypresses in such a way to preserve and protect the lush natural environment and create an intimate old-fashioned neighborhood atmosphere. Narrow streets are routed around trees and other natural landmarks. Gazebos, wooden bridges, picket fences, fruit orchards, and vegetable and flower gardens transport guests to a quieter place in time. Fittingly, with all the attention Dean has paid to the environment, Steinhatchee Landing has been designated as one of eight destinations in the "AAA Audubon Natural Florida Journeys," a listing of places where visitors can learn about the state's ecosystem and wildlife.

With the charm and beauty of a nineteenth-century village in mind, Dean contracted with the University of Florida's School of Architecture to design buildings in keeping with Florida heritage. The delightful result includes Victorian-style Georgia and Florida "Cracker" cottages with screened porches, swings, rockers, and ceiling fans. Historic in concept but modern in amenities, they vary in size and design. An imposing Victorian-style house actually contains three apartments. Although for rent by the night, week, or month, most of the cottages are privately owned and therefore decorated and furnished according to their owner's taste. Six of the cottages were known as the Spice Girls even before that music group skyrocketed to fame: Cinnamon, Vanilla, Clove, Saffron, Pepper, and Ginger. The Presidential Retreat, a large, homey house, is so named because former first couple Jimmy and Rosalynn Carter stayed there when they hosted a family reunion on the property several years ago. Another cottage boasts three bedrooms and a private screened pool. Every cottage also features a kitchen, living room, and dining room or dining area.

Although it's incredibly easy to do absolutely nothing without a trace of guilt, those who desire a little more activity find myriad choices. The best solution is to spend some therapeutic do-nothing time with a sprinkling of activities. Very family-friendly, the resort offers opportunities for swimming, boating, fishing, and much more. Scalloping lends itself to family fun because the shelled seafood is found in shallow, clear water, providing easy targets for children. In fact, the Marine Fisheries Commission reports that the Steinhatchee River surpasses all others in Florida in its scallop population. In addition, bird-watching and nature photography are popular pastimes.

The resort's own restaurant is open for dinner Thursday through Saturday nights and Sunday for brunch. Naturally, seafood is prominently featured with crab bisque, oyster and shrimp appetizers, and entrees such as the crab cake dinner, Grouper Matanzas, pecan grouper, or shrimp and pasta. Poultry and steak are also featured and a popular entree is Land and Sea—crab cakes and New York strip. There are daily specials, and the desserts are to die for.

Never one to rest on his laurels, Dean has purchased an 1813 hotel from Georgia, had it dismantled, and plans to reassemble it on the Steinhatchee Landing property and convert it into a restaurant and nine suites. Stay tuned.

HOW TO GET THERE: Steinhatchee Landing is located on State Road 51, 8 miles west of its intersection with U.S. 19. From north or south, the easiest travel route is I-75, west on U.S. 27, then U.S. 19 to State Road 51.

Governors Inn 📱
Tallahassee, Florida 32301

INNKEEPERS: Charles W. Orr, general manager

ADDRESS/TELEPHONE: 209 South Adams Street; (850) 681-6855 or (800) 342-7717 in Florida; fax (850) 222-3105

ROOMS: 40 rooms and suites; all with private bath, telephone, television, writing desk, robes.

RATES: $119 to $149 for rooms, $149 to $159 for junior suites, $179 to $189 for loft bedroom suites, $189 to $219 for suites; single or double occupancy; includes continental breakfast, morning newspaper, and nightly turndown service; $10 for each additional person; football weekends and some special events require a minimum two-night stay; rates may be higher during special event periods.

OPEN: Year-round.

FACILITIES AND ACTIVITIES: Airport transportation service, valet parking, laundry/valet service, room service, access to a nearby fitness club with a pool and hot tub. Nearby: Old and New Capitols, Knott House Museum, Tallahassee Museum, Florida Caverns State Park, Natural Bridge Battlefield State Historic Site, Pebble Hill Plantation, Torreya State Park, Wakulla Springs State Park.

BUSINESS TRAVEL: Meeting space for up to sixty; audiovisual equipment; in-room desks; fax and copy service, in-room telephones with dataports on request.

*V*isitors to the state Capitol in Tallahassee, official and unofficial, were delighted when a historic commercial building located within sight of the Capitol was converted into the intimate Governors Inn, which is the crowning touch in the Adams Street Commons project to reestablish a sense of history to the heart of the city. Restaurants, shops, brick streets and sidewalks, period streetlights, and planters overflowing with flowers and lush greenery round out the attractive project.

You'll know you're in for superior service the minute you pull up in front of the hotel and turn your car over to valet parking. Inside, the inn conveys the slow-paced flavor of a far simpler time coupled with all the modern amenities and services. Instead of a cavernous and often overly ostentatious lobby, there's a small registration area. You step down into a cozy two-story Florida Room where guests congregate for afternoon refreshments, continental breakfast each morning, or informal gatherings throughout the day. Those of you who don't live in Florida might mistake this description for a conservatory-like room filled with plants and blending almost imperceptibly with the outdoors. In the case of the Governors Inn, however, the Florida Room is more like a gentleman's library from the turn of the century. Richly paneled walls glow in the warm light of reading lamps, and tapestry- and leather-covered furniture provide comfortable seating.

Comfortable guest rooms, some of which are located in a modern addition, are reached by way of a picturesque hallway, the size of a small street, topped with original exposed heart-pine beams and well-lit by skylights. Forty bed chambers and suites, which are named for former governors, feature hand-polished antiques such as black-oak desks and rock-maple armoires as well as all the modern creature comforts, such as queen- and king-size beds in many rooms and television with the Movie Channel and ESPN. For a special event we'd treat ourselves to the lovely Spressard Holland Suite with its romantic four-poster bed, separate living room, and whirlpool bath.

We love the comfortable feel of the inn and appreciate its friendly staff. Although many of the guests are high-powered legislators, lobbyists, and others on government business, each and every guest—no matter how humble—is made to feel welcome and at home.

HOW TO GET THERE: From the airport, turn right onto Capital Circle (Route 263), go 1³⁄₁₀ miles to the light at Springhill Road; turn left and go 2 miles to the light at Orange Avenue; turn right and go 1³⁄₁₀ miles to South Monroe Street (Highway 61), turn left and go 1⁷⁄₁₀ miles to downtown where you will pass the State Capitol on the left. Past the Capitol, turn left at Jefferson Street and go 1 block to Adams Street and turn right. Governors Inn is on the right and offers valet parking.

Wakulla Springs Lodge
Wakulla Springs, Florida 32305

INNKEEPER: Bill Roberts, manager

ADDRESS/TELEPHONE: 550 Wakulla Park Drive; (850) 224–5950; fax (805) 561–7251

WEB SITE: www.unr.net/~skerr/wakulla_springs.htm

ROOMS: 27; all with marble floors, private marble bath, telephone. One room with a king-size bed, five with queens, remainder doubles and/or twins.

RATES: $65 to $90 weekdays, $75 to $90 weekends.

OPEN: Year-round.

FACILITIES AND ACTIVITIES: Restaurant. In the park: glass-bottom boat rides, swimming, snorkeling, picnicking, nature trails, hiking, bicycling. Nearby: Tallahassee, Florida Caverns State Park, Natural Bridge Battlefield State Historic Site, Torreya State Park, Lake Jackson Mounds State Archaeological Site, Thomasville, Georgia.

BUSINESS TRAVEL: Meeting rooms and restaurant can accommodate up to one hundred persons for meetings and retreats; glassed-in terrace for receptions.

*I*f you're a fan of old movies as we are, you may recognize Wakulla Springs, the world's largest and deepest freshwater spring, from the classics *Tarzan, Creature from the Black Lagoon,* and *Airport 77.* We did, and so we first went to Wakulla Springs State Park to see the springs and the wildlife that lives in and around it. Imagine our pleasant surprise when we discovered the historic Wakulla Springs Lodge, a two-story Moorish-style inn built in 1937 by financier and railroad magnate Edward Ball.

Ball designed the lodge using many arches, hand-wrought iron, imported Italian marble and hand-made ceramic tiles. Little changed except for improvements in safety and comfort, the lodge offers a nostalgic glimpse into life in Florida in the 1930s. Today the inn is operated by the Florida State University Center for Professional Development. The dining room is renowned for its cuisine and is a favorite destination for locals to dine.

The huge lobby is characterized by exposed beams, gray-and-pink checkerboard marble floors, and walk-in marble fireplace. It's the ceiling, however, which is the most amazing. Kaiser Wilhelm of Germany's court architect painted the ceiling with flamingos, other wildlife, palms, and tropical scenes Ponce de Leon might have seen when he explored Florida looking for the Fountain of Youth in the mid-1500s, as well as many colorful stenciled designs. Large walls of windows in the lobby and dining room overlook the springs. Check out Old Joe, a stuffed alligator who lives in a glass case in the lobby.

Each guest room with its private marble bath is filled with antiques and offers beautiful views of the park. Furnishings for most of the guest rooms are simple thirties and forties reproductions. Particularly large rooms have fancier furniture and a seating area.

The major attraction in the park, of course, is the incredible water-filled sinkhole, which was formed from the eroded bed of ancient limestone filled by natural springs. Archaeological evidence indicates that Florida's first human residents lived near the springs site as much as 12,000 years ago; beasts such as mastodons lived there even before that. Mastodon bones have been dredged from the 185-foot depths of the spring, and the soil nearby has revealed ancient hunting tools.

A part of any visit to the lodge and park is the thirty-minute glass-bottom boat ride along the Wakulla River and the springs, where you're sure to see alligators floating on logs or stretched out in the sun along the riverbanks, the large population of year-round birds, or some of the 2,000 waterfowl that make the park their winter migratory home. The crystal-clear waters don't seem anywhere as deep as they are and reveal fish, water plants, and other surprises. On dry land, the park's 1,500 acres of mature upland hardwoods contain some of the state's champion trees.

HOW TO GET THERE: Wakulla Springs State Park is just 14 miles south of Tallahassee. Take U.S. 319 south from the capital city and 2 miles beyond Capital Circle, take the left fork onto FL 61 and travel 7½ miles to FL 267. Turn left, and the park entrance is immediately on the right.

Old Joe

While you're staying at the Wakulla Springs Lodge, or even if you're just visiting the park or eating in the dining room, be sure to take a gander at Old Joe, a stuffed alligator in the lobby. He was an 11-foot alligator who inhabited the springs for many years—some say he was 300 years old. Usually found stretched out in the sun opposite the swimming area, he is said never to have bothered anyone. He became a mascot to the park because he was so much beloved by the locals, but he was killed by a poacher in 1966. The Fish and Wildlife Service had Joe stuffed and traveled with him to schools around the state for many years. Then it was decided that he should have a more dignified retirement; now he resides in a glass case at the hotel. On New Year's Eve, even Old Joe gets a party hat.

Select List of Other Florida Inns

Addison House

614 Ash Street
Amelia Island, FL 32034
(904) 277-1604 or (800) 943-1604

1876 home; 14 rooms, some whirlpool baths; full breakfast.

The Coombs House Inn

80 Sixth Street
Apalachicola, FL 32320
(850) 653-9199

Two Victorian mansions; 18 rooms.

The Clewiston Inn

108 Royal Palm Avenue
Clewiston, FL 33440
(941) 983-8151

Greek Revival inn; 48 rooms

Live Oak Inn

444-448 South Beach Boulevard
Daytona Beach, FL 32114
(904) 252-4667

Historic inn; 12 rooms; near Intracoastal Waterway.

The Villa Bed and Breakfast

801 North Peninsula Drive
Daytona Beach, FL 32118
(904) 248-2020

Historic Spanish-style mansion; 17 rooms; pool, spa; near beach.

Harrington House Beachfront B&B

5626 Gulf Drive
Holmes Beach, FL 34217
(941) 778-5444

1923 home and guest house; 12 rooms.

Seminole Country Inn

15885 Southwest Warfield Boulevard
Indiantown, FL 34956
(561) 597-3777

Historic inn; 28 rooms.

Crown Hotel

109 North Seminole Avenue
Inverness, FL 34450
(352) 344-5555

Historic downtown hotel; 34 rooms, pool, English pub, restaurant.

Kona Kai Resort

MM 97.8 Bayside
Key Largo, FL 33037
(305) 852-7200 or (800) 365-STAY

1940s bayside retreat; 11 suites; beach, pool, hot tub, tennis court.

Center Court Historic Inn and Cottages

916 Center Street
Key West, FL 33040
(305) 296-9292 or (800) 797-8787

Historic cottages; 14 rooms; pool, hot tub, exercise pavilion, pond with waterfall.

Courtney's Place

720 Whitemarsh Lane
Key West, FL 33040
(800) UNWIND-9

Historic guest cottages and inn; 10 rooms; pool, beach club membership, deluxe continental breakfast; pets welcome.

The Curry Mansion

511 Caroline Street
Key West, FL 33040
(305) 294-5349 or (800) 253-3466

Victorian mansion; 28 rooms; pool, private beach club.

Heron House

512 Simonton Street
Key West, FL 33040
(305) 294–9227 or (800) 294–1644
New England Cape Cod/Key West conch house style; 21 rooms.

Pilot House

414 Simonton Street
Key West, FL 33040
(305) 294–8719 or (800) 648–3780
Victorian; 14 suites; kitchens, hot tub.

The Club Continental

2143 Astor Street
Orange Park, FL 32075
(904) 264–6070 or (800) 877–6070
1923 Mediterranean style; 22 rooms; restaurant, pub, seven tennis courts, three pools.

Southern Wind Bed & Breakfast

18 Cordova Street
St. Augustine, FL 32084
(904) 825–3623
Turn-of-the-century mansion and carriage house; 15 rooms; full breakfast.

Historic Tavernier Hotel

91865 Overseas Highway
Tavernier, FL 33070
(305) 852–4131 or (800) 515–4131
1928 cluster of buildings; 17 rooms.

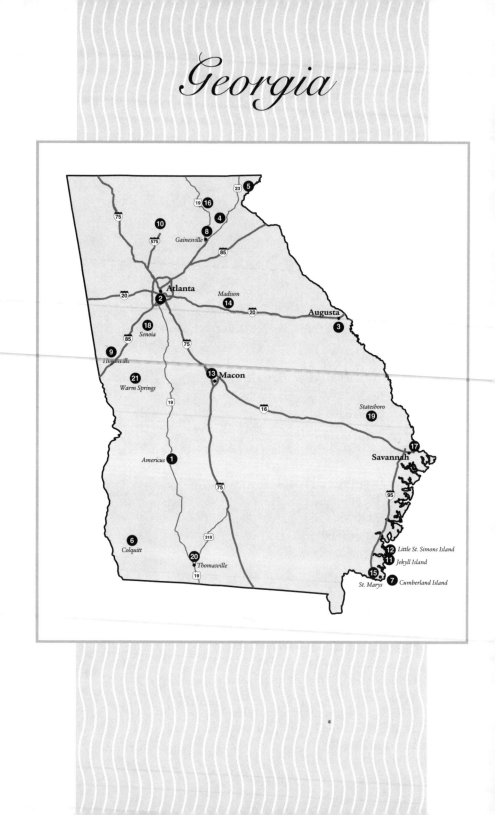

Georgia

23
5
19
16
4
75
10
8
575
Gainesville
85
20
Atlanta
2
Madison
14
20
Augusta
18
3
85
Senoia
9
75
Thomasville
21
13 Macon
Warm Springs
19
16
Statesboro
19
Americus
1
Savannah
17
95
6
Colquitt
12 Little St. Simons Island
11 Jekyll Island
319
15
20
7 Cumberland Island
19
Thomasville
St. Marys

Georgia

Numbers on map refer to towns numbered below.

*A Top Pick Inn

Windsor Hotel Americus
Americus, Georgia 31709

INNKEEPER: Mary Thompson

ADDRESS/TELEPHONE: 125 West Lamar Street; (912) 924–1555 or (888) 297–9567; fax (912) 924–1555, ext. 113

ROOMS: 53, plus 6 suites; all with private bath, ceiling fan, telephone, cable television with movies, clock radio, coffeemaker.

RATES: $68 to $72 for standard guest rooms, $99 for junior suites, $129 for executive suites, and $159 for tower suites; children under fifteen stay free in the same room with their parents.

OPEN: Year-round.

FACILITIES AND ACTIVITIES: Grand Dining Room restaurant, Floyd's Pub. Nearby: Plains, Jimmy Carter National Historic Site, Andersonville, Andersonville National Cemetery.

BUSINESS TRAVEL: Function areas to accommodate up to 200.

What attracted us to the Windsor Hotel in the first place was its whimsical castlelike appearance, with its enchanting, eclectic mix of architectural elements—particularly the distinctive towers, variety of European-influenced roof lines, and the unusual assortment of window styles. Depending on your vantage point, you could envision yourself in Amsterdam, Austria, Germany, or some fairy-tale European kingdom, not in a small west-central Georgia town. We felt we owed it to ourselves to check this inn, and we were enchanted.

What brought this opulent pleasure palace to sleepy Americus? Strange as it may seem now, in the last century Americus was a popular winter destination for northern hunters and vacationers. In the midst of Victorian excess, a simple lodge or hotel simply wouldn't do. So in 1892 this extravagant five-story edifice was erected. Unfortunately, after many years of misuse and disuse, the hotel had deteriorated and was in danger of destruction when it was rescued by the town, rehabilitated to its present form, and opened as an inn in September 1991.

Although the interior is a little less exuberant than the exterior, it is characterized by a gorgeous three-story atrium trimmed in golden oak, marble floors, antique chandeliers, soaring columns, and a grand staircase that rises from the lobby, and splits into twin staircases before completing its ascent to the restaurant and ballroom on the second floor. Very convenient for guests, the Americus Welcome Center is located off the lobby, as is the Tog Shop.

Our spacious, high-ceilinged junior suite retained a nostalgic feel with period reproductions, suitable fabrics, a sitting area, ceiling fan, and plantation shutters, at the same time providing all the modern creature comforts. Standard guest rooms are similar to the junior suites, but without the seating area. The two most romantic accommodations are the two tower suites

located in the round tower—one is the Honeymoon Suite and the other the Carter Suite, named for former President Jimmy Carter and Mrs. Carter, who stayed there to dedicate the hotel on its grand reopening.

After a wonderful night's sleep, the next morning, a Sunday, we slept late and then went down to the historic restaurant for a gargantuan brunch. Tiny white tiles on the floor, dark furniture, and generous use of palms and other lush greenery served to authenticate the turn-of-the-century ambience.

Manager Mary Thompson has been on board since the hotel reopened, along with a dedicated and loyal local staff whose sole purpose in life is to make sure that you are comfortable and content.

HOW TO GET THERE: From I-75, take either GA 27 or U.S. 280 west until they are joined by GA 49. Follow GA 49; as it enters Americus it is called Forsyth Street. Just past the post office, turn left at the light onto Lamar Street. The hotel is on the right.

Ansley Inn
Atlanta, Georgia 30309

INNKEEPERS: Phil and Joretta Rosner; Morris Levy, owner

ADDRESS/TELEPHONE: 253 Fifteenth Street; (404) 872-9000 or (800) 446-5416; fax (404) 892-2318

WEB SITE: www.ansleyinn.com

E-MAIL: reservations@ansleyinn.com

ROOMS: 22; all with private bath; most with single or double whirlpool tub, hair dryer, iron and ironing board, telephone, cable television, clock radio, wet bar, coffeemaker; some with gas-log fireplace. Evening turn-down and in-room breakfast on request. Limited handicap access.

RATES: $129 to $159 for rooms and suites in the main house; $109 to $129 for rooms in the annex; all include hot breakfast buffet, afternoon snacks, and beverages.

OPEN: Year-round.

FACILITIES AND ACTIVITIES: Concierge, free pass to Australian Body Works. Nearby: Woodruff Arts Center, Atlanta Botanical Garden, Piedmont Park, MARTA rapid rail Arts Station,

BUSINESS TRAVEL: Near midtown and downtown business districts; fax machine, computer ports in guest rooms.

*I*f we didn't already live in Atlanta and were traveling there, we'd love to stay at the lovely Ansley Inn. The philosophy of the owner and innkeepers of this B&B inn is to offer residential flavor with the service of a first-class hotel. The beautifully restored English Tudor mansion offers not only sumptuous accommodations but also impeccable service.

One of the things we'd find especially appealing is the inn's location in Midtown's elegant, historic Ansley Park neighborhood, conveniently near the Woodruff Arts Center where we spend a lot of time visiting the High Museum of Art and attending performances of the acclaimed Atlanta Symphony Orchestra and the Alliance Theater. In addition, the Atlanta Botanical Garden, Fourteenth Street Playhouse, and Piedmont Park are within easy walking distance.

Built in 1907 as the home of clothier George Muse, the magnificent yellow-brick house, with the addition of an annex, spent many years as a boarding house for women and later for men before becoming this gracious inn. Now fully restored, the Ansley Inn is accented with antiques, burnished hardwood and gleaming Italian marble floors, massive fireplaces, crystal chandeliers, and Oriental rugs.

Each individually decorated guest chamber, named for an Atlanta street in the main house, features a private bath. Most have a whirlpool tub, period and reproduction furnishings, a wet bar, telephone, and cable television. Many rooms boast gas-log fireplaces and four-poster rice beds. Those in the main house feature high ceilings or cathedral ceilings, large windows, and formal furnishings. Those in the annex are more casual and intimate.

A lavish breakfast buffet including hot beverages, juices, assorted breads, cereal, and fresh fruit is served in the spacious, barrel-vaulted formal dining room, which features the original ornate gesso ceilings and twin crystal chandeliers. You can also order eggs any style, bacon, hash browns, and French toast. For special occasions you can request breakfast in your room. Coffee, a selection of teas, and juice are available in the dining room throughout the day and evening. In the late afternoon the tantalizing aromas of freshly baked cookies and freshly popped popcorn draw guests to the cozy common room, with its beamed ceiling and fireplace surrounded by ceramic tiles. In good weather guests may want to take their breakfast or snacks out on the front terrace.

HOW TO GET THERE: From I-75/85, exit at Fourteenth Street and go east to Peachtree Street. Turn left and go 1 block to Fifteenth Street; bear right. The inn is just ahead on the right. Pull into the circular driveway to register; you will be directed to the parking lot.

Shellmont
Atlanta, Georgia 30308

INNKEEPERS: Ed and Debbie McCord

ADDRESS/TELEPHONE: 821 Piedmont Avenue Northeast; (404) 872-9290; fax (404) 872-5379

WEB SITE: www.innbook.com/shell.html

ROOMS: 4, plus 2-bedroom carriage house; all with private bath, queen beds, and dataport phones; carriage house with television.

RATES: $100 to $120 in the main house; $129 to $170 in the carriage house.

OPEN: Year-round.

FACILITIES AND ACTIVITIES: Located in historic midtown Atlanta. Nearby: restaurants, historic sites, city shopping areas, cultural activities.

It's taken the McCords a lot of undoing to get this B&B inn back to historic basics. Until Ed and Debbie bought it, their classic Victorian home had been in the same family since it was built in 1891. As generations of a family will do, earlier inhabitants had papered and painted many layers over the original walls and wood and plaster ornamentation. But now you can see it as it was originally designed and built.

The family that owned it kept records and photographs showing the original decor, including colors, wallpaper patterns, and elaborate stenciling. The McCords have replicated everything that they couldn't restore.

The outside of the house is blue, green, and yellow. Inside are a mind-boggling number of Victorian touches. For instance, there's a weird little room called the Turkish Room, which isn't really Turkish at all but is done in a style that Victorians imagined must be Turkish. At the foot of the stairs is a good-sized choir stall with room for an organist and singers to entertain assembled guests. Above the stall are five elaborate stained-glass windows that Ed and Debbie believe are by Tiffany, though they're still trying to verify it.

Shellmont has been listed as a City of Atlanta Landmark Building, one of only thirty-three, and it is listed on the National Register of Historic Places.

But fascinating as all this is, especially if you're interested in history and architecture, the real fun of staying at the Shellmont is the time you spend with Debbie and Ed. The amount of attention they give guests is pretty much up to the guests. But if you'd like to sit in front of the fire in the Turkish Room and do needlework and chat, Debbie will whip out her stitchery and join you in a minute.

Ed, a native of Atlanta, can entertain you endlessly with stories about the city and with suggestions on where to go for food, shopping, and sight-seeing.

One of the restaurants Ed and Debbie recommend for dinner is the Abbey. It's in an old church building, within walking distance, and specializes in veal, venison, and seafood.

It would have been fun to be here to see the couple who honeymooned at the inn and returned a year later to share their anniversary celebration with Debbie and Ed with a champagne picnic—including pieces of their original wedding cake, frozen—on the floor.

One wonders if they had room for Shellmont's full breakfast, which includes juice, fruit, homemade breads, and entrees such as egg soufflé. Maybe they settled for something simpler, such as the cereal, dried fruit, and yogurt that is available on the sideboard.

For your own creature comforts, the McCords have an icemaker and a coffee/hot water area as well as a phone just for guests in an upstairs nook.

HOW TO GET THERE: From I-75/85 north, exit 96, go through first traffic light, turn left at second light, cross bridge at third light (Piedmont Avenue), and turn right. Continue about 1 mile. The inn is on the corner of Piedmont and Sixth.

Partridge Inn 👥
Augusta, Georgia 30904

INNKEEPER: Tom Haufe

ADDRESS/TELEPHONE: 2110 Walton Way; (706) 737-8888 or (800) 476-6888; fax (706) 731-0826

WEB SITE: www.partridgeinn.com.

ROOMS: 155 suites, studios, and executive rooms; all with private bath, telephone, and television.

RATES: $80 to $150, includes breakfast buffet and afternoon hors d'oeuvres.

OPEN: Year-round.

FACILITIES AND ACTIVITIES: Pool, parking deck, valet parking. Nearby: historic districts, art and history museums, Riverwalk promenade and park, Cotton Exchange Welcome Center, Meadow Garden historic home, Augusta Canal, Confederate Powderworks, monuments; water sports, hiking, bicycling, fishing.

BUSINESS TRAVEL: One mile from downtown and Georgia Medical College. Guest room telephone with dataport; eight meeting rooms; copy machines, fax.

We were first enchanted by the quarter mile of verandas and private porches on the five-story historic inn, one of only three Georgia inns chosen to be a member of the National Trust for Historic Preservation's Historic Hotels of America. You can hardly imagine anything more Southern than relaxing in a rocker while sipping a cool drink on one of the verandas. Next we were captivated by our suite—a comfortable living room, a bedroom with a king-size bed, a private bath, a fully equipped kitchen, and, best of all, our own small private veranda with comfortable wicker chairs.

Perched on one of the highest spots in Augusta to catch the cool breezes, what began as a private residence in 1879 was enlarged over the years until it became one of the first all-suite inns in the country. Somewhere within the rambling structure is the framework of the original house. Today, faithfully restored and graciously furnished in period reproductions, some of the suites have been modified into studios and executive rooms to provide a larger number of accommodations. Sizes of suites vary from an efficiency to a multiroom apartment. Most of the multiroom suites offer a full kitchen, sitting room/dining area, bedroom, and private bath.

A complimentary hot breakfast buffet is served each morning in the informal cocktail lounge. In good weather we like to take ours out on the expansive second-story veranda. Afternoon hors d'oeuvres are offered in the cocktail lounge. Lunch and dinner are served in the formal plantation-style dining room.

HOW TO GET THERE: From I-20, take exit 65 onto Washington Road. At Berckman Road, turn right. Bear left onto Highland, then turn left onto Walton Way. The inn is on the right soon after you pass Augusta College. There is a parking deck in the rear.

Glen-Ella Springs
Clarksville, Georgia 30523

INNKEEPERS: Barrie and Bobby Aycock

ADDRESS/TELEPHONE: 1789 Bear Gap Road; (706) 754-7295

WEB SITE: www.glenella.com

E-MAIL: info@glenella.com

ROOMS: 16 rooms and suites; all with private bath; some with fireplace; some with wheelchair access.

RATES: $100 to $180, single or double; includes full breakfast. Inquire about discounts for weeknights and stays of more than three nights.

OPEN: Year-round.

FACILITIES AND ACTIVITIES: Dining room, with wheelchair access, open to guests and public most days, reservations requested; available for private parties; brown bagging permitted. Conference room. Swimming pool, seventeen acres with nature trails along Panther Creek, herb and flower gardens, mineral springs. Located in northeast Georgia mountains near historic sites. Nearby: restaurants, golf, horseback riding, boating, rafting, tennis, hiking, Tallula Gorge State Park, Chattahoochee National Forest.

*W*e think we're in love! Country inns are usually elegant or rustic. This one-hundred-year-old place is both. The suites are beautifully finished and furnished with fireplaces, refinished pine floors, walls and ceilings, whirlpool baths, and such niceties as fresh-cut pansies floating in crystal bowls.

The fireplace in the lobby is made of local stone, flanked with chintz-covered chairs.

An especially nice swimming pool, surrounded by an extra-wide sundeck that seems posh enough for any Hyatt hotel, overlooks a huge expanse of lawn and gardens that ends in woods. Both the pool and the lawn are great for kids.

The dining room could be called "subdued country," but there is nothing subdued about the food. It is simply spectacular—some of the best in the South, compliments of Barrie and her kitchen staff.

We have eaten here more times than we can remember and have *never* had a bad (or even fair) meal—they have all been wonderful. Dan's favorite is the rack of lamb; Carol's is either the low-country shrimp and grits entree or the fresh trout sautéed and dressed with lime juice, fresh herbs, and toasted pecans.

The story here is that Barrie, a wonderful cook, had wanted a restaurant for a long time. But the Aycocks also wanted to work and live away from the city. They bought Glen-Ella even though the old hotel needed a tremendous amount of renovating. Bobby and Barrie have an album of pictures that show the condition of the inn when they bought it.

They figured that here Barrie could have her restaurant, and since the inn was so far out in the country, lots of guests would spend the night. They do. And lots of other guests, who come for longer stays just to be in the country, enjoy the added pleasure of five-star quality food.

You can get a copy of the *Glen-Ella Cookbook*, with some of the inn's best recipes, at the front desk or you can order it by calling or writing the inn.

Every time we visit we find something new has been added—corporate-challenge obstacle course, state-of-the-art conference facility, upgraded rooms, etc.

And now there's one more bragging point for Barrie and Bobby: The hotel has been added to the National Register of Historic Places.

HOW TO GET THERE: From Atlanta, take I–85 north to I–985, traveling through Gainesville. Stay on this four-lane road past Cornelia and Clarkesville heading toward Clayton. It will become U.S. 441. After the stop-light at the Tom Arrendale Interchange (GA 365), go 7 miles and turn left on G. Hardman Road, then turn right back onto Historic Old 441. After ¼ mile turn left on Orchard Road and follow the signs for 3½ miles to the inn. From Clarkesville go north on Historic Old 441 for 8½ miles to Orchard Road. Follow the signs for 3½ miles.

English Manor Inns
Clayton, Georgia 30525

INNKEEPERS: Susan and English Thornwell

ADDRESS/TELEPHONE: U.S. 76; (706) 782–5789 or (800) 782–5780; fax: (706) 782–5780

ROOMS: 42, including 9 suites; all with private bath; suites with fireplace and whirlpool bath; some kitchen facilities.

RATES: $99 to $139; includes full breakfast and heavy afternoon refreshments; a two-night minimum is required for holidays, special events, and most weekends.

OPEN: May through November and Christmas/New Year holiday period (early December and January through April will open for groups of thirty or more).

FACILITIES AND ACTIVITIES: Lunch and dinner served for groups; swimming pool, hot tub, croquet.

BUSINESS TRAVEL: Ideal for small meetings and retreats.

*O*ur first visit to English Manor was for a hilarious mystery weekend written and produced by the property's energetic and imaginative mistress, Susan Thornwell. We had such a ball, we've been back to the inn numerous times for special events and quiet weekends alone, trying out a different guest room every time. We've never been disappointed. Another time we were visiting, our car broke down and had to be towed to a nearby town for repairs, which were to take several days. Susan and English lent us one of their cars for the week so that we could get back to Atlanta.

Seven inn buildings, ranging from a 1912 farmhouse to rustic stone cottages, sprawl across seven heavily wooded acres adjacent to the Chattahoochee National Forest. The first structure on the property, which is the most elegant and formal, began as a Sears kit house with a full-length veranda. The Thornwells have enlarged it several times so that it now houses a music room, formal parlor, dining room, and forty-two guest rooms and suites with private baths, some with fireplaces and/or whirlpool baths. Gorgeous wallpaper, plush carpeting, period antiques, and elaborate bed linens characterize this house.

Next the Thornwells began building other guest houses. Each of these other structures is more casual than the main house. Ranging from three to seven bedrooms, these buildings feature a common room with comfortable seating, a fireplace or wood stove, games, and puzzles as well as full kitchen facilities and charming country decor. Families and small groups traveling together have discovered how ideal it can be to take over an entire building for a family reunion or business meeting. Each guest house also boasts a porch with comfortable chairs and rockers.

In the morning a full breakfast is served at the vast dining room table in the main inn and provides a good opportunity to get to know your fellow guests. Seven gourmet menus are rotated so that you could stay for a week and have a different repast every morning. If any guests have dietary restrictions, all they have to do is let the staff know in advance and their menu will be modified accordingly.

Although the inn makes a perfect base from which to explore the northeast Georgia mountains or to engage in whitewater rafting, hiking, sight-seeing, or antiques and crafts shopping, the swimming pool and hot tub, numerous porches and fireplaces, and kitchen facilities may persuade you to never leave the property.

HOW TO GET THERE: From U.S. 23/441, turn east onto U.S. 76. The inn is about a mile ahead on the right. Registration is in the main inn.

The Christmas Pig

One Christmas, English Manor decided to throw a Dickens of a Christmas Celebration for those who like to travel at Christmas. Christmas dinner was included among the many features of the package. The inn was full and the roast pig had to be large enough to feed the crowd, but the size of the pig caused some logistic problems. First, where could Susan marinate the pig? The solution: in one of the deep claw-foot tubs. Next problem: The pig wouldn't fit into the oven. The solution: Susan called a nearby restaurant and they agreed to cook it. Next problem: How could they get the pig to the restaurant and back? The solution: Among the Thornwells' collection of vintage Lincolns was a purple hearse, so into the hearse went the pig and off to the restaurant. The Christmas feast was a great success, and the hilarity reached ever-greater heights when the guests learned how the pig eventually came to the Christmas table. The roast pig story is just one example of your hostess's ingenuity and sense of humor. Expect the unexpected at English Manor Inns.

Tarrer Inn ❤ 👪
Colquitt, Georgia 31737

INNKEEPERS: David McCleskey and Pat Webb

ADDRESS/TELEPHONE: 157 South Cuthbert Street; (912) 758-2888 or (888) 282-7737; fax (912) 758-2825

ROOMS: 12; all with private bath, telephone, television, coffeemaker; some provisions for the disabled.

RATES: $89 to $105, includes full breakfast.

OPEN: Year-round.

FACILITIES AND ACTIVITIES: Restaurant. Nearby: Spring Creek Park for bird-watching and fishing.

*U*nless you're from southwest Georgia, you might not know what a mayhaw is. We didn't when we first moved to Atlanta twenty years ago, but we were soon educated. A mayhaw is a tart, but delicate, swamp berry similar to a cranberry that can be made into jellies and sauces. This is important because Colquitt is the Mayhaw Capital of the World and the home of the annual Mayhaw Festival. The town also hosts a popular folk production called Swamp Gravy Tales. If you're in town for these events or just using it as a base from which to explore the southwestern corner of the state, the place to stay is the Tarrer Inn.

Built in 1866 as a boardinghouse, by the turn of the century the structure had become a full-fledged hotel known as the Hunter House. During this elegant period, white horse-drawn carriages picked up travelers from the train depot and brought them to the hotel in style. Restored to its former splendor, the inn continues the tradition of hospitality, recapturing the graceful nuances of days gone by with elegant surroundings updated with modern conveniences.

An elegant formal reception room is embellished with heavily carved Victorian sofas, chairs, a fainting couch, and ottomans covered in plush burgundy velvet dripping fringe. Opulent draperies, an ornate gilt mirror, Corinthian columns, Oriental carpets, and a tapestry complete this turn-of-the-century vision. One day while we were enjoying the excesses of this room, we struck up a conversation with an elderly man who told us he had met his future wife in this very room at a reception more than fifty years ago. Later, when they were newly married, the hotel had become apartments, and they lived in the room where they had met. Hearing that the hotel had reopened, they returned for a nostalgic visit. He said they were ecstatic about the restoration.

Our favorite spot is the second-story porch, where we can sit in comfortable wicker chairs or rockers, fanned by slowly turning paddle fans while we watched the slow pace of life on the town square.

Each of the twelve guest chambers is appointed in a distinctive motif and furnished with exquisite antique treasures from the Victorian era. We particularly liked the hand-painted or faux-finished fireplace mantels, surrounds, and screens. Embroidered bed linens add another touch of elegance.

Although most of the rooms feature queen-size beds, a few have twin beds. Every room, however, has a private bath, television, and coffeemaker.

Other amenities include fresh flowers and nightly turndown service with a chocolate left on your pillow.

As attractive as all these features are, there's one more reason to stay at the Tarrer Inn: the wonderful food. Noted for its fine dining—rich in the traditions of Southern cooking—the inn's dining room serves lunch Wednesday through Friday, dinner Friday and Saturday, and brunch Sunday. Included in the room rate, your full breakfast will feature Southern delicacies such as pecan waffles and quiches.

HOW TO GET THERE: Colquitt is located at the intersection of U.S. 27 and GA 91. Follow the signs to the historic downtown commercial district and the courthouse square, where the inn is located on one corner.

Greyfield Inn
Cumberland Island, Georgia

INNKEEPER: Brycea Merrill

ADDRESS/TELEPHONE: For reservations, contact 8 North Second Street, Box 900, Fernandina Beach, Florida 32035-0900; (904) 261-6408

WEB SITE: www.greyfieldinn.com.

ROOMS: 11, plus 4 suites; only 6 rooms have private en-suite bath; 2 others have adjoining bath; the remainder share baths; the only shower is in an outside bathhouse; rooms vary in size and have twin, double, queen- or king-size beds.

RATES: Rooms range from $275 to $350; $375 to $395 for suites; all double occupancy; includes three meals, naturalist's tour, bicycles, and ferry transportation to and from Fernandina Beach. Weekends require a two-night minimum.

OPEN: Year-round.

FACILITIES AND ACTIVITIES: Dining room, bar, bicycles, nature tours.

BUSINESS TRAVEL: Ideal for small corporate meetings and executive retreats.

*A*s writers, isolated Cumberland Island and the exclusive Greyfield Inn have always presented us with a great dilemma. Do we tout their many attractions to our readers, or do we keep the best-kept secrets on the East Coast all to ourselves? Well, that decision was taken out of our hands when John F. Kennedy, Jr., chose the supersecluded spot for his top-secret wedding to Carolyn Bessette. Since then, pictures and information about the island and the inn have been splashed around the world. Fortunately, restrictions on visitation to the island keep it peaceful and untamed.

Healthy dunes, oceans of sea oats, long stretches of deserted beach, and dense, scrubby maritime forests characterize Cumberland Island—one of the most pristine islands in America. For almost one hundred years, the Manhattan-size island was owned by the wealthy Thomas Carnegie family, and on this sanctuary they built several mansions for themselves and their nine children in the late 1800s. Among the homes were Dungeness (since destroyed by fire), Plum Orchard, and Greyfield. Greyfield was built in 1901 for Lucy and Thomas's daughter, Margaret Ricketson. In 1972 the family donated all but 1,300 acres of the island and all but one of the mansions to the United States, and it was designated as a National Seashore to preserve and protect the island from development. The island  is operated by the National Park Service and access is only by ferry. Visitation is severely limited to 300 day-trippers and campers per day. The National Park Service ferry operates between the island and St. Marys, Georgia, once or twice a day, depending on the season. (The inn operates its own ferry, which makes three exclusive runs between the island and Fernandina Beach on Amelia Island, Florida.)

The family maintains Greyfield on the acreage they retained, and Margaret's daughter, Lucy Ferguson, opened up her home as an inn in the 1960s as an elite refuge from the hectic everyday world. Lucy's children and grandchildren operate the inn now as if they were welcoming old friends into their home. At Greyfield you can easily imagine that you are in the august company of such as the Carnegies and Kennedys at leisure—a throwback to a more gentile time. Expect eccentric charm, but not a decorator look. The inn is furnished with family heirlooms and antiques, many of them original to the house, and some of them suffer from the passage of time and exposure to the salt sea air.

Although it isn't visible from the house, endless vistas of deserted beach are only steps away through a stand of scrub growth that protects the inn from all but the most severe storms. For nonbeach time, our favorite place to relax is on the spacious front veranda. Heavily shaded by deep overhangs, sheltered by ancient live oaks, and cooled by a gentle sea breeze, the veranda is furnished with comfortable rockers and two immense porch swings. Filled with plump, colorful cushions and throw pillows, these swings make the perfect place to read a book, snuggle with your love, sip a cool drink, take an afternoon nap, or all the above.

For most of its existence Greyfield was not air-conditioned, and therefore the inn was closed each August. Recent addition of air-conditioning permits the inn to remain open year-round. Guests in the know realize that winter is a particularly pleasant time for a getaway at Greyfield. Fires blaze from the living room and dining room fireplaces, encouraging guests to gather around after a blustery walk on the beach. Cooler temperatures make vigorous hiking, biking, and long walks on the beach more pleasant; the bug population has all but disappeared; and there are even fewer visitors. Storms often deposit a wealth of shells on the deserted beaches.

Fine dining is integral to the Greyfield experience, and all meals are included. A full country breakfast is served in the dining room each morning. Lunches are prepared picnic style and packed into knapsacks or baskets for you to take with you. Depending on your choice of activities for the day, you might feast at the beach, near the ruins of Dungeness, or on the front veranda. If you've been off at the beach or exploring the island, be sure to be back in time to get cleaned up for hors d'oeuvres before dinner. The evening meal is a more formal affair, served in the dining room with candlelight and flowers, and gentlemen are requested to wear jackets. The centerpiece of the gourmet meal might be seafood, Cornish hen, lamb, or beef, but it will be accompanied by homemade breads and fresh vegetables and topped off by a mouthwatering dessert. The wine list, although limited, is excellent. At other times during the day, the inn maintains a well-stocked bar in the old gun room where guests help themselves on the honor system.

Some things to know before you go: The only telephone is a radio-phone to the mainland and is reserved exclusively for emergencies. There are no stores on Cumberland Island, so bring everything you think you will need. The inn shop stocks a limited supply of sunscreen, film, cigarettes (for out-

Cumberland Island
National Seashore

We plead guilty. We and other travel writers tend to use the phrase "get away from it all" somewhat cavalierly to mean any junket away from home or to describe any place that's not a big city. Very few wilderness areas exist anymore that can be accurately described this way.

One of the exceptions is Cumberland Island, the largest of Georgia's barrier islands known as the Golden Isles. Imagine an island the size of Manhattan with only a handful of widely scattered buildings on it, a place where there are no paved roads and few service vehicles, a haven where there's no store or tourist trap and only one indoor overnight accommodation, the Greyfield Inn.

Why go there? For paradise on earth. Miles and miles of deserted, wide, hard-packed beach are backed by gentle dunes, anchored by gently waving sea oats, where shore birds and loggerhead turtles make their homes. You're likely to see small herds of wild horses galloping down the beach or armadillos scuttling across the crushed seashell roads. Deer, bobcats, alligators, birds, and other wildlife are more plentiful than people.

You have three options for visiting the island: Take a day trip, camp out, or stay at the inn. But plan ahead—only 300 visitors are allowed to experience Eden each day, so you need reservations for the National Park Service or inn ferry, the only way to get there. Campers need to make reservations far in advance. Actual campsites can't be reserved, however, so you may end up with a spot at the semideveloped campground or a primitive campsite far removed from everything. For campers and day-trippers: No matter how long you're staying, take everything you need. There are no stores or food outlets.

Day-trippers are at a disadvantage because they can see so little of the island in such a short time—especially if they spend much time on the beach—so we recommend several days to a week of camping or at the inn. The following itinerary is doable for a daytripper, however; visit the small Ice House Museum, near the ferry landing, which displays artifacts from thousands of years of the island's fascinating past—Indian, Spanish, and English occupation and the opulent era of Carnegie ownership. Take a ranger-guided walk through ancient maritime forest to the beach, and on the way see Dungeness, the ruins of one of the Carnegie mansions. Plum Orchard, a well-preserved Carnegie mansion, is open for occasional tours, so call ahead if you want to see it. Spend whatever time you have left photographing or painting the stunning scenery, hiking, fishing, bird-watching, or whatever your imagination dictates.

A trip to Cumberland Island is an experience like no other and is well worth the effort. You'll never forget experiencing heaven.

For information about Cumberland Island National Seashore, call (912) 882-4335; for day ferry reservations, call (912) 261-6408.

door smoking only), over-the-counter medications, and insect repellent. Pack according to the season and weather and bring some rain gear. Ferries depart to and from Greyfield only three times a day, so plan accordingly.

If you've been searching for a place where it's more than OK to do nothing, this is it.

HOW TO GET THERE: Get specific directions when you make your reservations—you can only get to the inn via their ferry from Fernandina Beach on Amelia Island, Florida.

The Dunlap House
Gainesville, Georgia 30501

INNKEEPERS: David and Karen Peters

ADDRESS/TELEPHONE: 635 Green Street; (770) 536-0200 or (800) 276-2935; fax (770) 503-7857

WEB SITE: www.bestinns.net

E-MAIL: dunlaphouse@mindspring.com

ROOMS: 9; all with private bath, telephone, and television; some with fireplace; some with wheelchair access.

RATES: $85 to $155, single or double; includes full breakfast and refreshments on arrival.

OPEN: Year-round.

FACILITIES AND ACTIVITIES: Nearby: restaurants, Helen and tourist activities, North Georgia mountains, Lake Lanier, Quinlan Art Center.

BUSINESS TRAVEL: Excellent work area in room. Fax, direct-dial computer access available.

The Dunlap House has become an "innkeepers' choice"; that is, we get letters from other innkeepers telling us how much they've enjoyed staying at the Dunlap House. That's high praise. The Dunlap innkeepers live on the property and offer a personal style of Southern hospitality. David and Karen Peters want you to feel that you are coming into a friendly, upscale Southern home, which just happens to be a B&B inn. They'll offer you a drink and goodies to enjoy while you register and get settled in your room.

Dunlap House is an elegantly renovated 1910 house listed in the National Register of Historic Places. The furnishings are period reproductions that include many pale pine pieces. The overall effect is bright and light, not the darkness we sometimes associate with historic homes.

In the front lobby area, a few small round tables with chairs make a good place to have a social drink in the evening if you bring your own. And the white wicker–furnished porch is our choice of locations for the full breakfast of fresh fruit; hot muffins or bread; French toast, eggs, or casseroles; fruit juice; and coffe or tea. Some people prefer breakfast on a tray in their room, but we like being outside with those healthy plants.

As for dinner, Rudolph's on Green Street is a neighboring restaurant in an old English Tudor–style house with a solid granite foundation and

exposed beams in the living room. The offerings include standards such as prime rib of beef and fresh Georgia trout, as well as some more elaborate continental entrees, including veal prepared a couple of different ways.

While you're out eating entirely too well, the staff at the inn are busy freshening your room, pressing your suit, taking care of your laundry, making sure there's a clean terry robe in the room, and, if you've asked for it, arranging to accommodate your special dietary needs at breakfast.

HOW TO GET THERE: From I-985, take exit 6 to Gainesville. Stay on the same road to the corner of Ridgewood Avenue and Green Street. Turn left at the light and park behind the inn.

The Grand Hotel ¢¢
Hogansville, Georgia 30230

INNKEEPERS: John Hardy Jones and Glenda Gordon

ADDRESS/TELEPHONE: 303 East Main Street; (706) 637-8828 or (800) 324-7625; fax (706) 637-4522

WEB SITE: www.gomm.com

E-MAIL: grandhtl@aol.com

ROOMS: 5, plus 5 suites; all with private bath, gas-log fireplace, television; some with whirlpool bath.

RATES: $100 to $125; includes full breakfast.

OPEN: Year-round.

FACILITIES AND ACTIVITIES: Tearoom, old-fashioned sweet shop, gift shop. Nearby: pick up a brochure for a driving tour of historic homes from the City Hall on Main Street or from the Troup County Chamber of Commerce on Bull Street; located midway between Newnan and LaGrange, which are filled with historic sites and antiques shops; not far from Warm Springs, Pine Mountain, and Callaway Gardens.

*L*ocated in the center of the commercial district of quaint, historic Hogansville, the Grand is a small nineteenth-century Italianate-style hotel. Its position on a corner permitted the original builders to incorporate a covered first-story promenade and a second-story porch wrapped around two sides—both replete with yards and yards of gingerbread.

On the first floor, barrel-vaulted ceilings and paneling in the diminutive lobby and up the staircase have been restored to their former splendor. Guest rooms and a large comfortable guest parlor are found upstairs, where sky-lights pour sunlight into the opulent sitting area, which is separated into two areas by ornate arches and columns. This area acts like a magnet, drawing visitors to read, watch television, or get to know one another. In good weather, however, you're more likely to find everyone outside on the expansive second-story porch or on the patio overlooking the rear garden.

Furnished with antiques appropriate to the turn of the century, the spacious, high-ceilinged guest rooms and suites feature queen-size beds, private baths, gas-log fireplaces, and cable television. Decorative themes for the guest chambers range from Georgian to Victorian to Mediterranean. Several rooms are further enhanced by two-person whirlpool tubs and/or direct access to the porch. Suites boast the luxury of a separate sitting room, some have a daybed, making them ideal for those traveling with an additional adult.

Downstair spaces are occupied by an old-fashioned sweet shop, a gift shop, and a Victorian tearoom that is open from 11:00 A.M. to 2:00 P.M. Monday, Tuesday and Thursday through Saturday. Full tea costs $12.95; Junior Tea is $8.95.

HOW TO GET THERE: From I–85, take GA 100 west about 4 miles to Hogansville. The hotel is on the left.

The Woodbridge Inn ¢¢¢
Jasper, Georgia 30143

INNKEEPERS: Brenda and Joe Rueffert

ADDRESS/TELEPHONE: 411 Chambers; (706) 692–6293

ROOMS: 18; all with private bath, telephone, and television. Pets welcome.

RATES: $40 to $72, single or double; breakfast not served. Children free.

OPEN: Year-round.

FACILITIES AND ACTIVITIES: Lunch on Wednesdays and Sundays; dinner every night except Sunday and Monday; full bar service. Swimming pool. Nearby: short drive to restaurants; tennis and golf; Amicalola Falls State Park hiking; Carter's Lake swimming, sailing, and fishing; Amicalola River and Talking Rock Creek whitewater canoeing.

The following is one guest's view of the inn's food: "I went to the restaurant early. A cheery man with a black mustache was digging flower beds around the front porch of the inn. Seeing my camera, he said, 'Take my picture,' and struck a bunch of comic poses.

"While I was tasting a wonderful seafood chowder that the waitress had recommended and eating crackers topped with a homemade cheese-spread from a crock on the table, I asked who the funny man working out front was.

"'That's Joe, the owner and the chef,'" my waitress said.

"Made me nervous. How was he going to cook my dinner if he was outside with a shovel? Especially something as out-of-the-ordinary as venison fillet in a pepper-and-cognac sauce or sweetbreads with mushrooms? Not to worry. I finally decided on the sautéed sweetbreads and somehow Joe got back into the kitchen and shortly produced the best calf sweetbreads I've ever tasted. They were lightly browned and delicately crisp on the outside, perfectly moist and tender inside, mixed with whole sautéed mushrooms that were still firm and juicy and a splash of light wine sauce. Everything was so good that I ate slowly for a long time."

Accolades like this are not unusual at the Woodbridge Inn. Guests tend to linger over dinner, hating to leave the dining room to go to their rooms. The dining room is in a historic old hotel that was built in the mid-1800s. The guest rooms are in a separate, newly built lodge a few steps away on the side of a hill with a magnificent view of the mountains.

The lodge is contemporary with siding that matches the exterior of the restaurant. The rooms have either patios or balconies, depending on whether you're on the first floor or on one of the other two floors. Inside they're quiet and simple but luxurious, with ceiling fans and Broyhill furniture. One room has spiral steps going up to a sitting area with a sofa so that guests don't feel confined to a bedroom. Another nice touch is a coffeemaker in each room. The owners have recently finished six more rooms in the old hotel over the restaurant.

The Woodbridge is not just for the older generation; our youngest son takes his wife there for romantic weekend getaways.

HOW TO GET THERE: Jasper is in the mountains, about an hour-and-a-half drive north of Atlanta. From the south, take I-75 to 575, then follow the signs into Jasper. From the north, take U.S. 53 off I-75 into Jasper. In Jasper, go north on Main Street. Cross over a small wooden bridge on the right and go into the parking lot.

Jekyll Island Club Hotel
Jekyll Island, Georgia 31527

INNKEEPER: Kevin Runner.

ADDRESS/TELEPHONE: 371 Riverview Drive; (912) 635-2600 or (800) 678-8946; fax 9912) 635-2818

WEB SITE: www.jekyllclub.com

E-MAIL: Via Web site

ROOMS: 134 guest rooms and suites; all with private bath—some whirlpool baths—television, VCR, clock radio; some fireplaces.

RATES: $89-$119 for a standard single, $99-$189 for a double, $149-$279 for specialty rooms and suites. In general, room rates are per room based on double occupancy. Bed-and-Breakfast Getaway packages are available for $49–$69 Sunday through Thursday or $59–$79 Friday and Saturday per night per person. Modified American Plan is available for $48 and Full American Plan for $64—both per person per night.

OPEN: Year-round.

FACILITIES AND ACTIVITIES: Four food outlets, elevator, concierge; staff fluent in five languages; private Surfside Beach Club, heated outdoor pool, nine tennis courts (one indoor, five lighted), laundry, dry cleaning; tours of the property, bicycle rental, complimentary transportation throughout the island. Nearby: Summer Waves water park, indoor/outdoor tennis, sixty-three holes of golf, deep-sea fishing, biking, horseback riding, carriage rides, historic tours, 20 miles of bicycling and jogging paths, miniature golf, dolphin watch tours.

BUSINESS TRAVEL: Six miles off the coast of Georgia, 12 miles from Brunswick and its airport, between Savannah and Jacksonville, Florida, airports. Ideal for small corporate meetings and retreats; ten meeting rooms provide space for banquets up to 160 and receptions for up to 400 guests; some secretarial services.

A couple of summers ago, we took our two young grandchildren (a boy and a girl) to the grand, whimsically turreted Victorian-era confection called the Jekyll Island Club on state-owned, environmentally protected Jekyll Island. It was their first hotel experience of any kind, and they were convinced we were staying in a fairy-tale castle.

No matter how sophisticated a traveler *you* might be, you're probably not so jaded that you'll escape being impressed by relaxing in luxury at what was once one of the most exclusive clubs in this country. In fact, the entire island was an elite playground for the fabulously wealthy. In the last century one hundred millionaires, including Astors, Goulds, Vanderbilts, Pulitzers, Rockefellers, Macys, Goodyears, and Morgans, purchased the mile-and-a-half-wide, 9-mile-long island off the coast of Georgia. They used it as a winter hunting retreat and for other recreational pursuits when they weren't in residence at their mansions in this country's major cities, at their palatial "cottages" in Newport, or at one of their other homes.

The group commissioned the construction of a vast, rambling, sixty-room clubhouse with a grand dining room, lounge, library, other public rooms, and sweeping verandas on the Intracoastal Waterway side of the island, and it opened to its first guests in January 1888. In 1896 Sans Souci, an adjacent building of six large apartments (the island's first condominiums), was added, and an annex attached to the clubhouse was constructed in 1901. Between 1888 and 1928 many member families built their own "cottages" nearby. Ranging up to 8,000 square feet, these mansions had one eccentricity—they had no kitchens because everyone ate at the clubhouse.

The membership, however, began to dwindle during the Depression, and then the U.S. government requested that the resort not be used during the entirety of World War II. In 1947, the state of Georgia purchased the entire island and the club. The state attempted to operate the clubhouse, Sans Souci, and Crane Cottage as a resort complex, but sadly it closed in 1972. In 1978 the 240-acre club district was designated a National Historic Landmark and a massive restoration began, making it the largest revitalization project in the Southeast. Beginning in 1986, a total of $20 million have been invested in restoring the club and its leaded art glass, ornate woodwork, and Rumsford fireplaces, and it has reopened as a hotel.

As one of today's discerning guests at the Jekyll Island Club, you can revel in a combination of natural beauty, elegant architecture, upscale amenities, and superb personal service akin to those enjoyed by the original millionaires.

Just as we and our grand-children did, luxuriate in turn-of-the-century appointments such as Victorian fireplaces in some guest chambers and cus-tom-made mahogany period reproduction furnishings—two-poster beds, armoires, chairs and sofas, and desks and tables —enhanced by rich fabrics, plush carpeting, and modern private baths. Some rooms have whirlpool baths, televisions, VCRs, clock radios, and multiple-dataport telephones. Good taste and attention to detail combine to redefine the meaning of being pampered. These features and amenities have earned the resort four stars and four diamonds from the major rating organizations and inclusion in the National Trust for Historic Preservation's Historic Hotels of America.

Dining options include gourmet continental cuisine with an emphasis on seafood in the opulent Grand Dining Room, delicatessen/bakery fare at Cafe Solterra, and fast-food and snack items at both the Surfside Beach Club and the Poolside Bar and Grill in season. J.P.'s Pub offers an intimate envi-ronment for cocktails and conversation. In good weather you'll want to take your drink out onto one of the vast verandas.

While you're on the island, be sure to take a guided tour of the historic district. The district includes Faith chapel and several of the cottages, which contain impressive collections of decorative arts as well as historical photographs and documents related to the club era.

HOW TO GET THERE: From I-95, take U.S. 17 east to the Jekyll Island Causeway and cross to the island. Follow the signs to the hotel.

The Lodge on Little St. Simons Island 🏠
Little St. Simons Island, Georgia 31522

INNKEEPER: Debbie McIntyre

ADDRESS/TELEPHONE: Little St. Simons Island (mailing address: P.O. Box 21078); (912) 638-7472 or (888) 733-5774; fax (912) 634-1811

WEB SITE: www.pactel.com.au/lssi

E-MAIL: lssi@mindspring.com

ROOMS: 2 in main lodge with private bath; 4 in River Lodge, all with private bath; 4 in Cedar House, all with private bath; 2 in Michael Cottage share bath; 3 in Helen Cottage share 2 baths.

RATES: $250 to $450, single; $325 to $550, double; includes all meals, wine with dinner, island activities, and ferry service. Minimum two-night stay. Inquire about longer-stay and off-season discounts.

OPEN: Year-round.

FACILITIES AND ACTIVITIES: Bar in lodge; collection of books about native birds, plants, animals, and marine life; swimming pool, stables, horseshoes, ocean swimming, birding, naturalist-led explorations, beachcombing, shelling, fishing, canoeing, hiking biking, fly-fishing schools.

*T*his is truly a special place. It is a 10,000-acre barrier island still in its natural state except for the few buildings needed to house and feed thirty guests. You can get there only by boat. Such creature comforts as nice bathrooms and ice machines have been added, but they rest unobtrusively in the natural scene.

When we visited, we felt welcomed as though we'd been visiting there for years.

You will marvel at how much you can do in a short time. The permanent staff includes three naturalists. One of the naturalists loaded us into a pickup truck and drove us around the island to help us get oriented. We walked through woods and open areas and along untouched ocean beaches. We saw our first armadillo. We gathered more sand dollars than we'd ever seen in one place before. We saw deer, raccoons, opossums, and more birds than we could identify. Serious bird-watchers plan special trips to Little St. Simons to observe the spring and fall migrations.

We even rode horseback with one of the naturalists to view some eagle and stork nesting sites.

When we weren't out exploring the island, we played bocce ball, swam, and just soaked up some rays. In the evening we sat in front of the fire in the lodge, chatting with the other guests and inspecting the photographs on the walls. They're standard hunting-camp pictures: rows of men grinning like idiots and holding up strings of fish, hunters with rifles grinning like idiots, and people climbing in and out of boats grinning like idiots.

One of the best meals we had while we were there was roast quail, served with rice pilaf and little yellow biscuits. As Carol polished off an unladylike-sized meal and finished her wine, she realized that she was grinning like an idiot. After dinner, with no thought of television, she retired to the comfortable bed in a simple, pleasant room and fell asleep instantly, still grinning.

We hear that The Helen House, an elegant 1928 tabby cottage, was opened to guests recently. We haven't seen it personally yet, but the reports we hear are good.

HOW TO GET THERE: When you make your reservations, you will receive instructions on where to meet the boat that takes you to the island.

1842 Inn 📱
Macon, Georgia 31201

INNKEEPER: Phillip Jenkins

ADDRESS/TELEPHONE: 353 College Street; (912) 741–1842; reservations (800) 336–1842; fax (912) 741–1842

WEB SITE: www.1842inn.com

E-MAIL: the1842inn@worldnet.att.net

ROOMS: 21; all with private bath, telephone, and television, some with whirlpool and fireplace; some with wheelchair access.

RATES: $95 to $155, double; single $10 less; includes continental breakfast and other inn courtesies.

OPEN: Year-round

FACILITIES AND ACTIVITIES: Beverages from bar at nominal charge, meeting rooms. Nearby: restaurants, easy access to Macon Historic District walking tours, Cherry Blossom Festival in March. Access to private dining and health clubs and country club for swimming, tennis, and golf, horse-drawn carriage rides.

BUSINESS TRAVEL: Located five minutes from business district. In-room computer and modem setup; excellent work surface; limited secretarial service; copier and fax available. Conference facilities on site for up to twenty (sixty using nearby property).

*S*carlett's Tara might not exist, but if you are looking for a very good substitute, Phil Jenkin's 1842 Inn is a good bet. Every time we visit Phil, we fall in love with his place all over again.

This B&B inn started with a strong-minded owner who was determined to get the restoration done right, then work on service. The new owner and manager has taken it from there.

When you start with a Greek Revival antebellum house of this beauty, it's hard to see how anyone could go wrong; but when the earlier owners bought the property, the house had passed its glory years, was divided into apartments, and had fallen into disrepair.

Such a building has a continuing life (life implies growth and change) as its fortunes wax and wane over the years. Originally it was smaller, with only four columns. About the turn of the century, the house was enlarged, columns were added, and elaborate parquet floors were laid over the original heart-of-pine floors.

Now, fully restored, this main house is connected by a courtyard to a Victorian cottage that was moved from Vineville Avenue to the rear of the inn and refurbished to provide additional rooms. One wonders: In another generation, what next?

When you stay at the 1842, you may find the history interesting, but if you're like us, you want to know more about your creature comforts. They're all here, including full handicap facilities, blackout linings in the draperies for late sleepers, and walls that are insulated to keep your room quiet. Some rooms have a second television set in the bathroom so that you can watch while you enjoy the whirlpool.

The furnishings are a mix of fine antiques, period reproductions, Oriental rugs, and luxurious towels and linens. The beds are all king- or queen-size period reproductions with custom-made mattresses.

The inn offers all the services of a fine European hotel: continental breakfast delivered to your room with flowers and a paper, turndown service with mints on the pillow, shoe shines while you sleep, and robes in guest rooms.

The inn has begun winning coveted awards from other inn guides—which shall remain nameless in this guide!

One of the most pleasant touches is the addition of what Phil calls "formal evening hospitality." This means really elaborate hors d'oeuvres and beverages in the parlors, with piano music, to separate the workday from evening relaxation. Whenever he's there, Phil plays the piano himself. Piano-playing innkeepers are pretty rare, but Phil enjoys doing it because it gives him a chance to socialize a bit with guests, something the keeper of a successful business inn doesn't often get to do.

HOW TO GET THERE: From I-75, take exit 52 to Forsyth Street. Turn left on College Street.

Brady Inn ![icon]

Madison, Georgia 30650

INNKEEPERS: Chris and Lynn Rasch

ADDRESS/TELEPHONE: 250 North Second Street; (706) 342–4400; fax (706) 342–9287

ROOMS: 7; all with private bath.

RATES: $60 to $150; includes full breakfast.

OPEN: Year-round.

FACILITIES AND ACTIVITIES: Restaurant. Nearby: historic Madison full of architectural treasures; Heritage Hall, Madison-Morgan Cultural Center; casual and fine dining; antiques and crafts shopping, boutiques.

*I*t was a dark and stormy night (or so the stories often start) when we were scheduled to stay at the Brady Inn. Even so, the first thing we noticed when we arrived was the cheerful-looking carousel horse on the front porch, which immediately lightened our mood. When our hosts, Chris and Lynn, greeted us, they gave us the bad news that they had a family emergency and couldn't get an inn-sitter. Rather than call and cancel our reservation or turn us away at the door, they met us with open arms, showed us around, made sure we were comfortable and knew where our breakfast items were, gave us the keys, and left us on our own as we were the only guests that night. That's the kind of friendly folks they are. We spent a delightful evening and following morning pretending that we lived in the charming Victorian cottage. Despite the bad weather, with a blazing fire in the parlor fireplace, we were as cozy as can be. Of course, if the weather had been fabulous, we would have loved sitting in rockers on one of the verandas.

Actually, the Brady Inn is two separate turn-of-the-century cottages connected by a vast veranda. The house in which we stayed was built in 1895; the adjoining cottage, in 1910. Both cottages are characterized by high ceilings, stained glass, intricate moldings, heart-pine floors, and working fireplaces. We particularly admired the ornate fretwork in the central hall of the older house. Both houses are filled with appropriate antiques and well stocked with books, magazines, puzzles, and games. There's a television in the common room.

Spacious, elegant guest rooms—which are furnished with antique sleigh beds or ornately carved beds, are also well supplied with dressers, armoires, and some seating—feature private baths. You can easily believe you're at your grandmother's house. Two connecting rooms can be used as a suite.

The Brady Inn is well known in Georgia's heartland for its restaurant, where lunch is served daily and dinner by appointment only. This cheerful room with lots of windows is where your full breakfast will be served.

Madison has enough charming small-town attractions to keep you busy, but is also an ideal base from which to explore nearby Millidgeville and Eatonton.

HOW TO GET THERE: Within the city limits, U.S. 129/441 is Main Street. From Main Street, turn west onto either Thomason or Burney and go 1 block. The inn is on Second Avenue between the two streets.

Riverview Hotel ¢¢¢
St. Marys, Georgia 31558

INNKEEPERS: Jerry and Gaila Brandon

ADDRESS/TELEPHONE: 105 Osborne Street; (912) 882–3242 or (888) 882–1807

WEB SITE: www.gacoast.com/navigator/stmarys.html

ROOMS: 18; all with private bath and television.

RATES: $45, single; $55, double; includes tax and continental breakfast.

OPEN: Year-round.

FACILITIES AND ACTIVITIES: Breakfast, dinner Monday through Saturday (5:00 to 10:00 P.M.); wheelchair access to restaurant. Lounge (closed Sunday), self-guided tours of St. Marys historic district. Nearby: Crooked River State Park and King's Bay Submarine Base, hour's drive to Okefenokee Swamp, access to Cumberland Island by ferry.

You can't tell an inn by its name. We've seen places called inns that were motels, and here's a place called a hotel that's really an inn. Sitting on the banks of the St. Marys River, across the street from the ferry to Cumberland Island National Seashore, the Riverview has a sitting room, a veranda with rockers, and an old-fashioned lobby with big brown-and-white tiles on the floor. The rooms are furnished, without frills or ruffles, with heavy country-style furniture.

The Brandon family (Jerry and Gaila) renovated the 1916 building in old-time style and furnished it with simple country furniture appropriate for the campers, bicyclists, and hikers who tend to gather in St. Marys.

If you are here before a ferry is scheduled to leave for Cumberland Island, the lobby will probably be full of knapsacks and backpacks, whose owners are eating in Seagle's Restaurant in the hotel, along with everybody else in town.

The restaurant has been renovated with wood siding, Irish green accents, a gallery for local artists, and some original brick walls exposed for the old-fashioned flavor. The restaurant, which is leased out, is not operated by Jerry and Gaila, but they do fix an expanded continental breakfast for their guests and will provide picnic lunches that you can take on the ferry or on a hike.

The food is fantastic! We thought the stuffed shrimp were surely the best thing possible until we tasted the fried rock shrimp, which are sweeter than regular shrimp and were fried in a delicate homemade batter resembling tempura batter. If you ask ahead of time, you can enjoy equally good food on your trip to Cumberland Island or Okefenokee Swamp by asking the Brandons' staff to pack a picnic for you.

Before he took up innkeeping, Jerry was a chemist and a tournament bridge player. He got involved with the Riverview Hotel because it was a family place and he wanted to continue the tradition. If you really want to make his day, show up asking for a fourth for bridge. At least that used to make his day. But Jerry is now the mayor of the town and so busy that he's harder to pin down than he used to be. Still, it never hurts to try.

If you're just exploring Georgia, you'll like St. Marys. It's historic but handles its tourism in a low-key way. The local people don't get all gussied up for it.

HOW TO GET THERE: From I-95, take Route 40 east straight into St. Marys and down to the water. The inn is on the right.

Spencer House Inn
St. Marys, Georgia 31558

INNKEEPERS: Mary and Mike Neff

ADDRESS/TELEPHONE: 200 Osborne Street; (912) 882–1872;
fax (912) 882–9427

WEB SITE: www.spencerhouseinn.com

E-MAIL: spencer@eagnet.com

ROOMS: 13, plus 1 suite; all with private bath, telephone, clock radio,
cable television, ceiling fan.

RATES: $80 to $125 for rooms, $145 for the suite; includes breakfast
buffet and afternoon iced peach tea; $15 for each additional person;
holidays and special events require a minimum stay.

OPEN: Year-round.

FACILITIES AND ACTIVITIES: Parlor, breakfast room, elevator. Nearby:
Orange Hall, Toonerville Trolley of cartoon fame, thirty-eight National
Register sites, McIntosh Sugar Mill tabby ruins; tennis, golf at Osprey
Cove and Laurel Island Links, deep-sea fishing, sea kayaking; Cumber-
land Island National Seashore, Okefenokee National Wildlife Refuge,
Georgia's Golden Isles; Amelia Island, Florida.

BUSINESS TRAVEL: Thirty-five minutes from Jacksonville, Florida,
airport.

*Y*ou'll love the first- and second-story verandas of this B&B inn, just
as we do. It's perfect for relaxing with a book and a cool drink, eating breakfast in good weather, getting to know your fellow guests,
or just people watching as tourists come and go through the quaint historic
district of St. Marys.

Captain William T. Spencer, the collector of customs in St. Marys from
1871 to 1873, built this gracious Victorian structure as a hotel in 1872. Over
the intervening years it served many purposes or sat abandoned. Today,
fully restored and painted a cheerful pink, the building has returned to its
original use. Original moldings, high ceilings, heart-pine floors, many windows, antiques and period reproductions, and appropriate fabrics add
warmth and beauty.

Different guest room sizes and configurations, as well as a variety of furniture and fabrics, ensure that every guest chamber has its own distinctive
personality. While retaining the charm of yesteryear, each room features
modern conveniences, such as a private bath with a claw-foot tub or shower,

television, and telephone. An elevator provides easy access to all three floors.

A generous full breakfast is served buffet style in the breakfast room each morning and will feature one of the chef's daily specials such as cranberry-pecan bread pudding, a frittata, or other specialty. Although the bright, cheery breakfast room is delightful, we prefer to take our breakfast out on one of the verandas.

Mary and Mike are only too delighted to sit down with their guests to give advice about area sight-seeing and help them get tickets on the Cumberland Island ferry, reserve tee times, or make restaurant reservations. For an additional fee they'll be glad to prepare a picnic lunch for you to take to the wilds of Cumberland Island or the Okefenokee Swamp.

St. Marys is the departure point for the National Park Service ferry to Cumberland Island. Because the ferry leaves in the morning, many who are going to camp out on the island for several days arrive in St. Marys the night before to enjoy a night of luxury and comfort at the Spencer House Inn before going on to their primitive camp site. On the day of their return, others immediately check in to the inn from the late-afternoon ferry to celebrate their return to civilization. Our personal recommendation is to do both—we're not enthralled with roughing it for very long.

HOW TO GET THERE: From I-95, exit onto State Route 40. As you enter St. Marys, Route 40 becomes Osborne Street. The inn is on the left at the corner of Bryant and Osborne. Parking is at the side of the inn or on the street.

The Stovall House
Sautee, Georgia 30571

INNKEEPER: Ham Schwartz

ADDRESS/TELEPHONE: 1526 Highway 255N; (706) 878–3355

ROOMS: 5; all with private bath; 1 with wheelchair access.

RATES: $50 single; $80 double; includes continental breakfast. Children under age four free; children ages four to eighteen $11.

OPEN: Year-round.

FACILITIES AND ACTIVITIES: Dinner, brown bagging permitted, wheelchair access to dining room. Located in the Northeast Georgia mountains. Nearby: lakes, rivers, creeks, waterfalls, and state parks for fishing, hiking, rock climbing, snow skiing (in season).

*T*his inn is the quintessential family homestead—rolling fields, a huge vegetable garden, a big white house with the kind of front porch people really sit on, and a lively assortment of kids and animals.

Ham is a zany, enthusiastic innkeeper who has brought a home of the 1800s back to life by restoring, renovating, decorating, and then welcoming guests as family. He says that he wants the place to feel like home away from home.

Not that many of us have homes with mantels and doors handmade of walnut, working fireplaces in all the downstairs rooms, heart-of-pine floors, and an original telescoping bed (the first Hide-A-Way) made in 1891.

Ham's particular genius is being able to blend his passion for restoration with a sense that history is about living, not about museums. Stovall House is on the National Register of Historic Places and has won two important awards for restoration. But you enjoy the inn not for its awards but for how it feels to stay here.

To give you an idea of how special the place seems to some guests, one man made a weekend reservation and confided to Ham that he planned to give his girlfriend an engagement ring while they were there. Another guest liked the place so well that she worked the Stovall House logo in needlepoint for Ham. Guests often plan birthday and anniversary celebrations here.

Just being in a room can be a celebration. In some of the upstairs rooms, you can go to sleep watching stars and wake up to see the sun rise through skylights strategically placed in the dormers.

Even though people celebrate romantic milestones at the inn, you don't have to live on love alone while you are here. The food is good—and fresh!

Some of the vegetables come from that huge garden I mentioned. The menu features homemade soups, fresh vegetables fixed in as many different ways as Ham and the staff can think of, and such delicacies as poached trout. The restaurant was named one of the top fifty restaurants in Georgia by the publication *Georgia Trend*.

Ham is deeply involved behind the scenes in the restoration of the old Nacoochee School, which dates back to the 1800s, and its development as an arts and community center. It has performances of everything from the Savannah Symphony to children's theater. Ham has enjoyed performing in some of the plays himself.

HOW TO GET THERE: Sautee is 5 miles east of Helen, Georgia, on Highway 17. At the Sautee Store, turn onto Highway 255 (Lake Burton Road). Drive about 1½ miles. The inn is on the right.

17 Hundred 90 Inn
Savannah, Georgia 31401

INNKEEPERS: Rita Dow; Dick and Darlene Lehmkuhl, owners

ADDRESS/TELEPHONE: 307 East President Street; (912) 236–7122 or (800) 487–1790; fax (912) 236–7123

WEB SITE: www.bbonline.com/ga/savannah/1790/

E-MAIL: 1790inn@email.msn.com

ROOMS: 14; all with private bath and a small refrigerator; king- or queen-size beds; some with gas-log fireplace.

RATES: $119 to $189; includes full breakfast and complimentary bottle of wine.

OPEN: Year-round.

FACILITIES AND ACTIVITIES: Restaurant and cocktail lounge. Nearby: Savannah historic district, River Street, shopping, fine dining, nightlife; beaches of Tybee Island.

The first night we stayed at the 17 Hundred 90 Inn, Carol woke up in the middle of the night with the feeling that someone else was in the room. When she opened her eyes, a woman in a long dress and with her hair in a bun was standing beside the bed peering down at us. She instantly evaporated into thin air, so obviously she was just curious and meant us no harm. When we related our tale over breakfast with owner Dick Lehmkuhl the next morning, instead of thinking we were crazy, he reassured us, "That's only Anna Powell, the first owner; she's our resident ghost. Your room is the one from which she jumped out the window to her death when her sailor boyfriend jilted her." We've stayed in the same room ever since, but she's never visited us again. Dick says other ghostly manifestation such as lilting piano music when no one is playing the piano occasionally delight guests.

Named for the year in which the brick foundation was laid, the historic inn and restaurant recently celebrated its 208th birthday. Upstairs you'll find luxury, Old South charm, and gracious pampering in the splendidly appointed guest rooms, which are filled with antiques, period reproductions, and appropriate wall coverings and fabrics. Gas-log fireplaces add romance to twelve of the rooms. One of our favorites is the largest, with its king-size bed on a dias and its spacious sitting area, but some romantics prefer the two rooms with mirrored ceilings.

As much as we love the spacious, high-ceilinged guest rooms, the heart of the inn is the cellar. Here you'll find the gastronomic delights of one of Savannah's most popular restaurants and cocktail lounges, where the intimate atmosphere is enhanced by low ceilings, brick walls, and dim flickering light cast by the glow of blazing fires in the twin walk-in fireplaces. *Gourmet* magazine has called the dining room the most elegant in Savannah. *Georgia Trend* magazine singled out the restaurant and lounge as the in place to be for "financiers, businesspeople, and professionals," and, we might add, politicians. Gourmet Diners Club has honored the establishment with its Silver Spoon award for eight years. During a stay at the inn, no matter how long or short, treat yourselves to a dinner of continental cuisine accompanied by fine wines in the restaurant. Another night, you might get back to the inn in time for complimentary hors d'oeuvres in the lounge. So generous are they that you won't even have to worry about dinner that evening.

The full gourmet breakfast served in the Garden Room typically includes a casserole, wonderful banana-nut bread, fresh fruit, juice, and coffee or tea. Later in the day the Garden Room becomes a popular lunch spot for Savannahians.

Outside your door is the Savannah historic district, which you can explore on foot for days.

HOW TO GET THERE: I-16 ends as it merges into Montgomery Street. Pass the Civic Center on the right and go 2 more blocks to York Street and turn right. Go 7 blocks and turn left onto Lincoln. The inn is at the corner of Lincoln and President Streets. Parking is on the street.

Ballastone Inn 🍋
Savannah, Georgia 31401

INNKEEPER: Jean Hagens

ADDRESS/TELEPHONE: 14 East Oglethorpe Avenue; (912) 236-1484 or (800) 822-4553; fax (912) 236-4626

ROOMS: 13, plus 3 suites; all with private bath, telephone, television, and VCR; 11 with working fireplace and Jacuzzi; some with wheelchair access.

RATES: $195 to $225 standard, $255 to $285 superior, and $315 to $345 suites ($60 more during high season and for special events such as St. Patrick's Day); includes full breakfast, high tea, hors d'oeuvres, brandy, and chocolates.

OPEN: Year-round.

FACILITIES AND ACTIVITIES: Full-service bar, landscaped courtyard. Located in Savannah historic district. Nearby: restaurants, antiques shops, Savannah riverfront, historic sites.

BUSINESS TRAVEL: Located five minutes from business district. Telephone in room, fax available. Inquire about corporate rates.

The Ballastone Inn is the kind of place that indulges the whims and idiosyncrasies of even the most crotchety traveler. Each time we stay at this B&B inn we're impressed with the good humor and ease with which the staff carry in extra luggage, rearrange schedules, and hasten check-in for a group of what we consider unusually demanding guests.

A few other nice things the staff will do for you include serving your breakfast at whatever time you choose—either in your room, in the tea or main parlor, or in the courtyard—and arranging everything from restaurant reservations and theater tickets to sight-seeing tours and airline flights. They'll even polish your shoes if you leave them outside your door at night.

Like many other old buildings in Savannah, the inn has been restored with special attention to authenticity, using Scalamandré fabrics and Savannah Spectrum colors. The colors were developed by chipping old buildings down to the original paint and matching it.

The most impressive thing about the inn is the absolute faithfulness with which the fabric, carpet, and eighteenth- and nineteenth-century furniture and art have been combined to fit the period of the house.

To give you a better idea of the rooms, consider the one called Scarlett's Retreat, a popular room at the Ballastone. It has an English canopy bed, a small sitting area, and a gas fireplace. The walls are painted spruce green and the drapes and bedding blend softly in more shades of green and white. The hardwood floors are set off with Oriental rugs.

Last year they purchased all new bedding. As one of the hostesses explained, "Just to look nice isn't enough—it has to *feel* good too.

The Ballastone also upgraded their food service over the past year. They now serve a full breakfast (you select what you want and where you want it served the night before), high tea at 4:00 P.M. each day, hors d'oeuvres at 6:30 P.M., and chocolates and brandy at bedtime.

HOW TO GET THERE: Take I–16 east to its end in downtown Savannah, where it merges into Montgomery Street. Turn right at the second stoplight onto Oglethorpe Avenue. Go 4 blocks to Bull Street. The inn is next to the Juliette Gordon Low House.

East Bay Inn

Savannah, Georgia 31401

INNKEEPERS: Glen Anderson

ADDRESS/TELEPHONE: 225 East Bay Street; (912) 238–1225 or (800) 500–1225; fax (912) 232–2709

WEB SITE: www.eastbayinn.com

E-MAIL: info@eastbayinn.com

ROOMS: 28; all with private bath, telephone, television, and coffeemaker.

RATES: $99 to $189; includes deluxe continental breakfast, morning newspaper, evening wine and sherry, turndown service with a sweet treat.

OPEN: Year-round.

FACILITIES AND ACTIVITIES: Restaurant; elevator. Nearby: Savannah's historic district, fine dining, shops, theater, nightime entertainment; beaches of Tybee Island.

BUSINESS TRAVEL: Fax and copy service; meeting planning services; meeting and banquet facilities ideal for small groups.

Charm, romance, an atmosphere reminiscent of Savannah's nineteenth century; elegant surroundings; personalized service; and a location just off River Street and the bustling waterfront make the East Bay Inn an extremely attractive place to stay in the city's historic district. This is a great place to people watch—especially during the three-day St. Patrick's Day celebration.

During the 1880s the building in which the inn is located was a cotton warehouse with offices on the third floor. Later the downstairs was occupied by a drugstore and then abandoned for many years. In 1984 it was fully restored and adapted for use as an inn. Despite its checkered past, the structure maintains its original crown moldings, hardwood floors, and Savannah bricks.

All public areas and the twenty-eight intimate guest rooms are furnished with antiques and period reproductions, porcelains, antique maps, Oriental rugs, and artwork by Audubon and Catsby. Well-proportioned, high-ceilinged guest rooms, some with exposed brick walls, feature a queen-size four-poster rice bed and offer all the modern conveniences such as a private bath, telephone, cable television, and coffeemaker. In this well-run small hotel, the friendly staff are always ready to help you in any way and to answer questions and make suggestions about their favorite city.

A continental-plus breakfast is served each morning, and this is a good opportunity to get to know your fellow guests. So is the relaxed social hour in the evening, when wine and sherry are served. Skyler's Restaurant serves Asian gourmet cuisine.

HOW TO GET THERE: I–16 ends and merges into Montgomery Street. Pass the Civic Center on the right as well as Elbert, Liberty, and Franklin Squares. Turn right onto West Bay Street and go 7 blocks. The inn is on the right opposite Emmett Park. Off-street parking is available next to the inn.

The Eliza Thompson House
Savannah, Georgia 31401

INNKEEPERS: Carol and Steve Day

ADDRESS/TELEPHONE: 5 West Jones Street; (912) 286–3620 or (800) 348–9378; fax (912) 238–1920

WEB SITE: www.bbonline.com/ga/savannah/elizathompson/index.html

ROOMS: 25; all with private bath, telephone, and television.

RATES: $89 to $199 per room; includes deluxe continental breakfast and daily wine-and-cheese reception. Dessert and coffee from 8:30 to 11:30 P.M. each evening.

OPEN: Year-round.

FACILITIES AND ACTIVITIES: Located in the Savannah historic district. Nearby: restaurants, antiques shops, Savannah riverfront, historic sites.

*J*ust down the street from our favorite breakfast and lunch spot, Mrs. Wilkes' Boarding House, is one of Savannah's wonderful B&B inns, The Eliza Thompson House. This 1847 townhouse and carriage hosue have been lovingly restored to their original grace and beauty, including the courtyard, which has been landscaped with Old South formality, including fountains, and the parlor, where guests may sip sherry and relax with one another after the day's activities. The Eliza Thompson House is owned by Carol and Steve Day. They continue a vigorous program of refurbishing and redecorating. One wonderful change is that they've had the old pine floors in the parlor refinished, and they've painted the room a rich blue and centered an Oriental rug there to create a social setting for guests to chat.

The Days have added such niceties as delivering breakfast to your room on a silver tray, providing a modified breakfast of coffee and fresh breads if you have to leave early, ironing the bed linens, providing good reading lights by the beds for people who like to read in bed, and, most recently, nine new marble bathrooms.

The mix of guests is interesting—travelers en route to farther places, tourists exploring Savannah, and an increasing number of men and women who find inns more congenial than motels when they're in Savannah on business. It makes for good conversation.

If you like Civil War lore, you'll be interested in hearing about how Eliza Thompson (the house was built for her in 1847), a beautiful red-haired widow, entertained here in traditional gracious Southern style and feared that Sherman would destroy her home when he marched into Savannah.

HOW TO GET THERE: From the north, exit from U.S. 17A; turn left onto Oglethorpe. Go to the second light and turn right on Whitaker. Go to Jones and turn left. From I-95, take I-16E and then the Montgomery Street exit. Immediately turn right (at the Civic Center) onto Liberty. Take Liberty to the first stoplight at Whitaker. Go right on Whitaker for 3 blocks, then turn left on Jones. A small sign identifies the inn.

Foley House Inn
Savannah, Georgia 31401

INNKEEPERS: Inge Svensson-Moore and Mark A. Moore

ADDRESS/TELEPHONE: 14 West Hull Street, Chippewa Square;
(912) 232–6622 or (800) 547–3708 outside Georgia; fax (912) 231–1218

WEB SITE: www.foley inn.com

E-MAIL: foleyinn@aol.com

ROOMS: 19; all with private bath, telephone, television, VCR; some with whirlpool bath; some with fireplace. Limited smoking; restrictions on children.

RATES: $145 to $275 single or double occupancy; includes full breakfast, afternoon and evening refreshments; minimum stay may be required.

OPEN: Year-round.

FACILITIES AND ACTIVITIES: Some fireplaces and whirlpool baths. Nearby: Savannah historic district, casual and fine dining, shopping, nightlife, Forts Jackson and Pulaski, beaches of Tybee Island; golf, bicycle rental, boating, tennis.

BUSINESS TRAVEL: Savannah airport is 15 miles away; all guest room phones have a dataport.

Although you'll be prepared for the Southern hospitality everyone expects in Savannah, you'll be surprised that the Foley House Inn also has a touch of Danish charm because one of the innkeepers is from Denmark. *National Geographic Traveler* compliments Inge Svensson-Moore for her successful "fusion of continental with Southern." That is only one of the many compliments the B&B inn has received from the national media.

Honored by *Vacation Magazine* as one of the Ten Most Romantic Inns in the country, by *National Geographic Traveler* as one of the Twenty-five Top Southern Inns, and featured on the Home and Garden Television Network in *Great Homes across America*, Foley House Inn occupies a pair of elegant 1896 Federal-style town houses. Restored in the most minute detail, every cornice, joist, and sill has been renewed by a master craftsman.

Each of the nineteen spacious guest rooms and suites is an individual masterpiece, handsomely appointed with period furniture, hand-colored engravings, and Oriental rugs. All the rooms in the main house are blessed with a four-poster bed and a gas-log fireplace. Fifteen of the rooms boast a fireplace. Many chambers are enhanced by a whirlpool bath, but all offer telephone and television as well as a VCR on which you can play movies borrowed from the inn's extensive film library. Guest rooms in the main inn are decorated in the opulent Victorian style, while those in the carriage house display a more casual country look.

A hearty full breakfast can be served in the privacy of your room, or you might prefer to join your fellow guests in the stunning lounge or, in good weather, out in the courtyard. If you're staying several days, a sweet breakfast of such dishes as waffles or French toast is alternated with a more traditional breakfast of quiches, omelettes, or other egg dishes. Two events are eagerly looked forward to in the afternoon: when a formal afternoon high tea including cakes and other sweets is cleared away, hors d'oeuvres follow. Be sure to arrange your daily schedule to get back to the inn in time to enjoy one or both of these repasts. Either or both will surely cut down on the amount of dinner you need. Late in the evening, cordials and a fine selection of wine are available to wind up the day.

Foley House Inn Tidbits

- During the 1800s it was believed that gargoyles could ward off evil spirits, so the original owners used gargoyles to adorn several fireplaces.

- The exquisite parlor chandelier is from the set of *Gone with the Wind*, as is the candelabra at the foot of the stairway.

- Some believe that the restless spirit of Honoria Foley, the original owner, stills dwells in the house.

- During the restoration of the two houses that make up the inn, a human skeleton was found in the wall between the two. No one has been able to solve the mystery of who it was or how it got there.

- If you had an eagle eye out when you saw the movie *Forrest Gump*, you may recognize Chippewa Square in the heart of Savannah's historic district as the place where parts of the movie were filmed. Gracious Foley House Inn overlooks this lovely square.

HOW TO GET THERE: I–16 ends and merges into Montgomery Street. Immediately after you pass the Civic Center on the right, turn right onto West Oglethorpe Street. Go 3 blocks and turn right onto Whitaker Street. Go 2 blocks and turn left at West Hull Street. Foley House is on the northwest corner of Chippewa Square.

The Forsyth Park Inn
Savannah, Georgia 31401

INNKEEPERS: Virginia and Hal Sullivan

ADDRESS/TELEPHONE: 102 West Hall Street; (912) 233–6800

ROOMS: 9, plus 1 cottage; all with private bath, television, and telephone; some with Jacuzzi and working fireplace.

RATES: $135 to $225, single or double; includes continental breakfast and evening refreshments.

OPEN: Year-round.

FACILITIES AND ACTIVITIES: Located in Savannah historic district, opposite Forsyth Park. Jogging, tennis courts, playgrounds for children, picnic area, and touch garden for the blind in the park. Nearby: restaurants, historic sites, Savannah riverfront, historic lighthouse, forts, beaches.

*V*irginia Sullivan and her son, Hal, bought this fine old B&B inn and reopened it March 1, 1988. They've been going strong ever since. You can find more opulent inns in Savannah, but none more friendly. Hal and Virginia serve good wine chilled in a silver bucket at their nightly social hour when guests really do join them in the parlor or on the patio to chat. Moreover, Hal and Virginia are good at providing the little favors that sometimes make the difference between an okay stay and a really comfortable one.

Here's an example: A guest spent the night at the inn on the Friday before St. Patrick's Day, a wild-and-woolly weekend in Savannah. We shared the Sullivan's excitement for the upcoming day, and we were to photograph the wonderous parade. However, our fellow guest just wanted to get out of town early Saturday morning before all the commotion started, long before people were thinking about breakfast, so she told the Sullivans she probably would be gone before they were even up. Before she went to bed, they brought a tray with a percolator, filled and ready to plug in, a croissant and a couple of muffins, and three pieces of fresh fruit. Next morning, she was on the road before sunrise, fed and full of coffee and feeling very, very good about Hal and Virginia as innkeepers.

Meanwhile, back at the inn, we found the rooms done in period furnishing with four-poster king- and queen-size beds and (glory) windows that you can actually open if you want to. Some of the rooms have inter-esting fireplaces and antique marble baths.

An addition that we enjoyed is the grand piano tucked under the staircase.

Our visiting on St. Patrick's Day weekend taxed Virginia and Hal's skills in recommending eating places that wouldn't be packed to the gills with par-tying Irish (and Irish "wannabes"), but that had a positive side because in the course of the conversation we discovered that they know Savannah inti-mately.

Virginia says that the inn attracts quite a few women business travelers. "They enjoy the friendliness and security," she says.

HOW TO GET THERE: At Savannah take the U.S. 16 exit off I-95. Go north on Montgomery Street to Liberty. Turn right on Liberty. Continue to Whitaker, which is one-way. Follow Whitaker to Hall Street. The inn is on the corner.

The Gastonian 💙
Savannah, Georgia 31401

INNKEEPER: Anne Landers

ADDRESS/TELEPHONE: 220 East Gaston Street; (912) 232–2869 or (800) 322–6603; fax (912) 232–0710

WEB SITE: www.gastonian.com

E-MAIL: gastonianinn@aol.com

ROOMS: 14, plus 2 two-room suites; all with private Jacuzzi bath with showers, fireplace, television, and telephone; 1 with wheelchair access.

RATES: $195 to $350, single or double; includes full sit-down Southern breakfast or silver-service continental breakfast in your room, afternoon tea and/or wine and nightly turndown service.

OPEN: Year-round.

FACILITIES AND ACTIVITIES: Sundeck, hot tub, off-street lighted parking, garden courtyard. Nearby: restaurants, carriage tours of historic district, Savannah riverfront shops, museums, beach, wildlife refuge.

*B*ack more years ago than we care to remember, when we were doing the travel columns for the *Guinnett Daily News,* we were asked to write a new B&B/inns column for them. One of the first B&Bs we reported on was The Gastonian, then recently opened by Hugh and Roberta Lineberger and already gaining a reputation as one of the most romantic inns in the Southeast. The Linebergers had invested a million and a half of their own and $900,000 of the bank's, Hugh says, calling it a poor investment but a "hell of a love affair."

How could you not love it? The B&B inn comprises two 1868 historic buildings sitting side by side and a two-story carriage house, joined by a garden courtyard and an elevated walkway.

The guest rooms are filled with English antiques, exotic baths, Persian rugs, and fresh flowers. The most outrageous bath is in the Caracalla Suite (named for a Roman emperor); it has an 8-foot Jacuzzi, sitting on a parquet platform draped with filmy curtains, next to a working fireplace. The fixtures here are of solid brass. In another room, they are of sculptured 24-karat gold. Each bath is unique and styled to complement the theme of its room—French, Oriental, Victorian, Italianate, Colonial American, or Country. All the inn's water runs through a purification system, which means, Hugh says, that you have to go easy on the bubble bath.

The public rooms are equally lavish, furnished with English antiques, satin damask drapes, and Sheffield silver. By 1996, both the Linebergers and The Gastonian were firmly established as the inn was expanded to sixteen rooms. Later that year, due to health reasons, the Linebergers sold their "love child" to Anne Landers (an innkeeper from suburban Atlanta, not the advice columnist).

"When I walked in the back door, it was love at first sight," says Anne, who has invested another $150,000 refreshing and upgrading the inn. The interiors have been painted; the gardens replanted; and a new phone system, commercial laundry, and reservation system have been added. However, the most important feature, the ambience of this ultraromantic inn, has remained.

HOW TO GET THERE: From I-95, take I-16 to Savannah. Take the Martin Luther King exit and go straight onto West Gaston Street. The inn is at the corner of East Gaston and Lincoln Streets.

The Kehoe House 🎔 📱
Savannah, Georgia 31401

INNKEEPER: Melissa Exley

ADDRESS/TELEPHONE: 123 Habersham Street; (912) 232-1020 or (800) 820-1020; fax (912) 231-0208

ROOMS: 13, plus 2 suites; 13 with private bath, telephone, cable television, clock radio, hair dryer, robe; some with private porch and/or sitting area; wheelchair accessible; not suitable for children.

RATES: $95-$250, includes a full gourmet breakfast as well as English afternoon tea and hors d'oeuvres, nightly turndown, and daily newspaper; $230 to $280 for St. Patrick's Day weekend; two-night minimum required for stays with Friday, Saturday, or Sunday arrival from October 1 through May 1.

OPEN: Year-round.

FACILITIES AND ACTIVITIES: Elevator, executive fitness area, billiards, table tennis, honor bar, twenty- four-hour concierge service, laundry service, limited room service. Nearby: historic Isaiah Davenport House, Savannah's historic district, casual and fine dining, shopping, nightlife; beaches of Tybee Island; Forts Jackson and Pulaski; golf, tennis.

BUSINESS TRAVEL: Entire fourth floor used as conference room, small boardroom; full secretarial services; corporate rates Sunday through Thursday.

This magnificent red-brick Victorian mansion, built in 1892 on Columbia Square, was unusual in being a single house in turn-of-the-century Savannah when town houses were the rule. Listed on the National Register of Historic Places, the three-story Kehoe House operates as a luxurious, intimate European-style B&B inn concentrating on exceptional personal pampering, which has earned it four stars and four diamonds from the major hotel rating services.

We've watched this property since it was a boarded-up derelict, hoping against hope that it would be saved and convinced that it would make a perfect inn or bed-and-breakfast. We'd idly wonder how much it would cost to purchase and fix up, but we knew without even asking that the answer was way more than we could ever afford or even borrow. Imagine our delight when we learned that such a project was in the works. Over several more trips to Savannah, we watched the progress with fascination and pleasure.

Now gleaming wall paneling, woodwork, and floors set off exquisite antiques, period reproductions, important artwork, Oriental carpets, and elegant fabrics in the public spaces and commodious guest chambers. Sumptuous guest rooms are found in the main house, two suites and a common parlor are found in the town house next door.

Some of the extraordinarily beautiful guest rooms feature canopy beds and/or private or shared upstairs porches. Generally considered the most romantic of the guest accommodations, the Limerick Suite boasts a four-poster bed and overlooks Columbia Square.

A full gourmet breakfast is served each morning and consists of eggs any style; bacon; grits; fresh fruits and juices; and freshly baked muffins, biscuits, and pastries. As if that weren't enough, a daily special is offered, which might be French toast with link sausage, eggs Benedict, omelettes, or whatever strikes the chef's fancy.

In addition to running one of the most successful inns in Savannah, Melissa Exley has found time to get married and have two children. As she points out, "This requires a great staff, and that is exactly what I have."

HOW TO GET THERE: I–16 ends and merges into Montgomery Street. Pass the Civic Center on the right and go 2 more blocks to York and turn right. Go 7 blocks and turn left onto Lincoln, then right onto President. The inn is on the corner of Habersham and President Streets. Parking is on the street.

Magnolia Place Inn
Savannah, Georgia 31401

INNKEEPERS: Kathy Medlock, Rob and Jane Sales

ADDRESS/TELEPHONE: 503 Whitaker Street; (912) 236–7674; outside Georgia, (800) 238–7674; fax (912) 236–1145

WEB SITE: www.magnolia.com

E-MAIL: b.b.magnolia@mci2000.com

ROOMS: 15; all with private bath and telephone; 7 with Jacuzzi; 14 with fireplaces.

RATES: $145 to $250, single or double; includes continental breakfast, high tea, and evening cordial.

OPEN: Year-round.

FACILITIES AND ACTIVITIES: VCRs and film library. Located in Savannah historic district, overlooking Forsyth Park, which offers jogging, tennis courts, playground for children, picnic area. Nearby: restaurants, within walking distance of riverfront.

BUSINESS Located five minutes from business district. Telephone in room with direct dial for modems; fax available. Corporate rates.

This B&B inn has a verified ghost who's been known to open and close doors and make other noises in distant rooms, turn on televisions and air conditioners, and move things around. According to legend, the ghost of Magnolia Place is the original owner, a cotton magnate who lost his fortune when the boll weevil hit and who committed suicide by falling down the steps. Others say he died of an overindulgence of oysters. Either way, staff members say the ghost is a strong and positive presence.

But ghost stories aside, the real attraction of Magnolia Place is in its exotic furnishings, your luxurious accommodations, and the top-notch service of the staff.

Some examples: Jacuzzis and gas fireplaces in some of the rooms, English antique furnishings, and prints and porcelains from around the world. The butterfly collection in the parlor is famous. Also, the staff can arrange private tours of Savannah if you'd rather not be herded along with a group.

The parlor, where high tea with imported teas, wine, and benne seed cookies is served in the afternoon, used to be a ballroom. Its fireplace is rimmed with tiles from Portugal, hand painted to look as though two rose trees rise from pots at floor level and "grow" up so that their bloom-laden branches nearly meet under the mantel. Around the room, pieces of Japanese cloisonné and Chinese porcelains catch your eye.

If you ask for a dinner recommendation, they'll mention Elizabeth on Thirty-Seventh—a well-known gourmet restaurant in a turn-of-the-century home nearby—the Pink House, or Bistro Savannah.

While you're at dinner, the staff at the inn are busy turning down your bed and placing pralines and madeira in your room, checking on your supply of Neutrogena amenities, and handling any personal requests you've made for extra service.

Personal attention like this attracts corporate and international travelers and celebrities, discreetly unidentified, as well as tourists. Best we can figure, the ghost hangs around, too, because he can't find such good service anywhere else.

HOW TO GET THERE: From I-95, take I-16 east onto Montgomery Street. Turn right on Liberty Street and then right on Whitaker. Coming from Charleston, take 17 north over the Savannah River Bridge. Immediately turn right on Oglethorpe and follow it to Whitaker. Turn right on Whitaker. Park behind the inn.

The Mulberry
Savannah, Georgia 31401

INNKEEPER: Jay Rettberg, general manager

ADDRESS/TELEPHONE: 601 East Bay Street; (912) 238–1200; fax: (912) 236–2184

WEB SITE: www.savannahhotel.com

ROOMS: 122 rooms and suites, all with private bath, television, telephone, coffeemaker, hair dryer, iron and ironing board; some with VCR and refrigerator.

RATES: $145 to $209, includes afternoon refreshments; special package rates including ones for Christmas and New Year's.

OPEN: Year-round.

FACILITIES AND ACTIVITIES: Elevator, pool, restaurant, tavern, concierge services, laundry service. Nearby: in the heart of the Savannah historic district and just steps from River Street and the waterfront; casual and fine dining, night spots, shopping; Forts Jackson and Pulaski; beaches of Tybee Island.

BUSINESS TRAVEL: Telephone dataports in guest rooms; meeting rooms; fax and copy services.

On our first visit to The Mulberry several years ago, given its gracious public spaces and well-proportioned guest rooms as well as its luxurious decor, we were quite surprised to learn that the structure in which the inn is housed actually began life as a Coca-Cola bottling plant. Another success story in Savannah's many restorations and innovative adaptive use projects, the simple gray-brick building now houses an intimate inn wrapped around a charming courtyard.

Recently refurbished again, the inn offers 122 guest rooms and suites that provide you with luxurious surroundings as well as all the comforts of home. Public spaces feature antiques, oil paintings, gleaming hardwood floors covered by vibrant Oriental carpets, and crystal chandeliers—all of which bring back Savannah's nostalgic past

Well-equipped to anticipate your every comfort, guest rooms are furnished with elegant period reproductions, enhanced with reproductions of old Savannah patterns in the fabrics, and supplied with modern conveniences. Luxurious suites offer a living room with a wet bar and deluxe amenities.

Enjoy three meals a day in the Courtyard Cafe overlooking the lushly planted courtyard, or stop in for cocktails in Sgt. Jasper's Tavern. Sit out in the courtyard to soak up sun or to read a good book. In inclement weather take your book into the cozy living room. Afternoon tea and desserts are served here in the late afternoon. If you have spare time, work off some of those pesky extra calories in the swimming pool.

At press time, a new addition to the historic building was being prepared to offer twenty-three new guest rooms, a hot tub, and a fitness center. For those of you who have visited before, this new addition will take the place of the parking lot.

HOW TO GET THERE: I-16 merges into Montgomery Street. Pass the Civic Center on the right and Elbert, Liberty, and Franklin Squares. Turn right on West Bay Street and follow it to the intersection of Houston Street. The inn is on the right.

Olde Harbour Inn
Savannah, Georgia 31401

INNKEEPER: Glen Anderson

ADDRESS/TELEPHONE: 508 East Factors Walk; (912) 234-4100 or (800) 553-6533; fax (912) 233-5979

WEB SITE: www.oldeharbourinn.com

E-MAIL: info@oldeharbourinn.com

ROOMS: 24 suites; all with private bath, fully equipped kitchen, cable television with HBO, telephone, clock radio.

RATES: $129 to $199 for studios and living/dining room suites; $169 to $229 for balcony or two- bedroom loft suites, includes continental breakfast, cordials in the afternoon, and nightly turndown service with a treat.

OPEN: Year-round.

FACILITIES AND ACTIVITIES: Kitchens, breakfast room, library. Nearby: Savannah's historic district, fine dining, shops, theater, nighttime entertainment; beaches of Tybee Island.

*O*ne of the things we liked so much about staying at the Olde Harbour Inn is its proximity to River Street and the busy waterfront. From our tiny balcony, we loved watching the bustling little tugboats guiding the gigantic ships up the Savannah River and the paddlewheel tour boat setting out, as well as getting a bird's-eye look at the tourists and town folks on River Street's Riverfront Plaza. The Olde Harbour Inn is an ideal vantage point during Savannah's fabled St. Patrick's weekend, but make reservations way, way in advance—a year ahead wouldn't be too soon.

Built in 1892, this three-story, bluff-side B&B inn is steeped in Savannah history. Originally the offices, warehouse, and shipping center of the Tide Water Oil Company, the structure has had many lives. The failure of a developer's dream turned into a boon for the traveling public in Savannah. Several years ago the structure was restored and modified as condominium apartments. With such an advantageous location, it's hard to understand how they failed to sell, but they did, permitting the building to be converted into an all-suites hotel.

Unusual elements of the original construction have been retained, including beams fashioned from various parts of old sailing vessels and gray bricks that were the first compressed bricks used in Savannah. Every luxurious accommodation—all of which overlook the river—is either a studio apartment or a full apartment with a fully equipped kitchen, living/dining area, and one or more bedrooms, some in lofts. Each is furnished in appropriate period reproductions.

Public spaces include the sunny Marine Room where a deluxe continental breakfast of hot biscuits, muffins, fresh fruit, cereals, juices, and hot beverages is served; the elegant Grand Salon where guests gather in the late afternoon for candlelight wine, sherry, and hors d'oeuvres; and the comfortably furnished library, which is well stocked with books, magazines, and newspapers.

All of Savannah's historic district is at your doorstep.

HOW TO GET THERE: I–16 ends and merges into Montgomery Street. Go past the Civic Center on the right as well as Elbert, Liberty, and Franklin Squares, then turn right onto West Bay Street. Go 10 blocks and turn left onto the Lincoln ramp. Follow the ramp down and turn right onto Factors Walk. The inn's entrance is on the left.

Planters Inn
Savannah, Georgia 31401

INNKEEPER: Natalie Alman

Address/Telephone: 29 Abercorn Street; (912) 232–5678 or (800) 554–1187; fax (912) 232–8893

WEB SITE: www.savannah-online.com/historicinns/planters

ROOMS: 56 rooms and suites; all with private bath, telephone, and television; some with fireplaces.

RATES: $110 to $160 includes continental breakfast and afternoon tea, newspaper, and turndown service.

OPEN: Year-round.

FACILITIES AND ACTIVITIES: Elevator, valet parking, bicycle rental, access to a health club.

BUSINESS TRAVEL: Conference facilities, hospitality suites, secretarial services.

A lovely small B&B inn restored to its 1912 glory, the Planters Inn successfully blends the warmth and charm of an intimate inn with the services of a grand hotel. An award-winning landmark building on lovely Reynolds Square in the heart of Savannah's historic district, the inn was created and recently refurbished with lavish attention to detail.

The inn features a sumptuous pink-marble lobby with intricate moldings, soaring columns, and immense gilt-frame mirrors. Elegantly furnished with comfortable period sofas and wing chairs done in copies of period fabrics, the lobby is the gathering place for breakfast and afternoon tea—affording the opportunity to meet and mingle with your fellow guests.

We loved our spacious and luxurious guest chamber, which, like all the others, features high ceilings, a private bath, Baker period furnishings, and lavish bed and window coverings done in reproductions of the finest Old Savannah–style textiles. Individually decorated, some of the guest rooms boast four-poster rice beds and comfortable seating areas.

Depending on your appetites, two options are available for breakfast. A complimentary continental breakfast buffet, which was more than ample for us, is set out in the lobby. For those with bigger appetites, a more elaborate breakfast is available from room service at an additional fee. After a strenuous day of sight-seeing and checking out other inns, we literally collapsed in the lobby in time for afternoon tea. A wide choice of hot and cold beverages and generous helpings of cakes and other desserts soon revived us and kept us going until dinnertime.

Among the other amenities at the inn are newspapers delivered to the room and evening turndown service with a sweet left on your pillow. Bicycle rentals and access to a health club satisfy those who yearn for physical exercise in addition to their sight-seeing, shopping, and dining pleasures.

With the Planters Inn as your home base, you're only steps from Savannah's bustling riverfront, where renovated cotton warehouses now contain quaint shops, casual and fine dining establishments, and nightlife.

HOW TO GET THERE: I–16 ends and merges into Montgomery Street. Go past the Civic Center on the right as well as Egbert, Liberty, and Franklin Squares. Turn right onto West Bay Street and go 6 blocks to Abercorn where you will turn right. The inn faces Reynolds Square. Parking is on the street or across the street in a parking garage.

The President's Quarters 📱
Savannah, Georgia 31401

INNKEEPERS: Stacy K. Stephens and Hank Smalling

ADDRESS/TELEPHONE: 225 East President Street; (912) 233–1600 or (888) 592–1812; fax (912) 238–0849

WEB SITE: www.presidentsquarters.com.

E-MAIL: pqinn@aol.com

ROOMS: 9, plus 7 suites; all with private bath, ceiling fan, small refrigerator, television, VCR, telephone, robes, hair dryer, and clock radio; some with Jacuzzi and/or steam shower; some with gas-log fireplace, balcony, loft bedroom, private entrance. Restricted smoking; provisions for the disabled.

RATES: $137 to $157 for rooms, $177 to $225 for suites, based on double occupancy, includes continental-plus breakfast, afternoon refreshments, nightly turndown, newspaper, complimentary fruit and bottle of wine. An occupancy charge of $20 for each additional person above the age of ten. Honeymoon, anniversary, and St. Patrick's Day packages.

OPEN: Year-round.

FACILITIES AND ACTIVITIES: Room service, elevator, pool, outdoor hot tub. Nearby: Savannah's historic district, casual and fine dining, shopping, nightlife; Fort Pulaski; beaches of Tybee Island.

BUSINESS TRAVEL: Writing desk and dataport; dining areas in the George Washington and Woodrow Wilson suites are appropriate for small board meetings; Presidential Cabinet Club membership for frequent business travelers.

On our way to a weekend stay at The President's Quarters, we had car trouble and were stuck on I-95 for three hours at night. After thousands of cars had passed us without stopping, a friendly University of Georgia student came to our rescue. By the time he called for a tow and we got to the inn, it was about midnight and we were frustrated and exhausted. The kindly night staff had lit our fireplace and, as soon as we were settled in, served us hot tea, cakes, and liqueur. That's the kind of pampering you can expect at this B&B inn.

Just to orient you, this mirrored pair of back-to-back brick Federal-style town houses, built in 1855 on Oglethorpe Square in the heart of what is now Savannah's huge historic district, was the backdrop for one of the scenes in the television miniseries *Roots*. The prestigious Owens-Thomas House museum, noted for its superior Regency architecture, is next door.

Inside, well-proportioned rooms, which feature ceilings as high as 13 feet, are filled with antiques and period reproductions and embellished with appropriate Savannah-style fabrics. Only a small amount of space is devoted to the cozy lobby, where breakfast and afternoon refreshments are set out daily. The rest is dedicated to luxurious guest rooms and suites.

Each guest chamber is dedicated to a president, and each is accented with portraits, photos, and framed newspaper clippings, handwritten notes, and other memorabilia relating to that president. Beds, which range from double to king size, may be four-poster, canopy, or old-fashioned high beds. Every room boasts a ceiling fan, cable television, and a VCR. Plush terry-cloth robes are provided as well. Select rooms offer a gas-log fireplace, Jacuzzi tub and/or steam shower, and a queen-size sofa bed. Some rooms have the added attraction of a balcony or courtyard. The fourth floor offers loft suites.

A sumptuous continental-plus breakfast of homemade sweetbreads, waffles, quiches, pastries, cereal, granola, and fruit can be served in your room, in the formal parlor, or in the enclosed patio. We always make plans to be back at the inn in late afternoon to enjoy the popular deluxe afternoon tea, which consists of cakes, salads, cheeses, wine, and other refreshments. Then we can have a light dinner later in the evening. The President's Quarters also offers nightly turndown service with Savannah sweets and port or sherry, newspapers, valet service, a splash pool, an outdoor hot tub, and off-street parking—a rarity in the historic district.

HOW TO GET THERE: I-16 ends and merges into Montgomery Street. Go 2 blocks past the Civic Center on your right and turn right onto York. Go 6 blocks to Oglethorpe Square. Just past the square, turn left. The inn is on the east side of the square at President Street.

The River Street Inn
Savannah, Georgia 31401

INNKEEPER: Nannette Neighbors

ADDRESS/TELEPHONE: 115 East River Street; (912) 234-6400 or (800) 253-4229; fax (912) 234-1478

WEB SITE: www.savannahhotels.com

ROOMS: 44; all with private bath, television, telephone, coffeemaker.

RATES: $129 to $189, double occupancy; includes breakfast, afternoon refreshments, morning newspaper, evening sweet. (Rates are $195 to $345 and require a minimum stay during the St. Patrick's Day celebration.) Children under the age of sixteen stay free in the parents' room using existing bedding.

OPEN: Year-round.

FACILITIES AND ACTIVITIES: Elevator, billiard room, restaurants, lounge, use of nearby athletic club, concierge service. Nearby: Savannah's historic district, fine dining, shops, theater, nighttime entertainment; Fort Pulaski; beaches of Tybee Island.

BUSINESS TRAVEL: Meeting and conference facilities for up to 150; secretarial services available.

*B*ecause of its location right in the heart of the action fronting on Factors Walk and overlooking River Street, Riverfront Plaza, and the busy Savannah River waterfront, we think The River Street Inn is an ideal headquarters for visiting Savannah's historic district. We love being only steps away from casual and fine dining, shopping, nightlife, and even a museum of seafaring. We can pop downstairs to Huey's for New Orleans-style beignets or to Savannah Sweets nearby to stock up on to-die-for pralines. Carol loves taking pictures of tugboats at all times of day and night, in all kinds of weather, at work and at rest. We can look right out our window or step just outside the door to add to our collection of tugboat shots.

Built in 1817 as a place to sample, grade, store, and export cotton, the structure was enlarged by adding three stories in 1853. As a result, a series of alleys and walkways were created between the bluff above and the building. Known as Factor's Walk after the factors who graded the cotton, these alleys and bridges are one of the River Street Inn's most unusual features. Best of all, the intimate hotel preserves the charm of the past with the amenities and conveniences of the present.

Beautifully restored, the structure has been reincarnated as a delightful inn where you'll find gleaming pine floors, intricate moldings, and exposed brick. Gracious high-ceilinged, well-appointed guest rooms, which range in decor from sea captain to English chintz, are furnished with antiques and period reproductions. Many feature a queen-size four-poster bed, decorative fireplace, hardwood floors with Oriental rugs, brass bathroom fixtures, French balcony, and floor-length windows providing an impressive view of the Savannah River.

Get your day off to a fun-filled start by going downstairs to Huey's for breakfast. We think beignets (square doughnuts covered with brown sugar) and coffee are more than adequate, but if you're hungrier, you get a made-to-order breakfast. By afternoon, what with sight-seeing and shopping, you're bound to be dragging. Just get yourselves back to the inn for a pick-me-up of wine and hors d'oeuvres.

Dining options include the previously mentioned Huey's, which serves breakfast, lunch, and dinner with a Cajun flair, and Tubby's, which specializes in seafood and serves lunch and dinner.

HOW TO GET THERE: The inn is easily accessible from I–16 and I–95 as well as U.S. 17 and U.S. 17A via Montgomery Street. Turn right at West Bay Street and go ½ mile to the gazebo at Emmet Park. The inn is on the left, with its entrance and parking on the East Bay Street level.

The Veranda ♥ 👥
Senoia, Georgia 30276

INNKEEPERS: Bobby and Jan Boal

ADDRESS/TELEPHONE: 252 Seavy Street; (770) 599–3905; fax (770) 599–0806

ROOMS: 9; all with private bath, robes, turndown with a surprise on your pillow.

RATES: $99 to $135; includes full Southern breakfast, afternoon refreshments, and evening desserts.

OPEN: Year-round.

FACILITIES AND ACTIVITIES: Restaurant, gift shop; some adaptation for the disabled; popcorn and chocolate chip cookies are available twenty-four hours a day. Nearby: antiques shopping, Callaway Gardens, Little White National Historic Site, Warm Springs, Franklin D. Roosevelt State Park, Pine Mountain Trail.

*B*obby (female) and Jan (male) are congenial, voluble hosts who make their guests feel like valued friends or family members visiting them in their home. We especially like to get Jan aside to tell us about his vast and varied kaleidoscope and ornate walking stick collections, which are displayed around the inn. We'd never realized there could be so many kinds—and there's a story behind every one. You'll be so enthused about kaleidoscopes that you'll surely want to buy one or more in the gift shop to take home for your own pleasure or to give as gifts. Check out Jan's kaleidoscope Web site at www.kaleidoscope.com.

But back to the inn. Built in 1906 as the Hollberg Hotel, the neoclassical structure with the wraparound porch supported by classic Doric columns has been restored and returned to its original use. Besides being listed on the National Register of Historic Places, the inn was named the 1990–91 inn of the year by *B&Bs, Inns, and Guest Houses in the U.S. and Canada.*

Located on a large corner lot with gardens to admire or while away some time in, the inn features spacious rooms with high ceilings. One of the twin parlors is set up as a music room with a working 1860 Estey reed organ and a Wurlitzer player piano with numerous music rolls. Needless to say, this room is a popular gathering place where complete strangers get to know one another through rollicking sing-alongs. If you'd like things a little more decorous, retreat to the sitting room in the upstairs hall, which you'll find amply stocked with books and games, to an old-fashioned swing on one of the porches, or to a stone bench in the garden.

Guest rooms, which are furnished with simple antiques more reminiscent of a boardinghouse than a house museum, all offer private baths. Some boast decorative fireplaces. Of particular interest are the Honeymoon Suite, which has a Jacuzzi, and the front bedrooms, which can be closed off to create a suite for a family or friends traveling together.

A full Southern breakfast, included in the room rate, is served in the formal dining room, which is also open to the public for lunch and for a five-course dinner by reservation. Afternoon tea and evening desserts are served here to guests as well.

HOW TO GET THERE: From GA 85, turn west onto Seavy Street. The inn is at the corner of Seavey and Barnes Streets. Alternately, from GA 16 turn north at Broad which becomes Seavy.

The Historic
Statesboro Inn and Restaurant
Statesboro, Georgia 30458

INNKEEPERS: Garges family

ADDRESS/TELEPHONE: 106 South Main Street; (912) 489-8628 or (800) 846-9466; fax (912) 489-4785

WEB SITE: www.statesboroinn.com

E-MAIL: frontdesk@statesboroinn.com

ROOMS: 16, plus 2 suites; all with private bath, telephone with dataport, television, ceiling fan, coffeemaker; some with private porch, fireplace, and/or whirlpool bath.

RATES: $75 to $85 for rooms; $100 to $120 for suites; includes full breakfast.

OPEN: Year-round.

FACILITIES AND ACTIVITIES: Restaurant, bar, several common rooms and porches. Nearby: Georgia Southern University museum, Herty Nature Trail, historical and architectural walking tours, Magnolia Garden, tours of Braswell Foods and Sunny South Pecans.

BUSINESS TRAVEL: Telephone dataports in rooms; reception, banquet, and conference facilities for large groups.

*K*ing Cotton built these two gracious side-by-side turn-of-the-century mansions, which today provide elegant accommodations as well as superb dining. Elegantly restored, the inn is listed on the National Register of Historic Places. Exterior architectural elements of note include wraparound porches, small second-story porches, and screened-in porches. Inside, you'll admire the 14-foot ceilings and burnished floors and woodwork. The gardens are beautiful year-round and provide additional places to relax in the company of others or alone.

The main house contains thirteen of the guest rooms and one suite; the sister house contains three additional rooms and a second suite. Lavish use of floral patterns and lace as well as antiques and period reproductions characterize the guest chambers and suites, most of which boast high or cathedral ceilings. Not surprising, the Honeymoon Suite is particularly romantic and features a whirlpool bath. The Executive Suite boasts two rooms, a private porch, and a queen-size hide-away bed, making it ideal for larger parties traveling together.

The well-known restaurant is presided over by a European chef who specializes in continental cuisine featuring steaks, chops, seafood, and homemade breads and desserts. A generous full breakfast is served to guests, and the dining rooms are open Wednesday through Saturday for dinner. Reservations are strongly recommended.

HOW TO GET THERE: From I–16, turn north onto U.S. 301/25, which runs through town. The inn is 1 mile north of Georgia Southern University.

Melhana,
The Grand Plantation Resort ♥
Thomasville, Georgia 31792

INNKEEPERS: Fran and Charlie Lewis

ADDRESS/TELEPHONE: 301 Showboat Lane; (912) 226–2290 or (888) 920–3030; fax (912) 226–4585

WEB SITE: www.melhana.com

E-MAIL: info@melhana.com

ROOMS: 25, plus 4 suites and honeymoon cottage; all with king- or queen-size beds and private bath (two are down the hall), plush bathrobes, television, desk, computer dataport, and multiline phone with conferencing capabilities; some with fireplace, whirlpool bath, and/or custom-made duvets and down comforters; twenty-four concierge. The entire interior of the facility is nonsmoking.

RATES: Rooms and suites in the Pink House are $250 to $450, the Hibernia Cottage is $450, and rooms in the Village section are $250 to $650; includes breakfast, afternoon tea, and use of recreational facilities. Ask about special packages—especially the Plantation Honeymoon, Swept Away, and Moonlight and Roses packages and those for Thanksgiving, Christmas, and New Year's; discounted rates are available from October 1 through December 30.

OPEN: Year-round.

FACILITIES AND ACTIVITIES: Complimentary airport shuttle service, heated pool, clay tennis court, croquet, fitness facility with personal trainer available by appointment, massage available by appointment, horse-drawn carriage rides on weekend evenings or by appointment. Plans in the works for an etiquette school, cooking school, visiting chef's program, and live theater productions. Nearby: historic Thomasville—the Rose City, Tallahassee, golf courses, skeet shooting, quail hunts in season, horseback riding, Birdsong Nature Center, Tall Timber Research Station, Maclay Gardens State Park, the Museum of History and Natural Science. Renowned Thomasville antiques show and sale first week in March, Rose Show and Festival in April, Victorian Christmas celebration from Thanksgiving through Christmas. The Florida Gulf Coast is one hour away.

BUSINESS TRAVEL: Eight miles south of Thomasville, 25 miles north of Tallahassee; rooms are executive friendly; twenty-four-hour concierge to assist with faxes, express mail, and special business needs; ideal for meetings and small corporate retreats; four meeting rooms with audio-visual equipment can accommodate up to one hundred, one with complete satellite hookup; corporate rates available.

We've all been told for years that the Old South with its traditional grand plantations was literally "gone with the wind." In actuality, hidden behind hedges, pine forests, and endless fields, America's greatest concentration of surviving working plantations—between seventy and one hundred—stretches between Thomasville, Georgia, and Tallahassee, Florida. In fact, this region of Georgia is known as the Plantation Trace. Until recently, all but the grandiose Pebble Hill Plantation, which is open for

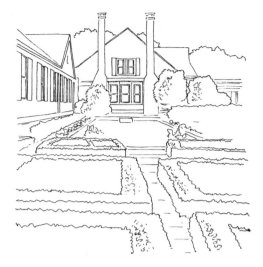

tours, were a well-kept secret. Happily, now you can experience for yourselves the gracious, luxurious, romantic Old South way of life. Melhana Plantation is a truly magical place where your everyday cares will melt away in its luxurious surroundings.

The heart of the sprawling pink Greek Revival mansion was built in 1825 and it has been added onto various times over its long life, creating the graceful manor house you see today. Seven exquisite guest rooms and four opulent suites grace the manor house—now known as the Pink House. Each high-ceilinged guest chamber is uniquely furnished and decorated to ensure its own distinct personality, but each is appointed with lovely antiques and/or period reproductions, as well as opulent fabrics and every possible amenity such as down comforters. Hibernia Cottage, a honeymoon hideaway in the fanciest creamery we've ever seen, guarantees complete seclusion for newlyweds or other romantics, and eighteen other guest chambers have been fashioned out of the many splendid Greek Revival outbuildings. A docent is available to give tours of the extensive property. Our favorite was the stately poolhouse. Two clues alerted us that this traditional brick building held its own surprises—one was the whimsical fountain and the other was the porthole windows. Stretching back from the brick facade and enclosed in glass is a delightful heated pool surrounded by comfortable seating as well as hothouse plants such as orchids and staghorn ferns. There are men's and ladies' dressing rooms, a brick and marble walled courtyard, and even a sitting area with a fireplace. Had we been able to stay longer than one night, this is where we would have spent most of our time—alternating refreshing dips with losing ourselves in a good book.

Another treat at the plantation is the Showboat. What looks like a typical Southern mansion on the outside reveals a private theater inside where the first private screening of *Gone with the Wind* was shown in 1939. Today the Showboat—completely paneled in pecky cypress—is used for screenings, productions, meetings, receptions, and other events. The extensive gardens include a walled vegetable garden supplying fresh herbs and vegetables are raised for use in the restaurant, a winter garden, sunken garden, marble goldfish pond with koi, and endless borders blooming flamboyantly depending on the season. Peacocks and hens strut their stuff for your entertainment. In good weather the wicker-filled veranda has its appeal; in inclement weather the delightful, formal Hogan and Hanna Rooms provide an elegant background for afternoon tea or a before-dinner drink.

White-gloved waiters serve you with elan in the princely Chapin Dining Room restaurant appointed with linens, fine china, crystal, and silver. Since this is a plantation, we expected that the cuisine would be Southern and we weren't disappointed, but the innovative, updated cuisine offers sophisticated surprises. One of us began our meal with traditional fried green tomatoes with the unexpected addition of a topping of grilled Gulf shrimp and Vidalia onion and tomato relish, while the other feasted on pan-fried softshell crab. Then we moved on to share cold zucchini soup and lobster bisque. Although it was extremely difficult to pass up the duck breast and roasted quail, we opted to try the New Zealand rack of lamb and the baked stuffed Gulf grouper combined with fresh Maryland jumbo lump crab meat. Regretfully, we had to pass on dessert: buttermilk pie, chilled seared pears with raspberry sorbet and chocolate sauce, carrot cake, or marble cheesecake with Amaretto sauce. Reservations and jackets for gentlemen are required.

After such a gargantuan dinner followed by a fabulous night's sleep in our four-poster bed, we were surprised to be hungry the next morning. It must have been the fresh air and clean living, because we managed to put away respectable portions of the signature breakfast pinwheel omelette accompanied by sweet potatoes, grits, hash browns, and biscuits.

HOW TO GET THERE: Follow U.S. 319 (Tallahassee/Thomasville Rd) south from Thomasville 4 miles; watch for the sign on your right.

Historic Thomasville

Find true Southern elegance among the stately oaks and pines and thousands of rose bushes in Thomasville—the Rose City. In the last twenty years of the nineteenth century, great weather, reputed curative powers for consumption and other respiratory illnesses, abundant game and game birds (along with the development of the modern shotgun), and the fact that the railroads' southern routes ended in Thomasville made the area an astoundingly popular resort destination. During Thomasville's heyday Northern socialites flocked to the area from fall through spring rather than chance the malaria epidemics in Florida. Presidential candidate William McKinley visited in 1895 and showered the area with praise about the pine forests, the generous helpings of Southern hospitality, and the magnificently beautiful spring season. He is even quoted as having said that the skies were as "blue and clear as those of Italy." Grand hotels, seasonal vacation "cottages," and plantations blossomed. Due to the immense wealth and varied tastes of the Northern visitors, an astounding array of architectural styles are represented in Thomasville.

More than fifty historic homes from the Winter Resort Era still grace Thomasville's streets, and more working plantations survive south of the city than anywhere else in this country. Several historic homes are open for tours or operate as bed-and-breakfasts, and you can tour the house, outbuildings, and grounds at magnificent Pebble Hill Plantation. Thomasville's Big Oak, a more than 300-year-old live oak is the largest live oak east of the Mississippi.

Begun in 1922 and held each April, the Thomasville Rose Show and Festival features more than thirty fun-filled activities, including an elegant plantation ball. Held the second Thursday and Friday in December, Thomasville's Downtown Victorian Christmas relives the grandeur of days gone by. Residents and shopkeepers dress in Victorian finery and stroll through the beautifully decorated historic downtown—selected as one of the top twenty Main Street towns in America. Horse-drawn carriage rides, carolers, hot wassail, and roasted chestnuts add authenticity to the celebration.

Susina Plantation Inn
Thomasville, Georgia 31792

INNKEEPER: Anne-Marie Walker

ADDRESS/TELEPHONE: 1420 Meridian Road; (912) 377–9644

ROOMS: 8; all with private bath. Pets accepted with advance arrangement.

RATES: $125 single; $150 double; includes breakfast and three-course dinner. Children under six free. No credit cards.

OPEN: Year-round.

FACILITIES AND ACTIVITIES: Lighted tennis court, swimming pool, fishing pond, jogging trails. Nearby: antiques and gift shops in Thomasville, golf, 22 miles to Tallahassee, Florida.

Our hostess, Anne-Marie Walker, is a rare combination of innkeeper and gourmet chef. She has been winning gastronomic kudos and running one of Georgia's most wonderful antebellum-era inns for as long as we've been writing about them.

The night we were there, Anne-Marie served dinner on English bone china to a total of six guests at a 12-foot-long antique table. Anne-Marie decides what to prepare according to the quality and availability of ingredients. The other guests had already eaten here the night before, and as we sipped our wine and chatted before dinner, they talked mostly about the previous night's meal, which included an eggplant appetizer they all raved over. Our dinner lived up to the advance praise. It was one of the best meals we've had anywhere, not because it was elaborate or exotic, but because every item was perfectly prepared. A green salad with feta cheese practically crackled with crispness on chilled plates. The appetizer, zucchini boats with shrimp, tantalized us with herb flavors we couldn't quite identify. The loin of pork served with a mustard sauce was juicy and tender inside, browned and crusty outside. The potatoes were browned and just crispy enough to give your teeth something to notice before getting to the mellow insides. And we

had all the big Swedish biscuits we could eat.

All this feasting took place in the dining room of an 1841 Greek Revival plantation home hidden back on a country road on 115 acres dotted with live oaks and the requisite Spanish moss.

The mansion has eleven fireplaces, a spiral staircase, and wide center halls in true plantation style. The rooms are huge, furnished with antiques and Oriental rugs. Our room had a claw-foot tub with an added shower in the bath and a four-poster canopied queen-size bed. The wallpaper, draperies, and spread, all in a deep blue floral pattern, matched. Windows look out into the tops of old live oaks.

We've had letters from people thanking us for telling them about Susina, specifically because they found its honesty romantic.

In addition to being a first-class cook, Anne-Marie is a flexible, accommodating innkeeper. Three of the guests, women traveling together, had gotten their schedules confused and arrived at Susina a day early. Fortunately, it was the middle of the week and not too busy, so Anne-Marie was able to settle them into rooms and make them dinner. She did it so well that before they left they presented her with a large antique china serving platter that looks right at home on her dining-room buffet.

HOW TO GET THERE: Susina is on the Meridian Road, 12 miles south of Thomasville and 22 miles north of Tallahassee. Follow Susina signs off Route 319.

Hotel Warm Springs
Warm Springs, Georgia 31830

INNKEEPER: Gerrie Thompson

ADDRESS/TELEPHONE: 17 Broad Street; (706) 655–2114 or (800) 366–7616; fax (706) 655–2406

ROOMS: 14 rooms and suites; all with private bath, television, and clock radio.

RATES: $70 to $175, includes full Southern country breakfast and afternoon social hour with soft drinks.

OPEN: Year-round.

FACILITIES AND ACTIVITIES: Formal parlor, social parlor, small garden with old-fashioned double swing, soda fountain/ice cream parlor, gift shop. Nearby: town, shops, and restaurants of Warm Springs, Little

White House National Historic Site, Franklin D. Roosevelt State Park, Pine Mountain Trail, Callaway Gardens.

BUSINESS TRAVEL: Ideal for small meetings and retreats.

We've stayed at this delightful B&B inn so many times, we're almost considered family. Once when we arrived, Dan was handed some spackle and a trowel to help plaster rooms not opened yet. Owner Gerrie Thompson is a whirlwind of energy who almost never relaxes. The only way we've ever found to get her to slow down is to take her out to dinner.

What's the big attraction in Warm Springs? Well there are many—several of which are connected with Franklin D. Roosevelt, who built and maintained a home there. This became the Little White House during his presidency so that he could have easy access to the beneficial mineral waters for relief from his polio. But Warm Springs today is so much more; besides that, it's a very convenient base from which to explore west-central Georgia.

Drive into the tiny crossroads that is Warm Springs and you'll be transported back to the 1930s and 1940s when FDR often came to town to stay at his Little White House. The town nearly died on April 15, 1945, when the president expired at his home there. When his funeral train pulled out of town, Warm Springs went into a deep slumber from which it did not awaken until the late 1980s, when a group of entrepreneurs renovated many of the downtown buildings for use as gift and antiques shops and restaurants catering to visitors from all over the world who come to visit the Little White House National Historic Site.

Gerrie, one of the most intrepid of these entrepreneurs, restored the three-story, buff-colored brick hotel to its 1941 appearance. Usually the first person you'll see when you step into the lobby, with its 16-foot ceilings and black-and-white tile floor, is Gerry behind the original reception desk. Not only is she probably on the phone taking reservations but she's also probably engaged in creating some craft masterpiece to sell in the hotel's gift shop. There's also a soda fountain and ice cream parlor where you can taste Gerrie's homemade peach ice cream. We swear she never sleeps.

This is all the casual visitor to the Hotel Warm Springs will see, but a serene world awaits overnight guests upstairs. The second-floor mezzanine serves as a large, gracious formal sitting room where guests are encouraged to congregate. There's also a small, casual game room/social parlor where guests can watch television, work on a gigantic jigsaw puzzle, or play cards or checkers. The third-floor mezzanine serves as the breakfast room.

In FDR's Day

Longtime residents still remember the 1930s and '40s, when FDR's chauffeur-driven convertible would pull up to the drugstore located downstairs in the Hotel Warm Springs so the president could get a Coke without getting out of the car and so he could linger and chat with the townsfolk. As likely as not little Fala, the Scottie, would be bounding around in the back seat, giving his master licking kisses from time to time. This was the heyday of Warm Springs and a boon for the Hotel Warm Springs where Secret Service agents, journalists, and visiting dignitaries would stay when FDR was in town.

In FDR's day, the hotel management decided that with such august guests and national and international scrutiny, the staff should be dressed in a more dignified manner than they had been heretofore. It was decreed that all the waitresses were to wear crisp white uniforms. Unfortunately, some details got lost in the translation. First of all, when the uniforms arrived they were all one size, but they were handed out anyway. You can just imagine how ridiculous that looked on the thin, medium, and heavy alike. Then the waitresses were directed to check out electric irons so they could take care of their uniforms at home. No one had bothered to find out that the girls were from homes so poor that they had no electricity. That problem was finally solved by allowing them to iron their uniforms at the hotel before they started their shift. Get Gerrie to tell you all about it.

Spacious, simple guest chambers are filled with Roosevelt memorabilia, antiques, collectibles, and the unadorned furniture of the thirties and forties. Modern amenities include a private bath, queen-size bed, and television. Some bathrooms have original re-enameled claw-foot tubs with reproduction antique showers. The Moncrief Room is furnished entirely with heirlooms from Gerrie's family—the prize item being the hundred-year-old iron bed. In addition to a bedroom and separate parlor, the Presidential Suite boasts original oak furniture made in Eleanor Roosevelt's Val-Kill Shop. A red, heart-shaped double Jacuzzi dominates the Honeymoon Suite. Gerrie keeps telling us to come try it out for our anniversary, but so far we've never been able to get our act together to do so. Gerrie has developed a special package for honeymooners that includes a night in the suite along with champagne, chocolates, strawberries, fresh flowers, and breakfast in bed. Maybe we should renew our vows.

HOW TO GET THERE: Hotel Warm Springs sits at the crossroads of U.S. 27 and GA 85 west.

Select List of Other Georgia Inns

Atlanta's Woodruff Bed & Breakfast Inn

223 Ponce de Leon Avenue
Atlanta, GA 30302
(404) 875-9449 or (800) 473-9449

Historic apartment building; 12 rooms and suites; continental or full breakfast.

Biltmore Suites

30 Fifth Street
Atlanta, GA 30308

Historic all-suite hotel temporarily closed for multimillion dollar renovation; 62 suites; some penthouse suites with rooftop whirlpool bath; continental breakfast.

Burns-Sutton House

124 South Washington Street
Clarkesville, GA 30523
(706) 754-5565

1901 mansion; 7 guest rooms and 2 suites; gas-log fireplaces; full breakfast.

The Charm House Inn

108 South Washington Street
Clarkesville, GA 30523
(706) 754-9347

1907 Greek Revival mansion; 5 rooms; restaurant; full breakfast.

The Blueberry Inn

Town Creek Church Road
Dahlonega, GA 30533
(706) 396-9150

Country setting, new reproduction of a 1920 farmhouse and barn; 12 rooms; full breakfast.

Mountain Top Lodge

Old Ellijay Road
Dahlonega, GA 30533
(706) 864–5257 or (800) 526–9754

Country setting, rustic lodge of new construction; 13 rooms; some with fireplace and/or whirlpool bath.

Smith House Inn

202 South Chestatee
Dahlonega, GA 30533
(706) 864–3566 or (800) 852–9577

1884 Victorian home and carriage house operating as an inn since 1922, 16 rooms; continental breakfast; famous family-style restaurant, gift shop.

Black Swan Inn

411 Progress Avenue
Hawkinsville, GA 31036
(912) 783–4466

1905 mansion; 6 rooms, continental breakfast; restaurant.

Fieldstone Inn and Conference Center

3499 U.S. 76
Hiawassee, GA 30546
(706) 896–2262 or (800) 545–3408

Casually elegant inn on the shores of Lake Chatuge; 62 rooms and 4 suites; restaurant, pool, fitness center, tennis courts, hot tub, dock, lawn games, meeting facilities.

Lake Rabun Hotel

Lake Rabun Road
Lakemont, GA 30552
(706) 782–4946

Lakeside setting, rustic stone hotel built in 1922; 16 rooms, 1 with fireplace; most rooms with shared baths; continental-plus breakfast.

The York House

P.O. Box 126
Mountain City, GA 30562
(706) 746–2068 or (800) 231–9675

Country setting, 1896 inn; 12 rooms, 1 suite with fireplace; continental-plus breakfast.

Bed and Breakfast Inn

117 and 119 West Gordon Street
Savannah, GA 31401
(912) 238-0518

Two 1853 Federal-style townhouses with carriage houses; 14 rooms and suites; continental-plus breakfast.

Catherine Ward House Inn

118 East Waldburg Street
Savannah, GA 31401
(912) 234-8564

1886 Italianate mansion, 10 rooms and suites; courtyard; full breakfast.

Hamilton-Turner Inn

330 Abercorn Street
Savannah, GA 31401
(912) 233-1833

French Second Empire–style; 14 guest rooms and suites; working fireplaces; full Southern breakfast and afternoon tea.

The Marshall House

123 East Broughton Street
Savannah, GA 31401
(912) 644-7896 or (888) 782-9244

Restored landmark property in the center of the historic district; 68 rooms.

1810 West Inn

254 North Seymour Drive, NW
Thomson, GA 30824
(706) 595-3156 or (800) 515-1310

Country setting, 1810 farmhouse; 10 rooms, 1 cottage; some working fireplaces; continental-plus breakfast.

Holly Ridge Country Inn

2221 Sandtown Road
Washington, GA 30673
(706) 285-2594

Country setting, a stately Victorian and an older farmhouse; 10 rooms; continental or full breakfast; pond.

Kentucky

Numbers on map refer to towns numbered below.

* A Top Pick Inn

Jailer's Inn
Bardstown, Kentucky 40004

INNKEEPERS: Fran and Challen McCoy

ADDRESS/TELEPHONE: 111 West Stephen Foster Avenue;
(502) 248-5551 or (800) 948-5551

ROOMS: 6; all with private bath; 2 with Jacuzzi, 2 with wheelchair access, 3 with television.

RATES: $65 to $105, single or double; includes full breakfast.

OPEN: Year-round.

FACILITIES AND ACTIVITIES: Nearby: restaurants, whiskey distilleries, My Old Kentucky Home State Park, Bardstown Historical Museum, Shaker Village; 35 miles from Louisville.

"*I* guess I'm sentenced to life imprisonment," Fran McCoy likes to say. Considering that she owns the two jails here, how could she resist that line?

The B&B inn was a jailer's residence until 1987. Fran and Challen purchased it in June 1988 and opened the prison section for tours almost right away. At that time, they didn't know it had been built by Fran's great-great-uncle. The front building, known as the "old" jail, was built in 1819 of native limestone. It had two cells and an "upstairs dungeon" for prisoners. The stone building behind this, built in 1874, was known as the "new" jail. Once it was operating, the front building became the jailer's home.

Fran and Challen turned the "old" jail into an inn decorated with antiques and Oriental rugs, except for the former women's cell, which is done entirely in prison black and white and contains the two original bunks plus a waterbed. The floor is tiled in a black-and-white geometric pattern, the mirror over the sparkling 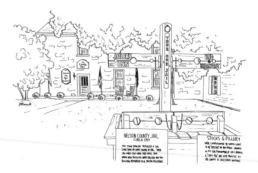 white sink has a white frame, and a picture on the white brick wall has a black frame. Fran says she loves it. Well, we're sure it's better than it was.

A much prettier room, the favorite of many guests, is the Garden Room, which looks out over the courtyard and is decorated in aqua green with wicker and wrought iron and lots of flowers. The Garden Room bedspreads are cross-stitched quilts in floral patterns. The courtyard is a favorite gathering place for savoring your full Southern breakfast, chatting with other guests, and trying to envision how it was as a work yard, with prisoners crushing limestone, and were visited by their relatives, or as the site of the county gallows.

The Victorian Room, a feminine room with flowered wallpaper, a tall mirrored vanity, lace-edged bed covers, and old-fashioned flowered hats on a stand in the corner, pleases guests, too.

Fran, who did all the decorating herself, takes obvious pleasure in the results. When she talks about it, though, it comes out sounding strange: "I just love my jails," she says.

HOW TO GET THERE: The inn is just off Court Square in downtown Bardstown. Highway 31-E runs directly to the square.

The Mansion Bed & Breakfast
Bardstown, Kentucky 40004

INNKEEPERS: Dennis and Charmaine Downs

ADDRESS/TELEPHONE: 1003 North Third Street; (502) 348–2586 or (800) 399–2586; fax (502) 349–6098

WEB SITE: www.bbonline.com/ky/mansion/index.html

E-MAIL: ddowns@bardstown.com

ROOMS: 7, plus 1 cottage; all with private bath.

RATES: $85 to $125, double occupancy includes breakfast and fresh flowers; $15 for each additional person; children older than age ten are welcome.

OPEN: Year-round.

FACILITIES AND ACTIVITIES: Nearby: historic Bardstown, the second oldest city in Kentucky.

A "truly dignified, aristocratic and striking example of Greek Revival architecture" is the way the National Register of Historic Places describes the 1851 Greek Revival Johnson villa that houses The Mansion Bed & Breakfast. Filled with history, stunning inside and out, exquisitely furnished and decorated, and surrounded by lush gardens, The Mansion is the very epitome of what a gracious B&B inn should be.

From the moment you step through the columned portico and enter the vast entry hall, you'll be wowed by the grandeur. Admire the original solid-brass chandelier with Waterford crystal prisms, the 10½-foot-tall gold-leaf mirror, and the 1876 rosewood Steinway square piano, then gaze up the stairwell of the freestanding elliptical staircase, which is the only one in Kentucky that turns first to the right instead of the left. The handrail is solid cherry, the steps are ash, and the spindles mahogany. Original mantels with fluted pilasters and fluted friezes grace the parlors.

Overnight guests are treated to a deluxe continental breakfast elegantly served in the formal dining room using china, silver, crystal, and fine linens.

In the well-proportioned bed chambers, high ceilings, Victorian-era antiques, and hand-crocheted bedspreads, dust ruffles, and pillow shams make every one inviting. Among the concessions to modern-day life are private baths and king-size beds—many of them romantic four-poster iron canopy beds draped with fabric. Located up under the eaves with cozy alcoves created by the sloping ceilings, two rooms have an additional twin bed, making them suitable for those traveling with an additional person. A former summer kitchen has been transformed into a snug cottage, which is particularly popular with those desiring a little additional privacy.

The equally beautiful three-acre grounds put on a colorful display spring through fall. In spring the estate is awash in the pastels of dogwood, pear, and apple blossoms. Summer showcases the feathery mimosa blooms, while fall is ablaze with brilliant maples.

HOW TO GET THERE: Follow U.S. 31 south from Louisville to Bardstown. U.S. 31 becomes North Third Street.

Weller Haus
Bellevue, Kentucky 41073

INNKEEPERS: Mary and Vernon Weller

ADDRESS/TELEPHONE: 319 Poplar Street; (606) 431–6829 or (800) 431–HAUS (4287)

WEB SITE: www.bbonline.com/ky/weller/

ROOMS: 5 in two buildings; all with private bath and television; 1 with whirlpool tub for two.

RATES: $75 to $145, double; $10 less, single; includes full breakfast.

OPEN: Year-round.

FACILITIES AND ACTIVITIES: Located in historic district across the river from downtown Cincinnati. Common kitchen. Nearby: restaurants.

*H*ere is small-town America, past and present. Two Victorian Gothic houses sit side by side, with a black iron fence dividing lawn from sidewalk. The American flag flies from a porch. Perennials bloom in a small garden out back.

The two houses constitute one homestead-style B&B inn. The main house is gray with blue-and-white striped awnings. The great room in this house has a cathedral ceiling. Guests check in and also have breakfast here.

Breakfast is not just a grab-a-doughnut affair, either. It's a full breakfast with homemade muffins, coffee cakes, and breads, served in high Victorian style.

In the buff-colored brick house next door, guests gather in an ivy-festooned kitchen where even the ceiling is covered with ivy-patterned wallpaper. You can get drinks here, use the microwave oven, and make tea or coffee. Guests often get to know one another sitting around the kitchen table. It doesn't matter which house your room is in, you may use the common areas in both places. Guests going back and forth have worn a footpath across the lawn.

Throughout both houses you find good collections of antique porcelains, pattern glass, linens, and the like, along with comfortable antique furniture. Because the spaces remain uncluttered, however, none of this is overpowering.

One of the nicest accommodations is Margaret's Porch Suite, two rooms furnished in the Art Deco style of the 1920s, with bold colors. The suite has a

private entrance, porch, and very comfortable whirlpool tub for two. Of course the Dream Suite is the special-occasion spot, with its Eastlake furniture and a big whirlpool tub. A simpler room, Nancy's Garden Room has a Steamboat Gothic brass bed, with stenciled flowers over the doors and windows.

Such touches make an impression on guests. Mary Weller says she thinks carefully about the decorating and where to put things. For instance, guests often comment on the picture of a medieval woman in a garden that Mary hung close to the floor near a bed so that it's the first thing you see when you wake up in the morning.

That's the small-town feeling of the house—a place where someone has taken the time to attend to the little details as we might have done in a slower time. As for the town itself, Mary likes to tell about the guest who went out for a run and worried everybody by not coming back as soon as they expected him. Turns out he ended up having coffee and a visit on the porch with some folks whose house he passed. That's good stuff.

HOW TO GET THERE: From I-471 take exit 5 toward Newport and Bellevue onto Dave Cowens, which is also Kentucky Highway 8. Turn right. The Ohio River will be on your left. After a few blocks this road becomes Fairfield Avenue. Turn right on Washington Street. Go 2 blocks to Poplar Street and turn right. The inn is at 319 Poplar.

Boone Tavern Hotel
of Berea College
Berea, Kentucky 40404

INNKEEPER: David Van Dellan

ADDRESS/TELEPHONE: College post office, Box 2345 (Main and Prospect Streets); (606) 986-9358 or (800) 366-9358; fax (606) 986-7711

WEB SITE: www.berea.edu/Publications/Boone-Tavern.html

ROOMS: 58; all with private bath, television, telephone.

RATES: $70 to $90, double occupancy; $10 each for additional guest in the room. Because the student employees of the hotel are working for their tuition, tipping is not permitted.

Confederate Flag Birthplace and Other Historical Tidbits

At the beginning of the Civil War, Nancy Johnson—wife of Lt. Governor and later acting Governor William E. Johnson V and mother of powerful Kentucky politician Ben Johnson—was on a committee of Southern women charged with selecting a design for the flag of the Confederacy. She favored the design created by art teacher Nicola Marschall of Marion, Alabama, and it was the one chosen. Immediately, Mrs. Johnson and her servants set to work stitching the now famous "Stars and Bars."

When she finished, a gala ceremony was held on the front lawn on March 3, 1861, for the first public raising of the flag (keep in mind that this was before the first shot was fired at Fort Sumter). It is reported that more than five thousand people were in attendance. Federal authorities issued an arrest warrant for the Johnsons but it was never served. The Yankees did come and cut down and burn the flagpole, but they couldn't find the flag: Mrs. Johnson had hidden it in the cellar. It is reported that when she went to retrieve it later, mice had shredded it to bits.

Legend has it that in 1863 Confederate General John Hunt Morgan hid out for two days and three nights in the house after his escape from a Columbus, Ohio, prison.

William Johnson was retained to defend the followers of the infamous Quantrill-Pence-James gang, and the family long treasured a red sash Quantrill was wearing when he was killed and a hat Jesse James was wearing when he escaped from Union militia men. Ben Johnson owned the first bicycle in Nelson County and the first car—an Oldsmobile for which he paid about $750.

OPEN: May be closed in January for renovations.

FACILITIES AND ACTIVITIES: Restaurant, campus tours, college activities such as lectures, art exhibits, concerts, theater productions, and sports. Nearby: Churchill Weavers, Appalachian Museum, Whitehall State Shrine, Boonesborough State Park, Bybee Pottery, Kentucky Horse Park, Shakertown, The Red Mile racetrack, Fort Harrodsburg, Cumberland Falls State Park.

BUSINESS TRAVEL: Forty-two miles from Lexington off I-75; meeting rooms to accommodate up to one hundred persons.

Can you imagine being expected to house, feed, and entertain 300 guests in your home over the period of one summer? Just the thought of such an undertaking makes us shudder, but in 1908 that's exactly what Nellie Frost, the wife of the Berea College president, did. After this ordeal, she suggested to her husband that perhaps the college should build a guest house to accommodate future college visitors. We can almost feel her sigh of relief when the college did just that. The result is this elegant, white three-story hotel with immense columned porticos.

Just to get any misunderstandings out of the way up front, the name of the inn is a misnomer. To us and maybe to you, the word *tavern* conjures up a drinking establishment, probably rustic in style or, at the very least, casual. We've already described the hotel as luxurious rather than rustic; now we have to tell you that no alcoholic beverages are served here because the county is dry. The hotel simply took its name from Kentucky's famous frontiersman, Daniel Boone.

Beginning with its opening in 1909, the Boone Tavern Hotel, which is located in the midst of the campus, has been operated by the college's hospitality management students as part of Berea College's extensive work-study program in which students work in lieu of tuition payments. The handiwork of students in the woodworking and arts and crafts departments are prominently displayed throughout the inn.

A gilt-framed portrait of the sixteenth president by Fred Walker peers down from over the graceful white fireplace and surveys the warm, magnificent Lincoln Lounge, which is furnished with camelback sofas and other pieces befitting such a sumptuous room.

Berea College Crafts

The unique Appalachian heritage of Berea College dates to
1855, when the school was founded by forward-thinking
John G. Fee as the South's first nondenominational inter-
racial college on land donated by Cassius M. Clay. Clay
described the college as a "historic monument to human
equality."

The college's long-established student crafts program
traces its roots to a practical and utilitarian beginning.
"Homespun Fairs" were held on the campus as early as
1896. At these fairs, parents sold hand-woven items to help
finance their children's education. The woven items
became so popular that looms were established on the campus so that the students could learn weaving skills. Wood-
craft, begun in the late 1800s, provided tables, chairs, and
other furniture needs for the college.

Eventually these extracuricular activities were incorporated as departments of the college. The weaving department produces couch throws, baby blankets, placemats,
and napkins. Fine furniture is handcrafted, with most
pieces being of Colonial design. Contemporary pieces can
be made to order, however. For most of the twentieth century, students in the department have also produced
wooden puzzles and marble games as well as candleholders;
a variety of cutting boards and chopping blocks; and the
popular wooden board game, skittles.

Broom-making has been a college craft since about
1920. Each handmade broom is unique in style and color as
the blending of native wood handles and natural and mul-
ticolored broomcorn results in a one-of-a-kind product.

New in the last quarter century are the ceramics and
wrought-iron programs. Potters produce vases and a variety of bowls, mugs, casseroles, and pitchers. Functional,
well-designed wrought-iron articles include fireplace sets,
boot and shoe scrapers, and hanging plant brackets.

All Berea craft items are available at the Log House
Craft Gallery, Boone Tavern Gift Shop, retail outlets in
Berea, and by catalog.

Guest rooms are well appointed and furnished with reproduction American traditional furniture created by students in the woodworking department and accessorized with student handiwork weavings and other crafts. Each features a private bath.

Although the hotel is an ideal place to stay when visiting the college or any of dozens of nearby attractions, the food served in the dining room, where three meals are served daily, has won the hostelry much of its acclaim. Considered a perfect blend of elegance and down-home Southern hospitality, the dining room serves simple Kentucky-style meals of meat and vegetables. Be sure to try the spoonbread (a cornbread soufflé) and chess pie. Many traditional dishes were developed by Richard T. Hougen, who managed the dining room from 1940 to 1976. Some favorites are Chicken Flakes in a Bird's Nest, Jefferson Davis Pie, Cinnamon Kites, and Boone Tavern Cornsticks. You can take home these and other recipes by purchasing one or more of Hougen's cookbooks. Reservations are required for meals, and although breakfast and lunch are casual affairs, dressy casual attire is required for dinner.

College tours depart from the hotel and include the Berea College Museum, which emphasizes the rich history and culture of Appalachia and the fascinating history of Berea College itself, and the Log House Craft Gallery, which showcases the fine woodworking and crafts skills of Berea College students and other local artisans as well as the Wallace Nutting Collection of Early American Furniture.

HOW TO GET THERE: Berea College is located at the junction of U.S. 25 and U.S. 21.

The Amos Shinkle Townhouse ♥
Covington, Kentucky 41011

INNKEEPERS: Don Nash and Bernie Moorman

ADDRESS/TELEPHONE: 215 Garrard Street; (606) 431–2118 or (800) 972–7012; fax (606) 491–4551

WEB SITE: www.bbonline.com/ky/shinkle

ROOMS: 7, three in main house, four in carriage house; all with private bath and television. Smoking and no-smoking rooms available.

RATES: $79 to $140, double; $10 less, single; includes full breakfast. Children under six free in room with adults.

OPEN: Year-round.

FACILITIES AND ACTIVITIES: Located in historic district across the bridge from downtown Cincinnati. Meeting space for groups up to fifteen. Nearby: walking distance to restaurants; Ohio River recreation, boating, cruises.

*T*his is the house the entrepreneur Amos Shinkle and his family lived in during the Civil War while his castle was being finished. A tour brochure for the historic district calls the structure a "modest Italianate home." Compared to a castle, maybe. But unless you are accustomed to castle life, you'll find The Amos Shinkle Townhouse posh.

The ceilings in this B&B inn are 16 feet high, with Rococo Revival chandeliers, plaster moldings, and cornices. Beyond the front entry a mahogany staircase, still with the original murals on the walls and crown moldings that continue on the second-floor landing, ascends to guest rooms furnished with antiques. The master bedroom has a fireplace, a four-poster bed, and a maroon-tiled bath with a crystal chandelier and a whirlpool tub.

Downstairs, comfortable couches and chairs clustered near the fireplaces make elegant places to read or chat. You're welcome to play the baby grand piano, too.

Behind the main house in the carriage house are simpler rooms decorated in Early American style. This building served as stable quarters in the 1800s. The horse stalls have been turned into sleeping accommodations for children.

A brick-and-grass courtyard between the two buildings includes places to sit under umbrellas when the weather is nice. During the growing season, pots of geraniums, petunias, and black-eyed Susans brighten the area. Tall hollyhocks and mature shrubs soften the austere lines of the carriage house.

Quite apart from the visual and architectural interest of the town house, staying here evokes a sense of old Southern hospitality. Be sure to spend some time talking with the resident innkeeper, Bernie Moorman. He used to be the mayor and maintains active involvement with the community. He likes to tell guests how special the area is historically and culturally, and he'll do almost anything to make sure you like it here. Bernie says everyone at the inn will help you arrange everything from restaurants to tickets for the horse races.

Even breakfast reflects their willingness to cater to your schedule. You order, from a full menu, anytime from 7:00 to 9:30 A.M. during the week or 8:00 to 10:00 A.M. on weekends. Your eggs, pancakes, French toast, or whatever come to you cooked to order. Be sure to try the goetta, a regional sausage-like dish of cooked ground pork, pinhead oatmeal, and spices. Bernie says their goetta, made by Dick Fink, is the best in the area. I say if you wanta spenda day in luxury you gotta getta night here.

If you are a baseball fan, the Cincinnati ballpark is only a ten-to fifteen-minute walk (or a forty-five minute car trip) from the house.

HOW TO GET THERE: From I–75/71 take exit 192 onto Fifth Street, which is one-way going east. Drive 9 blocks to where Fifth Street ends at Garrard Street. Turn left and go 2½ blocks north. The inn is on the left.

Beaumont Inn
Harrodsburg, Kentucky 40330

INNKEEPERS: C. M. (Chuck) and Helen W. Dedman

ADDRESS/TELEPHONE: 638 Beaumont Drive; (606) 734-3381 or (800) 352-3992; fax (606) 734-6897

WEB SITE: www.beaumontinn.com

ROOMS: 33; all with private bath, telephone, and television. No-smoking rooms available.

RATES: $85 to $105, double; single $20 less; includes continental breakfast.

OPEN: Mid-March to mid-December.

FACILITIES AND ACTIVITIES: Lunch and dinner. Swimming pool, tennis courts, shuffleboard, gift shops. Nearby: boating, fishing, and swimming on Herrington Lake; golfing; Keeneland Race Track; Shaker Village; Old Fort Harrod State Park.

BUSINESS TRAVEL: Well-equipped conference facilities; corporate rates; telephone in room.

*H*arrodsburg is in the heart of Kentucky's horse country, an area crammed with historic sites and gorgeous scenery, but the truth is that a lot of people go to the Beaumont Inn mainly to eat. The inn's food and service are famous.

When you make your dinner reservations, you have a choice of a 6:00 P.M. or a 7:30 P.M. seating. A bell rings right on the appropriate hour to announce dinner, and you are immediately shown to a table with your name on it. We have it on very credible authority that roast beef and the ham, which is aged two years, are fantastic choices. An appetizer such as the cream of celery soup is included in the cost of the meal. Then it seems that the food keeps coming for an hour.

After your salad, the server will bring your entree and a tray full of serving dishes from which you will be served such side selections as mashed potatoes and gravy, lima beans, corn pudding, and mock scalloped oysters. The server will return several more times to offer seconds and refill the basket of biscuits.

For dessert, try the crisp meringue shell filled with vanilla ice cream and fresh strawberries.

You'll barely have time to stroll around the grounds admiring the lush greenery and take a quick look at some of the antiques inside the inn after dinner before it's time to turn in. Then it will be breakfast time, and the whole incredible flow of food starts all over again, with an overwhelming number of choices, including a stack of the lightest, tastiest batter corn cakes you ever sunk a tooth into. The full breakfast is $4.00 extra, but you still get the continental breakfast, too, if you want it.

HOW TO GET THERE: In Harrodsburg, turn left off South Main at the United Presbyterian Church onto Beaumont Avenue and then right onto Beaumont Drive.

Shaker Village of Pleasant Hill
Harrodsburg, Kentucky 40330

INNKEEPER: James C. Thomas

ADDRESS/TELEPHONE: 3501 Lexington Road; (606) 734–5411 or
(800) 734–5611; fax (606) 734–5411

WEB SITE: www.shakervilageky.org

ROOMS: 81 in fifteen buildings; all with private bath, television,
and telephone. Inn especially suited for children.

RATES: $56 to $80, single; $66 to $78, double; breakfast extra.

OPEN: Year-round except Christmas Eve and Christmas Day.

FACILITIES AND ACTIVITIES: Breakfast, lunch, dinner open to guests
and public by reservation. Shaker Village preserves thirty-three original nineteenth-century buildings as they were used by the community
of Shakers living in the village, they are open for tours. Craft stores,
Shaker craft and farming demonstrations. Nearby: cruises on the *Dixie
Belle* riverboat.

"That's the closet," our guide said. We were in one of the guest rooms
and she was pointing to a strip of heavy pegs along the wall. The
Shakers hung everything, from their clothes to their utensils and
chairs, on such pegs. Guests at Shaker Village do the same.

The rooms are furnished in the same sparse, simple style of the Shakers:
rag rugs; streamlined, func-
tional furniture; trundle beds;
plain linens. Only the modern
bathroom, telephone, and television set in each room make it
different than it originally
would have been.

Like other communities of
plain people, the Shakers made
up in the bounty of their table
for what they lacked in knick-
knacks. The Shaker-town menu, which says, "We make you kindly welcome,"
does the same. Shakers, wherever they lived, adopted the food of the area. In

Kentucky, this means fried chicken, country ham, fried fish, roast beef, and large sirloin steaks. Fresh vegetables (some from the garden on the premises) and salads are passed at the table, as are breads from the bakery. The smell of baking bread distracts you much of the day at Shaker Village. And for dessert, Shaker lemon pie tops off everything. It's an unusual lemon pie, made with a double crust and whole sliced lemons, plus eggs and sugar, because the Shakers didn't waste anything—not even lemon peels.

Although the meal is bountiful, the dining rooms in the old Trustees' House resemble the guest rooms in their simplicity. The wood floors are polished and clean but unadorned. The tables and chairs are typical, functional Shaker design, and the place settings are plain white dishes. It adds up to a fascinating, almost-insider's view of unusual people whose way of life is almost gone except in this re-creation.

Many special events, including weekends of Shaker music and dance, are held during the year. You can write for a yearly calendar to help you plan a trip according to your interests.

HOW TO GET THERE: The entrance to Shaker Village is off U.S. Route 68, 7 miles northeast of Harrodsburg and 25 miles southwest of Lexington. Signs mark the drive clearly.

Gratz Park Inn 📱
Lexington, Kentucky 40507

INNKEEPERS: Liz Holmes

ADDRESS/TELEPHONE: 120 West Second Street; (606) 231-1777 or (800) 752-4166; fax (606) 233-7593

WEB SITE: www.gratzpark.com

E-MAIL: gratzinn@aol.com

ROOMS: 38; plus 6 suites; all with private bath, telephone, cable television, clock radio. Accessible to the handicapped.

RATES: $89 to $149 during low season, $130 to $199 in high season (April, July, and October), double occupancy; includes continental breakfast, evening turndown, fresh flowers in the room, daily newspaper; rate for each additional person is $10. Children younger than age eighteen are free in the room with the parents; minimum stay required for special events.

OPEN: Year-round.

FACILITIES AND ACTIVITIES: Elevator, restaurant. Nearby: universities, downtown business district, historic residential districts; convention center, sports arena, race course, Kentucky Horse Park; antiques shopping, art galleries, casual and fine dining, nightlife, performing arts, museums; water sports, golf, hiking, horseback riding.

BUSINESS TRAVEL: Meeting facilities to accommodate up to fifty; in-room phone with dataport.

*I*magine our surprise when we were chatting with the manager during our stay at this gracious historic Southern inn to learn that it was originally built as the first medical clinic west of the Allegheny Mountains. Whatever its origins, the 1916 Federal-style structure has made a very successful transition to an elegant inn where such luminaries as Sharon Stone, Albert Finney, Nick Nolte, and Ashley Judd have stayed.

In addition to our luxurious guest room, the elegant public spaces, the scrumptious food, and the personal attention, one of the other things we liked so much about the Gratz Park Inn, Lexington's only historic inn, was its desirable location in the heart of downtown's historic district, known as Gratz Park. We could stroll around the compact district admiring the beautiful old homes, then take a short walk to the commercial district centered around Triangle Park, with its dramatic wall of cascading fountains—especially striking when lit at night—to restaurants, shops, the Convention Center, and the Rupp Arena. The University of Kentucky and Transylvania University are within walking distance, and it's just a short hop by car to Keeneland Race Course, the Kentucky Horse Park, and world-renowned horse farms.

At the inn, antiques and artwork highlight the nineteenth-century ambience. The cozy lobby's original hardwood floors, beautiful antiques, and fireplace make it a popular gathering place. Each spacious guest room is decorated differently, but each features antique reproductions, including a mahogany four-poster bed, regional artwork, and all the modern conveniences. Why, you can even hook up your laptop and log on to several major online newspapers or check out what there is to see and do in town on one of several Lexington area Internet links.

An ample continental breakfast is served each morning, coffee and fruit are always available in the lobby, and lunch (weekdays) and dinner (Tuesday through Saturday) are served in the inn's restaurant, Jonathan at Gratz Park, where the cuisine is Southern with a gourmet twist. Try the fried oyster–stuffed beef filet with mushroom gravy, barbecued tuna with white cheddar grits and asparagus, or seafood Burgoo (a Kentucky dish) of shrimp, Little Neck oysters, and crawfish simmered with potatoes, corn, okra, and black-eyed peas.

HOW TO GET THERE: Convenient to both I–25 and I–27, from I–75 take exit 113 south onto Paris Pike south. As you get into town, the street name changes to Broadway. Continue to Short Street and turn left. Continue to Limestone and turn left. Follow it to West Second Street and turn left. The hotel is on the left.

Inn at the Park
Louisville, Kentucky 40208

INNKEEPERS: John and Sandra Mullins

ADDRESS/TELEPHONE: 1332 South Fourth Street; (502) 637-6930 or (800) 700-PARK; fax (502) 637-2796

WEB SITE: www.bbonline.com/ky/innatpark

E-MAIL: innatpark@aol.com

ROOMS: 7; all with private bath, television and telephone; 3 with whirlpool tub. Outdoor smoking areas available.

RATES: $79 to $149, double or single; includes full breakfast and snacks.

OPEN: Year-round.

FACILITIES AND ACTIVITIES: Located in Old Louisville neighborhood near Central Park. Nearby: walking distance to restaurants; University of Louisville; Bellarmine and Spalding colleges; Louisville Zoo; antiques shops on Bardstown Road; Ohio River Cruises on the historic *Belle of Louisville* sternwheeler.

BUSINESS TRAVEL: Located five minutes from downtown Louisville, ten minutes from Louisville International Airport. Telephone and desk in room; fax and copy service available.

One of the most striking features of this B&B inn, which started out as an 1886 mansion with Richardsonian Romanesque architecture, is an absolutely awesome staircase. It's the kind you expect Scarlett—nipped at the waist, flounced, and hoop-skirted, to come sweeping down. Also the inn has 10,000 square feet of space, hardwood floors, 14-foot ceilings, marble fireplaces, crown moldings, second- and third-floor balconies, and a perfect location right by Central Park in the Historic District, Old Louisville. You can take walking tours right from the inn. If you do, you'll realize that the inn looks almost new—not old and needing attention, as old buildings sometimes look as time passes. Because the mansion was completely restored in 1985, it looks now very much as it must have when it was new.

John and Sandy Mullins, who had been planning to become innkeepers "someday," jumped at the opportunity to take this one when circumstances called the previous owners away.

Before she left, the previous innkeeper, Theresa Schuller, gave the Mullinses a crash course in running the Inn at the Park, so they were able to take over with a full house during a busy convention without missing a step. They've been busy ever since, and

their inn has developed a reputation as a great spot for a romantic getaway. Couples book months in advance to get the room and date they want.

The place looks romantic. The Mullinses have decorated with warm Victorian colors, designer linens, and a combination of antique and reproduction furnishings. Some of the rooms have four-poster king-size beds that look romantically old and feel comfortably contemporary. (People apparently just weren't as big in earlier days as we've become now. Or else they didn't mind sleeping cheek to cheek.)

For business travelers who care more about utility than romance, the rooms also have desks and telephones that make a convenient work setup.

For the more romantically inclined, we suggest you check out the two new suites in the Carriage House with their whirlpool tubs and fireplaces.

And for guests in both categories, there are some really nice, out-of-room amenities, including complimentary beer, wine, and soft drinks plus a "munchies" cabinet in the Butler's Pantry.

But breakfast is a high point of staying here. You have a choice of juice, the inn's homemade granola, yogurt, home-baked breads and muffins—all that goes into a generous continental breakfast—in addition to a choice of two different entrees each day.

Sandra Mullins says she likes to think they've taken the success of an already well-established inn and built on it. No matter who's done what, guests like it.

HOW TO GET THERE: From I-65, take exit 135A onto West St. Catherine Street. Drive west to Fourth Street and turn left. Go 2 blocks to 1332 South Fourth Street.

Old Louisville Inn
Louisville, Kentucky 40208

INNKEEPER: Marianne Lesher

ADDRESS/TELEPHONE: 1359 South Third Street; (502) 635-1574; fax (502) 637-5892

ROOMS: 11, including 1 suite; all with private bath (one down the hall), suite with whirlpool bath and fireplace.

RATES: $75 to $195, private bath; single or double; includes full breakfast.

OPEN: Year-round.

FACILITIES AND ACTIVITIES: Located in the Old Louisville neighborhood. Nearby: walking distance to restaurants; University of Louisville; Bellarmine and Spalding colleges; Louisville Zoo; antiques shops on Bardstown Road; Ohio River Cruises on the historic *Belle of Louisville.*

*T*his B&B inn, all 12,000 square feet of it, was originally built in 1901 as a private home for the president of the Louisville Home Telephone Company. Apparently, that newfangled invention paid off in the early days, too!

The building was restored in the 1970s. It's in a section of Old Louisville where most of the homes are equally large and elaborate. If you're interested in architecture and history, you'll like staying here.

For one thing, 12,000 square feet and three stories makes a lot of room for things with aesthetic appeal: carved mahogany columns, murals on 12-foot ceilings, and a good-sized lobby. Everything seems to have a story, and Marianne likes telling her guests about the place.

The inn has a parlor with a fireplace and lots of books; a game room has everything from an "antique" Monopoly set to television. But you probably will want to spend more time in the neighborhood, looking at the old homes and perhaps taking the walking tours. The Old Louisville Neighborhood Council has produced a tour booklet and has done a wonderful job of describing the buildings in the area and explaining their significance. The tour for Third Street (where the inn is located) alone contains thirty-three entries.

After a day of walking, you will be grateful to retreat to your room, maybe to soak in a tub in one of the marble baths with original fixtures. (They've been modernized to include showers.) Your bed will be covered with an antique quilt, in keeping with the neighborhood you've toured.

Breakfast, on the other hand, is contemporary and includes granola, fruit, and yogurt if you want it, served with freshly squeezed orange juice. Some mornings you may be offered omelettes or Belgian waffles. The inn is famous for its popovers.

Given the size of the inn, it's important to mention that the place is professionally run. This isn't someone's little hobby; this is a serious, well-established inn, and if you stay here, you can expect to be treated to professional hospitality.

HOW TO GET THERE: From I-65, take the St. Catherine exit. Stay in the left lane and turn left on Third Street. Go 3 blocks; the inn will be on the left. Pull in the drive and stop at the side door to check in. You will be directed to off-street parking behind the carriage house.

Bed and Breakfast at Sills Inn
Versailles, Kentucky 40383

INNKEEPERS: Tony Sills and Glen Blind

ADDRESS/TELEPHONE: 270 Montgomery Avenue; (606) 873-4478 or (800) 526-9801; fax (606) 873-7099

WEB SITE: www.sillsinn.com

E-MAIL: SillsInn@aol.com

ROOMS: 12 rooms and suites; all with private bath, cable television, VCR, stereo CD player, and telephone; 9 with whirlpool bath; some with sitting room, porch, and/or deck.

RATES: $69 to $89 for guest rooms, $99 to $159 for suites, single or double occupancy; includes full gourmet breakfast, complimentary snacks, newspaper; $20 for each additional person. Children are not encouraged.

OPEN: Year-round.

FACILITIES AND ACTIVITIES: Porch, library, two-person whirlpools. Nearby: antiques shops, Nostalgia Station Toy and Train Museum, Bluegrass Railroad Museum, Buckley Wildlife Sanctuary, Jack Jouett House, Labrot and Graham Distillery, Shakertown Village at Pleasant Hill, Keeneland Race Course, Kentucky Horse Park.

BUSINESS TRAVEL: Ten minutes from Lexington, in downtown Versailles; all rooms have a work area and telephone with dataport; also some meeting space, copy, and fax service.

*U*ltra romantics will find many things to love about the Sills Inn. First of all, most of this B&B inn's superb rooms are located in an elegant three-story 1911 Queen Anne Victorian mansion with its big inviting wraparound porch. Second, nine of the nostalgic accommodations boast a two-person whirlpool tub—some heart shaped. And not to be neglected, we must mention the food, the attentive staff, and the location in historic downtown Versailles.

High ceilings, tall windows, opulent Victorian-era antiques, and king- or queen-size beds characterize the guest rooms in the main house. The Tara and Victorian suites in the main house feature gorgeous sitting rooms, and the Penthouse suite has a private deck. The English, French, and Oriental suites in the modern annex boast sitting area, private porches, and a wet bar with a microwave and refrigerator. Considered the most romantic of all, for one thing because it is the most secluded, the French suite features a crystal chandelier, French antiques, king-size bed, two-person whirlpool and two-person shower, and a private porch.

Breakfast is a substantial affair served in the formal dining room or on the delightful sunporch. Fresh fruit and juices as well as freshly baked muffins accompany an entree such as Eggs del Sol, eggs Benedict, baked stuffed French toast, or spinach soufflé.

One of the things we love about the inn is the lobby library, which is packed with books on Kentucky history, horses, and genealogy and an astounding collection of 1,500 cookbooks. Items with a horse theme as well as local arts and crafts are for sale in the sunporch gift shop.

HOW TO GET THERE: Exit from I–75 at exit 115 and head west on KY 922. Turn west (right) on New Circle Road, then turn west (right) on KY 60 at exit 5-B (it is approximately ten minutes to Versailles). Follow the business route to downtown, and at the courthouse turn left onto Main Street. At the second traffic light turn left at Montgomery Avenue. The inn is 2 blocks ahead on the right. Pull into the driveway and park in the back.

Select List of Other Kentucky Inns

Otter Creek Park Lodge
850 Otter Creek Park Road
Brandenberg, KY 40108
(502) 583-3577

Rustic, secluded lodge; 22 rooms, 12 cabins; restaurant.

Mary Ray Oaken Lodge at Dale Hollow Lake State Resort Park
6371 State Park Road
Burkesville, KY 42714
(502) 433-7431 or (800) 325-2282

New construction; 30 rooms; restaurant; hiking, horseback riding, water sports.

Barkley Lodge in Lake Barkley State Resort Park
Blue Springs Road
Cadiz, KY 42211
(502) 924-1131 or (800) 325-1708

Rustic complex of a main lodge with 124 rooms and suites and 13 individual cabins; restaurant, pool, lake, sauna, steam room, whirlpool, fitness center, marina, golf, tennis, racquetball, water sports, boat rentals, hiking.

General Butler State Resort Park Lodge
U.S. 227
Carrollton, KY 41008
(502) 732-4384 or (800) 325-0078

23 rustic cottages and 56 motel-style rooms in main lodge; restaurant; beach, lake, nature trails, minigolf.

Dupont Lodge and Cottages at Cumberland Falls State Resort Park
7351 KY 90
Corbin, KY 40701
(606) 528-4121 or (800) 325-0063

72 rooms and suites, 27 cottages, some with fireplaces; two restaurants; hiking trails, waterfall, fishing, whitewater rafting, horseback riding.

Pennyrile Lodge and Cottages at Pennyrile Forest State Resort Park

20781 Pennyrile Lodge Road
Dawson Springs, KY 42408
(502) 797-3421 or (800) 325-1711

24 rooms in lodge, 13 cottages; restaurant; beach, lake, minigolf, water sports, hiking, tennis.

Rough River Lodge and Cottages at Rough River Dam State Resort Park

450 Lodge Road
Falls of Rough, KY 40119
(502) 257-2311 or (800) 325-1713

40 rooms in lodge, 15 cottages; restaurant; beach, lake, water sports, marina, nature trails, golf, minigolf, tennis, Lady of the Lake *cruise boat, small airport.*

Lure Lodge in Lake Cumberland State Resort Park

5465 State Park Road
Jamestown, KY 42629
(502) 343-3111 or (800) 325-1709

63 rooms in lodge, 30 cottages; restaurant; pool, whirlpool, sauna, minigolf.

Pumpkin Creek Lodge in Lake Cumberland State Resort Park

5465 State Park Road
Jamestown, KY 42629
(502) 343-3111 or (800) 325-1709

Original lodge in the park; 13 rooms and suites; shares facilities with Lure Lodge.

Kenlake Hotel and Cottages

542 Kenlake Road
Hardin, KY 42048
(502) 474-2211 or (800) 325-0143

Rustic lodge overlooking Kentucky Lake; 48 rooms, 34 cottages; restaurant, pool, indoor tennis center and outdoor courts; boat rentals, water sports, golf.

Kentucky Dam Village Inn

KY 641
Gilbertsville, KY 42044
(502) 362–4271 or (800) 325–0146

86 rooms in rustic lodge, 72 cottages; restaurant; lake, beach, water sports, pool, boat rentals, gold, tennis.

Barren River Lake Lodge in Barren River State Park

1149 State Park Road
Lucas, KY 42156
(502) 646–2151 or (800) 325–0057

51 rooms in lodge, 22 cottages; restaurant, lake, beach, pool; water sports, nature trails, golf, minigolf, horseback riding.

Carter Caves State Resort at Carter Caves State Resort Park

Route 5, Box 1120
Olive Hill, KY 41164
(606) 286–4411 or (800) 325–0059

28 rooms, 15 cottages; restaurant; swimming, golf, water sports, hiking, tennis, horseback riding, cave tours.

May Lodge at Jenny Wiley State Resort Park

39 Jenny Wiley Road
Prestonburg, KY 41653
(606) 886–2711 or (800) 325–0142

49 rooms and suites, 18 cottages; restaurant; hiking, sky lift, lake, marina; Jenny Wiley Theater June through August.

Hemlock Lodge and Cottages at Natural Bridge State Resort Park

2135 Natural Bridge Road
Slade, KY 40376
(606) 663–2214 or (800) 325–1710

35 rooms, 10 cottages; restaurant; hiking, nature center, fishing, tennis, pool, sky lift, minigolf.

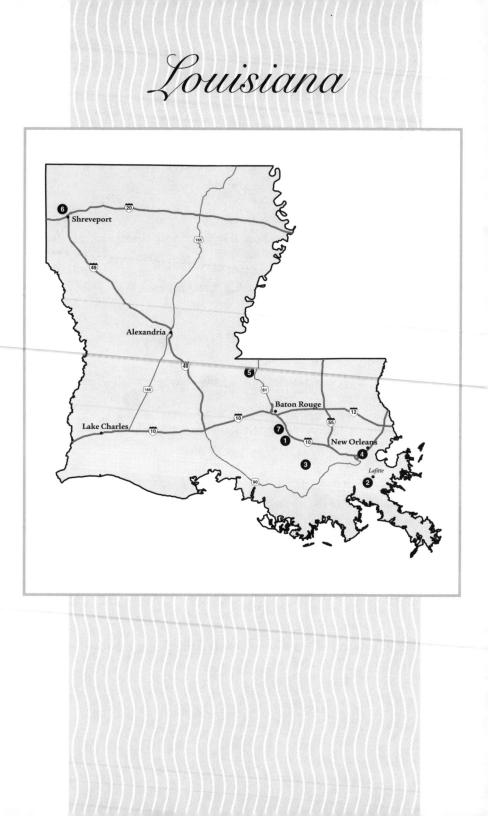

Louisiana

Louisiana

Numbers on map refer to towns numbered below.

* *A Top Pick Inn*

Tezcuco Plantation
Burnside, Louisiana 70725

INNKEEPER: Annette Harland

ADDRESS/TELEPHONE: Burnside (mailing address: 3138 Highway 44, Darrow, LA 70725); (225) 562–3929

ROOMS: 18 cottages; all with private bath and television; some with kitchen and fireplace.

RATES: $65 to $165, single or double; includes tour of plantation house and grounds, bottle of wine, and full Creole breakfast. $20 for each extra adult; $12.50 for each child.

OPEN: Year-round.

FACILITIES AND ACTIVITIES: Victorian-style restaurant, antiques-and-gift shop. Nearby: restaurants, plantation tour homes and historic sites, Mississippi River.

*T*ezcuco Plantation tries to give guests a feeling of what it would have been like to live on a working sugar plantation in the 1800s.

The original plantation house is an antebellum raised cottage (cottages were a lot bigger in those days) built about 1855 from cypress grown and cut on the property and from bricks made in the plantation's kiln.

Three of the original outbuildings remain. The others, long since gone from the grounds, have been replaced by moving in appropriate ones found on other plantations.

The overnight cottages are restored slave quarters, doubtless improved since slaves lived in them, with ruffled curtains, air conditioning, antique furnishings and artifacts, pecky cypress paneling, and the work of Louisiana artists on the walls.

Altogether there are thirty buildings on the plantation now, including a children's playhouse, a greenhouse and potting shed, an old shop with antique tools, a Civil War museum, and an African-American museum.

Guests sit in rockers on the porches of the little cottages, chatting back and forth from cottage to cottage in the old-time way.

For dinner, the people at Tezcuco will certainly suggest that you drive a couple of miles to Lafitte's Landing Restaurant next to the Sunshine Bridge on the Mississippi River, where John D. Folse, a chef much admired in the area, serves up wonderful, rich, and well-seasoned gourmet meals in his historic building.

On the grounds, the Tezcuco Plantation Restaurant is open from 11:00 A.M. to 3:00 P.M. to serve lunch. The offerings range from such comfortably familiar dishes as shrimp salad to more exotic choices, including fried alligator.

HOW TO GET THERE: Tezcuco is between Baton Rouge and New Orleans, near I-10. Coming from the north or the south on I-10, take exit 179 onto LA 44 south to Burnside. The plantation is 1 mile north of Sunshine Bridge on LA 44. Write for brochure with map.

Victoria Inn
Lafitte, Louisiana 70067

INNKEEPERS: Dale and Roy Ross

ADDRESS/TELEPHONE: Highway 45 Box 545B; (504) 689–4757 or (800) 689–4797; fax (504) 689–3399

WEB SITE: www.victoriainn.com

E-MAIL: DaleR13@aol.com

ROOMS: 11, plus 3 suites; all with private bath and television with VCR; suites have two-person whirlpool tubs and coffeemakers in rooms. No smoking in guest rooms.

RATES: $85 to $125, single or double; includes full breakfast.

OPEN: Year-round.

FACILITIES AND ACTIVITIES: Located on the Pen, a lake. Pier and covered dock with bar; pedal boat, sailboat, sailboard, and pirogue (motorless swamp boat) rentals; six acres of landscaped grounds, picnic tables; tea (hot or iced) is served each afternoon, complimentary drinks and snacks on arrival. Nearby: restaurants; swamp tours, Gulf and inland fishing charters, Sunday "Fais do do" at Bayou Barn. Tours to New Orleans (about one hour away) and plantations can be arranged.

Only 30 miles from New Orleans, LaFitte is a little bayou town that surprises you with its simplicity and offers a completely different view of Louisiana. Nothing much here but a few restaurants, places to rent boats, modest homes, and down-to-earth, friendly Cajun people.

Victoria Inn sits on six acres of landscaped grounds overlooking the Pen, a fishing lake in which crabs became trapped or "penned"—hence the name.

Dale and Roy Ross, the innkeepers, think one of the best ways to enjoy Victoria Inn is to rest and kick back for a few days after you've spent some strenuous days in New Orleans.

The buildings—a West Indies–style cottage, a Cajun cottage, and the family house—fit in with the overall simplicity of the region. Some of the guest rooms are named for what grows in the gardens: Magnolia, Jasmine, Rose, Ivy. The rooms are light, sunny, and brightly decorated. In the Magnolia Suite, for instance, the walls are a cheerful orange. In the sitting area, a loveseat covered in blue and orange chintz sits in front of a small white wicker table. In the bedroom, a frilly white spread and a canopy of netting set off the antique bed. And the Ivy rooms are garden-like in their combination of ivy-patterned fabrics, white wicker, and house plants.

What you eat when you crawl out of that bed in the morning reflects the local Cajun influence. You might choose among "mosquito toast" with bacon, a pecan waffle and bacon, and a crabmeat omelette, all served with fruit compote and juice. Whatever you choose, it will be beautifully presented on good china with white linens and fresh flowers. If you get up before most people, you may find coffee as early as 6:00 A.M. These early morning hours may be the best time for walking along the Pen, watching for the large variety of water birds that stay here.

If you are animal lovers like us, the innkeepers have one cat, two dogs, two horses, ducks, and chickens to help you deal with your separation anxiety.

HOW TO GET THERE: The inn is on a country road in Lafitte. You will receive a map or verbal directions on the telephone when you make reservations.

Madewood
Napoleonville, Louisiana 70390

INNKEEPERS: Keith and Millie Marshall, Michael Hawkins

ADDRESS/TELEPHONE: 4250 Highway 308; (504) 369-7151 or (800) 375-7151; for reservations, call 10:00 a.m. to 5:00 p.m.; fax (504) 369-9848

ROOMS: 5 in mansion, and 3 suites in the Charlet House; all with private bath; 1 with wheelchair access. Smoking only on porches.

RATES: $215, single or double; includes full breakfast and dinner.

OPEN: Year-round except Thanksgiving Eve and Day, Christmas Eve and Day, and New Year's Eve and Day.

FACILITIES AND ACTIVITIES: Dinner. Nearby: Mississippi River tour boats and tours of plantation homes.

*M*adewood feels like a house in the country—a fancy one, admittedly, a Greek Revival mansion with six white columns, but a house in the country nonetheless. Irises grow around the sides of the porches; you can see fields in every direction; pear trees on the property produce fruit for the inn, and the parking area is shaded by established old trees.

The mansion itself is filled with antiques, Oriental rugs, and crystal chandeliers. It has recently been painted and completely refurbished, but Madewood still feels like a home rather than a museum.

Upstairs, one room has been preserved as a dressing room—bathroom, complete with an old scoop-shaped metal bathtub that would have had to be filled and emptied with a bucket. It makes you appreciate the modern bathrooms now available to guests.

Old clothes are displayed in some of the tour bedrooms, laid out and hanging as though someone were just about to put them on.

You get a simpler sense from the rooms in the old slave cabin, a rustic little building with a working fireplace and tufted quilts on the beds.

At the rear of the house, the original open-hearth kitchen for the plantation home is still intact, set up with odd tables and chairs, an antique washing machine, and assorted pieces of cooking equipment so that you can imagine what it must have been like when meals for the family and guests were prepared there.

Wherever you stay, be sure you arrange to have Thelma or Clem Thomas and her daughter cook dinner for you. They are cooks who can tell you exactly what's in a dish—they just can't give you exact amounts. They stir things until they "feel right" and cook them until they "look right." Their menu includes chicken pies and shrimp pies, gumbos, corn bread, green beans, bread pudding, and Pumpkin Lafourche. Pumpkin Lafourche is a casserole of apples, raisins, pumpkin, sugar, butter, nutmeg, cinnamon, and vanilla; and don't ask in what proportions or for how long or at what temperature they baked it. Just enjoy.

Complimentary wine and cheese are served before dinner. Dinner includes an after-dinner drink in the parlor, where there's one of the tiniest old pump organs we've ever seen. A self-service honor bar is available for those who would like a drink during the day or later in the evening.

HOW TO GET THERE: From I-10, take exit 182, cross Sunshine Bridge, and follow bayou plantation signs to Highway 70, Spur 70, and Highway 308. The inn faces the highway.

Columns Hotel
New Orleans, Louisiana 70115

INNKEEPERS: Claire and Jacques Creppel

ADDRESS/TELEPHONE: 3811 St. Charles Avenue; (504) 899-9308 or (800) 445-9308; fax (504) 899-8170.

E-MAIL: columnshtl@aol.com

ROOMS: 20; all with private bath, in-room safe, clock radio.

RATES: $90 to $175; includes continental breakfast; $15 for each additional person; higher rates and minimum stay required during Mardi Gras, JazzFest, Sugar Bowl, and other special events. Not suitable for children.

OPEN: Year-round.

FACILITIES AND ACTIVITIES: Restaurant, full-service bar, elevator. Nearby: French Quarter museums, casual and fine dining, shopping, galleries, riverfront; Garden District, zoo, universities.

*L*ocated in an area known as Uptown on St. Charles near the Garden District, Audubon Park and Zoo, and Tulane and Loyola Universities, this is a very casual property. The one rule to follow is that there are no firm rules; in other words, go with the flow. Described as having a homey atmosphere with low amenities and high culture, the inn has a loyal, almost cultlike following.

Built in 1883 as a private residence, the Columns is one of the stateliest remaining examples of Italianate architecture in the city. Each of the guest rooms is individually and eclectically decorated with what has been called a "sophisticated mishmash." You're just as likely as not to find priceless antiques paired with Salvation Army rejects. The result is charming. For a particularly romantic occasion, stay in one of the two suites—the predominantly pink Suite 16 and the predominantly violet Pretty Baby Suite (named for the film).

Although out-of-town visitors come to the Columns for the overnight accommodations, locals flock to the restaurant and bar. One of New Orleans's three most-active bars, the award-winning Victorian Lounge is listed in *Esquire* magazine's Top 100. It's really hopping during the happy hour from 5:00 to 7:00 P.M. and whenever there is live entertainment with local New Orleans musicians. Two working wood-burning fireplaces in the bar and adjoining Avenue Room make the gathering place very cozy.

Albertens Tea Room serves lunch, dinner, and Sunday brunch under the stewardship of chef Betty Navia, who is Spanish but grew up in Paris. Continental breakfast consisting of banana bread, bagels, English muffins, juices, and hot beverages is served in the restaurant to overnight guests.

Jane, the night concierge, is a fountain of information—in her own words, "I love my city and my hotel."

HOW TO GET THERE: Take I-10 to downtown and exit onto the Pontchartrain Parkway. Take the Parkway to the St. Charles Street exit and turn right onto St. Charles Street Southwest. Follow it to the inn.

The Cornstalk Hotel
New Orleans, Louisiana 70115

INNKEEPERS: Debi and David Spencer

ADDRESS/TELEPHONE: 915 Royal Street; (504) 523–1515; fax (504) 522–5558

ROOMS: 14; all with private bath, telephone, television.

RATES: $75 to $185, double occupancy; includes continental breakfast and newspaper; higher rates and minimum stays required during special events such as Sugar Bowl, Mardi Gras, JazzFest, and the like.

OPEN: Year-round.

FACILITIES AND ACTIVITIES: Nearby: in the midst of the French Quarter—only a block from Bourbon Street—with casual and fine dining, nightspots, shopping, zoo, aquarium, riverboats, museums.

e were in the midst of writing an article about wrought and cast iron—their origins, uses, and designs. So when we saw the ornate 140-year-old fence with the unusual cornstalk design, we were intrigued. After we finished photographing and tracing it, we looked up and were charmed with the quaint house behind it and even further delighted to learn that it was an intimate B&B inn. Naturally, we had to investigate.

Built in the early 1800s, it was the home of Judge François Xavier-Martin, the first chief justice of the Louisiana supreme court and author of the first history of Louisiana. It is reported that Harriet Beecher Stowe was staying here when the sights at the nearby slave market inspired her to write *Uncle Tom's Cabin*.

Obviously, the house has been enlarged and remodeled several times to achieve its current appearance—mostly Greek Revival but with a battlemented tower. It is one of the most distinctive and photographed small inns in the French Quarter and has appeared as background in several movies.

Once inside the grand entrance hall lobby, you'll enter a quiet, more dignified world where brilliantly glowing crystal chandeliers reflect antique mirrors and ornate rosette scrolls, cherubs, and medallions float across the ceiling. Spacious, high-ceilinged guest rooms boast elegant antique furnishings such as carved and tester beds, as well as chandeliers, decorative fireplaces, and opulent fabrics.

You may enjoy your continental breakfast of pastries, muffins, juice, and hot beverages, accompanied by the morning newspaper in your room, on the front veranda, or the second-story balcony.

The Famous Cornstalk Fence

A real French Quarter landmark, the Cornstalk Hotel's famous fence never ceases to attract locals and visitors. Richly detailed ripe ears of corn shucked on their stalks seem ready to be harvested. Pumpkins form the base of the massive iron columns, which are entwined with pumpkin vines, leaves, and morning glories.

The story of the fence is that when an early owner brought his young bride to New Orleans from Iowa, she was terribly homesick for the waving fields of corn back home. To help her adjust to her new home, he had the fence made in graceful iron so that she could always see something of her native land.

Delta Queen
New Orleans, Louisiana 70130

INNKEEPERS: Various captains of the Delta Queen Steamboat Co.

ADDRESS/TELEPHONE: Robin Street Wharf, 1380 Port of New Orleans Place; (504) 586–0631 or (800) 543–1949; fax (504) 585–0630

WEB SITE: www.deltaqueen.com

ROOMS: 87 staterooms; all with private bath.

RATES: Approximately $200 per night per person; includes all three meals daily, snacks, and entertainment, depending on the season and itinerary.

OPEN: Year-round.

FACILITIES AND ACTIVITIES: Betty Blake and Forward Cabin Lounges, Orleans Room restaurant and theater, Texas Lounge bar, gift shop.

BUSINESS TRAVEL: Ideal for small executive retreats or incentive groups.

*A*t one time more than 11,000 steam-powered paddle wheelers plied the inland waterways which served as highways in the 1800s. Today only a few of these extraordinary boats remain and most of those are used as sight-seeing tour boats. Only three—one a genuine antique, the other two of new construction—offer overnight accommodations. Listed on the National Register of Historic Places and included as one of the National Trust for Historic Preservation's prestigious Historic Hotels of America, the *Delta Queen* is even a post office with its own postmark.

Fed on Twain stories and movies such as *Showboat*, we wanted to re-create the ambience of the steamboating paddle wheel era—the soul-stirring patriotic fervor, the slow pace of another era—for ourselves when we took our first cruise aboard the *Delta Queen*. That trip from New Orleans to Vicksburg and back to New Orleans created indelible, precious memories and friendships. All our expectations were surpassed. We totally agree with the company's slogan that a voyage aboard the *Delta Queen* is an "antidote to overstimulated lives." The soft swoosh, swoosh of the great steam pistons driving the enormous paddle wheel lulls you into a complete sense of well-being and detachment.

One of the incidents that still brings a fond chuckle was our adaptation of Afternoon Tea. We and two other couples (one from England) enjoyed the very staid-and-proper afternoon refreshments but then would repair to the Texas Lounge for Long Island iced teas (those lethal concoctions of all five white liquors). Some of our fellow passengers noticed what a good time we were having and joined us. Soon quite a crowd was doing the same. The afternoon gathering was soon dubbed "High" Tea.

Constructed in 1926, the *Delta Queen* worked a shuttle route on the Sacramento River with her twin, the *Delta King*. Commandeered by the U.S. Navy and painted gray during World War II, the boats ferried military personnel to ships in San Francisco Bay. After their heyday, they languished at the docks and even operated as a restaurant.

Then the Greene Line Steamers of New Orleans had the bright idea of providing overnight accommodations on the Mississippi River, sometimes

called the American Nile. The *Delta Queen* was completely overhauled and refurbished (using many parts salvaged from the *Delta King*) and put into service. For many years river cruising in America was a well-kept secret reserved for the wealthy, but gradually the news got out. Today cruising the Mississippi, Ohio, Tennessee, Arkansas, Atchafalaya, Cumberland, Red, and Kanawha Rivers has become so popular that the company has built two other paddle wheelers.

The military gray paint has been removed and the interior restored. Gleaming teak handrails line the decks, Tiffany windows sparkle in the brilliant sunlight or in the soft glow of lamp light, and crystal chandeliers sway gently as the vessel proceeds at her languid, almost silent, 5-mile-per-hour pace. Your surroundings are like those of a warm yet elegant nineteenth-century Victorian home, with warm paneling and a grand teak and brass staircase. Public spaces and most staterooms are filled with period furnishings—many of them genuine antiques—and opulent velvet- and tapestry-covered upholstered pieces. The small number of public rooms enhances the intimacy. You really get to know your fellow passengers and the crew.

Each stateroom has an individual Victorian personality that exudes charm and elegance enhanced by homespun touches such as patchwork quilts, collectibles, brass fittings, and wood-shuttered windows.

Your cruise, whether it be three days or two weeks, includes four sumptuous meals a day, including a fabulous five-course dinner each night, moonlight buffet, other snacks and treats throughout the day, professional showboat-style entertainment nightly, lectures, craft lessons, and calliope concerts (you can even learn to play a few notes on the difficult steam-powered instrument and get a certificate to take home to impress your family and friends). Drinks and shore excursions at many of America's most charming river cities and small towns are extra.

River Terms

When you're onboard for your first cruise, don't let your terminology show you up as a neophyte.

- First of all, it's a *boat* not a ship.

- When you come into a town, the place you tie up to is called a *landing*, not a dock.

- Sometimes in a very small town with no port facilities, the crew will simply throw a line around a convenient tree stump, that's known as *choke a stump*.

- *Mark Twain* was actually the pen name of Samuel Clemens. He took the name from the soundings being taken as the boat entered shallow water.

- A *tow* is a string of barges being pushed, not pulled, up and down the river.

- The *liar's bench* was just outside the pilothouse and is where the captain, pilot, and other crew members gathered to swap tall tales about the river. When Samuel Clemens/Mark Twain was a captain and pilot himself, this is where he heard or told many of the stories that later made him famous.

- Being able to *draw the river* is a requirement of every riverboat captain and pilot. Not only must they draw the course of every stretch of river on which they are licensed, but they must also be able to indicate on the map every sand bar or other obstacle—all from memory.

- Accompanying every cruise is a *riverlorian*, a historian and expert about the river, who gives lectures and informal chats about steamboats in general and the terrain, flora and fauna, and history of the current stretch of river being passed.

HOW TO GET THERE: You may board the *Delta Queen* at any of dozens of cities from New Orleans to Minneapolis/St. Paul or Pittsburgh to Galveston. Specific directions will be given with your cruise documents.

Hotel Maison de Ville and the Audubon Cottages

New Orleans, Louisiana 70130

INNKEEPER: Jean-Luc Maumus, managing director

ADDRESS/TELEPHONE: 727 Rue Toulouse; (504) 561–5858 or (800) 634–1600; fax (504) 528–9939

WEB SITE: www.maisondeville.com

ROOMS: 23 guest rooms, suites, and cottages; all with private bath, hair dryer, cable television with movies, modem phone jack, iron, and ironing board.

RATES: $144 to $725, includes continental breakfast with a fresh rose, newspaper. Not appropriate for children.

OPEN: Year-round.

FACILITIES AND ACTIVITIES: The Bistro at Maison de Ville restaurant, swimming pool, twenty-four-hour front desk, concierge. Nearby: French Quarter museums, casual and fine dining, nightspots, antiques shopping, boutiques; also not far away from aquarium, zoo, river cruises, Garden District.

BUSINESS TRAVEL: Modem jacks in rooms; meeting facilities for up to one hundred persons.

*W*hen we saw the inviting courtyards with their lush tropical flowers and greenery at the hotel and at the cottages, we could easily believe that in 1821 John James Audubon had produced a portion of his vast *Birds of America* series while he was living in one of the dwellings now named for him and that Tennessee Williams had worked on several of

his plays in the courtyard of the main inn where he stayed in Room 9. What glorious inspiration we would derive from these idyllic surroundings!

Maison de ville means *town house* in French and the main part of this intimate hotel is just that—a three-story dwelling erected sometime between 1800 and 1820 after a massive French Quarter fire destroyed the previous structure and most of those in the area. Four original slave quarters, which had been built at least fifty years before (mid-1700s), did survive and serve as additional guest quarters today.

One whimsical story about the house is that an early resident invented one of New Orleans's first cocktails. Since Antoine Amede Peychaud was an apothecary, it's certainly credible that he concocted potent drinks of brandy and bitters.

Nestled in a quintessential French Quarter setting wrapped around a hidden courtyard, the inn offers gracious accommodations as well as a renowned restaurant. The exterior is distinguished by a second-floor balcony with the requisite ornate iron balcony. Luxurious guest rooms feature antique furnishings such as ornately carved canopy beds, feather bedding, paintings and period accessories, and marble bathrooms with brass hardware. Modern conveniences include two-line phones with dataports, television, VCR, and hair dryer. Some rooms overlook Toulouse Street while others open onto the courtyard. The nearby cottages boast two bedrooms and two baths with a living room and dining room as well as their own courtyard and swimming pool.

Unless you stayed out partying too late the night before, you'll awaken eager to explore the French Quarter. Before you set off you'll want to savor the ample continental breakfast, which can be served in the privacy of your room or in the courtyard. Little touches say so much about an establishment. Your breakfast is served with a fresh rose in addition to the *Wall Street Journal* and the *Times-Picayune.*

Named New Orleans's Best Bistro by the Zagat Survey and the winner of numerous awards from *Wine Spectator, Gourmet, Bon Appétit,* and the *Times-Picayune,* the Bistro at Maison de Ville restaurant features creative nouvelle Creole cuisine in a jewel of a setting. Red banquettes, bentwood chairs, white table linens, ceiling fans, beveled-glass mirrors, and Impressionist paintings provide an intimate setting reminiscent of a Paris bistro. Menu items, which include traditional French favorites and New Orleans culinary selections, include Bistro Crawfish Remoulade, grilled Louisiana shrimp with sauce piquante, or andouille orzo jambalaya, and the signature crème brûlée for dessert. Lunch and dinner are served daily and reservations are recommended.

HOW TO GET THERE: From I-10 take exit 235-A (Orleans Avenue/Vieux Carre). Follow the ramp to Basin Street, staying in the left lane and making a U-turn at the sign NORTH RAMPART VIA TOULOUSE STREET/FRENCH QUARTER. From Basin Street turn right onto Toulouse Street, which cuts across Rampart Street. Follow Toulouse until you cross Bourbon Street. The hotel is on the left.

Hotel Provincial
New Orleans, Louisiana 70116

INNKEEPERS: Clancy, Verna, and Bryan Dupepe; Bryan Dupepe, Jr., general manager

ADDRESS/TELEPHONE: 1024 Chartres Street; (504) 581-4995; outside Louisiana (800) 535-7922; fax (504) 581-1018

WEB SITE: hotelprovincial.com

E-MAIL: via Web site

ROOMS: 94; all with private bath, telephone, and television; some with wheelchair access.

RATES: $99 to $275, single or double; breakfast extra. Children under seventeen free in same room with parents.

OPEN: Year-round.

FACILITIES AND ACTIVITIES: NuNu's Cafe open 7:00 A.M. to 10:00 P.M. for guests and public, bar, wheelchair access. Swimming pool, off-street parking. Located in the French Quarter 2½ blocks from Jackson Square. Nearby: restaurants, antiques shops, jazz, historic tours, aquarium.

BUSINESS TRAVEL: Meeting rooms for up to sixty; phones have dataports.

ood things seem to happen to guests here. Obviously an inn with ninety-four rooms isn't a cozy little hostelry just like home. But people seem to feel at home in the public spaces such as the courtyards and easily connect with other guests. The fact that the inn has been in the Dupepe family since its opening four decades ago (1999 is the fortieth anniversary) gives it a wonderful nontouristy feeling—as though you were visiting a prosperous friend or relative.

One guest told the story of sitting by the pool on a magical, warm New Orleans day. She got into a conversation with a woman from California who was publishing a book of recipes from a women's art club. The members met weekly to take turns posing for the group to practice painting nudes and then topped off the session with a gourmet lunch. The collected recipes were from these luncheons, and each was illustrated with the paintings done by

the club women (not exactly your typical women's club). You rarely have conversations like this in large anonymous hotels.

As one staff member put it, "It must be in the hotel's water; people relax, and the next thing you know they are making friends and sharing their innermost secrets."

And it's not just the guests; the staff also always seems to have a few minutes to talk—asking how you're liking your stay, suggesting their own personal favorite sights around town, or getting you a serving of Creole gumbo from the restaurant, "just to try." By the way, if you haven't had a really good bowl of Creole gumbo lately, this is the place to get one. Although the name of the restaurant has changed (from The Honfleur to NuNu's Cafe), the quality of the food is superb and now it's open for breakfast, lunch, and dinner. The cafe is supervised by a master chef whose offerings range from French bistro to New Orleans specialties. Local people flock to the cafe in addition to the guests from the inn. Calling it a cafe, seems to us, is a misnomer. This is not an eatery with checked table-cloths but a very elegant white-linen establishment with chandeliers, gilt framed mirrors, and the like.

The intimate hotel is actually a collection of low buildings, town houses, slave quarters, and old commercial buildings—nothing high-rise—unified by restoration and courtyards. Four of the five buildings are listed on the National Register of Historic Places and surround spacious tropical court-yards, two of which have swimming pools.

Each individually decorated, spacious bed chamber is furnished with Cre-ole antiques and French-style reproductions, which give the room a warm and relaxing ambience. Chandeliers or fans hang from the high ceilings; ornate plaster or wood moldings, period wallpaper patterns, chair rails, and paintings adorn the walls. Beautiful, romantic beds range from half-testers to highly carved headboards to brass. Magnificent bed coverings and win-dow treatments and elegant seating areas complete the picture. Everyday comforts such as cable television and a clock radio are beautifully integrated into the rooms.

HOW TO GET THERE: Exit I-10 at the Orleans Avenue/Vieux Carre exit (235A). Follow the right curve onto Basin Street and turn left onto Conti Street. At the first intersection, turn left onto Rampart Street. Go 7 blocks and turn right onto St. Philip Street. Go 5 blocks and turn left onto Chartres Street. The hotel is in the middle of the block.

Lafitte Guest House
New Orleans, Louisiana 70116

INNKEEPERS: Edward G. Doré and Andrew J. Crocchiolo

ADDRESS/TELEPHONE: 1003 Bourbon Street; (504) 581-2678 or (800) 331-7971

WEB SITE: www.lafitteguesthouse.com

E-MAIL: lafitteguesthouse@travelbase.com

ROOMS: 14; all with private bath and telephone, television, sleep (white noise) machines.

RATES: $109 to $189, single or double; includes continental breakfast, wine, and cheese each evening.

OPEN: Year-round.

FACILITIES AND ACTIVITIES: Off-street parking, $10 per night. Located in the French Quarter. Nearby: restaurants, antiques shops, jazz, historic tours.

When Lafitte was built in 1849, it was a single-family home. Today, as a guest house, it still feels more like a home than a hotel. We've attended meetings in the parlor and swear that something about the Victorian furniture, Oriental rugs, and elegant red velvet draperies made us all more cooperative than we would have been in an ordinary meeting room.

The guest rooms are decorated in period furnishings and have a kind of low-key calm that is a refreshing retreat from the outside activity of the Quarter. Many of them have the original black marble mantels over their fireplaces. Several have four-poster beds with full or half testers. The rooms in the main house are somewhat larger than those in the slave quarters and have simpler furnishings, but they have exposed brick walls that lend another kind of charm to a room, and, if anything, the sense of privacy is even greater in these rooms.

We especially liked the staff. Their approach is informal; instead of a conspicuous desk for checking in, they use an

unobtrusive antique table set well back in the hall so that when you come in the front door you see the Victorian parlor before you see anything resembling a hotel front desk. Even at the busiest times on the busiest days, the staff always has time to answer questions and provide helpful little extras.

New Orleans has so many good restaurants that recommending just one seems wrong. The inn staff all know a lot about city restaurants and tours and will talk to you about your own particular tastes, then make suggestions about where to eat and what to do. You can also exchange experiences and recommendations with other inn guests during the daily cocktail period from 5:30 to 7:00 P.M. over wine and cheese. As if that weren't enough, you'll also find a book of menus to browse. If this seems like a lot of emphasis on food, it is. As the innkeeper says, "Some people come just to eat!"

It is exciting to walk up and down Bourbon Street in the evening, full from a good meal, listening to the different music coming from each estab-

lishment along the way and enjoying the high spirits of the tourists and performers as they acknowledge one another.

HOW TO GET THERE: The inn is in the French Quarter. Bourbon Street is
between Dauphine and Royal.

Park View Guest House
New Orleans, Louisiana 70116

INNKEEPERS: Nick Ransom

ADDRESS/TELEPHONE: 7004 St. Charles Avenue; (504) 861–7564 or
(888) 533–0746; fax: (504) 861–1225

WEB SITE: www.parkviewguesthouse.com

E-MAIL: info@parkviewguesthouse.com

ROOMS: 22 rooms; 14 with private bath, all with telephone; some
with television.

RATES: $89 to $129; includes breakfast; $10 for additional guests in
the room.

OPEN: Year-round.

FACILITIES AND ACTIVITIES: Nearby: next door to Audubon Park
and Zoo; on the St. Charles trolley line with easy access to the French
Quarter museums, casual and fine dining establishments, nightspots,
shopping, riverfront, aquarium.

*L*ocated right on the St. Charles trolley line adjacent to the Audubon
Park and Zoo and near Tulane and Loyola Universities, the stately
three-story B&B inn, which looks as if it began life as an impressive
private residence, was actually built as a hotel for the Cotton States Exposi-
tion in 1884. Listed on the National Register of Historic Places, it is the
longest continuously operating hotel in New Orleans and offers guests a
taste of a less hurried era.

An architectural gem, the corner property features many-pillared wraparound verandas on the first and second floors. These porches and balconies
are favorite spots for guests to gather. Temple pediments and dormers characterize the third floor.

In impeccable condition, the inn's interior showcases high ceilings, hardwood floors accented by colorful Oriental carpets on the first floor and bur-

gundy carpet on the upper two floors. Twenty-two newly repainted guest rooms are light and airy and furnished with elegant antiques. Fourteen guest chambers feature a private bath, while the remainder share baths. Each room has a phone and a few have television.

The nightly rate includes a continental breakfast of croissants, juice, and hot beverages served in the formal dining room.

HOW TO GET THERE: Take I-10 to downtown and exit onto the Pontchartrain Parkway. Take the Parkway to the St. Charles Street exit and turn right onto St. Charles Street Southwest. Follow it to the inn, which is on the left.

Prince Conti Hotel
New Orleans, Louisiana 70112

INNKEEPER: Linda Eisenmann

ADDRESS/TELEPHONE: 830 Conti Street; (504) 529-4172 or (800) 366-2743; fax (504) 581-3802

WEB SITE: www.frenchquarter.com

E-MAIL: hotels@frenchquarter.com

ROOMS: 53 rooms and 3 suites; all with private bath, telephone, television, coffeemaker.

RATES: $95 to $175 for rooms, $185 to $215 for suites; includes morning newspaper; children younger than age twelve stay free in room with parents; rates are higher for special events such as Mardi Gras, Sugar Bowl, and JazzFest; $14 per night charge for parking.

OPEN: Year-round.

FACILITIES AND ACTIVITIES: Use of pool at Hotel St. Marie (2 blocks). Nearby: right in the heart of the French Quarter with museums, shopping, galleries, casual and fine dining, nightspots, riverfront, tour cruises, carriage rides.

BUSINESS TRAVEL: Telephone with dataport; meeting rooms.

"A prince among inns" is the way this deluxe European pensione–style B&B inn is described, and it is claimed that the best martini in New Orleans is served in the small hotel's The Bombay Club, the city's newest "veddy, veddy British" bar. Not being connoisseurs of martinis, we can't comment on the quality of those drinks, but we can attest to the fact that this is a delightful, elegant inn.

The three-story historic building is located in the heart of the French Quarter just a half block from Bourbon Street. Cheerful awnings overhang the entrance and lobby; traditional New Orleans lace-like cast-iron grillwork graces the second-floor balcony.

In contrast to some hotels' cavernous lobbies, the one at the Prince Conti is an intimate one-story affair with brick floors and French Provincial furniture. Individually decorated guest rooms are intimate as well, with low ceilings and a mixture of antiques and period reproductions plus all the modern conveniences. Because the Prince Conti is a sister hotel to the nearby Place d'Armes and Hotel St. Marie, guests also have privileges at those hotels. The swimming pool at the St. Marie is a big hit.

The Prince Conti normally offers its guests a complimentary continental breakfast. At press time, however, the breakfast was temporarily discontinued while the lobby was being moved and a cafe added, which will serve three meals a day. Once the construction is complete, the breakfast will be reinstituted and will be served in the cafe.

HOW TO GET THERE: Take I–10 to the St. Peter Street exit and follow St. Peter as it merges with Basin Street. Turn left on Conti and the inn is in the fourth block on the right.

St. Ann/Marie Antoinette
New Orleans, Louisiana 70130

INNKEEPER: Brett Smith

ADDRESS/TELEPHONE: 717 Conti Street; (504) 525–2300 or
(800) 537–8483; fax (504) 524–8925

ROOMS: 65; all with private bath, telephone, and television.

RATES: $129 to $199, single; $149 to $229, double; $239 to $299,
petite suites; breakfast extra.

OPEN: Year-round.

FACILITIES AND ACTIVITIES: Breakfast courtyard, swimming pool,
bar, valet parking. Located in the French Quarter. Nearby: restaurants,
antiques shops, jazz, historic tours.

BUSINESS TRAVEL: Secretarial service, dataport phones, day-time
meeting facilities; in the heart of the French Quarter.

The minute we got into the little lobby here and saw deep-green
plush carpeting, mirrored walls, and crystal chandeliers, we
started looking around for wealthy dowagers accompanied by
young heiresses sitting around and looking elegant, but most of the guests
were businesspeople and tourists like us.

The restaurant, which serves only breakfast, sets the tone. It has a wall of
brick painted white, pink marble floors, peach tablecloths, and silver trays. A
long wall of windows looks out onto a
brick patio with tropical plants and a
fountain, also set up for serving breakfast. You could order juice and croissants or go for something more
impressive—poached eggs on creamed
spinach with artichoke bottoms and
hollandaise sauce, maybe.

In keeping with the lobby and
restaurant, the bar has brass-topped
tables, green painted chairs, and panels
of stained glass in the ceiling. There's
more brasswork in the elevators. We
often see a lot of people busy polishing brass early in the morning.

The guest rooms are elegant, too, with French Provincial dressers and
desks, and luxuriously modern bathrooms, sixty-channel cable TV, dual port

telephones with multilingual voice mail. Nonsmoking rooms, irons, and ironing boards can be requested.

At dinner time, for a complete contrast, you can go next door to the Olde N'awlins Cookery, a simple restaurant with plain tables, bare floors, and the kind of Cajun and Creole cooking people line up for. Carol's favorite is deep-fried soft-shell crabs, but the barbecued shrimp, served in a big bowl of barbecue juice for dipping bread into, is probably the favorite dish of repeat customers. The waiter, who turned out to be an expatriate New Yorker who moved because he got tired of being cold, has made it a personal mission to teach tourists that barbecued shrimp in New Orleans has nothing to do with cooking on a grill or spit Yankee style.

There we all were, tourists and dowagers alike, breaking the legs off crabs and peeling the shells off shrimp, then licking the juice from our fingers before returning to the elegance of the St. Ann for an after-dinner drink in the Cypress Bar.

HOW TO GET THERE: The inn is in the French Quarter. Conti Street is between Bienville and St. Louis, in the block between Bourbon and Royal.

St. Charles Guest House
New Orleans, Louisiana 70130

INNKEEPERS: Joanne and Dennis Hilton

ADDRESS/TELEPHONE: 1748 Prytania Street; (504) 523–6556; fax (504) 522–6340

WEB SITE: log onto www.neworleans.com

E-MAIL: dhilton111@aol.com

ROOMS: 38; 26 with private bath, some with decorative fireplace, alarm clocks on request.

RATES: $35–$95 double occupancy; includes continental breakfast; each additional person in the room is $10; a minimum stay is required during special events such as JazzFest, New Years Eve, and Mardi Gras.

OPEN: Year-round.

FACILITIES AND ACTIVITIES: Swimming pool, extensive library.

hen we visited this unpretentious pensione-style B&B inn filled with nooks and crannies and eccentricities, we realized it certainly would not be for everyone. But for those who want to visit New Orleans on a shoestring, stay in a historic property, and meet some very interesting folks in the bargain, this could be a match made in heaven.

Although the guest house has been welcoming guests for forty years, Joanne and Dennis have been operating it for twenty years, and you can tell by their enthusiasm how much they love it. Dennis says their purpose in life is to offer safe, clean, affordable accommodations—and they've succeeded admirably.

The guest house, which is actually located in three adjoining turn-of-the-century Garden District homes, is so well known worldwide that it welcomes around 4,000 guests annually—many of them students, artists, writers, academics, world travelers, and others on a budget. Accommodations range from backpacker rooms at $35 per night to queen-bedded rooms with private bath at $95, with a variety of other accommodations in between. (A backpacker room isn't a hostel-style dormitory room as we feared, but rather a simple room with a double bed, no bathroom, and no frills that is available on a first-come, first-served basis.) Self-described as low tech, the quaint, eclectically furnished rooms have high ceilings, the simple necessities, and no telephones or televisions. There are pay phones in each house. We were left with the impression of a jumble of wallpaper patterns that were, perhaps, picked up at sales or flea markets, but the sense is also one of comfort and friendliness.

In good weather guests frolic in or around the pool. When the weather is less than ideal, they can borrow a book from the thousands located on bookshelves throughout the buildings. In the late afternoon fixings for tea or coffee are set out along with some kind of goodies.

Located 1 block off the St. Charles trolley line, the inn is conveniently located to the French Quarter, zoo, aquarium, and other New Orleans attractions.

HOW TO GET THERE: Take I-10 to downtown and exit onto the Pontchartrain Parkway to the St. Charles Street exit. Turn right onto St. Charles Street Southwest. Turn left on Jackson and go 1 block to Prytania and turn right. Follow it to the guest house, which is on the left.

The Soniat House Hotel 💟
New Orleans, Louisiana 70116

INNKEEPERS: Rodney and Frances Smith

ADDRESS/TELEPHONE: 1133 Chartres Street; (504) 522–0570 or (800) 544–8808; fax (504) 522–7208

WEB SITE: www.soniathouse.com

E-MAIL: Via web site

ROOMS: 31 rooms and suites; all with private bath and upscale amenities.

RATES: $145–$250 for rooms, $250 to $475 for suites, double occupancy; $7.50 for continental breakfast; $14 for valet parking.

OPEN: Year-round.

FACILITIES AND ACTIVITIES: Courtyard, honor bar, upscale ameni-ties, Nearby French Quarter museums, casual and fine dining, shopping, tours, carriage tours, riverboat tours, nightlife.

BUSINESS TRAVEL: Telephone with dataport; desks in some rooms; many business people like to work in the sitting room off the lobby.

*W*e love so many of New Orleans small hotels, inns, guest houses, and bed-and-breakfasts, it may be hard in reading the descriptions to tell which ones are really far above the others, so let us help you—this one is really special.

Considered by many worldwide to be New Orleans's finest small hotel, this thirty-one-room gem is located in a quiet residential section of the French Quarter, but it is still convenient to the action. The superb, intimate inn combines Creole style with Greek Revival detail to transport you back to the New Orleans of the 1830s, when the grand town house was built by Joseph Soniat du Fossat, the son of one of the earliest leading New Orleans families who made their fortune in sugar, corn, rice, and indigo. Thirteen children, in-laws, grandchildren, and the attendant staff explain the ample size of the house.

From the moment you enter the stone carriageway, which leads to a small registration area and a cozy sitting room, you'll be enchanted. An aura of adventure and romance hovers over the handsome house. You won't be surprised to learn that the inn has been named one of the Ten Best Small Hotels in America by *Condé Nast Traveler.*

In the Creole fashion, the original house turned its back on the street; a carriageway led to the courtyard where the life of the house took place. Built of red brick, the structure rises two stories with symmetrically arranged windows. Ample dormers open up the attic level. The main entrance, with its elegant paneled doorway flanked by sidelights and slender columns, was on the second floor. In the 1860s, when the fashion for ornate cast iron swept through the French Quarter, the extensive second-story gallery, with some of

the most elaborate ironwork in the area, was added. Created of representations of leaves and heavy clusters of grapes, it is one of the most complete examples of its kind in the Quarter.

Creole houses seldom wasted interior space on stairs, so the graceful spiral staircase rises from the courtyard to an open gallery that feeds into the second-story rooms. Because everything else in this house is symmetrical, it is believed that there was once a matching staircase where a small kitchen now exists.

On the second floor, the great central hall is embellished at each end by decorative doorways. The handsome rooms off this hallway are noted for their fine cornices and plaster ceiling medallions. Accommodations are impressive, with English, French, and Louisiana antiques the Smiths have collected during twenty-five years of world travel. Bedsteads, many of which have massive headboards, canopies, or half testers, were carved by New Orleans's finest cabinetmakers. Custom fabrics are chosen for each room to give it an individual style. Oriental carpets enhance the polished hardwood floors, and paintings by contemporary New Orleans artists enliven the walls. Fine antique books, lamps, and conversation pieces are carefully arranged throughout each room. Some guest chambers boast a balcony and/or whirlpool bath.

The management prides itself on attention to detail with extra touches such as high-quality soaps, extra-luxurious bed linens, and an honor bar. Some special luxuries include 200-count cotton percale bed linens, goose down pillows, and extra reading pillows. Your bed will be turned down at night. Registered guests and their friends may enjoy the hospitality of the well-stocked wine cellar and honor bar. Whether your visit involves business, pleasure, or both, the staff is ready to meet your needs.

One of the two lush and exotic courtyards contains a babbling fountain and a lily pond next to which you might choose to be served continental breakfast of Southern buttermilk biscuits, homemade strawberry preserves, sweet butter, freshly squeezed orange juice, and rich Creole coffee (extra charge) on a silver tray. You can also be totally decadent and have breakfast in your room. In the evening, the courtyard by candlelight is a romantic place for a before- or after-dinner drink.

To see more pictures and get more descriptions of this exquisite property, check out the October 1998 issue of *Architectural Digest*.

HOW TO GET THERE: Take the Esplanade exit from I-10 and turn toward the river to Chartres Street. Turn right; the hotel is 2 blocks on the right.

The Terrell House
New Orleans, Louisiana 70130

INNKEEPERS: Bobby Hogan

ADDRESS/TELEPHONE: 1441 Magazine Street; (504) 524-9859 or (800) 878-9859; fax (504) 529-9771

WEB SITE: www.lacajun.com

E-MAIL: info@lacajun.com

ROOMS: 9; all with private bath, telephone, and television; carriage house rooms with wheelchair access.

RATES: $85 to $150, single or double; includes full breakfast and evening cocktail.

OPEN: Year-round.

FACILITIES AND ACTIVITIES: Library of books about New Orleans and Louisiana, secluded courtyard. Nearby: fine restaurants, the French Quarter, the New Orleans Convention Center, the Riverwalk shopping-dining-entertainment center, St. Charles Avenue and the Garden District (where most antiques shops in the city are located), docks for the *Delta Queen* and other riverboats. Special golf packages available.

The Terrell House story is an interesting one. It was turned from a house into an inn by its owner, Freddy Nicaud, whose passions were the place, fine antiques, and Mardi Gras.

Freddy passed away early in 1994, just three weeks after enjoying a wonderful time at the Mardi Gras balls. His spirit is still reflected in Terrell House.

The house was built in 1858 by a wealthy New Orleans cotton merchant. It has twin parlors, marble fireplaces, gaslight fixtures, guest rooms that open onto balconies, and an outstanding courtyard.

As for the furniture, we'd heard about it from other innkeepers before we even visited. The inn is furnished with an excellent quality collection (much of it rosewood) of New Orleans furniture of the 1850s. Many pieces are by Prudent Mallard. Many of the antiques are from the Nicaud family. Freddy's mother was born in one of the beds; a spread was crocheted more than a hundred years ago by family members.

But Freddy loved to search out and bring home appropriate antiques, wherever he found them. He found the Waterford crystal chandelier that now hangs in the dining room in Boston. From Boston, Freddy flew home coach, but the pilot decided to belt such a delicate and fragile piece into a first-class seat.

He also found a full collection of small bedroom furniture, probably doll furniture or salesman's samples, from 1900 that enchants us every time we see it.

During one of our visits, Freddy, practically leaping through the door he was so excited, lugged in a wonderful Oriental carpet he'd found.

Since Freddy's death, the new innkeepers have kept up his tradition of elegant furnishings while upgrading all the baths with pedestal sinks and tile floors and adding a hot tub in the courtyard.

Another nice feature of the inn is its location in the Lower Garden District. Magazine Street is wonderful. It's undergone restoration and is full of antiques shops and restaurants. This neighborhood is quieter than the French Quarter; it's where the local people shop and eat away from the tourist area. Taxis are easy to find and inexpensive.

You can get as much or as little advice and attention as you want from the innkeepers. They know all about tours, tourist attractions, and interesting spots off the beaten path. Of course they know all about restaurants, too.

Bobby Hogan is a P.G.A. golf professional, so he has special knowledge for golf players, too.

HOW TO GET THERE: From I-10 East, take the Canal Street exit and turn right toward the river. Go 10 blocks to Magazine Street; turn right on Magazine to the 1400 block. From I-10 West, take Poydras Street exit. Go 10 blocks to Magazine Street and turn right to the 1400 block.

Barrow House
St. Francisville, Louisiana 70775

INNKEEPERS: Shirley Dittloff and Christopher Dennis

ADDRESS/TELEPHONE: 9779 Royal Street (mailing address: P.O. Box 2550); (225) 635-4791; fax (225) 635-1863

WEB SITE: www.topteninn.com

E-MAIL: staff@topteninn.com

ROOMS: 5, plus 3 suites in two buildings; all with private bath and television; telephone on request.

RATES: $95 to $115, double; $130 to $160, suites; inquire about single rates. Includes continental breakfast, wine, and cassette walking tour of Historic District. Full breakfast available at $5.00 extra per person. Cash and personal checks only.

OPEN: Year-round except December 22 to 25.

FACILITIES AND ACTIVITIES: Dinner for guests by advance reservation on weekends. Located in St. Francisville Historic District. Nearby: tour plantations and historic sites.

*L*oosen your girdle and listen to this: crawfish salad, chicken Bayou La Fourche (stuffed with crabmeat), jambalaya rice, pecan praline parfait. Served on good china with sterling silver flatware by candlelight on a flower-decorated table in the formal dining room, under the old punkah "shoo fly" fan. Oh, be still my heart!

We can tell you lots more about Barrow House, and we'll get to it, but how can Louisiana food like that, served with such style, come anywhere but first? You have to arrange for such dinners ahead of time, and you select from a number of different possibilities for each course.

After a meal—next day maybe—you can do penance by jogging down Royal Street with the locals, an enjoyable thing to do even if all you ate the night before was half a Big Mac.

"We want people to have a good time here," Shirley said. And they do. Beyond the food there's the house, an 1809 saltbox with a Greek Revival wing added in the 1860s that's listed on the National Register of Historic Places and furnished with 1860s antiques. Next to it, the Printer's House was built for the monks who founded the town. It dates from about 1780.

In the saltbox, the gorgeous antiques include a rosewood armoire by Prudent Mallard and a queen-size Mallard bed with a *Spanish moss* mattress. You don't have to sleep in that bed unless you want to, but one man, a doctor with a bad back, said it was the most comfortable bed he'd ever slept in.

Spanish moss was the traditional mattress filler used in Louisiana for 200 years. Shirley's informal tour of the house gives you a chance to learn how the mattress was made and to see all the fine antiques.

Similarly, the professionally recorded Historic District walking tour (with Mozart between stops) Shirley wrote guides you from Barrow House to twenty-three historic stops.

Food and antiques and tours matter, but unless good people are involved, it's probably more fun to go to Disney World. This will give you an idea about Shirley. Her inn came to our attention partly through an article on inns in the magazine *Louisiana Life*. Barrow House was included in the article because when the editor was married in St. Francisville, she dressed for the wedding at Barrow House. By the time she drove off, everybody who should have been crying was crying properly, and Shirley was carrying the bride's train. Shirley was crying, too.

Some people don't want too much personal fuss. Shirley says that she has to know when guests would rather be left alone. You'll get whatever amount of attention you want—no more. Probably the ultimate privacy is in the rooms and suites at the Printer's House. Here, the Empire and Victorian suites are the very best accommodations. Wherever you stay, expect to leave happy.

Shirley said, "It's great to have guests, and when they leave they hug you."

HOW TO GET THERE: Barrow House is behind the courthouse in the St. Francisville Historic District. You will receive a map after you make reservations.

Myrtles Plantation
St. Francisville, Louisiana 70775

INNKEEPERS: John and Teeta Moss

ADDRESS/TELEPHONE: 7747 U.S. 61; (225) 635–6277 or (800) 809–0565; fax (225) 635–5837

ROOMS: 10; all with private bath featuring claw-foot tubs.

RATES: $95–$195 includes continental breakfast and a historical tour of the house; $7 for ghost tour given Friday and Saturday nights after dark; limitations on children.

OPEN: Year-round.

FACILITIES AND ACTIVITIES: Restaurant. Nearby: Rosedown Plantation and Gardens, Greenwood Plantation, Nottoway Plantation, several other plantations; walking tour of St. Francisville; Afton Villa Gardens, Audubon State Commemorative Area; Casa de Sue Winery; Feliciana Cellars Winery, Baton Rouge, golf, Audubon Pilgrimage each March.

BUSINESS TRAVEL: Ideal for small corporate retreats.

It was thickening twilight and the heavy rain had stopped, but trickles of water still ran off the Spanish moss dripping from the ancient live oaks surrounding the darkened old French-style plantation house. Suddenly an eerie, flickering light appeared inside the house. "What's you want?" a husky female voice inquired. "Dis ain't no place to be at night. Too many people died here."

This was our introduction to the Myrtles, a B&B inn reputed to be haunted by so many ghosts that it has been named America's Most Haunted House by the Smithsonian Institution and the *Wall Street Journal* as well as being featured on several television programs. (Scientists measured, among other things, magnetic fields and temperature and pressure gradients, before reaching this conclusion.) We had arrived for a ghost tour, to be followed by an overnight stay if we were brave enough.

Originally built in 1796, the house has a history of elegance and intrigue. Ten murders have occurred here and a well on the property is said to hold the bodies of hundreds of slaves. Of the five bedrooms in the house, deaths occurred in four. The fifth was the master suite of an owner who made it only to the top of the stairs before dying of a gunshot wound.

Innocent enough looking, the 12,000-square-foot antebellum cottage (considered small in an era when houses up to 55,000 square feet were being built in the area) sits on a hill well back from the road in deep shadows created by immense magnolias and live oaks. The exterior is characterized by magnificent double dormers and lacy iron grillwork on the 120-foot-long veranda. Flickering wraith-like shadows cast by tendrils of Spanish moss drifting in the breeze create phantoms that intensify the eerie mood. Behind the house, a vast lawn stretches back to the gloom of a dark pond and deep woods.

Our raconteur guide took us on a tour of the darkened house by the light of one candle while recounted spine-tingling details of all the gory deaths. With quivering apprehension, we agreed to stay for the night. Once the lights were flicked on, the house was bathed in soft, friendly light as all the goblins disappeared until another night and the house was transformed into an intimate inn with elaborate plaster frieze work and faux bois as well as lovely antique furnishings and art treasures—many of French influence.

The members of our group retired to the front and back rocker-lined verandas with mint juleps to share our own mystical experiences with one another, and we all still went to bed that night hoping for some sign from beyond—just one that was not too scary. Much to our disappointment, nothing untoward happened beyond the pranks of one group member, who delighted in jumping out from behind doors or putting things in people's beds. Because everyone yearned to be spooked, the jokes were taken in good humor.

In addition to the elegant guest rooms in the main house, there is a garden cottage, which contains several more rooms and a cozy restaurant. Nothing unusual has ever been reported to have happened in the garden cottage, so if you're a little squeamish about the possibility of ghosts, perhaps you'd be more comfortable in one of those rooms. Kean's Carriage House Restauant serves lunch and dinner Wednesday through Saturday and Sunday brunch. The cuisine is that of traditional Louisiana, with choices such as gumbo, etouffée, and wild duck.

Assuming that you've had an uneventful night, you'll awaken refreshed and ready for a breakfast of muffins, pecan spins, fresh biscuits, fresh fruit and juices, and hot beverages.

Rosedown Plantation B&B

St. Francisville, Louisiana 70775

INNKEEPERS: Staff

ADDRESS/TELEPHONE: 12501 LA 10; (225) 635-3332.

ROOMS: 13; all with private bath.

RATES: $95–$145, double occupancy; includes continental breakfast; not suitable for children.

OPEN: Year-round.

FACILITIES AND ACTIVITIES: House and garden tour, swimming pool, tennis court. Nearby: Myrtles Plantation, Greenwood Plantation, Nottoway Plantation, several other plantations; walking tour of St. Francisville; Afton Villa Gardens, Audubon State Commemorative Area, Casa de Sue Winery, Feliciana Cellars Winery, Baton Rouge, golf; Audubon Pilgrimage each March.

*W*e went to Rosedown Plantation to see the world-famous gardens, which are considered one of the five most important historic gardens in the nation, but fell in love with the mansion and B&B inn accommodations as well. A monument to the splendor of the Old South, Rosedown was built in 1835 and named after a play the Turnbulls had seen on their European honeymoon. The majestic many-columned house sits at the end of an alley of majestic oaks and twenty-eight acres of gardens stretch out around it with 2,000 more acres beyond. This is the epitome of the Southern way of life long past.

Modeled after the gardens of seventeenth-century Versailles, Rosedown's formal gardens feature statuary, gazebos, and other garden ornaments. The Turnbulls were among the first Southerners to import azaleas, camellias, and other Oriental flora. Mrs. Turnbull tended the gardens herself and kept a meticulous journal from which the restoration was made. Naturally, a portion of the gardens is devoted to roses.

The scope of the family's wealth was so vast, they owned a race track and their own steamboat with space on it for horses and packs of hunting dogs. As with many Old South families, their fortunes declined after the Civil War, although family members lived in the house until the last descendant died in the 1950s. The mansion had never been modernized with electricity, and by that time it and the gardens were decaying badly, but the original family furniture was still intact. Then Catherine Fondren Underwood bought the property, restored the house and gardens, and opened them to the public.

The most convenient way to see the gardens and the plantation house at your leisure is to stay right on the property where bed-and-breakfast rooms are located in the 1950s house that was built for the Underwood family to live in during the renovations. Guest rooms, which are decorated in the manner of the bedrooms in the main house, feature private baths and queen-size beds—some of them romantic canopy beds. Although the guest house has no telephones or television, guests enjoy the swimming pool and tennis court. A minimal continental breakfast of muffins, hot beverages, and juice is offered in the morning. This is definitely an inn where the property itself far outshines the accommodations.

HOW TO GET THERE: Located at the intersection of U.S. 61 north and LA 10.

St. Francisville Inn
St. Francisville, Louisiana 70775

INNKEEPERS: Laurie and Patrick Walsh

ADDRESS/TELEPHONE: 5720 Commerce Street; (225) 635–6502 or (800) 488–6502; fax (225) 635–6421

E-MAIL: wolfsinn@aol.com

ROOMS: 9; all with private bath, cable television, telephone; some with king-size beds.

RATES: $55 to $75 double occupancy; includes full breakfast buffet; $10 for each additional person in the room.

OPEN: Year-round.

FACILITIES AND ACTIVITIES: Gift and coffee shop, courtyard, swimming pool. Nearby: adjacent to Parker Memorial Park; within walking distance of historic sites, churches, and shops; convenient to hiking, cycling, golfing, bird-watching.

*L*arge, twin, steeply pitched dormers centered by a smaller dormer, all lavishly trimmed with some of the best lacy gingerbread we've ever seen, characterize the darling Gothic revival Wolf-Schlesinger House built in 1880 in historic downtown St. Francisville. Streamers fluttering from the narrow gingerbread-topped columns of the full-length front veranda and the rockers and an old-fashioned porch swing on the veranda make you feel welcome.

Surrounded and shaded by more-than-century-old live oak trees festooned with Spanish moss, the house contains a guest parlor, general store gift shop, and a coffee shop. Guest accommodations are in a two-story wing wrapped around a New Orleans–style courtyard and swimming pool.

Overnight guests share the main house with the general public who come to dine or shop there. The inn's entry hall serves as a bar well supplied with sixty-five different beers and sixty wines from all over the world.

Sandwiches, light fare, and desserts are offered in the coffee shop from 8:30 A.M. to 5:00 P.M. Also located in the main house is Wolf's General Store, a gift and coffee shop, which purveys specialty items from Russian teacups to flavored coffees by the pound, lamps, china, jewelry, birdhouses, clothing, framed prints, bulk spices, cookbooks, jarred goods, and children's items.

The parlor serves as a sitting room for guests—a place where they can read, play cards, watch television, or play the baby grand piano. The veranda and courtyard are also popular with guests.

The first time we visited the inn, a small dirt courtyard in the rear of the main house separated it from the guest wing. The intervening years have obviously been good ones for the St. Francisville Inn, permitting the transformation of the courtyard with the addition of brick paving, lush landscaping, and a swimming pool. The guest chambers have been upgraded and are now furnished with a mix of antique and reproduction furniture and the added modern conveniences of cable television and telephone.

St. Francisville is a delightful, small, quiet town steeped in history and romance. Dozens of plantations and gardens open to the public ring the town.

HOW TO GET THERE: Take U.S. 61 to LA 10 and turn west. At the intersection of LA 10 and Route 3057, the inn is on your left.

Fairfield Place
Bed and Breakfast Inn

Shreveport, Louisiana 71104

INNKEEPERS: Jane Lipscomb

ADDRESS/TELEPHONE: 2221 Fairfield Avenue; (318) 222–0048;
fax (318) 226–0631

WEB SITE: www.fairfieldbandb.com

E-MAIL: via web site

ROOMS: 11; all with private bath, telephone, television, clock radio,
ceiling fan, hair dryer, robes, refrigerator, cold drinks, fruit.

RATES: $112 to $250 double occupancy; includes full breakfast and
afternoon tea; $14 for each additional person in the room; children
OK.

OPEN: Year-round.

FACILITIES AND ACTIVITIES: Some whirlpool baths, extensive gardens and grounds. Nearby: central business district, medical center,
casinos, Louisiana Downs Racetrack, Independence Stadium

BUSINESS TRAVEL: Writing desk and telephone with dataport in
guest rooms; meeting space; fax and copier available.

We met Janie about ten years ago at her turn-of-the-century Victorian B&B inn. She was up to her elbows in wallpaper paste—papering the outside of a claw-foot tub with Bradbury and Bradbury Victorian wallpaper to match the adjoining room. What a neat idea—we've seen it copied since, but Janie was the first. This little project is just one of the many this dynamo of artistic and business acumen dives into.

Since we first met her, Janie has acquired the house next door, another great 1890s Victorian home—this one Greek Revival—from its ninety-nine-year-old owner, who finally decided that he needed a smaller place. "The property was covered with thorn bushes—a little like Sleeping Beauty's castle, and while the house was wonderful, I don't think they ever threw anything out. We found empty ham cans from what must have been a weekly tradition of Sunday dinners that dated back forty-plus years. Luckily they had all been washed out."

It took four months simply to get the yard and gardens cut back and the house emptied before they could start the process of refurbishing and redecorating the fine old home to provide additional guest rooms as well as meeting and banquet space. Now the house and enlarged grounds are an integral part of this great property, which includes a full commercial kitchen where internationally known classical/Cajun/Creole Chef John Folse performed his magic last year while taping an episode of his PBS program at Fairfield Place.

Janie was also the first B&B owner to point out to us the tremendous potential for matching up business travelers—particularly business women—with B&Bs. Any vacationer will be enthralled by Janie's Victorian rooms and luxury suites in these two spacious, casually elegant, turn-of-the-century homes in the historic Fairfield-Highland district, but she also encourages business travelers to stay by providing an elegant, relaxing alternative to standard lodging.

Unlike anonymous, standard-issue, cookie-cutter hotels where you keep to your room and reluctantly awaken in confusion about where you are, at Fairfield Place you're a valued individual. Mingle with other guests in the library, which is well stocked with books by Louisiana writers; in the richly decorated parlor with a baby grand piano; on the first- and second-story verandas; in the New Orleans–style courtyard; or in the acre and a half of terraced and walled gardens.

Sleep as if on a cloud on a hypoallergenic feather bed, then awaken eagerly, knowing that you're cared about and pampered as an individual. King- or queen-size beds—some of them romantic four-posters—European and American antiques, paintings by Louisiana artists, Bradbury and Bradbury wallpapers, and writing desks characterize the bed chambers. Modern creature comforts include telephone, television, clock radio, ceiling fan, hair dryer, thick robes, and refrigerator, as well as cold drinks, fruit, books, and magazines. Some suites boast whirlpool baths and towel warmers.

A full gourmet breakfast is served in the dining room and might include Cajun coffee, fresh fruits and juices, a breakfast casserole, muffins, and pastries.

It's hard to guess what Janie will take on as her next "project," but rumor has it that one of her associates is in London attending a Cordon Bleu cooking course.

HOW TO GET THERE: From I–20 westbound, take the Fairfield Avenue exit and turn left onto Fairfield Avenue. The inn is about 11 blocks on the left. There is not a Fairfield Avenue exit eastbound, from I–20 eastbound, take the Line Avenue exit, turn right onto Jordan Street, then left onto Fairfield. The inn is about 7 blocks on the left.

Remington Suite Hotel 🖼

Shreveport, Louisiana 71101

INNKEEPERS: Dana McAlister

ADDRESS/TELEPHONE: 220 Travis Street; phone and fax (800) 444–6750 or (318) 425–5000

ROOMS: 22 suites, all with private bath with whirlpool, wet bar, refrigerator, television, telephone, desk.

RATES: $95 to $150 including continental breakfast; $199 to $250 for packages.

OPEN: Year-round.

FACILITIES AND ACTIVITIES: Access to pool, health club, racquetball courts. Nearby: jogging path, restaurants, nightlife.

BUSINESS TRAVEL: Desk, telephone with dataport.

The Remington has a very simple philosophy towards its guest services—you need only ask. Unprecedented attentiveness to guests along with unmatched attention to detail and extra-special upscale amenities give the intimate Remington a European ambience. A small hostelry of unusual elegance and style, the Remington provides an escape to a gentler time of Old World charm and beauty. The downtown Shreveport luxury property is larger than the typical bed and breakfast, but offers similar ambience, personal services, and even more amenities, making the Remington a perfect retreat.

Located in a restored historic commercial building with ornate wrought-iron balconies, the exclusive B&B inn offers twenty-two spacious suites as unique and distinctive as its guests. Suites range in size from extra-large sleeping rooms to one-bedroom suites with a sitting room to one-bedroom suites with a living room and dining room. Our favorites were the bilevel suites where the living area is well separated from the bedroom, which is reached by way of a romantic spiral staircase. All with one-of-a-kind in decor featuring deep rich colors and distinctive traditional furnishings, art, and appointments, the suites are similar only in their amenities. In addition to telephone and television, each suite boasts a wet bar, refrigerator, whirlpool bath, and spacious dressing room. Business travelers appreciate the large, well-lighted working desks and the dataport access for their laptops.

It is attention to detail, however, that sets the Remington apart. Fresh flowers adorn each suite. You can request luxurious robes and/or breakfast in bed. Around-the-clock concierge service is at your beck and call. Remington guests enjoy complimentary membership privileges at the prestigious University Club across the street, where you can avail yourselves of the pool and experience some of the finest dining in the city. Privileges are also extended to guests at the Cambridge Club and the Petroleum Club. Complimentary shuttle service is available to the airport and casinos.

Perfectly located a block from Shreveport's scenic riverfront, the inn is in the heart of the city's central business district where it's an easy walk to businesses, restaurants, and nightlife. Louisiana Downs racetrack is only ten minutes away and the casinos of Shreveport's twin Bossier City are just across the river.

HOW TO GET THERE: From I-20, take the Market Street exit and go north to Travis Street and turn right. The inn is on the left between North Market and Spring.

Nottoway Plantation Inn ♥
White Castle, Louisiana 70788

INNKEEPER: Cindy A. Hidalgo

ADDRESS/TELEPHONE: P.O. Box 160 (River Road, LA 1);
(504) 545-2730; fax (504) 545-8632

WEB SITE: www.louisianatravel.com/nottoway/

E-MAIL: nottoway@worldnet.att.net

ROOMS: 13; all with private bath, telephone, television; children welcome.

RATES: $125–$250, double occupancy; includes prebreakfast wake-up call, full breakfast, fresh flowers, tour of mansion.

OPEN: Year-round except Christmas Day.

FACILITIES AND ACTIVITIES: Tour of mansion, swimming pool, restaurant serving lunch and dinner, meeting space. Nearby: Baton Rouge museums, Old and New Capitols, USS *Kidd*, casinos, restaurants, nightlife, shops, galleries.

BUSINESS TRAVEL: Thirty miles from Baton Rouge; meeting space for up to 250; food and beverage service.

*I*t rose from the fog obscuring the tranquil surface of the Mississippi River and its banks like a mysterious castle floating on the clouds. That's how the big white mansion appeared to us the first time we saw Nottoway Plantation house from aboard the *Delta Queen,* cruising upriver from New Orleans. Little wonder that the few remaining antebellum homes along the river are dubbed "Ghosts along the Mississippi." Later, when we landed for a tour, the fog burned off and the sun came out, transforming the mansion into a gigantic wedding cake. It's little wonder that this relatively uninhabited area has taken the name White Castle from the plantation house that dominates it.

As hard as it is to believe, when this magnificent neoclassical mansion was completed by John Randolph in 1859 with modern innovations such as hot and cold running water and a gas lighting system, it wasn't the largest plantation home in the South. Soaring two-story columns across the front support vast verandas on both levels. Magnificently detailed paneling, molding, and plaster frieze work as well as original hand-painted Dresden door-

knobs, marble fireplaces, and exquisite furnishings characterize the interior.

Only a few years after the mansion's completion, the Civil War waged in the area and the mansion might have met the same unfortunate fate as many other opulent homes of the extravagantly wealthy planter class—being burned to the ground by Union troops. Legend has it that a Union gunboat fired on the mansion, but when Mrs. Randolph appeared on the front gallery, the captain recognized her and the house where he had been a guest before the war. He came ashore and offered her protection. As a result, Nottoway is now the largest surviving plantation home in the South.

You can hardly imagine rooms more romantic than Nottoway's stunning white double parlors, so it's only natural that many weddings are held there. How ultraromantic—to be married at Nottoway and then to spend your honeymoon there, perhaps in the Bridal Suite, which features a private courtyard and a swimming pool, or in Cornelia's Room on the third floor of the mansion with sweeping views of the river.

Guest accommodations are located in the mansion and the connected annexes, which once served as children's rooms or servants' quarters, as well

Nottoway Plantation Trivia

- The mansion occupies 53,000 square feet.
- There are seventy-two rooms.
- Two hundred windows and 165 doors add up to an opening for every day of the year.
- The mansion is surrounded by twenty-two columns.
- The bell pulls to summon the servants are silver.
- A crystal chandelier is by Baccarat.
- The doorknobs and keyhole covers are hand-painted Dresden china.
- It was the first house in the area to feature hot and cold running water, gas lighting, coal-burning fireplaces, and walk-in closets.
- The house has a ten-pin bowling alley.

as in an overseer's cottage and the honeymoon cottage. Those in the main house (two on the first floor, four on the second floor, and two suites on the third floor) are the most elegant. Four rooms located in the overseer's cottage aren't quite as formal.

No matter where your bed chamber may be located, you'll be pleasantly awakened by what the staff calls a prebreakfast wake-up call consisting of hot sweet-potato muffins, coffee, and juice delivered to your room to tide you over until you're dressed and ready for breakfast in the formal dining room. The generous full breakfast consists of such items as eggs, sausage, grits, cereal, waffles, juices, fruits, and hot beverages. Other amenities include fresh flowers in all the guest accommodations and chilled champagne in the suites or a carafe of sherry in the other guest rooms.

Use the inn as a base from which to explore the many plantations in the surrounding area, or stay on the property and do little or nothing. Tour the house, of course. Spend time sitting on the verandas, watching the slow-paced river traffic glide by or reading a good book. Stroll through the acres of lawns shaded by the broad canopies of ancient oaks. Swim or sun yourself around the pool. When hunger strikes, Randolph Hall, a restaurant located on the grounds, serves Cajun and Southern cuisine for lunch and dinner.

HOW TO GET THERE: From Baton Rouge, take I-10 west to the Plaquemine exit, then take LA 1 south for 20 miles. The inn is on the left.

Select List of Other Louisiana Inns

Bienville House Hotel
320 Decatur Street
New Orleans, LA 70130
(504) 529-2345 or (800) 535-7836

Intimate French Quarter inn; 81 rooms, 2 suites; pool, restaurant.

Chateau Motor Hotel
1001 Chartres Street
New Orleans, LA 70116
(504) 524-9636

Quaint hotel in the French Quarter; 39 rooms and 6 suites; pool; continental breakfast, restaurant, lounge.

Creole House
1013 St. Ann
New Orleans, LA 70116
(504) 524-8076 or (800) 535-7858

Small French Quarter inn with 30 rooms, courtyard

Fairchild House Bed and Breakfast
1518 Prytania Street
New Orleans, LA 70130
(800) 256-8096

1841 Greek Revival home and two adjacent guest houses in the Lower Garden District; 14 rooms; continental breakfast, afternoon tea, wine and cheese.

The Frenchmen
417 Frenchman Street
New Orleans, LA 70116
(504) 948-2166 or (800) 831-1781

Two quaint, unassuming town houses in the French Quarter; 25 rooms; pool, whirlpool; continental breakfast.

French Quarter Courtyard

1101 North Rampart Street
New Orleans, LA 70116
(504) 522-7333 or (800) 290-4233

Intimate inn just outside the French Quarter; 50 rooms and suites; pool, lounge.

French Quarter Guest House

623 Rue Ursulines
New Orleans, LA 70116
(504) 529-5489 or (800) 529-5489

Intimate guest house in the French Quarter; 12 rooms.

Grenoble House

329 Dauphine Street
New Orleans, LA 70112
(504) 522-1331

Nineteenth-century inn in the French Quarter; 17 suites; pool, hot tub, kitchen facilities.

Historic French Market Inn

501 Rue Decatur
New Orleans, LA 70130
(504) 561-5621 or (800) 451-6536

1700s inn; 68 rooms, 6 suites; continental breakfast; courtyard, pool.

Hotel Chateau Dupre

131 Rue Decatur
New Orleans, LA 70130
(504) 569-0600 or (800) 285-0620

Historic inn in the French Quarter; 43 rooms, 11 suites; continental breakfast.

Hotel St. Helene

508 Rue Chartres
New Orleans, LA 70130
(504) 522-5014 or (800) 348-3888

Intimate French Quarter inn; 26 rooms; courtyard, pool, some whirlpools; continental breakfast, complimentary champagne.

Hotel St. Marie

508 Rue Chartres
New Orleans, LA 70116
(504) 522-5014 or (800) 348-3888

Historic French Quarter inn; 93 rooms, 1 suite; pool, restaurant.

Hotel St. Pierre

911 Burgundy Street
New Orleans, LA 70116
(504) 524-4401 or (800) 535-7785

Eighteenth-century French Quarter inn; 66 rooms and 9 suites; pool, some kitchen facilities; continental breakfast.

Hotel Villa Convento

616 Ursulines Avenue
New Orleans, LA 70116
(504) 522-1793

1840s Creole town house in the French Quarter; 25 rooms; continental breakfast.

The Lafayette Hotel

600 Saint Charles Avenue
New Orleans, LA 70130
(504) 524-4441 or (800) 733-4754

Historic four-diamond inn overlooking Lafayette Square; 44 rooms and suites; Mike's on the Avenue restaurant; bar, hot tub.

Landmark French Quarter Hotel

920 North Rampart Street
New Orleans, LA 70116
(504) 524-3333 or (800) 535-7862

98 rooms and one suite; pool, restaurant, lounge.

La Salle Hotel

1113 Canal Street
New Orleans, LA 70112
(504) 523-5831 or (800) 521-9450

Small hotel on Canal Street; 60 rooms.

Le Richelieu

1234 Chartres Street
New Orleans, LA 70116
(504) 529-2492 or (800) 535-9653

Extra-special French Quarter hotel; 69 rooms, 17 suites; restaurant, lounge, pool.

New Orleans Guest House

1118 Ursulines Street
New Orleans, LA 70116
(504) 566-1177

1848 Creole cottage; 14 rooms; continental breakfast.

Old World Inn

1330 Prytania Street
New Orleans, LA 70130
(504) 566-1330

1920s town houses outside the French Quarter; 20 rooms; 10 with private baths; continental breakfast.

The Pelham

444 Common Street
New Orleans, LA 70130
(504) 522-4444 or (800) 451-6536

Historic inn just outside the French Quarter; 60 rooms; restaurant, lounge.

Place d'Armes

625 St. Ann
New Orleans, LA 70116
(504) 524-4531 or (800) 366-2743

Quaint French Quarter inn at Jackson Square, nine adjoining buildings; 74 rooms and 8 suites; courtyard, pool; continental breakfast.

Prytania Inns

1415, 2041, and 2127 Prytania Street
New Orleans, LA 70130
(504) 566-1515

Antebellum buildings near the French Quarter; 40 rooms; full gourmet breakfast.

St. Louis Hotel

730 Bienville Street
New Orleans, LA 70130
(504) 581-7300

Built in 1970 to resemble French Quarter inns; Louis XVI French restaurant; 79 rooms, petite suites; and one-bedroom suites, use of pool at St. Ann.

St. Peter Guest House

1005 St. Peter
New Orleans, LA 70116
(504) 524-9232 or (800) 535-7815

Historic French Quarter inn; 29 rooms and suites; continental breakfast.

Ursuline Guest House

708 Rue Des Ursulines
New Orleans, LA 70116
(504) 525-8509 or (800) 654-2351

Eighteenth-century Creole cottage and slave quarters; 13 rooms, 1 suite; continental breakfast; hot tub.

The Whitney Inn

1509 St. Charles Avenue
New Orleans, LA 70130
(504) 521-8000

Nineteenth-century town house in the Lower Garden District; 19 rooms, 5 suites; continental breakfast.

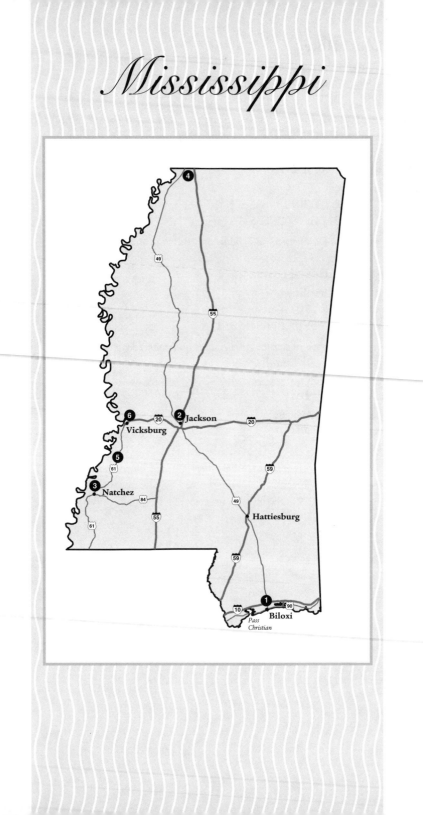

Mississippi

Mississippi

Numbers on map refer to towns numbered below.

* A Top Pick Inn

The Father Ryan House ♥
Bed & Breakfast Inn
Biloxi, Mississippi 39530

INNKEEPER: Rosanne McKenney

ADDRESS/TELEPHONE: 1196 Beach Boulevard; (228) 435-1189 or
(800) 295-1189; fax (228) 435-1189

WEB SITE: www.frryan.com

E-MAIL: reservations@frryan.com

ROOMS: 9 in main house, 4 in cottages; all with private bath, cable television, coffeemakers, and telephone. Smoking outside only.

RATES: $92 to $165, double; single $15 less; $15 for each additional
guest; includes full breakfast.

OPEN: Year-round.

FACILITIES AND ACTIVITIES: Swimming pool, Gulf of Mexico ocean
beach. Nearby: restaurants, Biloxi Lighthouse, Keesler Air Force Base,
Jefferson Davis home at Beauvoir, Gulf Shores National Seashore, golf
courses, floating gambling casinos, art galleries and museums.

BUSINESS TRAVEL: Excellent work space and light in rooms; direct telephone lines, dataports; fax available.

> *Just a hundred feet away*
> *Seaward, flows and ebbs the tide;*
> *And the wavelets, blue and grey*
> *moan, and white sails windward glide*
> *o'er the ever restless sea.*
>
> —Father Abram Ryan, Sea Rest

So Father Ryan described this place. He was the poet laureate of the
Confederacy and a close friend of Jefferson Davis, president of the Confederacy. Father Ryan wrote some of his best-known poetry while he
lived in this house, which was built about 1841. Legend has it that when Father
Ryan was in residence, he erected a cross on the front steps to indicate that a

priest lived there. When he left for the last time, the cross was blown away in a storm, but a palm seed took hold in its place. Towering over the house today and known as the Rather Ryan Palm, it extends a welcome to visitors.

Standing just 20 feet from the beach, but across a busy highway, this is one of the oldest remaining structures on the Gulf Coast, and it has been faithfully restored according to information in Father Ryan's letters and other contemporary sources. Today it is a B&B inn.

To further heighten the mood, his poetry, written in calligraphy, is displayed throughout the house, as are books about him, some of his letters, and more poetry. Margaret Mitchell's *Gone with the Wind* lies open to her mention of Father Ryan's visit.

But don't suppose that the historicity of the house means it's dark and gloomy. In fact one guest who saw it for the first time said, "How did you make it so light?"

Windows, mainly. Roseanne says that the English architect who added the second and third floors at the turn of the century "went crazy with windows," an uncommon approach at the time because homes were taxed according to the number and size of their windows. "Apparently it didn't matter," Roseanne says.

The guest rooms in the house, including the ones that once would have been Father Ryan's bedroom, study, and a room for an orphan boy he took in, are quietly elegant, almost understated, furnished with handcrafted beds and antiques dating back to the early 1800s. All the comforters and pillows are of down.

Concessions to modern travelers include private bathrobes, cable television, and telephone with dataports. Some guest chambers boast whirlpool tubs. Four additional rooms are available in the historic cottages next door and behind the pool.

The inn has several appealing common areas. Upstairs a large room that runs all the way from the north to the south side of the house overlooks the Gulf on one side and the courtyard and swimming pool on the other. Upstairs, the library has floor-to-ceiling shelves filled with books, including many about the South and Mississippi. Rolling ladders help you reach the high shelves. Empire furniture from the 1860s, upholstered in a light cream-colored fabric, lends dignity without being overbearing. In addition to a formal dining room, there is the Lemon Room—a bright closed-in porch with Mexican tile floors, high ceilings, and antique converted brass gaslight fixtures—where breakfast is served unless you request (free) room service.

No matter where you take your breakfast, it will be special. Anita, the chef, was trained in San Francisco and brings a California flair and expertise with herbs to the kitchen. Each breakfast includes a savory or fruit bread, fruit prepared in various ways—poached pears or yogurt-fruit soup, for instance—and a main dish that may be anything from cheese blintzes to

Recipe from Chef Anita Velardi, The Father Ryan House Bed and Breakfast Inn

Fruit Clafoutis
(sweetened fruit custard)

2 cups fresh or canned cherries, apricots, or blueberries
  (*must be stemmed, pitted, or drained)
2 tablespoons butter
½ cup granulated sugar
2 eggs
6 tablespoons flour
confectioners sugar

Butter individual ramekins or ovenproof 8-inch dish with one tablespoon butter. Sprinkle fruit with ¼ cup granulated sugar. (If using presweetened canned fruit, use less sugar.)

Place sweetened fruit in bottom of individual ramekins or ovenproof dish. Distribute evenly. Make a smooth batter of milk, eggs, 1 tablespoon butter (melted), remaining granulated sugar, and flour. Add flour, 1 tablespoon at a time, and incorporate before adding next tablespoon. Pour batter over fruit. Bake at 400 degrees for approximately 20 minutes, then reduce heat to 325 for another 10 minutes. To test doneness, insert knife in custard—if comes out clean, custard is ready. Serve sprinkled with powdered sugar.

puffy oven pancakes with fruit. That's a breakfast that gives you zing for exploring the area or going off to a day's work if you're a business traveler, but relaxing on the property is a good option, too.

HOW TO GET THERE: The inn is on Highway 90, 6 blocks west of the I-110 off ramp, 4 blocks west of the Biloxi Lighthouse, and 2 blocks east of the main Keesler Air Force Base entrance. You will receive a brochure with a map when you make a reservation.

Green Oaks B&B 🖤
Biloxi, Mississippi 39530

INNKEEPERS: Oliver and Jennifer Diaz

ADDRESS/TELEPHONE: 580 Beach Boulevard; (228) 436–6257 or (888) 436–6257; fax (228) 436–6255

WEB SITE: www.gcww.com

E-MAIL: greenoaks4@aol.com

ROOMS: 8; all with private bath, cable television, telephone with dataport.

RATES: $88 to $155; includes breakfast, afternoon tea, mint juleps and snacks; $15 for each additional person in the room.

OPEN: Year-round.

FACILITIES AND ACTIVITIES: Beach; casino shuttle stops at the door; golf packages. Nearby: next door to the church Jefferson Davis attended, casinos, Biloxi Small Boat Harbor, casual and fine dining, shopping, museums, water sports.

BUSINESS TRAVEL: Telephone with a dataport; access to a fax machine.

Considered Biloxi's finest example of period architecture, the circa-1826 home is the oldest remaining beachfront residence and is listed on the National Register of Historic Places. Elegantly appointed with an impressive collection of fine period furnishings, including many family heirlooms, the house and historic outbuildings provide eight guest rooms and suites, each named for members of Judge Diaz's family. The family dates back to 1700, when the judge's first ancestor arrived on the Mississippi Gulf Coast with Pierre Le Moyne, Sieur d'Iberville, on his second voyage to the area.

The luxurious guest chambers in this B&B inn are well appointed with massive four-poster, full-tester, and heavily carved beds. The most popular room is the Carquot, with French doors that afford a breathtaking view of the Gulf of Mexico and provide access to the south gallery. This room boasts 14-foot ceilings, a spectacular mahogany full-tester bed carved by Clee, a bath with full-body shower, and a fireplace; but every room has its own specialty. In the main house, the Bosarge Room features a fireplace, the Ladner Room has the original chandelier and a claw-foot tub, and the Fountain Room features brick walls and an antique brass and wrought-iron bed. In the guest cottage, the Fayard Room has screened doors onto the front porch and a claw-foot tub, the Ryan Room displays hand-stenciled walls, and the Moran Room is actually a three-room suite.

Take a leisurely, romantic stroll around the two acres of landscaped grounds with twenty-eight live oaks overlooking the beach and Gulf of Mexico, or relax on the veranda with its unparalleled views.

Breakfast is an event, with gourmet selections served using china, crystal, and silver in the dining room overlooking the Gulf. There are always two to three courses featuring dishes such as Eggs Diane, Grits Jeff Davis, Cajun sausage, or, perhaps, poached eggs topped with hollandaise sauce and lump crab meat and accompanied by steamed asparagus all topped off with something like baked pears with caramel sauce or bananas Foster. The delicious breads are home baked. In the late afternoon, a traditional English tea is served with at least two sweet and two savory selections.

HOW TO GET THERE: Green Oaks is centrally located in Biloxi between New Orleans and Mobile. Take I-10 to I-110 South. Turn east on U.S. 90 (Beach Boulevard). The inn is located one mile east, between Bellman Avenue and Lee Street. Approaching from the west on Beach Boulevard, the inn is 2 miles east of the Biloxi Lighthouse.

Fairview Inn Bed and Breakfast 📱 💟
Jackson, Mississippi 39202

INNKEEPERS: Carol and Bill Simmons

ADDRESS/TELEPHONE: (601) 948–3429 or (888) 948–1908; fax (601) 948-1203

WEB SITE: www.fairviewinn.com

E-MAIL: fairview@fairviewinn.com

ROOMS: 8 rooms and suites; all with private bath, telephone, television and VCR, clock radio, hair dryer, robes; some with whirlpool bath and/or fireplace; one with wheelchair access.

RATES: $115 to $165, double occupancy; includes full breakfast, snacks, and complimentary wine; $15 for additional guests in the room.

OPEN: Year-round.

FACILITIES AND ACTIVITIES: Decks, formal gardens. Nearby: Old Capitol Museum, Governor's Mansion, New State Theater, the longest operating theater in the state.

BUSINESS TRAVEL: Meeting facilities in the study which doubles as a sitting room and conference room when needed; telephone with dataport, voice mail; work desk.

The first thing you'll notice as you drive up the sweeping circular drive is that the big white mansion flanked by mature magnolias and crape myrtles bears an uncanny resemblance to Mount Vernon. Owners Carol and Bill Simmons, in whose family the mansion has been since 1930, are quick to tell you, however, that the 1908 house has significant differences from the famous president's house, although the subtleties were lost on us.

Located in Old Jackson near the state Capitol, both the main house and the carriage house are Colonial revival, a style associated with formality and traditional Southern elegance. Classical detail and ordered proportions popularized by the famous designer and architect Palladio are readily apparent. The long, rectangular two-story, flat-roofed Georgian house is fronted by an immense portico supported by modified Corinthian columns.

Inside, the vast entry foyer of this B&B inn seems more like a small ballroom, with gleaming floors, crystal chandeliers, and fireplaces. The study, which is virtually unchanged since 1908, features quarter-sawn oak paneling, Tiffany lamps, a Herschede grandfather clock, an impressive collection of miniature toy soldiers, important oil paintings, and an extensive Civil War library that includes many first editions.

Guest rooms and suites are elegantly decorated with antiques and repro-ductions and given individual character by the use of lavish fabrics, acces-sories, and collectibles. In addition to all the modern conveniences, the rooms feature queen- or king-size beds as well as extra-special amenities like fine linens and upgraded toiletries. Some guest chambers boast a whirlpool tub and/or walk-in shower. The Hayloft, Tack, and Third Floor Suites offer ample sitting areas; the Executive Suite has a separate library/sitting room. The Carriage House Suite is popular with honeymooners.

Among the popular places to spend some quiet time, in addition to your room or the study, are the cheerful garden room with a piano, the porches, two decks with a hot tub, and the formal garden of box hedges and lilies, where you can admire a replica of the statue of *La Baigneuse* by French sculp-tor Jean Baptiste Allegrain, the original of which is found in the Louvre.

A full Southern breakfast of bacon and eggs or French toast, grits, and biscuits is prepared to order and served at the guests' convenience in the sunny Carriage Room, which connects the main house to the carriage house.

Fairview is the proud recipient of AAA's four-diamond designation. It was named *Country Inns* Inn of the Month in October 1994 and one of the magazine's Top Inns for 1994 (keep in mind that these accolades were earned in the first year of operation) and was selected by the National Trust for His-toric Preservation for inclusion in their 1998 calendar.

HOW TO GET THERE: From I-55 South, take exit 98A. Go west on Woodrow Wilson Drive and turn left onto North State Street. Go left at the Medical Plaza building onto Fairview. The inn is on the left. From I-55 North, take exit 96C and go west on Fortification Street to North State Street, then turn right. Turn right on Fairview as above.

———

Millsaps Buie House
Jackson, Mississippi 39202

INNKEEPERS: Judy Fenter, on-site innkeeper; Mary McMillan, Jo Love Little, and Jim Love, owners

ADDRESS/TELEPHONE: 628 North State Street; (601) 352–0221 or (800) 784–0221; fax (601) 352–0221

ROOMS: 10 rooms, 1 suite; all with private bath, telephone with dataport, radio, television, ceiling fan; some with decorative fireplaces.

RATES: $100 to $170, double occupancy; includes Southern breakfast; each additional person in the room $15; not suitable for children younger than age twelve.

OPEN: Year-round.

FACILITIES AND ACTIVITIES: Gardens. Nearby: 1½ blocks from the Capitol, Old Capitol Museum, Governor's Mansion, Museum of Art.

BUSINESS TRAVEL: Telephone with dataport, some rooms have desks.

Two of our most indelible memories of the Millsaps Buie House, a B&B inn, are of the beautiful stained-glass window on the landing between the first and second floors and the delicious pralines, which are left on your pillow when your bed is turned down at night. Carol collects praline recipes, and the family graciously parted with theirs. It has remained one of our favorites.

Back in the 1880s when the Millsaps Buie House was built, the elite of Jackson built their mansions along State Street near the Capitol. This extraordinary house with its impressive columned portico was constructed for the colorful financier and philanthropist Major Reuben Webster Millsaps. A founder of Millsaps College, he was also an officer in the Confederate Army. At his death the mansion passed to his nephew, Webster

Millsaps Buie, whose widow lived in the house for more than fifty years. After an abortive scheme to sell the house to an oil company for use as its offices and a near-disastrous fire, three Buie heirs (sisters and a brother) converted the family home into this wonderful inn—stately and formal, yet warm and inviting. You'll have realized from this recitation that the home has remained in the same family throughout its 112-year history—an incredible rarity in these days of far-flung families.

Created with the intent of providing a nineteenth-century urban retreat for twentieth-century travelers, the inn features 14-foot ceilings, hand-molded frieze work, bay and stained-glass windows, highly polished newel posts and handrails, and sparkling chandeliers. Guests admire the artistry with which the foyer, library, parlor with its grand piano, and dining room are furnished. When they're feeling more casual, guests may prefer to relax on the screened porches or in the courtyard or may want to wander around the one-and-a-half-acre grounds.

Ten luxurious guest chambers and one suite are handsomely accoutered with well-chosen period pieces—including the half-tester bed of the founder himself—as well as elegant fabrics and rich colors. Rooms on the third floor have a more contemporary decor. Most sport queen- or king-size beds, several have a sleeping porch, one has a balcony, and one even boasts an observatory.

Breakfast is a very special meal when a generous buffet of casseroles, cheese grits, breakfast meats, cereals, homemade breads and pastries, fresh fruits and juices, and hot beverages are served. In the late afternoon wine and hot hors d'oeuvres are offered at social hour.

HOW TO GET THERE: From I-55, take the High Street exit. Go west to the fifth traffic light and turn right onto State Street. The inn is the fourth building on the left.

The Briars 💟
Natchez, Mississippi 39121

INNKEEPERS: Newton Wilds and R. E. Canon

ADDRESS/TELEPHONE: P.O. Box 1245 (31 Irving Lane); (601) 446-9654
or (800) 634-1818; fax (601) 445-6037

ROOMS: 14; all with private bath.

RATES: $135 to $360, includes full Southern breakfast, honor bar,
popcorn, tea and coffee.

OPEN: Year-round.

FACILITIES AND ACTIVITIES: Pool, porches, gardens. Nearby: historic
Natchez, Natchez-Under-the-Hill, riverboat gambling, plantation and
historic town homes, casual and fine dining, shopping, special annual
events.

BUSINESS TRAVEL: Guest rooms with writing desk and telephone with
dataports.

If you're a Civil War buff, you know that Jefferson Davis, only president of the Confederate States of America, was Mississippi born and bred and that he lived out his last years at Beauvoir, his stately Biloxi home on the Gulf of Mexico. You probably also know that his second wife was Varina Howell, called the Rose of Mississippi. Davis and Varina were married in front of the lovely Adam-mantled fireplace of the gracious parlor at The Briars in February 1845. Little could they know as they left Varina's parents' house that Davis, a graduate of West Point, would go on to serve and become a hero in the Mexican War, be elected as a member of the United States Senate, and serve as the Secretary of War under President Pierce before the momentous split between the North and South. Imagine their simple wedding ceremony as you stand before the very same fireplace in this house, now a B&B inn. Dream about the social occasions that must have occurred in the 48-foot-long drawing room with its twin staircases and five Palladian arches.

Perched on a promontory overlooking the Mississippi River, The Briars is an excellent example of early Southern plantation-style architecture believed to have been designed by master architect Levi Weeks of Philadelphia. Constructed with elegance and delicacy of detail and a sophisticated plan, it was erected between 1814 and 1818. One of its most outstanding features is the 80-foot-long veranda with its ten slim Doric columns, where guests can lounge on the swings and rockers while they survey the activity on the river below and watch the cars crossing the two bridges that connect Louisiana and Mississippi.

Today many of the nineteen acres that remain of the original estate are devoted to formal and informal gardens with gazebos and fountains. More than a thousand azaleas and multitudes of camellias grace the gardens. The combination of the house and grounds creates a Utopia where you can find peace and beauty.

It won't come as surprise that the fourteen spacious guest rooms—seven of which are located in the main house, four in the guest house, two in the pavilion, as well as a suite in the old schoolhouse—are so beautifully furnished with antiques and reproductions, since the owners are interior designers. Despite the Old South ambience of the bed chambers, each also offers modern conveniences such as a private bath, robes, hair dryer, and cable television. Bedding ranges from extra-long twins to queens and kings. Some rooms have direct access to the verandas and/or gas-log fireplaces.

The full Southern breakfast, which is served in the pavilion, might include any one of three entrees such as crepes but is sure to include an ample quantity of freshly baked biscuits, traditional Southern grits, breakfast meats, juices, fruits, and hot beverages.

HOW TO GET THERE: Take U.S. 64 North to Government Fleet Road (South Canal Road); immediately turn right onto Beech Street, which turns into Irving Street. The inn is on your right.

Dunleith
Natchez, Mississippi 39120

INNKEEPER: Nancy Gibbs

ADDRESS/TELEPHONE: 84 Homochitto Street; (601) 448–8500; for reservations (800) 433–2445

ROOMS: 11, in courtyard wing and on second floor of main house; all with private bath, telephone, television, and fireplace.

RATES: $95 to $140, includes full Southern breakfast, welcoming lemonade, tour of the house, and snack in room; no children under age eighteen.

OPEN: Year-round except Christmas Eve, Christmas Day, and Thanksgiving.

*A*s a couple who are not very good at gardening but would like to spend much more time with plants, we found special pleasure in the grounds and gardens at Dunleith. Formal gardens are planted in colorful, low-growing flowering plants.

Dunleith is a B&B inn on forty acres of rolling pastureland, which leaves room for refreshing green space as well as for formal garden areas. The plantation has its own greenhouse to provide plants for the gardens as well as for the mansion. Perhaps most delightful of all, an old magnolia tree behind the house has grown so huge that park benches have been arranged under its arching branches so that you can sit in the shade and look out over the property. At night the grounds are lighted to give the feel of moonlight.

The lower floor of Dunleith is open for public tours. One of the remarkable attractions is the French Zuber wallpaper in the dining room. The paper was printed before World War I from woodblocks carved in 1855 and hidden during the war in a cave in Alsace-Lorraine. If you look closely, you can see small mildew stains that developed in the cave.

The bed-and-breakfast accommodations of Dunleith are on the second floor and in a group of courtyard rooms, away from the public eye.

Dan got nervous when they said that breakfast is served in what used to be the poultry house; his family comes from a farm background and he knew about chicken coops. But it turned out to be a wonderful big room, with brick walls and polished wood floors and skylights. The country decor included bright jars of canned hot peppers, and there were flowers everywhere. It was a great place to eat scrambled eggs, bacon, and sausage with cheese grits, biscuits, and pancakes.

The guest-room decor continues the country-and-floral theme with four-poster beds, live plants, and cute little country-store baskets filled with fruit, cheese, and canned juices. The rooms are named after trees. Dunleith is a National Historic Landmark.

HOW TO GET THERE: Highway 81 heading south into Natchez becomes Homochitto Street. Continue about 1½ miles. The plantation is on the left. Write for a map.

Linden
Natchez, Mississippi 39120

INNKEEPER: Jeannette Feltus

ADDRESS/TELEPHONE: (601) 445–5472 or (800) 2-LINDEN; fax (601) 445–5472

ROOMS: 7 rooms; all with private bath; some with claw-foot tub.

RATES: $90–$125 including full Southern breakfast and a tour of the mansion.

OPEN: Year-round.

FACILITIES AND ACTIVITIES: Seven acres with courtyard. Nearby: historic homes and plantations, museums; Natchez-Under-the-Hill, riverboat gambling, casual and fine dining, shopping, special annual events.

Lucky Jeanette Feltus is the sixth generation of her family to live at Linden, which dates to 1792. Most of the present manor house, however, was built between 1818 and 1849 when her ancestors bought it. Nearly all the furnishings, including Hepplewhite, Sheraton, and Chippendale pieces, are original to the house.

When we drove up the deeply shaded drive to this B&B inn set well back from the road in a park-like setting of ancient live oaks, the first thing we noticed were the unusual front verandas. A full-length, first-floor veranda is supported by numerous columns. On the second floor a smaller gallery over the entrance has four columns supporting a temple pediment. Shutters flanking all the windows give the house a more casual appearance.

A hearty breakfast, which may be served in the formal dining room or on the back gallery overlooking the courtyard, might consist of grits, sausage or other breakfast meats, a different egg dish every day, fruits, juices, and hot beverages. If you eat in the dining room, be sure to ask about the enormous lyre-shaped cypress punkah fan that hangs above the table. In the old days, it was pulled by slaves or servants to cool the diners and to keep flys off the people and food—earning it the nickname "shoo fly."

HOW TO GET THERE: Take U.S. 61/84 to Melrose Avenue; turn left on Melrose Avenue to Linden.

Monmouth Plantation 💙
Natchez, Mississippi 39120

INNKEEPERS: Ron and Lani Riches

ADDRESS/TELEPHONE: 36 Melrose Avenue; (601) 442–5852 or (800) 828–4531; fax (601) 446–7762

WEB SITE: www.monmouthplantation.com

E-MAIL: Via Web site

ROOMS: 13, plus 15 suites, in four buildings, four cottages; all with private bath, television, telephone, hair dryers, irons and ironing boards; some rooms with wheelchair access; 9 with whirlpool tub.

RATES: Rooms $140 to $180; suites $165 to $355, single or double, includes full Southern breakfast and house tour.

OPEN: Year-round.

FACILITIES AND ACTIVITIES: Five-course prix fixe candlelight dinner daily; honor bar for guests only. Twenty-six acres suitable for jogging, pond, croquet lawn. Nearby: Mississippi riverboat tours, tours of many historic Natchez homes.

BUSINESS TRAVEL: Conference facilities for up to one hundred; desk; ideal for small retreats.

Rated as One of the Ten Most Romantic Places in the USA by *Glamour* magazine and *USA Today*, as well as being named one of the Top 50 U.S. Inns and B&Bs by the Zagat Survey, Monmouth Plantation is a member of the prestigious Small Luxury Hotels of the World and the National Trust for Historic Preservation's Historic Hotels of America and the recipient of AAA's four diamonds. These affiliations should give you a clue as to how spectacular this intimate inn is.

At Monmouth Plantation, everything is on a grand scale—restorations, furnishings, gardens, and hospitality. In addition to operating as an inn, Monmouth is one of the mansions in Natchez open year-round for tours, so the staff includes three hostesses, all of whom can give you a mind-boggling amount of information about the history, architecture, and antiques of Monmouth

As an overnight guest, you're apt to be more concerned with the quality of the rooms than with knowing that the house was built in 1818, that the table in the formal dining room is an Empire piece from New York, or that the water pitchers are made of coin silver. But once you see that the guest rooms are as luxurious as the rest of the house (complete with outstandingly nice, modern bathrooms) you kind of get into the history and elegance and can pretend that you always live this way.

Lavishly done in plantation-style, the guest chambers are the most elaborate we've seen anywhere, bar none—particularly the extravagant bed coverings and window treatments. In fact, we'd love to have had the concession on selling fabric, fringe, and other trimmings for the bedspreads, dust ruffles, and opulently festooned bed canopies and floor-to-ceiling draperies. It boggles the mind how many yards (more likely miles and miles) of fabric must have been required to create these royal-looking swags, pleated canopies, and trailing side curtains for the incredibly romantic beds. (There are a few rooms that don't have canopy or half-tester beds, so if that's something you really want in your room to complete a romantic fantasy getaway, be sure to say so.)

Guest chambers are found in the main house, the courtyard building, former kitchen and servant quarters, garden cottages, carriage house, plantation suites building, and Quitman's Retreat building, but you don't have to worry about getting downgraded accommodations in any of the outbuildings—all are top notch. In fact, more suites are located in the outbuildings than in the main house, and the two most opulent are in Quitman's Retreat. No matter where it is located, every bed chamber is a different, vibrant color and has touches that set it apart from the others. Many accommodations boast fireplace, whirlpool bath, and/or private porch. What is common to every room are the high-class amenities: thick terry robes, English toiletries, a welcome basket of pralines and cold drinks, and evening turndown service with a chocolate left on your pillow with a little note that says, "We're glad you're here. Sweet dreams."

Among the standouts are the General Quitman Room in the main house, furnished with pieces that belonged to the Mexican war hero and governor of Mississippi. Its only drawback is that it is on the public tour between 9:00 A.M. and 5:00 P.M. We were particularly impressed with the massive posts on the antique canopy bed in the Camellia Room—one of the garden cottages. Largest of all the suites, the Duke of Monmouth Suite features a king-size canopy bed, whirlpool tub and separate shower in the bathroom, and a fireplace in the sitting room. The two-level Lani's Suite boasts a sitting room, kitchen, and dining area with an antique spiral staircase leading up to the bedroom and bathroom with its whirlpool and separate shower. Most impressive of all, this suite has three working fireplaces—even one in the bathroom.

The owner Ronald Riches is a young, energetic redhead from California. The place was jumping with activity because they were trying to get some more restoration touches finished by spring in time for the famous Pilgrimage, when many homes are open for public tours. We thought he was one of the workmen and asked what he did. He said that he owned the place; then he thought for a minute. "Actually, I guess this house owns me," he said. Similar passion seems to have infected all the staff.

Ordinarily we'd associate such grand-scale elegance with coldness and formality, but here the staff seem to enjoy one another so much and everybody is so excited about each new project in the restoration that their enthusiasm is almost palpable.

Early-morning coffee is served in the study, followed by a full Southern breakfast, which is a formal affair served in the dining room. The charming brick patio in the rear of the mansion is the scene for afternoon hors d'oeuvres. Perhaps you'd like to order an icy cold mint julep to go with this treat, but save room for dinner.

Since our first visit, Monmouth has begun serving five-course candlelight gourmet dinners in the formal dining room, complete with the elegance of ornate silver and fresh flowers. In the Southern tradition, the food is plentiful. We aren't sure how anyone who eats it all can find enough room for Monmouth's traditional full Southern breakfast—eggs, grits, sausage, and biscuits—the next morning.

If the weather is good, don't neglect the twenty-six acres of grounds and gardens, a picturesque white bridge, pebbled paths, magnolias and moss-draped oaks—all of which make perfect places to stroll. The first time we were there, a Canadian television travel expert was filming a segment in the profusion of springtime blossoms. The gazebo is a delightful place to go with a good book. Fish in one of the two ponds, explore the walking trails, or challenge each other to a game of croquet.

HOW TO GET THERE: From the 61/84 bypass just outside Natchez, turn onto Melrose Avenue and follow Melrose to where it intersects with the John A. Quitman Parkway. You will see the mansion on a small hill. Turn left onto the parkway and then immediately turn left again into the Monmouth driveway.

Bonne Terre Country Inn and Cafe
Nesbit, Mississipi 38651

INNKEEPERS: June and Max Bonnin

ADDRESS/TELEPHONE: 4715 Church Road West; (601) 781-5100 for overnight reservations; (601) 781-5199 for dinner reservations

WEB SITE: www.bonneterre.com

E-MAIL: Max@BonneTerre.com

ROOMS: 12, plus 1 two-bedroom suite; all with private bath with whirlpool tub and telephone; some with fireplace.

RATES: $95 to $155, double occupancy; includes full breakfast, cheese or fruit tray, and sherry.

OPEN: Year-round.

FACILITIES AND ACTIVITIES: Restaurant, pool, lakes. Nearby: Memphis, Tunica casinos, golf, horseback riding.

BUSINESS TRAVEL: Ideal for small meetings and retreats; complete conference facilities with food service, audiovisual equipment.

*W*e admit it. We're terribly prejudiced when it comes to small inns and bed-and-breakfasts. Our preference is so strong for historic properties that we seldom like new ones. Bonne Terre is a rare exception—and that's because of its resemblance to a historic property, its superior setting, its fine restaurant, the quality of its amenities, and the warm, charming owners, Max and June Bonnin.

Although the inn is located only twenty-five minutes south of Memphis, it is secluded on one hundred acres of gently rolling farmland, pecan trees, and lakes. As you approach the inn on a long, winding gravel road, you'll see, carefully secluded from the highway, the three elegant classical white buildings with green roofs. Although the facility was built in 1996, you could easily believe that the gracious Greek Revival-style inn with full-length front and back verandas supported by columns on both levels was built as a private home in 1846. The flanking structures house a popular restaurant and a special-events facility used for conferences, weddings, and the like.

Simple elegance abounds throughout the main house, the interior of which can best be described as country chic. Public and guest rooms are decorated in casually elegant style with fine French and English country antiques and fine art that Max and June have collected during their world travels.

Each of the thirteen enchanting guest chambers, twelve of which are located in the main inn, has its own personality and offers its own delights. Light and cheerful, none of the rooms is overdone and might feature a wrought-iron bed, a canopy bed, a two-poster, or a fabric headboard—all in either queen- or king-size. All rooms boast a feather bed, whirlpool tub, and access to a porch or balcony with serene views of the lake, pecan groves, gardens, or the swimming pool. Most have a fireplace. Located above the stables, a huge two-bedroom, two-bath suite with a living room, fireplace, and kitchen is ideal for families or two couples traveling together. Special touches such as fresh flowers and a carafe of spring water make you feel you are visiting a considerate friend.

Bonne Terre Cafe is the heart of the inn. Reminiscent of a quaint French country cafe, the restaurant is decorated in rich colors and features a double-sided fireplace, oak bar, grand piano, and an open-style European kitchen. Walls of windows allow the sunshine in and permit you to enjoy the scenery. Six sets of French doors open onto a wraparound deck.

Here the European Cordon Bleu-trained chef prepares creative dishes using organically grown vegetables and herbs from the inn's own kitchen garden. The prix fixe dinners, which are $45 for three courses or $55 for four, feature seafood, beef, or whatever happens to catch the chef's fancy. Dinner is served Sunday through Thursday 5:30 to 8:30 P.M. and Friday and Saturday until 9:30 P.M. Folks will drive from Memphis for the champagne and live jazz Sunday Brunch, which is served from 11:30 A.M. to 1:30 P.M. on the first Sunday of the month (adults $22.50, children $11.00). A full breakfast of an entree such as Belgian waffles or an omelette as well as yogurt, freshly baked muffins and pastries, juice, and hot beverages is served here each morning.

Bonne Terre offers a true getaway opportunity where you can swim in the pool, fly-fish in one of the lakes, stroll through the gardens and grounds, go horseback riding, or simply relax in a hammock or a rocker on one of the porches.

HOW TO GET THERE: From Memphis, take I–55 to exit 287, Church Road. Go west on Church Road about 4⁴/₁₀ miles and look for the small sign on the left.

Oak Square Plantation
Port Gibson, Mississippi 39150

INNKEEPERS: Mr. and Mrs. William D. Lum

ADDRESS/TELEPHONE: 1207 Church Street; (601) 437–4350 or (800) 729–0240; fax (601) 437–5768.

ROOMS: 12 rooms; all with private bath, cable television, and telephone.

RATES: $85 to $125 includes full breakfast and afternoon refreshments; facilities for children limited.

OPEN: Year-round.

FACILITIES AND ACTIVITIES: An acre of grounds, porches. Nearby: Grand Gulf Military State Park, Civil War Battlefields, museums, historic district, Ruins of Windsor.

*P*ort Gibson, a small town rich in Southern heritage, is located on the Mississippi River. The third oldest town in Mississippi, it was incorporated in 1811 and saw considerable action during the Civil War. Fortunately General Grant referred to it as "too beautiful to burn" in May 1863. The entire town was Mississippi's first National Historic District, and its tree-lined streets and beautiful old homes offer visitors a quiet retreat into the past.

When visiting Port Gibson and its Civil War sites, what could be more natural than to spend a night or several at an authentic antebellum plantation home? Built in 1850, the big Greek Revival house at nearby Oak Square Plantation fills the bill. Actually constructed as the town house of a wealthy planter, the house was on the outskirts of town when it was built. The suburbs of Port Gibson have grown up around it, but the property still retains an acre of land.

A massive, square two-and-a-half-story mansion, this B&B inn displays large temple pediments on each side and a two-story veranda supported by six towering columns. Luxurious guest accommodations are in the mansion, carriage house, two guest houses, and servants' quarters.

Inside, the rooms showcase ornate millwork and spectacular chandeliers. One of the most spectacular architectural elements in the house is the massive divided staircase that leads to an unusual minstrel gallery where musicians played at long-ago balls and socials. Family heirloom antiques, some dating back to 1770, grace all the spacious rooms.

In the main house, high-ceiling bed chambers are kept light and airy by large windows. Furnished with eighteenth- and nineteenth-century antiques such as romantic extra-high, elaborately draped full- or half-canopy beds, these accommodations have an elegant Old South ambience but with the addition of modern amenities such as private baths with large vanities and marble or tile floors, as well as cable television and telephone. Nine rooms have queen-size beds, the other three have twins. Guests often choose the rooms in the outbuildings because they are fancier and more private. One of those buildings boasts first- and second-story porches, which are popular reasons to choose that location.

If you were a member of a wealthy family in antebellum days, you would have begun your day by being served a full Southern breakfast. To create that type of experience for you, the staff at the four-diamond Oak Square will bring on the yellow grits, bacon, eggs, sausage, homemade biscuits, homemade strawberry preserves, juice, and hot beverages. Afternoon refreshments are dependent on the weather—perhaps wine or iced tea in hot weather, hot chocolate or hot cider in cool weather.

HOW TO GET THERE: Located on the Great Mississippi River Road, U.S. 61, 1½ miles from the Natchez Trace Parkway.

Cedar Grove Inn ♥

Vicksburg, Mississippi 39180

INNKEEPERS: Ted and Estelle Mackey

ADDRESS/TELEPHONE: 2200 Oak Street; (601) 636–1000 or
(800) 862–1300; fax (601) 634–6126

WEB SITE: www.cedargroveinn.com

E-MAIL: Via Web site

ROOMS: 14 in the mansion, 2 in the pool house, 8 suites in the carriage
house; 5 cottages; all with private bath, cable television, and telephone;
some with patio; some with fireplace, whirlpool tub, wheelchair access.

RATES: $85 to $165, double; 10 percent less for single; includes full
plantation breakfast and tour of mansion.

OPEN: Year-round.

FACILITIES AND ACTIVITIES: Full cocktail service with piano and
gourmet candlelight dining at 6:00 P.M. Rooftop garden overlooking
Mississippi River; swimming pool and Jacuzzi set in a courtyard with
five acres of formal gardens, gazebos, fountains. Nearby: restaurants,
Mississippi riverboat tours, historic sites in Vicksburg.

Owner Estelle Mackey, dressed to kill in a billowing, low-cut ballgown
of an attractive pre–Civil War style, swung open the heavy front
door and invited us in when we visited Cedar Grove for the first
time. This isn't your normal everyday greeting at Cedar Grove, mind you, but
it was Pilgrimage time. At other times of year, you'll be just as warmly welcomed inside by longtime innkeeper and life-long resident of Vicksburg,
Rhonda Abraham (in normal dress). Voted the Best Antebellum Home in
Vicksburg, this magnificent estate makes a perfect place to capture *Gone With
the Wind* elegance and romance.

The place smells like dried rose petals when you enter. Just as you start
thinking that there was a softness about the atmosphere that most antebellum
tour houses lack, you see the cannonball lodged in the parlor wall, a patch in
the door, and a ragged hole in the parlor floor that has been framed and covered with heavy glass so that you could see through to the rooms below.
What is all this?

"Union gunboat cannonball, from the Civil War," the innkeeper said. "It came through the door and hit the parlor wall. Mrs. Klein, the owner of the house, insisted on leaving it there as a reminder after the war."

And the hole?

"War damage. After the fall of Vicksburg, Grant slept here for three nights. He turned the servants' quarters down below into a Union hospital for his soldiers. The Kleins were in residence at the time."

The present owners' and innkeeper's familiarity and personal fascination with the history of the house give any of them little stories to tell about every room of the mansion. Listening to them and knowing that the house is largely furnished with its original antiques adds a human note to the Civil War that you'll never get from reading plaques in museums or touring military memorials. They even knew that what we thought was a goldfish pond out in the yard actually, back in 1885, had been a catfish holding pond to keep the fish lively until it was time to eat them.

Ted and Estelle Mackey, the owners, have been working steadily assembling the furnishings, buffing the house, and manicuring the lawns to bring the property up to its pre–Civil War glory. They've done a tremendous amount since the first time and even since our last overnight visit and the place truly looks worthy of the waltzing of Jefferson Davis.

The Greek Revival home was built about 1840 by John A. Klein as a wedding present for his bride. Sure beats a set of Pyrex casseroles! The house survived the Civil War because it was used as a Union hospital and, it's rumored, because Mrs. Klein had family ties to General Sherman—a fact that caused her to be rejected by Vicksburg society during the war.

Superior guest accommodations are found in the main house, the two-story carriage house, or several humble restored cottages scattered around the five-acre grounds—some of them poolside. Each is lavishly decorated and furnished with period antiques and reproductions. Some of these furnishings are original to the house and were collected by the Kleins on their year-long European honeymoon. Romantic canopy and half-tester beds grace many guest chambers.

It's impossible to describe all twenty-nine rooms and suites here, but we must mention a few of the most exceptional bed chambers—many of which are named for Civil War heroes or *Gone with the Wind* characters.

Perhaps you'd like to sleep in the very room and the very bed where General Grant spent three nights after the fall of Vicksburg. Appropriately named for him, this room features a heavily carved and opulently draped canopy bed, original rosewood and cherry antiques, and a Prudence Mallard armoire bearing the master craftsman's signature mallard egg, as well as a marble bath with a whirlpool tub.

The two-story Library Suite is located in the original library, which Mr. Klein used as an office. A spiral iron staircase connects the extravagant scarlet Victorian sitting room with the bedroom. The General Lee Suite boasts king-size bed, working fireplace, entertainment center with surround sound, and private patio with a fountain. The Jefferson Davis Room sports a magnificent canopy bed with massive posts, ornately carved headboard, and fancy canopy drapings. Klein's Grand Suite, which was once the Klein children's music room, is especially spacious and well endowed with amenities including fireplace and whirlpool tub.

We enjoyed staying in the grand, white-columned carriage house. We had a separate sitting room and easy access to our second-story veranda, where we could relax with a cool drink on comfortable wicker while we surveyed the main house, gardens, statuary, fountains, original Italianate ironwork gazebo, catfish pond, greenhouse, arbors, courtyards, and swimming pool as well as glimpses of the Mississippi River in the distance. If we hadn't had such a wonderful vantage point, we could have gone up to the terraced garden on the roof of the big house to enjoy the views.

Bask in the luxury of the Old South and let the dedicated staff spoil you. Awaken to the sounds of Mozart and the aroma of fresh coffee, followed by a full Southern plantation breakfast. In the late afternoon or evening, relax to live piano music in the Mansion Bar, then enjoy a romantic candlelight dinner of New Orleans cuisine accompanied by fine wines in the cozy garden atmosphere of Andre's, an elegant restaurant voted the Best Restaurant in Vicksburg (additional charge). Delicacies include such mouthwatering dishes as New Orleans catfish off the grill and topped with Cajun crawfish etouffée or sushi-grade yellowfin tuna marinated in champagne with Andre's Creole seasoning, topped with crumbled hickory-smoked bacon, and served with lemon caper hollandaise sauce. Cap your meal with cappuccino and brandy bread pudding. Chef Andre's herb olive oil and cookbooks are for sale in the gift shop.

HOW TO GET THERE: From I-20, take the 1A Washington Street exit. Go north about 2 miles. Turn left onto Klein.

Chef Andre's recipe for Brandy Bread Pudding and Brandy Sauce

2 large loaves French bread (torn into 3-inch pieces) toasted

1 whole pound cake (strawberry glazed) torn into pieces

10 whole eggs

2 cans sweet condensed milk

3 cartons hazelnut creamer

3 tablespoons nutmeg

2 tablespoons cinnamon

1 pound melted butter

2 tablespoons almond extract

Toast French bread and add strawberry glazed pound cake. Place in baking pan (17 1/4-inch by 11 3/4-inch x 2 1/4 inch). Mix remaining ingredients with a large whisk. Pour over bread and cake. Cover with foil and bake 1 hour at 325 degrees. Uncover and bake 15 minutes at 350 degrees. Scoop out portions and pour hot brandy sauce over pudding. Top with chopped roasted nuts and sprinkle with powdered sugar. Garnish with a strawberry.

Cedar Andre's Brandy Sauce

10 egg yolks

2 cartons whipping cream

2 bags of powder sugar

2 cups of brandy

2 tablespoons of almond extract

1 pound of butter (melted)

Mix all ingredients well. Place sauce in a double boiler on medium heat and stir occasionally until bubbles, and serve.

The Corners Bed and Breakfast Inn
Vicksburg, Mississippi 39180

INNKEEPERS: Bettye and Cliff Whitney, Cliff (Jr.) and Kilby Whitney

ADDRESS/TELEPHONE: 601 Klein Street; (601) 636-7421 or
(800) 444-7421; fax (601) 636-7232

WEB SITE: www.thecorners.com

E-MAIL: cornersb@magnolia.net

ROOMS: 13, plus 2 two-bedroom suites and the two-bedroom Cottage
on the Green; all with private bath, television, and telephone; some with
fireplace; some with whirlpool tub; 2 with wet bar/kitchen. Smoking
outside only.

RATES: Double, $85 to $120, rooms; $120 to $140, suites; single, $10
less; four people in suite, $160; includes full breakfast, evening nonalco-
holic beverages, and tour of house.

OPEN: Year-round.

FACILITIES AND ACTIVITIES: Formal gardens and fountains. Nearby:
restaurants, Mississippi riverboat tours, historic sites in Vicksburg,
Vicksburg National Military Park.

*T*he Corners is the kind of B&B inn that earns recommendations
from other innkeepers. It's a champagne-and-flowers, romantic-
getaway kind of place. This two-story Victorian Louisiana raised
cottage–style mansion with Greek Revival and Italianate influence, along
with its associated outbuildings, on a bluff overlooking the Mississippi and
Yazoo Rivers exudes old Southern charm and romance in all its details,
inside and out.

The most distinctive feature of this house is its veranda trimmings.
Instead of round or square solid columns supporting the roof, these are flat
and cut out with the shapes of hearts, spades, and triangles, forming a lace-
like effect. These shapes are repeated in the spindles of the porch and stairway railings of the 70-foot veranda and were replicated for the first- and
second-story verandas of the new guest house. Unique to Vicksburg, these
pierced columns are known as Vicksburg Columns.

The guest rooms are furnished with canopied beds, period antiques, and
individual special features to set each room apart from all the others. For
instance the Eastlake Bedroom got its name for the 1870s Eastlake queen-

size half-tester bed, dresser, and night table that are a focal point in the room's personality. The room has 12-foot windows that open onto the back veranda, giving you a view of the gardens. It also has a fireplace. Similarly, the Library Bedroom really was the library when the mansion was a family home. It has cypress bookshelves, a queen-size bed with a tapestry drape, and a wood-burning fireplace. You can go on in your imagination to understand the nature of the Stained-Glass Bedroom, the Garden Rooms, the Blue Room, and so on.

Attached to the main house is the Guest Quarters, a one-story structure built in 1875 as a kitchen and servants' quarters. Today it features pine floors and fireplaces and houses two guest rooms with pencil-post beds, bathrooms with whirlpool tubs, and a veranda. The Galleries, a new two-story building, which resembles the main house but with full-length verandas on both levels (from which owner Bettye Whitney says, "You can see the horizon all the way to Texas"), was completed in 1997 to provide additional accommodations. Each of its four extra-large rooms boasts antique beds, superior linens, intimate seating areas, and whirlpool tub. Just across the street from the main house, with its back to the river, is the humble Cottage on the Green—a two-bedroom home with its own living room, kitchen, and dining area, making it ideal for families or two couples traveling together.

Walking through the public rooms downstairs, you may have a sense of having been here before, particularly if you have visited nearby Cedar Grove Mansion. Although the two buildings don't look the same from the outside (this one is a raised cottage with an elevated gallery instead of a columned portico), the Corners has the same floor plan and many similar features as Cedar Grove. John Alexander Klein, who owned Cedar Grove, built this house, with 13-foot-high ceilings, in 1872 as a wedding gift for his daughter.

As you eat your candlelight breakfast, served on antique porcelain and silver in the magnificent peach-and-white formal dining room, you can imagine how she must have lived. The food is as extravagant as the service, with entrees such as ham-asparagus quiche, eggs Benedict, and caramelized baked French toast, all served with fruit and good Southern biscuits.

Outside, the 70-foot gallery is as good a place to catch a breeze and view the grounds today as it must have been in the 1800s. Sip morning coffee or afternoon tea in the glassed-in, brick-floored, wicker-filled morning room (previously the rear veranda) overlooking the gardens, or relax in the late afternoon with cookies and a beverage in the striking, formally furnished double parlors with their floor-to-ceiling windows, twin fireplaces, gasolier-style chandeliers, and baby grand piano. End the day by marveling at the magical sunsets over the Mississippi and Yazoo Rivers from a rocker on the front veranda.

The parterre gardens helped earn The Corners a listing on the National Register of Historic Places. A parterre garden is one in which the growing areas are separated by formal brick walkways. Here flowers bloom much of the year, giant camelias in fall through winter, and bright cerise crape myrtles, some of which are over 100 years old, from roughly June through October.

HOW TO GET THERE: From I-20 near the state welcome center by the Mississippi River, take exit 1-A onto Washington Street. Turn left on Klein. You will receive a brochure with a map when you make reservations.

Select List of
Other Mississippi Inns

The Country Goose Inn
350 Highway 305
Olive Branch, MS 38654
(601) 895-3098 or (800) 895-3098

Lakeside cottages with picturesque surroundings; 15 rooms/5 baths; includes three meals; fishing and pedal boating, horseback riding.

Mockingbird Inn B&B
305 North Gloster
Tupelo, MS 38801
(601) 841-0286

1925 Arts and Crafts/Prairie–style house; 7 rooms are internationally themed; some with fireplace or whirlpool; includes full breakfast.

Anchuca
1010 First East Street
Vicksburg, MS 39180
(601) 661-0111

1830 Greek Revival; 6 rooms; pool; includes full breakfast and afternoon tea.

Annabelle
501 Speed Street
Vicksburg, MS 39180
(601) 638-2000 or (800) 791-2000

1868 Victorian main house and 1881 guest house; 7 rooms; pool; includes full breakfast.

Floweree Cottage
2309 Pearl Street
Vicksburg, MS 39180
(601) 638-2704 or (800) 262-6315

1870 Victorian; 8 rooms; includes full breakfast.

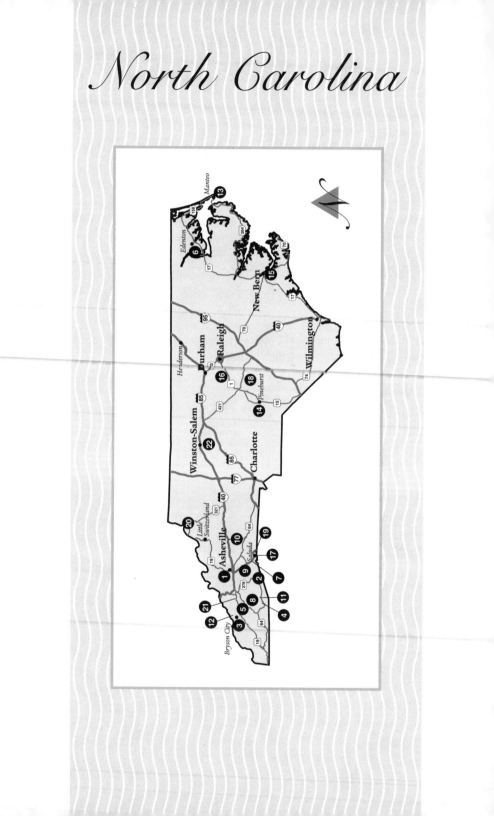

North Carolina

Numbers on map refer to towns numbered below.

* A Top Pick Inn

Albemarle Inn ♥
Asheville, North Carolina 28801

INNKEEPERS: Cathy and Larry Sklar; Zantui Rose, assistant innkeeper

ADDRESS/TELEPHONE: 86 Edgemont Road; (828) 255-0027 or (800) 621-7435; fax (828) 236-3307

WEB SITE: www.albemarleinn.com

ROOMS: 11; all with private bath, television, and telephone. No smoking inn.

RATES: $90 to $150 per room; includes full breakfast.

OPEN: Year-round.

FACILITIES AND ACTIVITIES: Swimming pool. Nearby: Biltmore Estate, Blue Ridge Parkway, crafts and antiques shops, hiking, rafting, golf; five minutes from downtown Asheville.

Béla Bartók wrote his Third Piano Concerto while he was at Albemarle Inn. We're not suggesting that a stay here will turn you into a composer, but much about this B&B inn does call to mind musicians, artists, and literary gatherings, including the classical and contemporary music playing in the background.

This building has been restored to its early elegance and is decorated with furniture and accessories that reflect its neoclassical heritage. New innkeepers have recently purchased the inn and are upgrading the already grand property to the next level. The old oak paneling has been stripped and refinished, bringing out its rich texture. The yard has been completely relandscaped, new carpet has been laid, and the bedding has  been upgraded with goose-down quilts and luxurious linens. Everything is bright and airy with a wonderful feeling of calm spaciousness.

One of the most notable features of the inn is a marvelous carved-oak staircase with a curved-frame glass window and an opposing curved balconylike landing. It looks like a setting for the balcony scene from *Romeo and Juliet*. At least one couple has been married on that spot.

Each guest room has a special feature, such as antiques or four-poster beds or decorative brass. Bartók's Retreat, for instance, is a bright, high-ceilinged room from which you can see a bit of the Blue Ridge Mountains. It has a queen-size sleigh bed, two comfortable upholstered chairs, and floral wallpaper in greens, sand, rust and deep red. This is one of the less expensive rooms.

At the other end of the scale, the Sunrise Suite, with a 10-foot ceiling and year-round sunporch, has two plaid wing-back chairs and a king-size bed dressed with a deep green spread that sets off the tan of the marbled wallpaper and the wine, navy, and green in its trim. All the second-floor rooms are grouped around a second living room.

Because the new innkeepers come from a different world (they were both New York lawyers), they have retained Zantui Rose as assistant innkeeper while they "learn the ropes." From what we've seen so far, they have the fundamentals down pretty well already. Larry puts the coffee on at 7:30 A.M.

They offer early-evening wine and cheese to give guests a chance to chat with them and with one another. A particularly nice gathering spot is the sun porch. When the windows are open you can hear all kinds of birds singing—the same sound that is said to have inspired Bartók.

The Sklars are working continuously to improve the inn and their service as innkeepers. The building, listed on the National Register of Historic Places, is in Grove Park, a nice residential section of Asheville, convenient to downtown and some fine restaurants.

HOW TO GET THERE: From I-240 at Asheville, take the Charlotte Street exit. Go north on Charlotte Street about $^9/_{10}$ mile to Edgemont Road. Turn right and drive another $^2/_{10}$ mile. The driveway is marked with a sign.

Cedar Crest Victorian Inn
Asheville, North Carolina 28803

INNKEEPERS: Jack and Barbara McEwan

ADDRESS/TELEPHONE: 674 Biltmore Avenue; (704) 252-1389 or (800) 252-0310; fax (828) 253-7667

WEB SITE: www.cedarcrestvictorianinn.com

E-MAIL: stay@cedarcrestvictorianinn.com

ROOMS: 8, plus 1 suite and 2 suites in guest cottage; all with private bath; suites with service kitchen and parlor, all with telephone, some with wheelchair access, some with fireplace. Smoking in designated areas on veranda only.

RATES: $135 to $220, double; single $6.00 less; full breakfast and afternoon and evening refreshments.

OPEN: Year-round.

FACILITIES AND ACTIVITIES: English gardens and croquet lawn. Nearby: restaurants, Biltmore House, crafts and antiques shops; easy access to the Blue Ridge Parkway and mountain activities.

*I*nnkeeper Jack McEwan talks of Cedar Crest as a kind of antidote to the Biltmore House, the famous mansion tourists come to Asheville to see. At the Biltmore House, everything is so massive, there are so many rooms, the furniture and art are so overwhelming, that you really can't relate to it. Then you return to Cedar Crest and see work of equal quality, purportedly done by some of the same craftsmen, in something closer to human scale.

Not that Cedar Crest is a modest little cottage. It's an 1890 Queen Anne–style Victorian mansion, so filled with splendid features that we think you'd have to stay about thirty days to see everything. The woodwork, first-

generation oak, is elaborate and different in every room: heavy and masculine in the library, for instance, and delicately ornate in the dining room.

Among other features we could absorb during our visit of less than thirty days: a grand corner fireplace with fluted columns, a beveled mirror, a gilded cherub, and splendid stained-glass windows in the foyer. In what used to be the maid's room, is a secret closet once used for hiding silverware. In one bathroom is what Jack swears is the largest tub (6 feet long) in Western North Carolina and in another what he says is the smallest tub (4 feet long). We noticed some pencil marks on the door frame of one of the bedrooms indicating the height to which "John" had grown in 1907.

A relatively recent addition to this B&B inn is what the McEwans called The Celebration Suite, a spacious third-floor retreat that simply oozes romance. The McEwans made a fabulous garland for the head of the bed in which wisteria vines, gauzy lace, Italian lights, cherubs, and flowers are artfully intermingled. This suite also has a two-person whirlpool tub and a television.

It all would have intimidated us almost as much as the Biltmore House were it not for Jack and Barbara's enthusiasm and apparently endless willingness to talk about the inn. They have backgrounds in the hotel business and a finely developed sense of hospitality. Being a guest at Cedar Crest goes beyond awe over the features of the building. The best example we can think of, and one Carol noticed immediately, is that after the guest-room sheets are laundered, Barbara insists on having them dried on a clothesline in the sun. In this day of automatic dryers, we feel a line-dried sheet is almost more of a wonder than a Victorian mansion. The English gardens and croquet lawn are just above what Barbara calls her "Victorian linen garden." The cottage sits just above this area.

Another aspect of the McEwans' hospitality is their willingness to help you find the best place for dinner. Asheville has lots of good food. One of their favorite places to recommend is the Weaverville Milling Company, a restaurant serving veal, steaks, trout, and the like in a building that was a grain mill from 1912 to 1965.

HOW TO GET THERE: Take exit 50 or 50B from I-40 in Asheville. After the exit, stay in the right lane to Biltmore Avenue. The inn is 1¼ miles north of I-40.

Richmond Hill Inn
Asheville, North Carolina 28006

INNKEEPER: Susan Michel

ADDRESS/TELEPHONE: 87 Richmond Hill Drive; (828) 252-7313 or (888) 742-4565; fax (828) 252-8726

WEB SITE: www.richmondhillinn.com

ROOMS: 12 in mansion, 15 garden house rooms, and 9 croquet cottages; all with private bath, telephone, and television; some with gas-log fireplace and Jacuzzi; 1 with wheelchair access. No smoking in guest rooms.

RATES: $135 to $375, per room; includes full breakfast and afternoon tea. Two-night minimum on weekends.

OPEN: Year-round.

FACILITIES AND ACTIVITIES: Dinner. Beer and wine available. Library, conference facilities, croquet court, gardens, waterfalls. Nearby: Biltmore House, Folk Art Center, crafts and antiques shops, Great Smoky Mountains National Park, Blue Ridge Parkway.

This is a luxurious inn with a heroic saved-from-the-wrecking-ball story. The century-old mansion was the home of a former congressman and diplomat, Richmond Pearson, and his wife, Gabrielle. It was one of the most innovative and elegant homes of its time. But it outlasted the people who wanted to live that way and could afford it. Toward the end, the Pearsons' daughter, Marjorie, then an elderly woman, lived alone in it, using just one room.

In subsequent sales and maneuvering, the building was scheduled to be torn down and then reprieved several times. Many community organizations, including the Preservation Society, campaigned and raised money to try to save the mansion. They also found the Michel family, who were willing to buy and restore it. It was moved, all in one piece, to its current spot on the hill.

The building was preserved where possible, and restored or re-created where necessary, with fidelity to the mansion's original state. Much work was done by hand as it would originally have been, rather than with electric tools. Now listed on the National Register of Historic Places, it is considered one of the best examples of a Queen Anne–style mansion remaining. It's a "must see" if you are interested in architecture and preservation.

Because of the fine woodwork, soaring ceilings, and generously sized rooms, the mansion makes a fine inn. Some guest rooms are named for Pearson family members who once lived in them, others for important guests

and, on the third floor, for Asheville-connected writers, such as Carl Sandburg. Each writer's room has a picture of the writer and a collection of his or her books.

Also re-creating the past, several hundred of Mr. Pearson's own books have been recovered and placed in the inn library along with books about North Carolina and those by North Carolina authors.

The restaurant reflects the mansion's history in being named "Gabrielle's," after Mrs. Pearson. The food, however, is clearly a product of modern times. Considered American and nouvelle cuisine, it features lighter sauces and more healthful preparation than earlier haute cuisine. We have been disappointed so often when we try crab cakes that we have almost given up ordering them. Gabrielle's turned out to be a wonderful exception, using jumbo lump crab meat in a striking presentation flanked by strips of red corn tortilla chips and laced with a grilled tomato–roasted pepper sauce. Fabulous!

The entree was a perfectly prepared filet mignon. A small sweet-corn flan and whipped Yukon Gold potatoes extended the effect of the filet while adding their own mild flavor in combination with a wonderful hunter sauce.

HOW TO GET THERE: From I–240, take the 19/23 Weaverville exit. Continue on 19/23 and turn at exit 251 (UNC–Asheville). Turn left at the bottom of the ramp. At the first stoplight, turn left again onto Riverside Drive. Turn right on Pearson Bridge Road and cross the bridge. At the sharp curve, turn right on Richmond Hill Drive. The mansion is at the top of the hill.

The Inn at Brevard
Brevard, North Carolina 28712

INNKEEPERS: The Yager family

ADDRESS/TELEPHONE: 410 East Main Street; (828) 884–2105; fax (828) 885–7996

ROOMS: 5 in main house; 10 in adjacent lodge; all with private bath. All lodge rooms are air-conditioned and have cable television. Smoking allowed only in some lodge rooms.

RATES: $79 to $150; includes full breakfast. Extra person in double room, $10. Inquire about off-season discounts and children's rates. Two-night minimum or $8.00 service charge on holidays and weekends.

OPEN: Year-round.

FACILITIES AND ACTIVITIES: Dining room Easter through Thanksgiving. All ABC permits. Brunch, Sunday only, 11:30 A.M. to 2:00 P.M.; dinner, Thursday and Saturday, 5:00 to 9:00 P.M. Meeting and banquet rooms. Nearby: Brevard Music Center, Pisgah National Forest, the Blue Ridge Parkway.

In 1998 the Yager family took over this wonderful Greek Revival inn from its former owners, Eileen and Bertrand Bourgets. For a number of years the Bourgets had added their own personal touch to this historic mansion and its adjacent lodge, which gave the property a somewhat New England/Irish flavor.

The Yagers have a different view of the property: They want to restore it to its Southern roots. Carpets are being taken up and the original heart-pine floors exposed and refinished. Fay Yager tells us, "We'd always heard that the original floors were badly damaged. What a wonderful surprise we had when we removed the carpeting and found the original heart pine in almost perfect condition. All it needed was a little sanding and cleaning—and a good coat of wax.

"Another wondrous surprise was when we moved into the bedrooms and discovered the fireplaces. The hearths had been covered over with plywood, flooring tile, and carpet; the actual fireplaces had been boarded over, and in some cases the mantels had been either covered over or removed  and stored. We are restoring all of them to their original beauty—and where we did not have the original, we have found a wonderful local craftsman who has built replicas from the pieces we do have."

Paints have been researched and true, bright period colors are being reapplied (blues, yellows, and even bright reds). The Yagers are also upgrading all the furniture with antiques and period reproductions. They've even found the bed that the Reconstruction governor of North Carolina slept in during his term in office.

This is still a work in progress, so we can't say for sure how it will all come out. But with the dedication the Yager family has shown thus far, the inn is a jewel that will shine even more brightly than it has in the past.

In the meantime, what about the food?

Fay's breakfast features three full courses: The first is a fruit dish, coffee (or tea), and juice; the second is a hot or cold cereal course; and the final is a hot entree such as Belgian waffles with pecans and blueberries. It makes our mouths water just thinking about it. The dinner menu will also return to more traditional, fine Southern cuisine.

By the time this edition of the book is out, the inn will be up and running, replete with its new clothes—stop by and see all the improvements.

HOW TO GET THERE: The inn is on Route 276 in the center of town. If you take Route 64 into town, go east on Main Street.

Fryemont Inn
Bryson City, North Carolina 28713

INNKEEPERS: Sue and George Brown and Monica and George Brown, Jr.

ADDRESS/TELEPHONE: : Fryemont Road (mailing address: P.O. Box 459) (828) 488–2159 or (800) 845–4879; fax (828) 488–6586

WEB SITE: www.fryemontinn.com

ROOMS: 37 in main lodge, 7 suites in 3 cottages; all with private bath. No smoking inn.

RATES: $47.50 to $79.50 per person, double occupancy; breakfast and dinner. Inquire about children's rates.

OPEN: Mid-April through October. Cottage suites open year-round; no meals included in winter.

FACILITIES AND ACTIVITIES: Breakfast and dinner open to public by reservation, picnic lunches available, full bar. Swimming pool, craft-and-gift shop. Located in the Great Smoky Mountains. Nearby: Blue Ridge Parkway, rafting, horseback riding, boating, fishing, historic sites, the Cherokee Indian Reservation.

*B*eing in this inn makes you feel rustic without sacrificing any creature comforts. Just entering the lobby gives you a sense of being in a different world. It's a huge expanse of space, finished in wormy-chestnut board and batten, with a stone fireplace big enough to burn 8-foot logs. Couches and chairs are grouped for conversation in front of the fireplace and around the rest of the lobby, along with a couple of good-sized tables with chairs for games or cards.

The Browns and their staff practice the kind of easy hospitality that encourages people to talk to them and to one another.

This is the kind of place that would have to have a porch with rockers for hardcore relaxing as well as for watching the view of the Smoky Mountains.

The dining room, too, is just what the location calls for, a large room with many windows and another stone fireplace.

At dinner, you could begin with soup and salad. Your choice of entrees might include fresh mountain trout, turkey with pecan dressing, and prime rib. The vegetables are fresh, served family style. It's nice to be able to order good wine to go with such a meal.

Outside, the poplar shingles of the inn make it seem to be covered in bark in such a way that the building blends into the surrounding trees and landscape as though it were itself a growing thing.

Inside and outside, everything is clean, polished, mowed, trimmed—the kind of perfectly kept place in the woods we fantasize about. The good thing is that it's you in the rocker or by the pool and somebody else out there on the property doing the cleaning, polishing, mowing, and trimming.

HOW TO GET THERE: Follow Route 74 west to Bryson City. Take Exit 67. Go ³⁄₁₀ mile to Fryemont Road, on the right. This goes directly to the inn.

Hemlock Inn
Bryson City, North Carolina 28713

INNKEEPERS: Morris and Elaine White

ADDRESS/TELEPHONE: P.O. Drawer EE, Bryson City; (828) 488–2885; fax (282) 488–8985

ROOMS: 26; all with private bath; some with wheelchair access. No air-conditioning (elevation 2,300 feet).

RATES: $134 to $181, double; single $25 less; includes breakfast, dinner, and all gratuities. Inquire about long-term rates in cottages. Inquire about children's rates.

OPEN: Mid-April to first Sunday in November.

FACILITIES AND ACTIVITIES: Dining room open to public by reservation; no Sunday-evening meal, picnic lunches available on request. Shuffleboard courts, skittles, Ping-Pong, walking paths in the woods, wildflower tours. Located in the heart of the Great Smoky Mountains. Nearby: rafting, fishing, hiking, birding.

*W*e like everything about this place, even if it is basically just an old motel, especially the way guests are encouraged to slow down, unwind, and actively enjoy nature. The inn offers guests a calendar of bloom, compiled by the Tennessee Department of Conservation, listing the more familiar flowers you can find blooming in the Great Smoky Mountains National Park each month from March through September. You can walk in any direction and find flowers.

The inn sits on sixty-five wooded acres with a couple of miles of hiking trails. Even sitting on the porch puts you in touch with the out-of-doors in a gentle way. The view of valleys and mountains is magnificent, and the lawn and landscaping complement that view while introducing enough order so that you don't feel you are roughing it.

The rooms blend into the scene, too. They're furnished with country antiques and furniture made by local craftspeople. It's all comfortable without being so overbearing as to take your attention away from the scenery and growing plants.

Now, dinner might distract you. The Whites don't think that studying wildflowers should mean you have to eat lamb's-quarters and sorrel. Substantial home-style Southern cooking in generous quantities becomes the high point of the day for many guests. The food is served on lazy Susan tables, inviting you to help yourself as often as you like.

A typical dinner includes country-fried steak, baked chicken with dressing, green beans, frosted cauliflower, apple-carrot casserole, okra fritters, and chess pie. Let's go back to that "frosted cauliflower." It's cooked with a topping of cheese, mustard, and mayonnaise that zips up the flavor and imparts a colorful gloss to the cauliflower—hence the name "frosted." The rolls are homemade, of course, as are the pumpkin and apple chips to spread on them. These "chips" also need explanation. They're pieces of fruit in a thick syrup, like preserves, and so many guests have become addicted that the Whites now offer jars of pumpkin and apple chips for sale.

HOW TO GET THERE: The inn is just east of Bryson City, about a mile off Highway 19 on top of a small mountain. The turn is marked by a hemlock inn sign. When you make reservations, you will receive a highlighted map with full directions from all interstate highways in whatever direction you will be traveling.

Nantahala Village

Bryson City, North Carolina 28713

INNKEEPERS: John Burton and Jan Letendre

ADDRESS/TELEPHONE: 9400 Highway 19 West; (828) 488–2826 or (800) 438–1507; fax (828) 488–9634

WEB SITE: www.nvnc.com

E-MAIL: nvinfo@nvnc.com

ROOMS: 11, in main lodge; all with private bath and television; 50 cabins, cottages, and privately owned homes; all with private bath; some with television; some with fireplace. No smoking in public rooms.

RATES: $50 to $270, single or double; $10 each extra person in room over regular number, up to maximum allowed. Rates vary seasonally. Meals extra. Children under thirteen free.

OPEN: Mid-March to January 1.

FACILITIES AND ACTIVITIES: Restaurant open to guests and public three meals a day, weekend brunch. Brown bagging permitted. Swimming pool, tennis courts, volleyball court, Ping-Pong, horseshoes, hiking trails, horseback riding. Nearby: Great Smoky Mountains National Park, rafting, fishing, bicycling.

*N*antahala Village has been a special place over many years. The bad news is that the old lodge burned down in 1997. The good news is that a new lodge building opened in mid-1998 and is better than ever. The architecture is classic, the number of rooms has been reduced to eleven, the amenities upgraded, there are now six meeting rooms, and the view from the restaurant is still spectacular.

The Village covers 200 mountain acres, so the place lends itself to out-door recreation, but the rebuilt stone lodge is a cozy place to relax inside, too. The rooms are spacious, furnished in country-style furniture. The beds are good. The showers are hot. We've stayed in some of the cabins, when we were traveling with friends, and we found each experience there just right, too. Innkeepers John Burton and Jan Letendre take care to book guests into cab-ins that fit their situations—no cliff-edge cabins for people with little kids, a romantic cabin well away from everyone else for honeymooners, and so on.

The food here has always been good in the almost-Thanksgiving-dinner style, and still is, but you now have choices of vegetarian entrees and other lighter food as well. In addition to country ham, trout, and rib eye, for instance, you could try Wild Forest Pasta, with a cheesy sauce of herbs and vegetables. Spinach lasagna and mushroom-cheese pie are other new favorites. A children's menu is offered at each meal so that you can order the kinds of things kids like in quantities appropriate to their appetites.

The view of the mountains from the dining room is so breathtaking, we like to take a long time to eat. The view remains perfect, as ever. And now, with committed, enthusiastic new ownership, Nantahala Village gets better and better. That's good news for all of us who love the mountains and the Nantahala Gorge.

HOW TO GET THERE: The inn is 9 miles southwest of Bryson City on High-way 19.

High Hampton Inn and Country Club 🤍 🏠

Cashiers, North Carolina 28717

INNKEEPERS: W. D., Will, and Becky McKee

ADDRESS/TELEPHONE: P.O. Box 338; (828) 743–2411 or (800) 334–2551; fax (828) 743–5991

WEB SITE: www.highhamptoninn.com

E-MAIL: Information@HighHamptonInn.com or Reservations@HighHamptonInn.com

ROOMS: 117 rooms and cottages; all with private bath; some with fireplace.

RATES: $82 to $101 for rooms in the inn per person, double occupancy, depending on the season and whether midweek or weekend; $62 for an additional person in the room; $53 for a child under six in the room with two adults. Ask about rates for the cottages and the colony homes, which are rented by the week but can also be rented for less than a week with a three-night minimum. All include full American plan (three meals daily), afternoon tea, many of the sports and recreation facilities; alcoholic beverages are extra; five-day/four-night Thanksgiving package $130 per person, double occupancy; golf and tennis packages.

OPEN: Closed November through March, with the exception of Thanksgiving weekend.

FACILITIES AND ACTIVITIES: Restaurant, tavern, cafe, gift shop, tennis and golf pro shops, exercise room, pool table, Ping-Pong, playground; lake, exercise room, fishing, swimming, boating; eighteen-hole golf course, six clay tennis courts; hiking trails, fitness trail, mountain biking, summer children's program, bird walks; bridge lessons and tournaments, golf schools and tournaments, wildflower workshops, watercolor and other art workshops, literary conference, Teddy Bear Picnic.

BUSINESS TRAVEL: Meeting rooms; ideal place for executive retreats.

*W*e'd been hearing about High Hampton for years from two couples who traditionally visited the mountain inn and resort for the annual Thanksgiving house party. They continually raved about the ambience and the food, so finally we simply had to check it out for our-

selves. Much to our delight we learned that the inn is everything they said and much more. The day we drove up the winding drive was a crisp, clear fall day, and the inn stood out sharply against the dark green and brilliant yellow and orange background of leaves changing on the mountain that rises in the distance behind the inn. We immediately felt at home in the rustic, wood-paneled inn, where the ambience is casual. We instantly knew that although there was plenty to do, we could engage in our favorite vacation activity—doing nothing. We can certainly see why so many people couldn't get through the year without at least one visit to High Hampton.

High Hampton is a true mountain getaway, located as it is in the stunning Blue Ridge Mountains of western North Carolina 50 miles from Asheville and 70 miles from Greenville, South Carolina—the nearest cities. No superhighways penetrate this remote area, only winding two-lane roads with a waterfall, mountain peak, deep valley, or other spectacular sight around every turn.

One man's dream, High Hampton was the summer retreat of South Carolinian Wade Hampton—Civil War hero, Reconstruction governor of South Carolina, and United States Senator. The entire 1,400-acre estate remained in the Hampton family until 1922, when it was acquired by the McKee family, who began operating it as an inn. Second and third generations of McKees still offer you their hospitality.

The rustic architecture of the wood-frame inn and guest cottages blend with the natural beauty of the surroundings. We particularly loved the great stone four-sided fireplace in the lobby that folks gather around in cool weather. The public and guest rooms are all furnished with comfortable, mountain-crafted furniture. Very little changes here except the seasons.

Cozy guest rooms are paneled with natural woods from the estate, applied in a board-and-batten pattern. Small and basic, the rooms have rustic furnishings, simple bedspreads and curtains, and a private bath. Bedding ranges from twins to kings. There are no telephones or televisions (oh, happy day)—you'll find those in the lobby if you can't live without them. Most people come to High Hampton for the serenity, the unparalleled scenery, the good food, and the other guests, anyway.

If you need more room to spread out, there are suites as well as cottages and colony homes with varying floor plans. Many of the cottages offer fireplaces. The Honeymoon Cottage is about as picturesque as you can get. Located on the lake shore and with its own little dock, it is a log cabin with a wraparound deck, a fireplace, and a waterwheel. The privately owned colony homes feature a great room, fireplace, fully-equipped kitchen, two to four beds with private baths, television and VCR, telephone, and top-of-the-line furnishings. Although these are ideal for families or groups traveling together, we think you're missing a lot of what High Hampton is all about if you don't stay in the inn itself.

Dining at High Hampton is an epicurean experience. First of all, the rustic dining room has two walls of windows so that you can enjoy the majestic scenery while you dine. All meals are served buffet style, and dinner might include fried chicken, fresh local trout, or prime rib accompanied by delicious soups, salad from the salad bar, fresh vegetables, freshly baked bread, and tempting desserts. Guests are assigned their own table and their own wait staff for the duration of their stay. About the only concession to the outside world of rules is that coats and ties are required for gentlemen for the evening meal—a relic of the past we cherish.

Another culinary tradition at High Hampton is Afternoon Tea, a holdover from a slower paced era when people made time for leisure and conversation. Today's guests find this afternoon break over tea, coffee, and cakes an excellent opportunity to get to know one another. Don't fill up so much that you spoil your dinner, though. Music and dancing are there for your enjoyment in the Rock Mountain Tavern, and other evening activities and entertainment are posted on the bulletin board.

The McKees know how to make you feel welcome. Last year Dan called the inn on Thanksgiving morning, fully expecting some staff person to say they were busy with the annual feast. Instead he talked to W. D. himself, who encouraged us to put the laptop in the car and "come up for the weekend."

Just so you'll know: High Hampton does not add a service charge to your bill, and it is not necessary to tip. For those who can't be parted from their pets, there are kennels.

HOW TO GET THERE: High Hampton is located near the intersection of U.S. 64 and NC 107 in Cashiers.

Jarrett House
Dillsboro, North Carolina 28725

INNKEEPERS: Jim and Jean Hartbarger

ADDRESS/TELEPHONE: Dillsboro (mailing address: P.O. Box 219); (828) 586–0265 or (800) 972–5623

WEB SITE: www.preation.com/jarretthouse/index.html

ROOMS: 18; all with private bath; some with wheelchair access. No smoking inn.

RATES: $70 to $80 per person, single or double; $5.00 each additional person; full breakfast included in room rate. No credit cards.

OPEN: April to October.

FACILITIES AND ACTIVITIES: Lunch, dinner; dining room, with wheelchair access, open to public; brown bagging permitted. "Eatin' and talkin' and rockin'."—Jim Hartbarger

*J*arrett House is famous for its food, so we'll tell you about that first. It's been a matter of pride since the inn began business back in the 1800s that the table be so generous that no one should ever have to ask for seconds. All we can say is that anybody who would dare eat more than is offered had better bring along a couple of Weight Watchers counselors.

For lunch try the country ham or fried chicken. That is the only choice except for a beverage. Everything else comes automatically—green beans, slaw, pickled beets with onion, candied apples, browned potatoes, and a seemingly endless supply of the lightest little biscuits you've ever tasted. A squeeze bottle on the table is filled with honey for the biscuits. Jim says that

after a full season he sometimes gets a little tired of country ham and fried chicken, but he never gets tired of those biscuits!

After all that, you'll wish you could order a cot to take a nap. And that's just lunch. After a big dinner here, a hospital bed may be called for.

But after-meal dozing is what the rockers on the porch are for.

For serious sleeping, the guest rooms, furnished in oak, walnut, and cherry antiques, are nice. Everything is squeaky clean, a feeling enhanced by the white chenille bedspreads. Most of the rooms have claw-footed bathtubs.

The double-wide hallway upstairs is lined with well-used antiques, old sewing machines, an unusual oak desk, and an interesting oak washstand. It all looks as if someone will be using it again in the next hour or so—no museum feeling here.

Downstairs, the Victorian parlor is almost eerie in the feeling it gives you that any second the old inhabitants will come in and sit down. In one corner, an old Bacon & Ravern piano that belonged to Jim's grandmother is partly covered by a lovely folded lace tablecloth. On the wall is a framed hanging of the Lord's Prayer that she crocheted when she was ninety-two years old. Something about its intricate detail and beauty makes just looking at it a prayerful act.

The sense of family pervades this inn in another manner, too. Jim and Jean's sons, Scott and Buzz, and their wives, Mary and Sharon, are all involved in its operation. To quote Jim, "We have acquired a legend and we will continue the tradition. . . ."

HOW TO GET THERE: Dillsboro is 47 miles west of Asheville. Routes 19A/441 and 23/19A form an intersection in town. The inn is on the corner at the intersection.

The Lords Proprietors' Inn
Edenton, North Carolina 27932

INNKEEPERS: Arch and Jane Edwards

ADDRESS/TELEPHONE: 300 North Broad Street; (919) 482-3641;
fax (919) 482-2432

WEB SITE: www.lordspropedenton.com

E-MAIL: reserv@lordspropedenton.com

ROOMS: 20; all with private bath, television, VCR, and telephone.

RATES: $225 to $275 MAP; $155 to $190 B&B (Sunday and
Monday only).

FACILITIES AND ACTIVITIES: Gift shop. Nearby: restaurants,
waterfront parks, guided walking tours of Edenton Historic District,
Hope Plantation tours, Somerset Place tours.

BUSINESS TRAVEL: Telephone and good work space in room,
fax available.

This inn has earned a reputation as one of the most elegant and gracious inns in the state. Three separate restored buildings—the White-Bond House, the Satterfield House, and the Pack House—in the historic district cluster around a lawn and gardens; these buildings house the guest rooms, three big parlors, and a library. Breakfast and dinner are served at the Whedbee House, set on a brick patio surrounded by dogwoods in the center of the complex. The Pack House was originally a tobacco barn that was sawed in half and brought to the grounds in two pieces. Its conversion created lodging with huge amounts of open space, vast floors, and soaring ceilings. The guest rooms open onto a balcony that runs around the inside of the building and overlooks the common rooms. The feeling of openness is accentuated by old pine floors that are covered only with area rag rugs, and a whimsical Brunschwig and Fils wallpaper border that runs around the room above the chair rail. Old chests and chintz upholstery fit comfortably into the scene.

Dinner at the inn, served only to guests, gets raves. The chef, Kevin Yokley, offers entrees ranging from roasted rabbit and pork with a porcini mushroom sauce to striped bass with a pistachio vinaigrette. The entrees change daily.

Edenton is on the Albermarle Sound. It differs from many waterfront communities in having kept the waterfront for parks and homes rather than commercial activities.

Edenton boasts a lot of history. Settled in 1685 and incorporated in 1722 as the first capital of the province of North Carolina, the town has kept alive the memories of its early leaders, men who signed the Declaration of Independence, supplied Washington's army in defiance of British blockades, and convinced the people of North Carolina to ratify the new United States Constitution.

Many of the people in the community are direct descendants of those early leaders. Those descendants and others who care have turned virtually the entire community into a project of historic preservation.

Arch and Jane Edwards have been deeply involved in the community and value their inn's place in it. Their hospitality extends to inviting guests to use their residential swimming pool and to tour their private home, Mount Auburn, an authentically restored waterfront plantation house of the 1800s.

HOW TO GET THERE: Edenton is 90 miles east of I–95 at the junction of Highways 17 and 32. Broad Street runs through the center of town.

Highland Lake Inn 🏛
Flat Rock, North Carolina 28731

INNKEEPER: Carrie Smith; Kerry and Larc Lindsey, owners

ADDRESS/TELEPHONE: Highland Lake Drive (mailing address: P.O. Box 1026); (828) 693–6812 or (800) 762–1376; fax (828) 696–8951

WEB SITE: www.highlandlake.com

E-MAIL: webmaster@highlandlake.com

ROOMS: 20 in lodge, 15 in inn, 10 cabins, 6 cottages; all with private bath, telephone, and television, except rooms in lodge; some with fireplace; some with whirlpool; some with wheelchair access and facilities for handicapped. No smoking inn.

RATES: $89 to $164, double, for rooms in cabins, lodge, and inn; single $10 less; breakfast extra. Children five and under free. Inquire about cottage rates.

OPEN: Year-round.

FACILITIES AND ACTIVITIES: Restaurant; Olympic-sized pool, lake, canoes, tennis, fishing, volleyball; one hundred acres of walking trails.

BUSINESS TRAVEL: Telephone and excellent work space in cabins; conference facilities.

egardless of what we tell you about Highland Lake Inn (and Conference Center), you'll find something more when you get there. This is a dream-in-process. The dreamers—Kerry, his brother, Larc, his parents, and other siblings—all stay involved with everything that happens. This place, which in earlier years variously functioned as a club, a boys' school, and a camp, has almost as many personalities as Sibyl. It's been an inn and conference center since 1985, a place that delights all who experience it, but somehow it has remained a secret from most of us. Perhaps the most fascinating thing about it is that Kerry and the family are creating a self-sufficient compound. That's the dream. The restaurant serves vegetables and herbs organically grown on the property; bakers make bread from Arrowhead Mills' organically grown grains, which are stone-ground in the inn's kitchen; eggs come from free-range chickens. If you stay in a cabin, you'll probably burn wood that was cut on the property in the fireplace.

Plans in the works include a closed-system fish farm for trout and tilapia. The overall concept is known, these days, as permaculture, a more sophisticated and realistic version of the homestead concept some of us tried to implement in the 1970s and 1980s.

The significance of all this to you, even if you don't care about such things in general, is threefold: First, the food has taste, texture, and color. If

you are one of those who complains that tomatoes don't taste like tomatoes anymore, wait until you eat here! When you taste an egg with a brilliant bright-yellow yolk produced by a free-range chicken, you'll be angry at the tastelessness mass-produced eggs force upon us.

Second, you can bring kids here to learn how to take an egg out of a chicken nest; watch goats being milked; see vegetables growing in family-sized gardens; and roam freely through lawns, and fields, and woods. The place is not totally self-sufficient and may never be, but children can get a sense of how it works.

Finally, this place is pretty, comfortable, and "far from the madding crowd," with lots of outdoor things to do, pleasant places for doing nothing at all, and, of course, that fabulous food.

So, we are discovering Highland Lake. Who knows what will have been added when you get here? Wood-fired bake ovens? More fruit and vegetable crops? Larger greenhouses?

Whatever. It will be wonderful.

HOW TO GET THERE: From I–26, take exit 22 and go west on Upward Road, which becomes Highland Lake Road at U.S. Highway 176. The entrance is at the waterfall; follow signs up the driveway to the office.

The Woodfield Inn
Flat Rock, North Carolina 28731

INNKEEPERS: Rhonda and Michael Horton

ADDRESS/TELEPHONE: U.S. 25 South; (828) 693–6016 or (800) 533–6016; fax (828) 693–0437

WEB SITE: www.woodfieldinn.com

ROOMS: 18 rooms; all with private bath and king- or queen-size bed; some with fireplace, whirlpool, and/or television; no telephones.

RATES: $119 to $169, includes breakfast; weekend package available for the annual Civil War reenactment includes two breakfasts, two dinners, tickets for both days, and tickets to the Southern Jubilee Ball.

OPEN: Year-round.

FACILITIES AND ACTIVITIES: Restaurant, verandas, patio, gift shop, walking trails, annual Civil War reenactment in September. Nearby: Flat Rock Playhouse, Carl Sandburg Historic Site, antiques and crafts shopping, casual and fine dining, hiking.

BUSINESS TRAVEL: Meeting space, secretarial assistance and audiovisual equipment for meetings; pavilion and gazebo for special functions.

*I*t was a bright, sunny Easter Sunday with a startlingly blue sky. Cheery tulips and daffodils danced in the gentle breeze. Folks began to drift in from church in their Sunday-go-to-meeting clothes. Families with little boys looking less than comfortable in their suits and giggling little girls in frilly dresses and ruffled socks lined up on the inn's veranda steps for their parents to take pictures for posterity. We had just visited the Carl Sandburg Historic Site practically next door and now waited patiently on the veranda for our turn at brunch in the dining room, taking advantage of the comfortable Flat Rock rockers in the meantime. Other parents rocked while children raced around the velvety lawns. It could have been any Easter since this wonderful inn was built as a stagecoach stop in 1852, when the highlands area was known as the Little Charleston of the Mountains because so many Low Country families escaped there from the oppressive heat of summer.

Steeped in history and romance, the inviting three-story inn sits on twenty-eight acres well back from the road on a rise at the top of a circular drive. Its most distinguishing feature is its double tier of verandas with their unusual double-X railings and deeply curved brackets topping the second-story columns. Inside, high ceilings, hardwood floors, and simple moldings characterize the unpretentious, yet appealing rooms. Victorian  antiques and curios adorn both public and guest chambers. Be sure to check out the huge hand-carved ebony chest large enough to hide an elephant and ask about the secret room where Confederate soldiers hid not only gold and silver but also the ladies of the house from Union troops, renegades, and scallywags from remote mountain coves. When the weather doesn't permit waiting and socializing out on the verandas, diners and guests alike gather around the fireplace in the graceful formal parlor, which is warmly furnished with Victorian-era antiques and accented with rich colors and interesting accessories as well as games, books, and magazines.

Upstairs, eighteen restful guest bed chambers all offer private baths. Many of them also boast gas-log fireplaces and French doors opening onto the veranda with majestic vistas in the distance. Two very special rooms sport whirlpool tubs. Different style beds from four-posters to sleigh beds as well as carefully chosen bed coverings and window treatments give every guest room distinct personality. Not at all overdone, the simple rooms are painted in warm, deep colors and adorned with just enough artwork and accessories to make them interesting without being overpowering. We wish we could have spent the night instead of merely passing through.

Breakfast is a substantial affair that begins with a generous bread basket, juice, and hot beverages. Don't fill up too much, though, because you'll soon be treated to a hot entree ranging from scrambled eggs to French toast to waffles and breakfast meats accompanied by such hearty side dishes as grits and/or hash browns.

Ample country-size portions are served to guests and the public for dinner and Sunday brunch at Squire's restaurant. Three dining rooms provide enough space for a crowd but still offer window tables and little out-of-the-way nooks intimate enough for a romantic meal à deux. Antique coverlets adorn the walls and the cozy fireplace blazes in cool weather. Walls of windows in the Garden Dining Room let the outdoors in—a particularly pleasant state of affairs in the spring and fall when the grounds blaze with color.

Dinner entrees might feature prime beef, North Carolina trout, pork chops, or tenderloin medallions accompanied by a bread basket, salad, and fresh vegetables. Wild turkey and swordfish make an appearance in season. A groaning-board Sunday brunch features eggs Benedict, other egg dishes, French toast, waffles, bacon, sausage, pork chops, breads, vegetables, and cobblers. Begin or end any meal with a Woodfield Inn tradition: Lemon Juleps, a lemon and whiskey drink with a twist of lemon peel instead of mint, on the veranda.

HOW TO GET THERE: The Woodfield Inn is located on U.S. 25, 2½ miles from Hendersonville. From I–26, take U.S. 64 west to Hendersonville, then turn south on U.S. 25. Pass through the town of Flat Rock. The inn is on the right just past the Carl Sandburg Historic Site.

Flat Rock Rockers

One of the previous owners of The Woodfield Inn was Squire Henry T. Farmer of the prominent Charleston family who made Flat Rock a popular summer destination for society's elite. During his tenure the inn was known as the Farmer Hotel, and even today the restaurant is called Squire's in his honor.

Something that annoyed Squire Farmer immensely was that no matter what kind of rockers he bought for the verandas, they creaked and crept across the floor when rocked. He put his brain and talents to work and developed a black-walnut rocker that didn't creep. These rockers were so well liked by visitors to the inn that they wanted to buy them, so he opened a furniture factory nearby to produce them. Unfortunately, the factory was forced to close down during the Civil War and his exact design has never been duplicated. Fortunately for all of us, two of those very original rockers survive and are actually in use on the veranda. (We can't believe they're not in a museum.) Try one out for yourself.

Innisfree Victorian Inn 💙
Glenville, North Carolina 28736

INNKEEPERS: Teri Federico and Brenda Crickenger; Henry Hoche, owner

ADDRESS/TELEPHONE: Highway 107 North (P.O. Box 469); (828) 743-2946

WEB SITE: www.innisfreeinn.com.

ROOMS: 10 rooms and suites; all with private bath, clock radio, ceiling fan; some with fireplace or woodstove, whirlpool tub, telephone, television with VCR, refrigerator.

RATES: Rates for the rooms in the main house are $119 to $249 week nights and during the off-season (November through May) and $150 to $290 for weekends and the peak season; $159-$239 week nights and off-season and $175 to $275 weekends and peak season for suites in the Garden House; based on single or double occupancy; includes candlelight breakfast in the tower for inn guests or breakfast delivered to the suite for Garden House guests, afternoon hospitality hour, Irish coffee by the fireplace in the evening, and Godiva chocolates; weekends require a two-night minimum, holidays a three-night minimum; wedding, honeymoon, and anniversary packages. Only the Garden House is suitable for children.

OPEN: Year-round.

FACILITIES AND ACTIVITIES: Gardens, verandas, walking trails, hammock, gazebo, private beach, games, small gift shop. Nearby: water sports, boat rentals, fishing, tennis, golf, hiking, snow skiing, antiques and crafts shopping, restaurants.

e have our dear friends Gelia and Tom Dolcimascolo to thank for recommending this delightful four-diamond B&B inn to us, but our own experience was even more magical because of the time of year. We're crazy about Christmas, so you can just imagine how enchanted we were to see the lavish Victorian decorations at Innisfree. Our first glimpse was of what seemed like miles of garlands draped around two stories of wraparound verandas and decks. Inside, a magnificent Christmas tree reached to the cathedral ceiling.

Even if you're not lucky enough to visit Innisfree at Christmastime, there are plenty of Victorian furnishings and accessories to admire. First, the stately house itself. Although it was built in 1989, it has many of the Victorian characteristics you'd expect—gables, verandas, gingerbread, and, the

most obvious, a three-story turret (more about it later). Perched on a hillside on twelve acres, the house boasts walls of windows overlooking Lake Glenville—the highest lake east of the Rockies—with the Blue Ridge Mountains providing a backdrop.

All the ornate moldings and woodwork that were so prevalent in turn-of-the-century mansions may be too costly to replicate, but the cathedral ceiling in the great room simulates the high ceilings of yore, and the marble mantelpiece is just as grand as any you'd see in a century-old house. Exuberantly furnished, the great room, breakfast room, and guest rooms feature antiques and reproductions, Oriental carpets, and carefully chosen accessories from years of world travel. Under the eaves is an informal observatory/TV/game room equipped with binoculars. Guest chambers are divided between the main house and a smaller garden house.

Every guest room or suite features a firm mattress, fine linens, plush towels, and good reading light, but each has its own charms. In the main house, rooms are named for Queen Victoria and Prince Albert as well as the English cities of Cambridge, Canterbury, and Windsor. The Queen Victoria Suite, the grandest of them all, boasts a tray ceiling; bay window; massive, ornate canopy bed; whirlpool bath; and even a bidet. The Windsor Room has a fireplace and an Italian lavatory with hand-painted blue irises and gilded dolphin faucets. Exotic Chinese headboards are the focal point in the Prince Albert Suite and Canterbury Room. The Cambridge Room features a private porch and separate entrance.

The Garden House, a small Dutch Colonial–style house with its own turret, located down the hill from the main house, contains five suites named for English authors: Lord Tennyson, Elizabeth Barrett, Emily Brontë, Charles Dickens, and Robert Browning. Offering more privacy than the big house, these suites boast a fireplace, wet bar, refrigerator, telephone (although why would you want one?), and a fireplace—some of them double-sided so that you can enjoy the fire in your bedroom and, the height of luxury, in your bathroom. Several offer garden tubs for two with spectacular views out the window. Because the tower dining area won't accommodate more guests than those staying in the main house, breakfast and evening liqueurs are brought to the Garden House Suites. Guests here will want to join those in the main house for afternoon refreshments, however.

We promised to say more about the turret or tower. Open to its rafters and surrounded with stained-glass windows, it is the striking setting for the ample breakfast of egg dishes, breakfast meats, juices, fruits, special breads, and hot beverages. You'll feel like royalty feasting by candlelight under the ornate chandelier. Later, whether you've had a strenuous day hiking, a leisurely day shopping for mountain crafts, or a do-nothing day with a good book, you'll enjoy gathering with your fellow guests for afternoon refreshments on the veranda in good weather or around a crackling fire in the great room in inclement weather. After you return from dinner Irish coffee and hot chocolate are waiting, and you'll find a Godiva chocolate on your pillow at bedtime.

HOW TO GET THERE: From U.S. 64 in Cashiers, turn north on NC 107 and go 6 miles. Watch for the signs to the inn on the left.

The Waverly Inn
Hendersonville, North Carolina 28792

INNKEEPERS: John and Diane Sheiry, Darla Olmstead

ADDRESS/TELEPHONE: 783 North Main Street; (828) 693–9193 or (800) 537–8195; fax (828) 692–1010

WEB SITE: www.waverlyinn.com

E-MAIL: waverlyinn@ior.com

ROOMS: 13, plus 1 two-room suite; all with private bath and telephone; no smoking indoors.

RATES: $109 to $149, double; $90, single; $165 to $185, suite; includes full breakfast.

OPEN: Year-round.

FACILITIES AND ACTIVITIES: Nearby: restaurants, hiking, tennis, miniature golf, antiques and crafts shops; easy drive to Biltmore Estate, Carl Sandburg home, Flat Rock Playhouse.

The Waverly opened its doors in 1898 and has never been closed since. Many of the guests come back year after year to this B&B inn to cool off. Hendersonville is a mountain town where people have gone for years to escape the summer heat. Even on the hottest days you can expect to sleep under blankets at night. But don't worry about unexpected heat waves. All rooms are air-conditioned just in case.

John and Diane Sheiry each have more than twenty years' experience in the hotel business. They chose Hendersonville and The Waverly because they wanted to get out of the fast-track life that kept John traveling most of the time and made it hard for them to nurture family life. It's not that they work less as keepers of a small inn but that now they can work together, at home. In recent years they have contributed a high level of innkeeping professionalism to the area.

Diane's sister, Darla, as third innkeeper, adds another family dimension to the mix.

Their values line up beautifully with the family orientation that has traditionally been typical of The Waverly, but there is growth here, too. These days, The Waverly attracts guests in addition to those escaping the heat: overnight travelers looking for a place more interesting than a motel and vacationers looking for lodging with a personal feel. The result is a fascinating mix. You can see it on the porch—young travelers, middle-aged couples, retired people, and families with children, not just occupying rockers side by side, but talking and actually listening to one another.

It's a good setup for socializing. In addition to using the porch, guests can gather in the library or in the Victorian parlor, where a fireplace is the focal point on nippy evenings. There are sitting rooms on all three floors.

John and Diane have renovated extensively and have furnished the place with the kind of turn-of-the-century mix you'd have expected to find originally in such a home.

Waverly still emphasizes service so complete you can only think of it as personal favors. John said, "We dote on our guests. We'll take you to church, get your car fixed, answer questions, and get your travel information."

Two additions to the inn's activities, Murder Mystery weekends and Wine

Lovers' weekends, each offered twice a year, are turning out to be a lot of fun for guests and for John and Diane. On weekends when these are scheduled, the inn accepts reservations only for people planning to participate, so you don't have to worry about arriving and finding yourself in the middle of *Murder, She Wrote* if that's not what you had in mind.

For the mystery weekends, the actors check in the same as any other guests, so you really have no idea who is a player and who is not until the whole thing is over. The wine weekends include a French meal and an Italian dinner, preceded by a tasting and discussion of five French or Italian wines and served with three more. Diane says that after either kind of weekend guests inevitably go home feeling they've made some new friends.

The Waverly Inn is listed on the National Register of Historic Places and is the oldest inn in Hendersonville.

HOW TO GET THERE: From I-26 take exit 18B, go west on Route 64 for 2 miles, then right on Main Street. The inn is 1 block up on the left.

Inn at Lake Lure 🏨 ⓒⓒ
Lake Lure, North Carolina 28746

INNKEEPER: Sherri Helps

ADDRESS/TELEPHONE: P.O. Box 10; (828) 625-2525 or (800) 277-5873; fax (828) 625-9655

WEB SITE: www.lakelureinn.com

E-MAIL: lakelureinn@wncguide.com

ROOMS: 50 rooms; all with private bath, desk with telephone, television, ceiling fan, coffeemaker.

RATES: $59 to $89 off-season, $109 to $150 in season, double occupancy, includes continental breakfast.

OPEN: Year-round.

FACILITIES AND ACTIVITIES: Restaurant (open only weekends during the off-season), informal dining porch, Moosehead Lounge, pool, Lake Lure, water sports. Nearby: casual and fine dining, antiques and crafts shops, Bat Cave, Chimney Rock Park, The Bottomless Pools, hiking, golf, boating, tennis, horseback riding, boat tours of Lake Lure.

BUSINESS TRAVEL: Twenty-five miles from Asheville; adjacent conference center will accommodate up to 125; several conference rooms, audiovisual equipment.

*W*hen it opened in 1928, the pleasant, three-story stucco Mediterranean-style hotel was called "the little Waldorf of the South," and it attracted such distinguished visitors as Calvin Coolidge, F. Scott Fitzgerald, Franklin D. Roosevelt, and Emily Post. During World War II it served as a place of rest and relaxation for Air Force officers. In more recent years, movie stars Patrick Swayze and Jennifer Grey stayed here during the filming of *Dirty Dancing*. Located across the road from a quiet cove on

Lake Lure, which *National Geographic* has called the most beautiful manmade lake in the country, the small hotel is backed by rocky escarpments and tree-covered mountains. With its historic building and long tradition of Southern hospitality, the inn is a member of the National Trust for Historic Preservation's Historic Hotels of America.

More standard than you'd expect from all these accolades, the inn is a comfortable place to stay with a family. Upgraded rooms feature period reproduction furniture; the rest are furnished with standard motel/hotel issue, but all have spectacular views of the lake or the mountains and the usual hotel amenities: telephone, television, and coffeemaker.

Public areas include the long columned lobby with comfortable seating areas—which doubles as a special events function area—a formal restaurant, informal restaurant, cozy bar, two terraces, and a swimming pool.

A complimentary continental breakfast of pastries, hot and cold cereals, fresh fruits and juices, and hot beverages is served each morning on the sun-porch or in the informal restaurant. White linen service for dinner and Sunday brunch are offered in the Tanner Dining Room. This handsome room features a fireplace with an ornate mantle, columns throughout, a wall of windows opening to a terrace and the pool, and antique sideboards and china cabinets. The varied menu features steak, chicken, and seafood dishes. You can choose from such specialties as smoked trout and crab cakes, old-fashioned venison stew, chicken with dumplings, linguine and shrimp, or roast duck, then finish off with desserts such as bread and raisin pudding with rum sauce or Lake Lure Mud Pie. The lavish Sunday brunch is extremely popular with residents as well as visitors.

Dominating the very small and cozy Moosehead Lounge is, of course, a gigantic moose head (when we saw it at Christmastime, it was jauntily adorned with a big red bow) as well as an ornately carved and mirrored bar back. Seating is at the bar and several high tables.

The inn is conveniently located across the street from the town beach and features a boardwalk to the town park and marina, which is equipped with picnic tables and is the departure point for boat tours of the lake. Interesting shops are nearby.

HOW TO GET THERE: The inn is located on U.S. 64/74 southeast of Asheville. You can take scenic U.S. 74 from Asheville or come south on I–26 to exit 18A and turn east on U.S. 64. From the south, take U.S. 108 to U.S. 9 and turn north to Lake Lure.

The Lodge on Lake Lure ♥
Lake Lure, North Carolina 28746

INNKEEPERS: Jack and Robin Stanier

ADDRESS/TELEPHONE: Charlotte Drive (mailing address: Route One, Box 519A); (828) 625-2789 or (800) 733-2785; fax (828) 625-2421

WEB SITE: www.lodgeonlakelure.com

E-MAIL: Info@lodgeonlakelure.com

ROOMS: 12; all with private bath, 1 with deck and fireplace.

RATES: $99 to $149, single or double; includes full gourmet breakfast. Inquire about discounts for mid-week or week-long stays; $15 for additional person; two-night minimum on weekends, three-night minimum on holidays; high season is April through November.

OPEN: Year-round.

FACILITIES AND ACTIVITIES: Lakefront, fishing, three canoes, boathouse and boat rentals. Nearby: restaurants, two golf courses, hiking, tubing, tennis, horseback riding, antiques and crafts shops.

"Our guests love our guests," Jack told us in summing up this B&B inn's ambience. We certainly hit it off with the innkeepers and several couples we met there. It was December and there was a nip to the air, so in the evening we all settled in by one of the fireplaces and got to know one another over several bottles of Biltmore Estate wine we'd each bought that day.

This wonderful ambience isn't an accident; it's one of the founding principles Robin and Jack have built their inn around, and came from a famous inn in Mexico they visited more than twenty-five years ago. What Robin liked most was that it "attracted great guests." So does their inn.

It's a matter of kindred spirits. People who are attracted to a very casual atmosphere—with overstuffed chairs pulled around a fireplace, rooms with wormy-chestnut walls, rustic pieces paired with fine art and antiques from around the world, displays of family photos and collectibles, breakfasts ranging from banana-buckwheat pancakes to eggs Benedict, innkeepers with more than a little sense of humor, outdoor activities, and a view to die for—are bound to like one another. If this describes you, we guarantee that this is the place for you and that you're destined to become one of this inn's great guests.

We'd like to make another observation: "Great innkeepers make great inns." The wonderful humor and pleasure with which you are met by Robin, Jack, the rest of the staff, and even the grandchildren and two handsome Labs—Muffin, the yellow, and Chip, the chocolate—rounds out the experience. They genuinely enjoy their guests and are always ready to swap some stories or share some new piece of information about the mountains, lake, or town.

For years Robin and Jack called their romantic suite the Something Suite because they didn't want prospective guests to think it was limited to honeymooners. Recently redecorated, it's finally been dubbed the Veranda Suite. Summer evenings at 5:00 P.M. cocktail time, Jack gets out their pontoon party barge to take whoever wants to join him on a tour of the lake, followed on their return by a glass (or two) of wine and a game of "Two Truths and a Lie" that helps the innkeepers and guests get to know one another. In the sunny breakfast room, the hanging rack of personalized mugs belonging to frequent guests attests to the fact that Robin and Jack are doing everything right.

Ever modest, Robin and Jack attribute the inn's success to something other than themselves. "The outside of the building doesn't tell the story; the view tells the story." Robin says. The lodge is built in European hunting-lodge style that sort of nestles into the steep lakeside without calling attention to itself. Inside, the high vaulted ceilings, hand-hewn beams, and the huge 20-foot-tall stone fireplaces (one with a large gristmill stone imbedded in it) in the two public lounges make you think of one of the National Park lodges built during the Depression, just not quite as imposing. But Robin is right—the key is really the view from the long row of windows in the sunporch/breakfast room, from many of the guest rooms, and from the great lower level open-air stone veranda that all overlook the deep blue of a crystal-clear mountain lake that *National Geographic* has dubbed the most beautiful manmade lake in this country and one of the top ten in the world, surrounded by steep hillsides of the Blue Ridge Mountains covered with a forest of pines and hardwoods and all capped with a clear sky dotted with puffy clouds.

The Staniers have capitalized on this wonderful gift of nature by taking advantage of the outdoor possibilities. They've filled the covered patio with rockers, hammocks, and other comfortable places to relax. From here a terraced path leads down the steep hillside to the water. Halfway down a deck with bench seating is another place to while away some time. At the water's edge, the boathouse is headquarters for swimming, fishing, and boating (there are three canoes, a paddle boat, and a sea cycle). Its rooftop deck provides yet another perfect spot to sit and enjoy the serenity and beauty that surround you.

Back inside, in addition to the great room with its grand piano, there's a more cozy library, with a woodstove insert in its stone fireplace, a television and VCR, and mounds of books, magazines, and games. The enclosed sunporch creates a light, airy scene for breakfast.

Cozy, comfortable guest rooms, all but two of which are in the main lodge, boast wormy-chestnut walls and furnishings with country charm—quilts; down comforters; simple locally produced beds, night tables, and dressers; and some four-poster or canopy beds. Private baths have been cleverly tucked wherever they'll fit (one is across the hall). Two rooms boast garden tubs. The extra-large Veranda Suite features a canopy bed, fireplace, and garden tub. Next door, a modern house offers two accommodations, one of which, the Cove Room, has a fireplace, soaking tub, and its own deck.

Although we didn't get to experience all the outdoor amenities of the lodge, we'd love to experience it in the summer as well as in the glorious beauty of spring and fall. In our humble opinion, this is a little piece of heaven.

HOW TO GET THERE: From I-26, take Highway 64/74 to Lake Lure. The lodge is on Charlotte Drive, just off Highway 64/74. Turn at the Lake Lure fire station opposite the golf course. Ask for a map when you make reservations.

Greystone Inn ❤

Lake Toxaway, North Carolina 28747

OWNERS: Tim and Bobo Lovelace

ADDRESS/TELEPHONE: Greystone Lane; (704) 966-4700 or (800) 824-5766; fax (828) 862-5689

WEB SITE: www.greystoneinn.com

E-MAIL: greystone@citcom.net

ROOMS: 33; all with private bath, Jacuzzi, television, and telephone; some with fireplace and private balcony.

RATES: $265 to $525, per couple; single $40 less; includes breakfast and dinner, afternoon tea and cakes, hors d'oeuvres, and all recreational activities except golf fees (greens fees waved weekends shoulder season). Inquire about children's rates. Off-season rates and several packages are available. Thanksgiving and Christmas are magical.

OPEN: Year-round.

FACILITIES AND ACTIVITIES: Library-lounge with full bar service. Lake for swimming, boating, waterskiing, and fishing; heated swimming pool, golf course, tennis courts, croquet, horseshoes, lawn games, use of boats, and spa. Nearby: hiking, scenic drives, antiques and resort shops.

BUSINESS TRAVEL: Meeting space for up to 30; can handle groups up to 60.

*R*inged by an exclusive resort community, placid Lake Toxaway sits among several thousand acres of heavily wooded highlands. Driving past beautiful lakeshore homes and a golf club, tennis courts, and swimming pool, we followed the road for quite some way before we ultimately came to the centerpiece of the community—the historic Swiss revival-style, four-star Greystone Inn and its new additions perched on a promontory peninsula overlooking the lake. In addition to the mansion, there are several two-story almost motellike buildings, although they do blend in architecturally with the historic house—that contain upscale rooms and suites and another structure that houses the Lakeside Dining Room, which offers a panorama of the lake.

Enter the inn through the enclosed sunporch, where white wicker entices you to relax to watch the activities on the lake, read a good book, visit with fellow guests, or even nap. This is also the location of a delightful afternoon

tea. Just beyond the sunporch is the first of two handsomely paneled lounges where you check in and a small gift shop. Behind the first lounge is a second one, which serves as a library and a cozy bar. In winter, fires blaze in both lounges. In good weather guests throw open the sets of French doors in the library and step out onto the stone terrace.

Early in this century the Greystone was built as the private mansion of Lucy Moltz. When she first decided that she wanted to build a summer place in the woods beside Lake Toxaway, her husband, apparently a practical man, suggested that she camp out there for a while first to see if she really liked it. This she did—in a tent with hardwood floors staffed with eleven servants. After a successful season of "roughing it," she had the 16,000-square-foot mansion called Hillmont built.

Owner Tim Lovelace has worked hard to keep the intimate feeling of visiting a private home, but make no mistake—most of us don't visit private homes as luxurious as this. Every room in the inn has a magnificent view of the lake or grounds and is furnished in antiques and period reproductions similar to the furniture Mrs. Moltz had. The television sets are hidden in armoires. The rooms are named after the wealthy and famous people who used to visit Lake Toxaway: Vanderbilt, Rockefeller, Wanamaker.

Although we're partial to the quaint charm and eccentricities of the sumptuous rooms in the mansion, those in the Hillmont and Lakeside Suites buildings have their own considerable appeal. They're very spacious and contain a large seating area or separate sitting room, as well as a fireplace, whirlpool tub, ceiling fan, and private porch—some of them screened.

Guests dine in the Lakeside Dining Room, where every table has a great view of the water and the cuisine is gourmet. Breakfast and dinner are included in the nightly rate. Lunch is available at the golf club for an additional cost. During the peak season, jackets are required for gentlemen.

Pampering is what a stay at the Greystone Inn is all about, and you can take that concept to new heights. Services at the Spa at the Greystone Inn are guaranteed to reduce tension and increase your sense of well-being. Half- and full-day packages as well as à la carte services include body care, skin care, massage therapy, and hair and nail care. Soft music and gentle touch can be followed by a cleansing session in the sauna.

But as lovely as everything is inside the inn, the outdoor activities thrilled us more. In good weather, Tim is available to lead hikes along Horse Pasture River past three magnificent waterfalls. During the warmer months, he takes guests out on the lake on the party boat to watch the sunset. What could be more romantic than a champagne cruise before dinner? When the leaves are in color, the beauty of sailing or canoeing along the lake's 13 miles of shoreline can be an almost religious experience. (See Facilities and Activities above for more.)

HOW TO GET THERE: The inn is in western North Carolina, 50 miles south of Asheville. It is off U.S. 64, 10 miles east of Cashiers and 17 miles west of Brevard. Turn into the Lake Toxaway entrance. It is clearly marked. Follow the signs 4 miles to the inn. Because you are driving steep, winding roads, it will feel longer, but keep going.

Cataloochee Ranch

Maggie Valley, North Carolina 28751

INNKEEPER: Tim Rice

ADDRESS/TELEPHONE: 119 Ranch Drive; (828) 926–1401 or (800) 868–1401; fax (828) 926–9249

WEB SITE: www.cataloochee-ranch.com

E-MAIL: info@cataloochee-ranch.com

ROOMS: 6; plus 6 suites, 12 cabins, 1 house; all with private bath; some with fireplace, whirlpool bath, and/or kitchen.

RATES: $145 to $185 for rooms in the ranch house, $165 to $210 for Silverbell Lodge suites, $195 to $275 for individual cabins; double occupancy; includes breakfast and dinner. Rates for four in a Silverbell Lodge suite are $335 to $355; $45 for each additional child younger than twelve and $60 for an additional guest older than twelve; rates for four in a cabin are $360 to $385; $50 for a child younger than twelve, $60 for a guest older than twelve.

OPEN: April 1 through November 30 and December 26 to January 3.

FACILITIES AND ACTIVITIES: Pond, pool, hot tub, horseback riding, tennis court, children's playground, ranch activities. Nearby: whitewater rafting, golf courses, Appalachian Trail, Great Smoky Mountains National Park, Cherokee Indian Reservation, Ghost Town in the Sky, Tweetsie Railroad, Cataloochee Ski Area.

BUSINESS TRAVEL: Meeting space will accommodate up to fifty; ideal for executive retreats.

*I*t doesn't get much better than this, we thought—sitting astride a horse surveying more than a thousand acres of mountaintop ranch with vistas of the Great Smoky and Blue Ridge Mountains in the distance and the town of Maggie Valley below. *Cataloochee* is believed to be the Cherokee word for "wave upon wave," and this is just what we saw from the Cataloochee Ranch—wave upon wave of mountain peaks. We quickly realized that whether you're a single person or part of a couple, family, or group of friends, anyone who loves the active outdoor life will revel in the exciting activities at the Cataloochee Ranch. And best yet, we didn't have to sleep on the ground or do our own cooking over a campfire. We found plenty of creature comforts.

In the olden days before everyone's life was so dominated by television, movies, video games, and the Internet, there was good, clean family fun of quite another sort, and you can discover or rediscover it at the ranch. In addition to swimming, fishing, horseback riding, and hiking, guests at the ranch join in storytelling, clogging, square dancing, lawn games, hayrides, bonfires, and marshmallow roasts. There's a tennis court as well and three entrances directly into the Great Smoky Mountains National Park.

A longtime family enterprise, the ranch with overnight lodging, which has evolved into a resort, was founded in 1933 by "Mr. Tom" and "Miss Judy" Alexander. When their first location was absorbed by the newly created Great Smoky Mountains National Park, they moved to the lofty 5,000-foot peaks of Fie Top Mountain in 1938. The property's sturdy stone-and-log cattle barn became the main ranch house, and several original cabins continue to provide comfortable accommodations. To these have been added several more cabins and the Silverbell Lodge, which contains six suites. Although Mr. Tom died in 1972 and Miss Judy in 1997, their daughters and their families continue to offer hospitality to new generations who'd like to experience the life of a simpler time.

We particularly liked the suites in the Silverbell Lodge. We thought the cathedral ceiling and fireplace in the living room and the loft bedroom were just right. The cabins are appealing, too. All of them have a fireplace, refrigerator, coffeemaker, and radio. Four of them boast a whirlpool, wet bar, and private deck. Several of the suites and cabins have an additional one or more bedrooms, which make them perfect for families or friends.

Although there are so many activities to tempt you away to the far reaches of the ranch, the good home cooking served family-style in the ranch house dining room may make you want to stay close by. The modified American plan provides you with breakfast and dinner daily. Lunch and box lunches are available at an additional charge. Fresh mountain-grown products are used to create the rib-sticking meals, and the breads, jellies, and preserves are homemade. Entrees might feature rainbow trout or wild game in season. Frequent outdoor barbecues or "steak outs" are a big hit with all ages.

There's so much to experience at the ranch, you couldn't possibly get the full benefit of a ranch vacation in a short stay, so one-night visits aren't encouraged. In fact, we recommend that you plan on at least a week to unwind from the stresses of your everyday life. So pack some jeans, a bathing suit, and a sweater or jacket for those cool evenings, and head for the hills.

HOW TO GET THERE: At the west end of Maggie Valley, look for the CAT-ALOOCHEE RANCH sign at the Ghost Town in the Sky attraction. The ranch is located 3 miles up the paved Fie Top Road.

The Tranquil House Inn
Manteo, North Carolina 27954

INNKEEPERS: Don and Lauri Just

ADDRESS/TELEPHONE: Queen Elizabeth Street (mailing address: P.O. Box 2045); (252) 473-1404 or (800) 458-7069; fax (252) 473-1526

WEB SITE: www.tranquilinn.com

E-MAIL: dljust@aol.com

ROOMS: 25; all with private bath, television, and telephone; some with wheelchair access. No-smoking rooms available.

RATES: $79 to $169, single or double, seasonal; includes continental breakfast buffet each morning and wine and cheese at check-in. No charge for one or two children under sixteen in the same room.

OPEN: Year-round.

FACILITIES AND ACTIVITIES: New restaurant on premises open for dinner, touring bikes. Nearby: walk to restaurants and shops; Fort Raleigh National Historic Site, Elizabeth II State Historic Site, Elizabethan Gardens, North Carolina Aquarium, all kinds of fishing.

*T*he Tranquil House Inn is strikingly attractive, inside and out. The building is a reproduction of a typical turn-of-the-century Outer Banks inn. The interior, done in cypress, furnished with light pine furniture and decorated with Oriental rugs, seems as bright and sunny as the docks outside. Stained-glass windows and handmade comforters in the guest rooms whisper luxury. Perhaps because of its location right on Shallowbag Bay, a sense of quiet permeates the place, even though it is close to Manteo's tourist activities.

And, nice as it is, you probably won't spend many daylight hours in the inn because there is so much to do in and around Manteo. The Manteo

Walking Tour takes a couple of hours and instructs you in much of the area's early history, including the mystery of the colony set up by Sir Walter Raleigh that disappeared sometime between 1587 and 1591, while its leader was away procuring supplies.

People fish and crab right from the docks here, and the inn has bikes if you want to pedal around the rest of the town.

We are Christmas nuts. We decorate at least one tree in every room in our house each year and look for new ornaments wherever we go. The reason we mention this is that Manteo is the home of one of the very first Christmas shops in the United States. Dan remembers visiting it when his family vacationed in the area during his childhood—and that was more than just a few years ago. Over the years, this wonderful shop has not lost its magic. This is a "must see."

When you need to sit down for a while, one of the most popular spots at the inn is on the second-floor deck, from which you can watch boats maneuvering in and out of their slips in the marina.

At dinnertime, the inn's restaurant, 1587, offers a variety of gourmet entrees, including such unusual dishes as seared salmon and puff pastry tower with flash-sautéed leeks, fried spinach, and lemon-artichoke beurre blanc. They also have an above-average wine list.

HOW TO GET THERE: Take Highway 64 from the west or Highway 158 from the north. Follow the signs for the Elizabeth II State Historic Site. You'll see the inn on the Manteo waterfront. Sir Walter Raleigh Street leads directly to the inn.

Pine Crest Inn
Pinehurst, North Carolina 28374

INNKEEPER: Peter Barrett

ADDRESS/TELEPHONE: Pinehurst; (910) 295-6121 or (800) 371-2545; fax (910) 295-4880

WEB SITE: www.pinecrestinnpinehurst.com

E-MAIL: frondesk@pinecrestpinehurst.com

ROOMS: 40; all with private bath, television, and telephone.

RATES: $59 to $88, per person, double occupancy, depending on season; single, $20 to $50 more; includes breakfast and dinner. Corner rooms $10 extra. Inquire about package rates including greens fees.

OPEN: Year-round.

FACILITIES AND ACTIVITIES: Breakfast and dinner open to the public, bar. Access to Pinehurst Country Club golf course and thirty-five other area courses. Nearby: tennis, horseback riding, skeet shooting; fishing, sailing, and swimming on Pinehurst Lake.

*Y*ou'll always find something going on at Pine Crest Inn. Most people come for the golf. Visitors at the inn are afforded access to the Pinehurst Country Club golf course and thirty-five other area courses; the inn is happy to set up times for you. Pinehurst is famous for the number and quality of its golf courses. But golf is by no means the only attraction at the inn.

The dining room is famous. Executive Chef Carl Jackson has been here more than sixty years; his assistant and nephew, Chef Peter Jackson, has been here about thirty years. Local folks as well as inn guests fill up the dining room regularly. The menu changes every day. It features everything from spaghetti to roast leg of spring lamb and homemade soups, breads, and desserts. The Happy Heart Dinner, a low-fat, low-cholesterol offering, is available each day. As for desserts, we find the Château Margaux Sundae elegant and appropriate to our growing interest in lower-fat diets. It's made of orange sherbet, orange slices, and Château LaSalle wine.

The inn has piano-bar music for dancing in the lounge. Sports talk in the bar is by no means limited to golf, popular as it is. The area also has good tennis and many horse farms. All these activities bring guests to the inn

For all its activity, the inn is definitely a family affair, the kind of place that includes the names and pictures of all the staff and many guests in its advertising. The easy hospitality makes you feel as though you've known everyone here forever.

HOW TO GET THERE: U.S. 1 and 15–501 go directly into Pinehurst. When you get into the town, follow the TO VILLAGE SHOPS signs to the market square. The inn is on Dogwood Road, 1 block from the center of the village.

The Fearrington House 💙
Pittsboro, North Carolina 27312

INNKEEPER: Richard M. Delany

ADDRESS/TELEPHONE: 2000 Fearrington Village Center; (828) 542–2121 or (800) 733–2785; fax (828) 542–4202

WEB SITE: www.fearington.com

E-MAIL: fhouse@fearrington.com

ROOMS: 31; all with private bath, television, and telephone, some with wheelchair access.

RATES: $165 to $325 per room; includes full breakfast, afternoon tea.

OPEN: Year-round.

FACILITIES AND ACTIVITIES: Fearrington House Restaurant, with wheelchair access, open to guests and public Tuesday through Saturday, 6:00 to 9:00 P.M., and Sunday, 6:00 to 8:00 P.M. The Fearrington Market Cafe is open Monday through Friday for lunch and dinner, Saturday and Sunday for brunch. Galloways Bar, shops, swim and croquet club.

BUSINESS TRAVEL: Meeting space to accommodate up to 200; computer-friendly telephones; fax and copy service.

"I

t's not so much where you go, but how you're treated that's hospitality" is founder R. B. Fitch's Fearrington Formula, which has earned The Fearrington House international renown as well as the coveted five-diamond rating for both its accommodations and its restaurant—the only establishment in North Carolina to do so. Who wouldn't like to investigate this extraordinary inn to see what it's all about? In this particular case, however, we decided to visit because R. B.'s special approach to development piqued our curiosity.

We'd been told that The Fearrington House isn't just a fabulous inn but a complete concept—but that's pretty nebulous. Right up until the very moment we arrived, we were still more than a little hazy about how an award-winning inn and restaurant, combined with a village of shops and services, residential neighborhoods, gardens and common spaces—all newly created from scratch out of farm land while leaving some of the fields and buildings intact—fit together as a whole.

Our first hint that we were on to something unique was when we came to the field of Belties (a rare breed of Scottish Belted Galloway cattle that are

black at both ends with a wide white band around the middle at the entrance to the planned community. We registered the signature silo, a former barn—now a special events facility—the graceful 1927 white-columned colonial-style home that now houses the restaurant, and numerous small many-gabled buildings scattered about a square with tasteful new neighborhoods stretching out beyond. As we drove up a flower-lined lane, so clever is the design that we weren't sure which was the inn—nothing looked big enough.

As it turned out, we were right to wonder. The inn rooms are scattered in multiple buildings in two areas. The original section, located behind the restaurant and wrapped around several courtyards, is contained in little houselike buildings with gabled roofs. Newly added rooms are connected to some of the businesses.

We knew we were in for an exceptional level of service when several blazer-clad staff members rushed out to unload our bags and escort us to registration, then whisked us to our magnificent accommodations across the square—an oversized room with subdued colors, a king-size bed, English-pine antiques, original art, a cozy little sitting area in a window alcove, an extensive entertainment system, and a huge bathroom with every amenity we could think of, including a heated towel rack. Fresh flowers adorned both our bed chamber and bathroom. In all, this was a room fit for royalty, and it wasn't even one of the most deluxe rooms; some feature separate sitting area, fireplace, and/or whirlpool bath. Distinctive touches such as ecclesiastical doors used as headboards or pine flooring from a workhouse along England's Thames river give each guest room its own personality.

If the good weather and our curiosity about the hamlet, the spectacular gardens, the fascinating shops, and divine eateries hadn't begged us to come out to explore, we could cheerfully have stayed cocooned in our room for the duration.

We headed back to the village center (a walk of less than half a block) to investigate. Explorations work up an appetite, so we stopped in the cozy Garden Room for a substantial afternoon tea of iced and hot English teas, cookies, tea cakes, scones, and cheese and crackers to tide us over until dinner.

Sophisticated regional cuisine prepared according to classical techniques blends Southern basics with haute cuisine. Today's chefs prepare staples such as grits or fried green tomatoes and exotic fare such as ostrich or antelope carpaccio for a prix fixe four-course dinner Tuesday through Sunday. Impeccable service and a comfortable and upscale atmosphere (jacket and tie for gentlemen are recommended) combine to make a perfect evening.

A hearty breakfast is served to guests on one of the restaurant's glassed-in porches. The mornings we were there, the choices included freshly squeezed juice, warm muffins and just-baked breads, yogurt, granola, fresh fruit, eggs to order, fried cheese grits, French toast with cinnamon syrup, and hickory-smoked bacon. If you're hungry at midday, grab a quick lunch at the deli or the Market Cafe. And don't forget about the afternoon tea.

We loved wandering through the gardens—drinking in both the sights and smells. If we had had more time, we could have used the sports facilities in the residential area: the swim and croquet club and the hiking and biking trails.

One last suggestion: If you're departing on a Tuesday afternoon, take home some produce, fresh baked goods, flowers, or local cheeses from the Fearrington Farmers' Market—an informal gathering of local producers. Definitely take home a whimsical item honoring the Belties: T-shirts, mugs, caps, and other souvenirs. We buy Christmas ornaments wherever we travel and were delighted to find charming representations of the Beltie. We got lots of comments on this addition to our "destination" tree.

HOW TO GET THERE: Fearrington is 8 miles south of Chapel Hill on U.S. 15/501 toward Pittsboro.

Fearrington Village

The twenty-year-old brainchild of R. B. and the late Jenny Fitch, the planned community is the result of their quest to build a low-key, high-style lifestyle for themselves and others when they bought the dairy farm that had been in the Fearrington family for almost 200 years. They combined all the elements they liked about places they'd traveled, particularly European villages, and strove to balance private space and common space, building structures and open land. What they created is a real village where people live and play, where shops and service businesses provide what residents and visitors need, and where guests can come to stay and play. These disparate elements blend into a coherent whole that could well be copied by developers and town planners nationwide.

Many of the original farm buildings have found new life as integral parts of the town. The former granary is home to the Market, which features a Mediterranean bistrolike cafe. Dovecote: A Home and Garden Shop, located in the old milking barn, is the starting point for formal garden tours with the director of landscape design. The Potting Shed, located in the old corn crib, sells more than 200 species of plants propagated from Fearrington's gardens.

In new buildings, McIntyre's Fine Books and Bookends is as comfortable as your own living room, but with enough books to keep you busy for life. Watermarks sells works of art on paper. Other shops purvey jewelry, pottery, and other specialties. A bank, travel agency, beauty shop, pharmacy, and medical clinic are on site too.

Another of the passions of the multitalented Jenny Fitch was gardening, and she developed the formal and informal gardens at Fearrington. Take a stroll or several around the knot, rose, perennial, and herb gardens.

Once they'd established a town, the Fitches started the restaurant. Jenny, who studied French cooking for seven years, was the first executive chef. The next best thing to eating at the Fearrington House is buying a copy of Jenny's *The Fearrington House Cookbook: A Celebration of Food, Flowers, and Herbs*.

The Fitches put their creative talents to work developing an inn that would meet their personal ideas of a luxurious getaway. Central to their philosophy is the Fearrington Formula: providing highly attentive, yet unobtrusive service. Although Jenny is gone, we wonder what R. B. will do next.

The Orchard Inn
Saluda, North Carolina 28773

INNKEEPERS: Kathy and Bob Thompson

ADDRESS/TELEPHONE: Route 176 (mailing address: P.O. Box 725); (828) 749–5471 or (800) 581–3800; fax (828) 749–9805

WEB SITE: www.orchardinn.com

E-MAIL: orchard@saluda.tds.net

ROOMS: 9 in main house, plus 3 cottage suites; all with private bath; some with fireplace and whirlpool tub. No smoking inn.

RATES: $119 to $195, single or double; includes full breakfast. Two-night minimum stay for advance reservations on weekends. Inquire about special conference rates.

OPEN: Year-round.

FACILITIES AND Dinner Tuesday through Saturday, open to public by reservation; brown bagging permitted. Conference room, gift shop, library, horseshoes, nature trail, hiking, birding. Nearby: antiques and crafts shops, Biltmore Estate, Carl Sandburg home.

This place simply overwhelmed me. It sits on eighteen wooded acres at the top of the Saluda rise, at an elevation of 2,500 feet. All you can see in any direction are treetops and mountains. It is unbelievably quiet.

As you enter the inn from the front porch, you step into a huge living room where beautifully arranged plants, paintings, antiques, and books all invite your attention. Guest rooms are also decorated in an upscale country style.

In the small cottages, the atmosphere is romantic, with whirlpool tubs, fireplaces, wormy-chestnut paneling, and twig furniture.

For many years this well-established inn has attracted guests from all over with gourmet cooking and easy hospitality. Kathy and Bob Thompson, who enjoyed the inn as guests for ten years prior to becoming innkeepers, have come to this place full of good humor and the energy and ideas of new innkeepers. They have certainly kept the inn's old following and are building their own coterie of new and repeat guests.

The food is still a draw, too. Award-winning chef Sallie Corley brings her native South Carolina talent for traditional dishes such as mountain trout, Low Country filet, and pan-seared quail.

For a romantic evening, dine on the glassed-in porch that overlooks the Warrior Mountain Range. As the day fades and candles are lit, classical music chases back the shadows, and from the nearby kitchen come the aromas of garlic, wine, and grilled meats. Back in 1985, a similar experience inspired the late travel writer Norman Simpson to call the Orchard Inn "quite magical." It still is.

HOW TO GET THERE: The Orchard Inn is in western North Carolina, on Highway 176 between Saluda and Tryon. From I-26 north of Hendersonville, take exit 28 and follow the connector road (West Ozone Drive) to Route 176. Turn left on 176, and drive ½ mile. The inn is on your right.

Pine Needles
Southern Pines, North Carolina 28388

INNKEEPER: Peggy Kirk Bell

ADDRESS/TELEPHONE: 1005 Midland Road (mailing address: P.O. Box 88); (910) 692-7111 or (800) 747-7272; fax (910) 692-5349

WEB SITE: www.golfne.com\pineneedles

E-MAIL: pneedles@ac.net

ROOMS: 72; all with private bath, television, and telephone.

RATES: Peak season rates from mid-March to mid-June and from September 1 to mid-November. Please call for rates. Inquire about off-season and special-package rates. Children under age four free.

OPEN: Year-round.

FACILITIES AND ACTIVITIES: Breakfast, lunch, dinner, lounge for guests only. Meeting and conference facilities, swimming pool, lighted grass tennis courts, private golf courses. Located in the sandhills of North Carolina, known for many golf courses and horse farms.

*S*omething new is always going on at Pine Needles, so whatever is written now, you can bet there will be more by the time you read this. It's not so long ago that the lobby and rooms were redecorated, so here's what you'll almost certainly find there: In the main lobby, a dark green carpet bordered in red and white dramatically sets off light country pine furniture and drapes and upholstery done in tweeds and a burgundy, green, and tan plaid known as Pine Needles Plaid. The plaid is used throughout Pine Needles, even on brochures.

The room has a vaulted ceiling and a raised-hearth fireplace in the brick wall along the far end. In the spring and summer, vases of flowers decorate the massive oak mantel.

The Bells built the inn mainly so that Peggy would have a place to teach golf. Certainly golf is the main attraction for most people who stay here.

Guests especially like knowing that the course will never be crowded, because play is restricted to guests of the inn, if the inn is full, or will include outside players to a maximum of 140 players in off-seasons. Pine Needles has added many golf learning centers, concentrated three- and four-day schools that take as many as sixteen people, intended for the intense golfer who wants a precise school to develop specific skills. It would be a good idea to write or call for more information, because schedules will certainly change often.

We don't golf, but we could still stay all but forever and have a good time. The other facilities are first-class, especially the large heated swimming pool. The food is good; the wine list is above average. The area is secluded and usually quiet. (Peggy and members of the family teach an amazing number of "Golfari" sessions, basically golf workshops, for groups ranging from all women to young people. If you want a quiet escape, it is important to make sure your visit doesn't overlap with a Golfari.)

Although Pine Needles has several different kinds of guest rooms, we think you can get an accurate picture of the new look if you know that many rooms have brass headboards but are still comfortable enough that you feel free to kick off your shoes and sprawl. The Pine Needles expression for it is "casual elegance."

During the off-season the inn offers a B&B package, but in the main season golf takes precedence.

HOW TO GET THERE: Pine Needles is ¼ mile off U.S. Highway 1 on NC Route 2 between Pinehurst and Southern Pines.

Stone Hedge
Tryon, North Carolina 28782

INNKEEPERS: Thomas and Shaula Dinsmore

ADDRESS/TELEPHONE: Howard Gap Road (mailing address: P.O. Box 366); (828) 859–9114 or (800) 859–1974; fax (828) 859–5928

ROOMS: 6 in inn, guesthouse, and stone cottage; all with private bath, television, and telephone; some with fireplace; some with kitchen.

RATES: $95 to $120, double; includes full breakfast. Inquire about single, corporate, and long-stay discounts.

OPEN: Year-round.

FACILITIES AND ACTIVITIES: Dinner for guests and the public Wednesday through Saturday, 6:00 to 9:00 P.M., and Sunday, noon to 2:30 P.M.; brown bagging permitted; wheelchair access to dining room. Swimming pool. Nearby: tennis, hiking, horseback riding, golf, antiques shops.

*S*ometimes when you've had a bad day, imagine yourself sitting on the inn's stone patio enjoying a panoramic view of the mountains and watching squirrels skitter along the stone fence around the patio. It soothes us every time.

The view from inside is just as lovely. The long window-wall of the dining room looks out over the patio and an expanse of flowers, shrubs, and a lawn that stretches down to the honeymoon cottage by the pool. Unspoiled woodland borders everything.

Throughout the interior flower arrangements echo the outdoor flowers. As you enter the dining area, you'll see a stone fireplace with an elegant hand-carved cherry-wood mantel. The exposed ceiling beams, doors, and all wood-work are made from cherry wood, too. And the carpet pattern resembles fallen autumn leaves. The effect is so pretty that it makes you feel like dressing up for dinner.

The couple who owns Stone Hedge considers being there a dream come true. They bring to their innkeeping, and especially the restaurant, their own special liveliness and joy.

Tom Dinsmore is the chef. A man who loves to experiment, he has designed an eclectic menu with specials ranging from traditional meals such as broiled mountain trout and Black Angus beef to novelties prepared especially for you by special arrangement. One enchanted guest wrote that the food was "big-city menus in a hometown setting" and raved over the fact that everything is so good that strangers at adjacent tables strike up friendships during dinner.

Breakfast, served in the main dining room, is an elaborate affair served with warm hospitality and a fabulous daytime view of the countryside.

The guest rooms are furnished mostly with locally purchased antiques. The cottage by the swimming pool feels almost like a private retreat.

Indeed, all of Stone Hedge, on its secluded twenty-eight-acre grounds, feels like a luxurious retreat, miles away from any other civilization. The same delighted guest said Stone Hedge was a "castle without a moat, knights without armor, maidens in no distress." But when you're ready to engage the world again, Tryon, with all its quaint stores and antiques shops, is only a couple of miles away.

HOW TO GET THERE: From I-26, take the Tryon exit (#36) to NC 108. Follow 108 toward Tryon for 2½ miles. Turn right on Howard Gap Road and follow the signs about 1½ miles to the inn.

Mast Farm Inn
Valle Crucis, North Carolina 28691

INNKEEPERS: Wanda Hinshow and Kay Phillip

ADDRESS/TELEPHONE: Star Route 1112 (mailing address: P.O. Box 704); (828) 963–5857 or (888) 963–5857; fax (828) 963–6404

WEB SITE: www.mastfarminn.com

E-MAIL: stay@mastfarminn.com

ROOMS: 9, plus 4 cottages; all with private bath; 1 with wheelchair access. No smoking inn.

RATES: $125 to $215, double; includes full breakfast.

OPEN: Year-round.

FACILITIES AND ACTIVITIES: Dinner for guests and the public by reservation; dinner Monday evenings for lodging guests only; Sunday lunch at 12:30 and 2:30 P.M.; no evening meal Sunday; brown bagging permitted. Located in the Blue Ridge Mountains, near Blue Ridge Parkway. Nearby: crafts shops, antiques shops, potteries, hiking, fishing, whitewater rafting.

The innkeepers consider it a good day when inn guests who meet sitting together at dinner adjourn to the porch afterward to continue talking for the rest of the evening.

They manage to learn a little about the interests of everyone who will be eating at the inn. In the half hour or so before the dining room opens people begin to congregate on the front porch, overlooking the flower gardens, to rock and chat and watch the mountains. The aromas that drift from the kitchen are so inviting that when the dining room opens, everyone moves very briskly.

We suggest starting with a fresh tossed salad with the best tomatoes you'll have tasted all summer. The entrees change daily and always include at least one vegetarian entree. Try the roast pork loin perfectly seasoned with garlic and black pepper. In addition there are side dishes of yam-and-apple casserole, succotash, and zucchini. Taste the smoked mozzarella-filled ravioli accompanied by grilled eggplant and parsleyed tomatoes in an herb seasoning. Chef Scott Houlman has attracted quite a following at the inn with his new Southern cuisine that concentrates on local foods and fresh vegetables and herbs from the garden in season.

In the morning, look around the property. Mast Farm is on the National Register of Historic Places and is considered a fine example of a restored self-contained mountain homestead. The springhouse, icehouse, wash-house, barn, blacksmith shop, gazebo, and cabin, as well as the main inn, look much as they must have amid the daily activity when Mast Farm was originally operated as an inn in the early 1900s.

Start the day off right with a breakfast of three-grain pancakes with a fresh blueberry-blackberry sauce; a delicious drink made of orange juice, frozen cubes of pineapple-grapefruit juice, and bananas; and a seemingly endless flow of coffee.

HOW TO GET THERE: At Boone, take NC 105 south about 5 miles to the VALLE CRUCIS sign. Turn onto SR 1112 (the road to Valle Crucis) and go 3 miles. The inn is on the left just before you get to the village of Valle Crucis.

Grandview Lodge
Waynesville, North Carolina 28786

INNKEEPERS: Stan and Linda Arnold

ADDRESS/TELEPHONE: 466 Lickstone Road; (828) 456-5212 or (800) 255-7826; fax (828) 452-5432

WEB SITE: www.bbonline.com/nc/grandview/

E-MAIL: sarnold@haywood.main.nc.us

ROOMS: 9 in main lodge and attached porch, plus 2 two-room apartments; all with private bath, two beds, and television. No smoking inn.

RATES: $105 to $115, double occupancy; $75, single; includes breakfast and dinner except Sunday dinner. Inquire about rates for single occupancy, children, and apartments. No credit cards. Minimum stay of two nights high season and holidays.

OPEN: Year-round.

FACILITIES AND ACTIVITIES: Lunch by special arrangement, dinner open to public by reservation, brown bagging permitted. Library, game room, shuffleboard courts. Nearby: golf at Waynesville and Laurel Ridge country clubs, tennis, outlet shopping, easy access to Blue Ridge Parkway and many historic sites.

*S*eems Stan came home one day from his corporate management job in Chicago and said, "I've had it. Let's do it or stop talking about it." The other dreamer, Linda, a home economist who'd recently taken some cooking classes at the Culinary Institute of America just in case, said, "Okay, let's do it."

So they bought themselves an inn—Grandview Lodge, here in their native North Carolina. They got here in the spring of 1986; their furniture got here a few days later; their first guests checked in a few days after that.

Everyone is living happily ever after.

Stan and Linda run the inn much as it has been operated for the past fifty years. It's furnished with what Stan calls "the kind of antiques you're not afraid to sit on, but definitely not rustic. More like Grandmother's house."

They've arranged two separate groupings of furniture in the living room, one for watching television and one for conversation and maybe (Stan hopes) bridge games.

Just as Stan says the furniture's not rustic, Linda says the cooking's not Southern in the old sense. She cooks with herbs from her garden, fresh garden vegetables that a neighbor brings pot-ready, fresh local fruits, and whole-grain flours. But you're not getting into health-nut meals—unless you consider barbecued beef ribs, corn pudding, and homemade ice cream hairshirt. Linda also makes her Chocoholic Tart that has in it two kinds of chocolate plus chocolate liqueur. Dinner is not served Sunday night.

So many guests ask for Linda's recipes that she wrote *Recipes from Grandview Lodge.* That book did so well she has written a second book, *More Recipes from Grandview Lodge,* both of which you can buy if you'd like to go home and try to cook likewise.

Grandview now offers one thing I'm relatively sure you can't find at any other inn in the South—an innkeeper who speaks Polish, Russian, German, and Hebrew. It sounds like a talent Stan might not get to use often in Waynesville, but the area is increasingly becoming known for its international folk-dance festivals, and in past seasons, dancers from eleven foreign countries came. Stan had a ball!

HOW TO GET THERE: From I-40, take U.S. 23-74 to exit 98 (West Waynesville). Turn east (follow the WAYNESVILLE signs). Turn left at the first traffic light onto South Main Street. At the second traffic light, turn right onto Allens Creek Road. Go exactly 1 mile. Turn left at the GRANDVIEW LODGE sign onto Lickstone Road and continue ⁴/₁₀ mile up a winding road to the Lodge driveway on your right. Stan and Linda will send a map when you make reservations.

The Old Stone Inn
Waynesville, North Carolina 28786

INNKEEPERS: Cindy and Robert Zinser

ADDRESS/TELEPHONE: 109 Dolan Road; (828) 456-3333 or (800) 432-8499

WEB SITE: www.bbonline.com/nc/oldstone

ROOMS: 18 rooms and 4 suites in 7 separate buildings; all with private bath and television.

RATES: $109 to $159, double; single, $15 less; includes full breakfast. Not appropriate for children.

OPEN: Closed January 1 to Good Friday.

FACILITIES AND ACTIVITIES: Restaurant; wine and beer available. Game room with television and piano, Wendell's Attic reading lounge; robes in cottages and Chestnut Rooms. Nearby: walking distance to Waynesville shops; short drive to hiking, biking, tubing, whitewater rafting, trout fishing, rockhounding, horseback riding; golf at five local courses; crafts museums and shops; Smoky Mountain Railway; thirty-minute drive to Cherokee or Asheville. Inquire about special mountain activity package.

*T*his rustic inn, which used to be known as Heath Lodge, sits under huge oak trees, surrounded by dogwoods, rhododendrons, and mountain laurels, at an elevation of about 3,200 feet, in the Smokies. In summer, the foliage shuts out the hot sun and almost all sounds of civilization. You feel isolated in the woods.

But you're not. A quick walk down the hill takes you into Waynesville, a community full of interesting crafts and art shops, a great Mast Farm store, and lots of interesting nooks and crannies. Even a bookstore.

People come to this place year after year, generation after generation. In recent years, the Zinsers have bought the lodge and, in addition to making friends with lots of guests, have systematically set about improving the property—renovating, refurnishing, upgrading everything from the rooms to the bedding and towels. They've also changed the food a bit. This is partly in response to the fact that whereas families once came for extended stays, guests now are more likely to be there a few days for a romantic getaway.

At one time the dining room served a one-price, no selection, family-style meal, but service is now from a menu. The food itself is still Southern regional, pretty much the same cuisine, only now you have more choices, with seatings at 6:00 and 8:00 P.M. as well as appetizers and wine in a guest lounge off the dining room from 4:00 to 8:00 P.M. This means you can have anything from a full-course meal in the dining room, with entrees such as marinated lamb chops or a tart of smoked gouda with wild mushrooms, to a light-bite sitting on the sofa beside the fire.

If you've been here before, you'll be surprised when you see the revamped guest lounge and dining room. The dining room has been made smaller and more intimate, seating about thirty-six people at small tables for two and four. In the new guest lounge, you'll find several seating groups of sofas and chairs, with rockers in front of the fire and lots of books, games, and puzzles. The space is comfortable, with stone walls, log ceiling, quilts, and fireplace working together to create a mountain atmosphere.

Both rooms are in a stone and log building with a huge fireplace, hardwood floor, and exposed beams. For more quiet moments, guests like the second-floor lounge; this is where we go to read.

The shady site, rustic buildings, comfortable rooms, and pleasantly served food (with wine or beer, a triumph in much of North Carolina) make this a great rejuvenating spot.

HOW TO GET THERE: From Highway 23, exit onto 276 south and continue to Dellwood Road, the second stoplight. Turn right and go ⁴/₁₀ mile to Love Lane, turn right, and drive uphill to Dolan Road. Turn left; the lodge is on your left.

Pisgah Inn on the Blue Ridge Parkway 🏞 ₵₵

Waynesville, North Carolina 28786

INNKEEPER: Bruce O'Connell

ADDRESS/TELEPHONE: Blue Ridge Parkway Mile Marker 408.6 (mailing address: P.O. Box 749); (828) 235–8228; fax (828) 648–9719

WEB SITE: www.pisgahinn.com

E-MAIL: pisgahinn@aol.com

ROOMS: 50, plus 1 suite with fireplace; all with private bath, television, and balcony or porch. Fully equipped rooms for the handicapped available. No smoking in some guest rooms.

RATES: $65 to $73, single; $70 to $78, double; $110, suite; breakfast extra. Children under twelve free with two adults.

OPEN: April through November, weather permitting.

FACILITIES AND Restaurant serves breakfast, lunch, and dinner daily. Beer and wine license. Gift shop, gas station, convenience store, laundromat, campground. Many hiking trails begin from the inn parking lot.

*P*isgah Inn is perched at an elevation of 5,000 feet above sea level, directly on the Blue Ridge Parkway. The original inn was built in 1918. That building is gone now, but its successor overlooks the same mountains from the same giddy height.

When you first drive up, you think that the inn looks like a motel, especially since you park right in front of it. But the minute you leave the car, that view makes everything else seem insignificant. There's nothing else like this on the Parkway.

The rooms are large and nicely furnished with modern furniture. Each room has huge windows and a porch facing out over the mountains. What you see through them is awe-inspiring: mountaintops in every direction.

Because of the inn's location, it's a good base for hiking excursions or driving jaunts. You can consult the trail maps or parkway road map, plot your day's hiking and sight-seeing, and come back for showers, sleep, and good meals.

The dining rooms have windows all around so that you can watch the day changing even as you eat. There's nothing like sipping a glass of wine while watching the sunset from 5,000 feet above sea level.

The restaurant serves good food at reasonable prices. The menu includes Southern favorites, such as country ham, along with fresh vegetables and homemade breads, but it's trout for which they're famous. It comes fresh daily from a trout farm lower on the mountain, and you can have it prepared any number of ways.

HOW TO GET THERE: The inn is directly on the Blue Ridge Parkway between Mileposts 408 and 409. Go south out of Asheville or north out of Brevard. The spectacular drive takes about thirty minutes.

The Swag 🏠 ♥
Waynesville, North Carolina 28786

INNKEEPER: Deener Matthews

ADDRESS/TELEPHONE: 2300 Swag Road; (828) 926-0430 or
(800) 789-7672; fax (828) 926-2036

WEB SITE: www.theswag.com

E-MAIL: dianem@theswag.com

ROOMS: 16 rooms, plus 3 cabins; all with private bath; 9 with fireplace
or woodstove; some with whirlpool or steam shower, 2 with wheelchair
access. No smoking inn.

RATES: $240 to $510 single or double, includes three meals daily,
tea-time cookies, and an hour of hors d'oeuvres. Extra person in room
$80 to $130. Children especially welcome. Two-night minimum stay.

OPEN: May through November (closed weekend before Thanksgiving).

FACILITIES AND ACTIVITIES: Restaurant, brown bagging permitted. Gift
shop, library, racquetball court, sauna, croquet, badminton, pond, 3 miles
of hiking trails with marked plants and trees on Swag property, special
interest events, entrance to hiking trails in Great Smoky Mountains
National Park. Nearby: Asheville and Biltmore Estate, Maggie Valley.

BUSINESS TRAVEL: Meeting space and the isolated location are ideal for
small meetings and retreats

"God lives here!" a guest told us when we visited this spectacular getaway. And we can readily believe it. First of all, we had twisted and
turned up dozens of hairpin turns while climbing the incredibly
steep dirt road to finally reach the lofty elevation of 5,000 feet. Once we got
there, we were so close to the sky, we could easily believe that God is within
easy reach. Second, on a clear day (and most of them are) the vista from this
250-acre privately owned mountaintop is more than 50 miles.

The inn is a collection of pioneer buildings that, back in the early 1970s,
were hauled up the mountain, where they were grouped about vast, grassy
grounds right at the edge of the Great Smoky Mountains National Park.

Everything is set up to make the most of the views and the outdoors: big
windows and porches, rockers and hammocks, picnic nooks, a path, and sev-

eral overlooks. We dropped into a pair of Adirondack chairs arranged along the brow of the mountain to contemplate the view, and we were mesmerized. You will be, too. As professional photographers, we found many spectacular shots to take—and we've sold quite a few of them.

Inside, the public and guest rooms vary in detail but have in common rough wood walls, exposed beams, and wood floors. The rustic ambience contrasts with such luxuries as coffee grinders and coffeemakers, hair dryers, terry-cloth robes, and handmade covers and rugs. From many of the rooms you have a view of the mountains from your windows or your private porch.

Accommodations are also offered in several cabins, including Chestnut Lodge. Recently this lodge was gutted so that its three guest rooms could be converted to two "super" rooms. Each of these new-and-improved accommodations now boasts a sleeping loft with a sofa, reading lamps, and a view as well as two bathrooms, one of which sports a whirlpool and separate steam shower and the other of which has a skylight shower. The lodge's common living room, which is often used for lectures in the special events series, has a new library loft with a Putnam rolling ladder to reach the high shelves.

You find more contrasts in the dining room. The room itself is rustic, with more wood walls and floors, plus tables that were handmade by a Tennessee furniture maker. Yet the service is professional. The food is sophisticated enough to include shredded jicama in a salad and simple enough to offer fresh trout without unnecessary extra trappings.

The library is filled with books stashed in old, stacked wooden crates, organized by category, and has an honor borrowing system. The collection ranges from local history to philosophy, with lots of mysteries, science fiction, and nature books as well. The inn also has a theological library.

What will come as a complete surprise to you is that deep in the bowels of the inn, burrowed into the mountain, is a racquetball court. So those Type-A personalities, to whom a stiff competition of some sort is their only idea of relaxation, won't have to worry about being bored. And when they're finished torturing their bodies, they can sweat off some more calories in the sauna.

The innkeeper's husband, Dan, is an Episcopalian priest in New York City; he's around infrequently. Throughout the inn you see extraordinarily good art with a religious theme. None of it is sentimental, nor do guests who are not Christian ever seem to find it bothersome. Without bowing to any dogma, The Swag practices hospitality as a joyful ministry.

You could drive down the mountain to find a church on Sunday, and you could drive to any number of tourist attractions in the area—but it seems to us that once you get up to the top of this mountain, walk in the woods, and look down on range after range of mountains following one another into the clouds, you've got all the entertainment and all the church you could possibly need.

HOW TO GET THERE: From I–40, take exit 20. Go south on Route 276 for $2\,^8/_{10}$ miles, turn right on Hemphill Road, and drive about 4 miles to the private road that winds up the mountain to the inn. The road is narrow and rough; it's only a few miles long, but will feel much longer.

Brookstown Inn
Winston-Salem, North Carolina 27101

INNKEEPER: Gary Colbert

ADDRESS/TELEPHONE: 200 Brookstown Avenue; (336) 725–1120; reservations (800) 845–4262; fax (336) 773–0147

ROOMS: 71; all with private bath and television; some with wet bar, garden tub, and private sitting room; some with wheelchair access. Two rooms equipped for the handicapped.

RATES: $95 to $115, single; $115 to $135, double; includes continental breakfast and evening wine and cheese party, cookies and milk at 8:00 P.M., turndown service, newspaper. Children under twelve, free; twelve and over, $20.

OPEN: Year-round.

FACILITIES AND ACTIVITIES: Nearby: restaurants, Old Salem, local colleges, galleries, museums.

BUSINESS TRAVEL: Located 3 blocks from business district. Meeting facilities, reception space, photocopier, fax available; dataports.

*A*s a B&B inn, this old building is in its fourth incarnation. It was built in 1837 by the Moravians to be a cotton mill. Then it became a flour mill and later a storage building for a moving company. The mill was restored as an inn and a complex of specialty shops and restaurants in 1984. It's listed on the National Register of Historic Places.

As often happens in building within an existing large structure, the new spaces are larger than average, with spectacularly high ceilings, surprising twists and turns, nooks and crannies, and a wealth of visual interest in exposed beams, old brick, and historic artifacts.

More specifically: On the fourth floor, in what originally was a dormitory for girls who worked in the cotton mill, renovators found and have preserved behind glass a plaster wall full of graffiti. The old factory boiler visually dominates Darryl's Restaurant. In guest rooms, architectural features of the original building, such as brick buttresses, unusual roof slopes, and interesting spaces, have been incorporated into the design of the room.

The decor throughout the inn is Early American, appropriate to the building and its Old Salem connection, without being oppressive. Quilts decorate lobby walls; country touches like hand-woven baskets, pieces of pewter, and silk flowers are scattered throughout the public areas. The huge open spaces keep it from feeling at all cluttered. In the guest rooms, furnishings are reproductions appropriate for the period set off with Wedgwood-blue stenciling around the windows. The poster beds are covered with handmade quilts.

In the breakfast room, which has brick floors and comfortable club chairs around the tables, your continental breakfast is served each morning.

The old Moravians were famous for their hospitality. Brookstown Inn is doing a remarkably good job communicating that spirit at the same time they offer the modern creature comforts you expect from a first-class hostelry.

HOW TO GET THERE: Coming from the west on I-40 Business, take the Cherry Street exit. Turn right when you come to the light at the top of the ramp, onto Marshall Street. Follow the inn signs, turning left onto Brookstown Avenue. The inn is on the right. Coming from the east on I-40 Business, take the Cherry Street exit. As you come to the light coming off the ramp, turn left onto First Street. Go 1 block, turn left on Marshall. Follow the inn signs, turning left on Brookstown.

Select List of
Other North Carolina Inns

Grove Park Inn
290 Macon Avenue
Asheville, NC 28804
(800) 438-5800

140 rooms in the historic core of this huge 510-room resort; restaurants, lounges, conference facilities, golf course, indoor pool, shops, fitness center.

Hanwood Park Hotel
1 Battery Park
Asheville, NC 28801
(828) 252-2522 or (800) 228-2522

Historic commercial building downtown, 33 suites, some with whirlpool; restaurants, bars, shops.

Balsam Mountain Inn
Seven Springs Inn off US 23/73
Balsam, NC 28707
(828) 456-9498 or (800) 224-9498

1908 neoclassical Victorian inn on twenty-six acres; 50 rooms; 100-foot-long porches, restaurant.

Archer's Mountain Inn
Route 2, Box 568-A
Banner Elk, NC 28604
(828) 898-9004

Stone-pillared lodge with 6 rooms, Annex with 8 rooms; The Wobbly, which contains the dining room; full breakfast.

Nu-Wray Inn
Town Square
Burnsville, NC 28714
(800) 368-9729

1833 stagecoach inn; 26 rooms; breakfast and dinner served to the public.

The Dunhill Hotel—an SRS Hotel
237 North Tryon Street
Charlotte, NC 28202
(704) 332–4141

Historic downtown financial district property built in 1929; 60 well-equipped rooms, penthouse; high-quality furnishings and art, award-winning Monticello restaurant; excellent for business travelers.

Culpepper Inn
609 West Main
Elizabeth City, NC 27909
(252) 335–1993

Colonial-style home built in 1935; 11 rooms, some with fireplaces and garden tubs; pool, full breakfast, other refreshments.

Ellerbe Springs Inn
Route 1, Box 179-C
Ellerbe, NC 28338
(800) 248–6467

1857 inn and guest house; 16 rooms, some with gas-log fireplace; Murder Mystery Weekends monthly; restaurant, full breakfast, other refreshments.

Radisson Prince Charles
450 Hay Street
Fayetteville, NC 28301
(910) 433–4444

Intimate 1925 Italian palazzo–style hotel; 83 rooms and suites, rooftop ballroom and terrace, executive level and lounge, exercise room, Chloe's restaurant, Babe's lounge.

Summit Inn
125 East Rogers Street
Franklin, NC 28734
(828) 524–2006 or (800) 524–3133

1898 mansion; 14 rooms, most with shared baths; dinner served Friday and Saturday; game room, children welcome.

The Claddagh Inn
755 North Main Street
Hendersonville, NC 28792
(800) 225-4700

Turn-of-the-century inn; 14 rooms; full breakfast.

Rubin Osceola Lake
P.O. Box 2258
Hendersonville, NC 28793
(828) 692-2544

Rustic lodge built in 1902; 80 rooms; restaurant; full breakfast, evening tea and coffee.

The Main Street Inn
270 Main Street
Highlands, NC 28741
(800) 213-9142

Turn-of-the-century inn; 20 rooms; full breakfast, afternoon tea; closed January to March.

The Old Creek Lodge
165 Highway 106
Highlands, NC 28741
(800) 895-6343

Rustic cabin-style lodge built in 1954; 19 rooms; continental-plus breakfast.

Darlings by the Sea
329 Atlantic Avenue
Kure Beach, NC 28449
(910) 458-8887 or (800) 383-8111

Quaint oceanfront inn with facsimile lighthouse attached; 5 whirlpool suites with wet bar; fitness center, courtyard, decks, luxury amenities; prestocked gourmet continental breakfast.

Lagoalinda Inn
333 Lakeshore Drive
Lake Junaluska, NC 28745
(828) 456-3620

Rustic lakeshore mountain inn built in 1925; 14 rooms; continental-plus breakfast; kitchen available to guests.

Eseeola Lodge

U.S. 221
Linville, NC 28646
(800) 742-6717

Rustic lodge; 29 rooms; breakfast and dinner included; golf course, tennis courts, swimming pool, croquet, children's recreation program.

The Switzerland Inn

Milepost 334 off the Blue Ridge Parkway
Little Switzerland, NC 28749
(828) 765-2153

Rustic Swiss chalet–style lodge; 55 rooms; restaurant, pool, tennis court, shops.

First Colony Inn

6720 South Virginia Dare Trail
Nags Head, NC 27959
(800) 368-9390

Beach inn with wraparound porches; 26 rooms; breakfast buffet, afternoon tea.

The Berkley Manor Bed and Breakfast

P.O. Box 220
Ocracoke, NC 27960
(800) 832-1223

Close to beach; 12 rooms, four-story tower; full breakfast.

Snowbird Mountain Lodge

276 Santeetlah Road
Robbinsville, NC 28771
(800) 941-9290

1940s stone and chestnut lodge; 22 rooms; full American plan.

Woodlands Inn of Sapphire

1305 U.S. 64 West
Sapphire, NC 28774
(828) 966-4709

Contemporary inn built in 1989; 14 rooms, some with fireplace and/or whirlpool bath; full country breakfast; closed December to February.

Pinebridge Inn

101 Pinebridge Avenue
Spruce Pine, NC 28777
(800) 356-5059

Former school built in 1930; 46 rooms; continental breakfast.

Freedom Escape Lodge and Retreat Center

530 Upper Flat Creek Road
Weaverville, NC 28787
(888) 658-0814

Rustic lodge built in 1984; 17 rooms, continental breakfast, other refreshments; lake gristmill.

Coast Line Inn

503 Nutt Street
Wilmington, NC 28401
(910) 763-2800

On the river walk next to the convention center; 50 rooms, continental breakfast; River's Edge Lounge.

The Inn at St. Thomas Court

101 South Second Street
Wilmington, NC 28401
(910) 343-1800 or (800) 525-0909

Quaint inn in the heart of the historic district; 34 suites, some with kitchen, whirlpool, fireplace; courtyard gardens.

Beau Rivage Plantation

6230 Carolina Beach Road
Wilmington, NC 28412
(910) 392-9021 or (800) 628-7080

Coastal resort near the beach; 30 suites; restaurant.

Miss Bettys Bed and Breakfast Inn

600 West Nash Street
Wilson, NC 27893
(800) 258-2058

Four late-nineteenth-century historic homes; 10 rooms, 4 executive suites; full breakfast; pool, antiques shop.

Tanglewood Manor House

NC 158
Winston-Salem, NC 27012
(910) 766-0591

Former residence of the brother of tobacco magnate R. J. Reynolds; 28 rooms, 6 cottages.

South Carolina

South Carolina

Numbers on map refer to towns numbered below.

* A Top Pick Inn

Belmont Inn ♥ ¢¢
Abbeville, South Carolina 29620

INNKEEPERS: Alan and Audrey Peterson

ADDRESS/TELEPHONE: 104 East Pickens Street; (864) 459–9625 or (877) 459–8118; fax (864) 459–9625.

ROOMS: 25 rooms and suites; all with private bath, cable television, telephone, clock radio, coffeemaker.

RATES: $49 to $99 double occupancy; includes continental breakfast.

OPEN: Year-round.

FACILITIES AND ACTIVITIES: Restaurant, lounge, porches. Nearby: Abbeville Opera House, Burt-Stark House, Abbeville County Museum, Trinity Episcopal Church, Richard B. Russell Lake; water sports, tennis, golf.

BUSINESS TRAVEL: Meeting and special space.

*W*e love quaint, sleepy little Abbeville which is primarily grouped around a delightful town square. This hamlet has two claims to fame. First it bills itself as the Birthplace and Deathbed of the Confederacy because the secession papers were first read in Abbeville in 1860 and the rebel cause died when the War Council formally disbanded here in 1865 during its flight from Richmond. Abbeville's 1908 Opera House, which brought a steady stream of performers to tread its boards, from vaudevillians such as Fanny Brice and Jimmy Durante to serious thespians, still attracts visitors to Abbeville with an impressive summer and winter season of theatricals.

Visiting stars and the fans who came to see them stayed in the sturdy brick hotel just across the street from the Opera House. Built in 1903 and originally called the Eureka, but now known as the Belmont Inn, it also catered to railroad and textile executives and remained in business long after the Opera House itself closed. Although the inn sat empty from 1972 to 1982, it was fully restored and reopened in 1984. Listed on the National Register of Historic Places, the intimate inn continues to offer delightful accommodations. The charm of the early twentieth century is reflected in the large rooms, high ceilings, fireplaces, and the sweeping veranda. We were delighted with its understated ambience when we stayed there one summer weekend.

Our light, airy room was simply and tastefully furnished with antiques and period reproductions. Its best feature, however, was its private veranda—

the only one in the inn. We enjoyed a queen-size bed (bedding in all the rooms is either twins or queens). Armoires were a matter of course here long before they became a popular way for most modern hotels to hide televisions and other amenities, simply because these rooms weren't built with closets. Although we had cable television, we never turned it on.

The inn's restaurant is the scene of an extensive twenty-item continental breakfast of fruits, juices, waffles, several kinds of muffins and Danishes, and hot beverages. The restaurant is also open to the public for dinner and Sunday brunch. Dinner, which innkeeper Alan Peterson describes as Southern fine dining, features such popular favorites as shrimp and grits with vegetables, sweet potato biscuits, and brandied peaches. At Sunday brunch, in addition to all the usual brunch items, there's a carving station and sometimes an omelette station. Folks look forward to the live entertainment at the Jazz Brunch held the last Sunday of every month.

For anyone who has ever been to the Belmont, the old lobby with its four fireplaces on the first floor has been converted to special function space and the new lobby is on the lower level with the aptly named Curtain Call Lounge, the perfect place for a drink before or after the show or during intermission. Be sure to look at the pictures showing the stages of the renovation, which are displayed near the bar.

Since the weather was pleasant while we were there, we took our after-breakfast tea and coffee out to the porch, as did some of our fellow guests—giving us all an opportunity to get to know one another and to trade suggestions about sight-seeing and shopping. Abbeville is filled with delightful antiques shops and boutiques.

Weekend theater packages include wine and cheese before the show, dinner, theater tickets, coffee and dessert afterwards, breakfast the next morning, and admission to the historic Burt-Stark House—all for $169, quite a good deal.

HOW TO GET THERE: From I-85, take the U.S. 76 exit and go south. Follow SC 28 south to Abbeville. At the square, turn left onto Pickens Street. The inn is on your left.

Abbeville Opera House

From Reconstruction to well into the 1920s, traveling troops of actors, musicians, and vaudevillians passed through Abbeville, where the citizens had an insatiable thirst for entertainment. The town's location on the rail line between New York and Atlanta made it a natural stopover. Many a one-night-stand production was performed in the town square alfresco or in a tent. Then the citizens got the bright idea of combining the need for a municipal office building with the desire for an opera house. The result, completed in 1908, is the handsome brick building that provides space for both.

The building's modest two-story facade fronts on the square and doesn't prepare you for the spacious interior. Because the lot slopes down in the back, the performance space is actually six stories tall and qualifies as an opera house because the stage area exceeds the seating area. The small but elegant theater provides seating for 350 on the main floor, a balcony, and four impressive boxes.

An orchestra pit is recessed under the stage. Backstage, three floors of dressing rooms have a hallway window onto the stage so that the performers could follow the action and not miss a cue. The back wall of the building stands over 100 feet tall. Built four bricks thick without restraining rods, it is believed to be one of the tallest freestanding brick walls in the western hemisphere.

Sets were changed with a rope-pulled system of counterweights balanced by sandbags on hemp ropes—hence the name "hemp house." This system is still in place. Abbeville's Opera House is the only remaining hemp house in South Carolina.

Between 1908 and 1930, the theater provided melodrama, minstrels, Shakespeare, and opera. The first production was *The Great Divide*, which was followed later that year by *The Clansman*, played with a troop of cavalry horses on stage. Beginning in 1920, silent movies came to the theater with musicians and full sound effects, but the advent of talkies spelled decline for all live entertainment. As fewer and fewer traveling shows passed through town, Abbeville's influence as a cultural center faded. The Opera House remained a movie theater until the 1950s, when its doors were closed. In the late 1960s the Abbeville Community Theater formed and through a community wide effort the Opera House was restored and reopened to theater once again. Today the community theater offers thirty-six weeks of live theater annually.

Willcox Inn
Aiken, South Carolina 29801

INNKEEPERS: Becky Robert

ADDRESS/TELEPHONE: 100 Colleton Avenue; (803) 649–1377 or (800) 368–1047; fax: (803) 643–0971

ROOMS: 30, including 6 suites and 5 junior suites; many with four poster beds and decorative fireplaces; all with private bath, one with claw-foot tub and telephone, some with dataport, television.

RATES: $95 to $145 weekends, double occupancy; children twelve years old and younger stay free in the parents' room; brunch is $14.95 for adults and $12.95 for children ages five to twelve.

OPEN: Year-round.

FACILITIES AND ACTIVITIES: Pheasant Dining Room, Polo Pub, elevator and other facilities for the disabled, valet service. Nearby: Aiken historic district, Hopeland Gardens, Aiken Historical Museum, Thoroughbred Hall of Fame.

BUSINESS TRAVEL: Meeting space for up to sixty; some telephones with dataports.

*W*e'd heard the story that in its heyday early in this century, the exclusive Willcox Inn was so discriminating about its clientele that the doorman would look down his nose to check a prospective male guest's shoes before admitting him. If the unfortunate guest's attire wasn't up to snuff, the verdict was "no spit-and-polish shine, no room at the inn." Although we made sure our shoes were shined—just in case—we were glad we wouldn't be under such exacting scrutiny when we checked in. Instead, we found a relaxing atmosphere of casual elegance.

In the last century Aiken was a popular winter getaway for wealthy Northerners who came for the mild climate and stayed for months on end, bringing with them not only trunks and trunks of clothing and a staff of servants but also their horses and grooms. At first, mammoth Victorian hotels provided grand accommodations for these visitors, but soon they began to build "cottages" of their own—huge mansions by present-day standards. Eventually all the large hotels burned down, were torn down, or fell down and were never replaced. That's when English butler Frederick Willcox got the idea that an intimate inn was needed to provide lodgings for the few visitors who were merely passing through.

Having salted away his earnings over the years, Willcox had the funds to start building his dream in 1898. When finished, the two-story white-columned inn, which is somewhat reminiscent of Mount Vernon, opened its doors in 1900. The inn's understated elegance gained a solid reputation, and it attracted wealthy business, social, and political leaders including Franklin D. Roosevelt, Winston Churchill, Harold Vanderbilt, Elizabeth Arden, and Count Bernadotte of Sweden.

World War I, the stock market crash of 1929, and the Great Depression, as well as the extension of the railroads into Florida and the increasing avail-ability of air transportation, set Aiken's tourism business way back. Today the town and the inn are enjoying a renaissance. Some of those Northerners and their horses still winter here. Aiken is the only town we know of where some of the streets are unpaved sandy tracks to protect the horses' feet—and the only one where WALK buttons at intersections are placed at the height for a person to push from horseback.

Over the last ninety-nine years, the Willcox has been expanded and reno-vated more than once, but it has never lost its rich patina of history. From the moment we stepped under the stately portico and through the inviting front doors into the warm, cozy lobby with comfortable seating areas pulled up around the two wood-burning fireplaces, we could feel the past come alive.

Exquisitely restored guest rooms each have a distinct personality created with antiques and reproductions and carefully chosen fabrics and wall cov-erings, but each exudes a romance all its own. Our spacious abode was a cor-ner suite with a decorative fireplace in its separate sitting room coupled with a large bedroom with a four-poster bed. Some suites boast a private porch.

Gourmet dining is offered in the refined atmosphere of the Pheasant Room restaurant. We enjoyed the complimentary continental breakfast of fresh fruit and juice, cereal, muffins, breads, pastries, and hot beverages. Some guests elect to order a more substantial breakfast from such choices as eggs Benedict, omelettes, or waffles from the menu at an additional charge.

Later that evening after a busy day of visiting Aiken's museums, gardens, and shops, we stopped in to the clublike Polo Pub for a nightcap. Its blend of wood and leather sets just the right "horsey" note for an inn in the midst of horse country. If you're lucky enough to be spending a Saturday night at the Willcox, Sunday brunch is an extravaganza offered from 11:00 A.M. to 2:00 P.M. that includes a wide variety of traditional breakfast selections as well as roast beef, turkey or ham, vegetables, salads, and desserts.

Use the Willcox Inn as a base from which to explore Aiken and nearby Abbeville and North Augusta, South Carolina, and Augusta, Georgia.

HOW TO GET THERE: From I-20, take exit 18 (Aiken) and turn right. Go 6½ miles to downtown and turn left at Park Avenue. Go 2 blocks to Chesterfield and turn right. The inn is 1 block ahead at the corner of Colleton and Chesterfield.

Beaufort Inn 🗝❤

Beaufort, South Carolina 29902

INNKEEPERS: Debbie and Russell Fielden

ADDRESS/TELEPHONE: 809 Port Republic Street; (843) 521-9000; fax (843) 521-9500

WEB SITE: www.beaufortinn.com

E-MAIL: bftinn@hargray.com

ROOMS: 11 rooms and suites, 1 two-bedroom cottage; all with private bath, desk, telephone with dataport, voice mail, clock radio, television and VCR, ceiling fan, refrigerator, coffeemaker, robes; some with fireplace and/or balcony.

RATES: $125 to $225 for rooms and suites, $300 for cottage, double occupancy; includes breakfast and afternoon tea; extra person $20.

OPEN: Year-round except Christmas Eve and Christmas Day.

FACILITIES AND ACTIVITIES: Restaurant, bar, verandas, courtyard garden, elevator. Nearby: historic Beaufort, home tours, museums; Intracoastal Waterway; boat tours, carriage tours; antiques and gift shops, sidewalk and waterfront cafes, Waterfront Park, beaches; fifty golf courses within a forty-five-minute drive; tennis, horseback riding, ecological tours.

BUSINESS TRAVEL: Telephone with dataport and voice mail; conference room can accommodate up to eight and features a wet bar, fireplace, wall-mounted presentation board, television with VCR; fax, copying, and other business services available. First-floor parlor can accommodate fourteen to twenty. Garden courtyard is also suitable for special functions.

*B*eaufort exudes romance. Located on the Intracoastal Waterway and shaded by ancient live oaks dripping with Spanish moss, the historic town is filled with nineteenth-century mansions, attractions, and folklore and is one of only three National Historic Landmark Districts in South Carolina. What is more natural when visiting Beaufort than to stay in a historic inn? A standout among several historic lodgings is the four-diamond Beaufort Inn, which has been named one of the Top Ten Inns in the Country by American Historic Inns and one of the Top Ten Most Romantic Inns in the USA by *The Road Less Traveled*.

Built as a private second home by a prominent Hampton, South Carolina, attorney in 1897, the structure became one of Beaufort's first boardinghouses. It operated as a hotel in the 1930s and eventually became run-down and neglected. Fully restored in the 1990s and opened as an inn, the stately, many-gabled Beaufort Inn provides a perfect balance of historic charm and modern conveniences, superior accommodations, excellent cuisine, and genuine Southern hospitality.

We visited in December when the inn was bedecked for Christmas and the first thing that caught our attention was the stunning, beautifully decorated three-story atrium, with a stairway climbing all three floors around its perimeter. Hanging down through the vast stairwell was an immense brass-and-crystal chandelier. Everything was draped with festive garland and tied with cheery red bows. What a perfect setting for the season.

The bustling downstairs is occupied by the formal restaurant, which has a fireplace, the casual Grill Room and Wine Bar, and a comfy, cozy library/sitting room with a fireplace. Handsome hardwood floors, ornate moldings, antiques and period reproductions, and crystal chandeliers are featured throughout. A first-floor veranda and a pleasant courtyard garden make great places to relax by yourself or gather with fellow guests in good weather. Everyday life will be the farthest thing from your mind.

The upper stories are occupied by luxurious guest accommodations. Light and airy, each spacious, graciously furnished guest chamber features a painting of the nearby plantation after which it is named—among them, Oak Grove, Orange Grove, Retreat, and Laurel Hill. Every room boasts a sitting area, king- or queen-size bed (it might be a romantic four-poster, canopy bed, or nostalgic iron bed), small refrigerator, and Caldwell-Massey bath amenities, plus all the conveniences you'd expect such as telephone and television. Wallpapers, window treatments, and bed coverings are carefully selected to give every room singular character. Some special rooms and suites boast a fireplace, wet bar, and/or private porch. In addition to accommodations in the main house, the Beaufort Inn has a charming two-bedroom cottage with a living room, dining room, and kitchen.

You may not have to lunch at all after breakfast at the Beaufort Inn (although there are dozens of pleasant restaurants in Beaufort). Imaginative hot breakfast entrees change according to the season and the whims of the chef, but they might consist of whole-grain French bread stuffed with Brie and sun-dried peaches, pecan pancakes, eggs Benedict with crab cakes, or a shrimp omelette. Regardless of the entree, the breakfast is accompanied by cereal, fresh fruits and juices, and a basket of hot biscuits and honey butter. You can enjoy your breakfast feast in the dining room, on the porch, or in your room.

Served in the elegant and quiet dining room by a fire blazing in the fireplace in cool weather, the inventive dinner menu might feature ginger-crusted sea bass with citrus glaze, filet mignon, duck with shallot sauce, or grilled shrimp with eggplant and risotto. Special entrees and desserts are created daily. Burnished paneling and leather dominate the casual Grill Room and Wine Bar, where you can order lighter, simpler fare as well as anything from the dining room menu. The extensive wine list includes popular vintages and hard-to-find reserve wines by the bottle and forty-eight wines from around the world that are available by the glass. Try the inn's Flights of Wine—two-ounce glasses of three different wines that complement one another.

HOW TO GET THERE: Beaufort is just thirty minutes from I-95 halfway between Charleston and Savannah. From I-95, take exit 38 east to U.S. 17 and turn left (north). At U.S. 21, turn right (east). As the road enters town it becomes Boundary Street. Turn right at Charles Street, left at Craven Street, and right at West Street. Watch for signs on the left indicating the inn's parking lot. You'll enter the inn from the rear.

The Rhett House Inn
Beaufort, South Carolina 29902

INNKEEPERS: Marianne and Steve Harrison

ADDRESS/TELEPHONE: 1009 Craven Street; (843) 524–9030 or (800) 480–9530; fax (843) 524–1310

ROOMS: 17; all with private bath, telephone, and television; 9 with fireplace; 8 with whirlpool tub.

RATES: $150 to $225, double or single (inquire for details); includes full breakfast.

OPEN: Year-round.

FACILITIES AND ACTIVITIES: Bicycles, country club membership for golf, tennis, swimming. Nearby: beach, walking and carriage tours of historic sites in Beaufort, one-hour drive to Charleston or Savannah.

BUSINESS TRAVEL: Located one hour from Charleston or Savannah. Telephone in room, fax available, conference facilities, twenty-four-hour desk.

*B*eaufort does something to people. Lured by tourist literature laced with phrases like "picturesque old port town" and "nestled along the Intracoastal" and "quaint historic community," people come to visit this place that time is supposed to have skipped over. And sure enough, it has.

Except for telling you that the only reason Sherman didn't burn Beaufort is because it was under Union occupation at the time, nobody gets very worked up over anything. Breezes really do "waft." The streets really are "tree-lined." Folks really do "stroll."

Next thing you know, you get to thinking that instead of visiting, you'd like to live there.

It happened to Marianne and Steve Harrison. They left their city lives behind and the result is Rhett House, a B&B inn that they restored to gleaming beauty and operate in a thoroughly professional manner.

The 1820 building has wraparound verandas with classic columns and porticos and beautifully curved entry stairs. Live oaks swathed in Spanish moss shade the house. The white exterior almost sparkles. The scene cries out to be a movie set for a Southern romance with violins playing in the background.

Across the street is an 1850s cottage, which Marianne and Steve bought in 1997 and restored as seven new luxury rooms, each complete with small refrigerators, minibar, coffeemaker, whirlpool tub, and fireplace.

All rooms are furnished with antiques, but everything has been chosen to keep the rooms light and bright, avoiding the slightly gloomy look we sometimes associate with antiques.

The room we stayed in was huge. It opened onto the courtyard garden, so that we could hear the fountain all night. The fireplace had a raised brick hearth. The drapes, rugs, and furniture were done in a country motif with blue-and-white gingham and ticking.

It seemed like a good idea just to stay there with the door open to the courtyard and spend the morning reading, but we didn't want to miss breakfast.

We sat around the dining room table, playing "Where are you from?" and "What's your favorite inn?" and digging into bowls of huge strawberries and plates of tiny poppy-seed muffins with unromantic vigor and a most un-Southern display of energy.

Marianne gave lots of advice about nice places to see in the area and how to get there. One of her favorite places (and ours, incidentally) is Hunting Island State Park, a 5,000-acre park just 16 miles from downtown Beaufort, with several miles of perfect swimming beaches that are also uncommonly good for shelling.

At the marina, the chamber of commerce provides more information than you can possibly use about Beaufort and the area, and it offers a nice brochure for a self-guided tour of historic sites.

This inn has been enjoying a lot of publicity and the presence of some celebrity guests, including Barbra Streisand and Nick Nolte. (Not at the same time, understand.)

HOW TO GET THERE: From I-95, take exit 33 to Beaufort. From Savannah, follow the signs to Hilton Head Island and then to Beaufort. The inn is 1 block from the Intracoastal Waterway at the corner of Craven and Newcastle Streets. Ask for a map when you make reservations.

Greenleaf Inn ¢¢
Camden, South Carolina 29020

INNKEEPER: Jack Branham

ADDRESS/TELEPHONE: 1308/10 North Broad Street; (803) 425-1806
or (800) 437-5874; fax (803) 425-5853

ROOMS: 10; plus 2 suites; all with private bath, telephone, clock radio,
cable television with a movie channel, some with decorative fireplaces;
children welcome.

RATES: $55 to $75: includes continental breakfast.

OPEN: Year-round.

FACILITIES AND ACTIVITIES: Restaurant and bar. Nearby: National
Register of Historic Places historic district, Historic Camden Revolutionary War Site, Camden Archives and Museum, Bonds Conway House,
Hobkirk Hill Battle Site, Springdale Race Course, Lake Wateree, Battle
of Camden site, Historic Boykin, Battle of Boykin's Mill site, golf, tennis, fishing, boating.

BUSINESS TRAVEL: Telephone with dataport.

*W*e were visiting Camden because Carol's mother's family lived
there before the Revolutionary War until the 1830s when they
migrated to Alabama, and Carol wanted to use the Camden
Archives for genealogical research. Whether you're visiting this lovely Southern town for its rich Revolutionary War history, your own genealogical
research, or to watch the world-renowned steeplechases at Springdale Race
Course, a good base of operations is the Greenleaf Inn.

Located on a shady tree-lined street of impressive historic homes just a
couple of blocks from the main downtown business district, the inn offers
elegant and comfortable accommodations in two adjacent houses and a cottage. By far the fancier of the two, the imposing McLean House—built in
1890—houses several elegant upstairs guest rooms and the locally popular
Avanti's Restaurant and pub downstairs. High ceilings, tall windows with
dramatic window treatments, antiques, rich fabrics, and decorative fireplaces
characterize the spacious bed chambers.

Next door, the Reynolds House, circa 1805, is much more basic, as befits
a home of its venerable age. Rooms are smaller, ceilings lower, and the furniture, bed coverings, and window treatments simpler. Although our bedroom
in this house was so simple as to border on nondescript, we liked its seclu-

sion from the restaurant and pub as well as the enclosed veranda that served as a cheery sun porch/sitting room, complete with comfortable wicker and lush plants.

Also on the property is a 1930s two bedroom cottage furnished with blond furniture. This comfortable little hideaway is a favorite with horse people who come to town for races, horse shows, polo matches, and fox hunting and want to stay some place comfortable and not at all fancy.

Italian cuisine is featured at Avanti's Restaurant, which is open to the public for dinner only on Monday and Thursday through Saturday. A generous continental breakfast is served to overnight guests each morning in Avanti's. The cozy pub, which sports a horsey theme with pictures of horse racing, is open the same hours as the restaurant.

Camden is a delightful small town with more than 250 years of history: from the Revolutionary War through the antebellum South and the Civil War through the turn-of-the-century era when the town became a winter playground for wealthy Northerners and their horses. Its present claim to fame is steeplechasing at the spring Carolina Cup and the fall Marion DuPont Scott Colonial Cup.

HOW TO GET THERE: From I–20, take the U.S. 521 exit north. The inn is 1½ miles past the intersection of U.S. 521 and U.S. 1.

Anchorage Inn
Charleston, South Carolina 29401

INNKEEPER: Barry Hutto

ADDRESS/TELEPHONE: 26 Vendue Range; (843) 723–8300 or (800) 421–2952; fax (843) 723–9543

E-MAIL: theanchorageinn@otmail.com

ROOMS: 17, plus 2 suites; all with private bath; some with whirlpool tub, telephone (some with dataport), and television. One room fully handicapped equipped.

RATES: $94, single or double, $230, suites, includes full continental breakfast buffet, turndown service, afternoon wine and cheese, evening sherry. Inquire about off-season rates.

OPEN: Year-round.

FACILITIES AND ACTIVITIES: Nearby: across from Waterfront Park. Walking distance to restaurants, Dock Street Theatre, Footlight Players Theatre, and the Old City Market; carriage tours.

BUSINESS TRAVEL: Located minutes from business district. Computer and modem setup, good work space, and telephone in room; fax available.

Anchorage means "safe harbor." The woman, a local historian, who opened this B&B inn in 1991 chose the name because it seemed to fit the location of the inn and the history of the building. The red-brick, two-story structure was built about 1840 as a warehouse in what used to be a commercial shipping district of the city. The shipping is long gone, of course, but people stay here because they've heard it's not only a safe harbor but also a comfortable one, noted especially for providing extra services that don't show up in any brochure. More about that in a minute.

The inn has a British feel, which many people find a pleasant change from the almost overwhelming Civil War emphasis of Charleston. Charleston was an important settlement for British colonists, so the taste of an Anglophile makes sense here.

When you come into the foyer, which is open to the second-story roof and skylights, you see the exposed post-and-beam construction of the original building. Then, in keeping with the period, you see a magnificent painted Chinese tea canister from the 1700s above the desk. Farther back, an English library with dark wood beams and paneling and big stuffed chairs arranged near the fireplace remind you of the pubs you'd visit on a trip through the British countryside.

The guest rooms have seventeenth century–style bedsteads and straight, paneled tapestry drapes. The Berber carpet suggests the sisal matting of the seventeenth-century floor coverings. But the conveniences are entirely of this century, with everything from hair dryers in the bathroom to spaces where you can hook up your computer and modem if you just can't stop working, even in a safe harbor.

That brings us to the highly personal service. The young, obliging staff are visibly proud of working in the inn. Moreover, they are local and pride themselves on providing both local information and all the service you need. A good example is the story of a woman who came to the Anchorage with a group from the San Francisco Museum of Modern Art. She became ill and said she just wished she could have a couple of poached eggs to settle her stomach. Like most inns in Charleston, the Anchorage does not cook food on the premises but serves a continental breakfast. But Sally Chapman, whose "official" job is handling public relations, went to the trouble of finding two fresh eggs and a cookbook so that she could prepare poached eggs for the ailing guest. Such service stands out anywhere.

HOW TO GET THERE: From I-26, take the East Bay Street exit to the heart of the city. Turn left on Vendue Range; the inn is in the middle of the block on the left.

Ansonborough Inn 💚
Charleston, South Carolina 29401

INNKEEPER: Kevin Eichman

ADDRESS/TELEPHONE: 21 Hasell Street; (843) 723–1655 or (800) 522–2073; fax (843) 577–6888

WEB SITE: www.aesir.com/ansonboroughinn

E-MAIL: ansonboroughinn@cchat.com

ROOMS: 37 suites; all with private bath, telephone, television, and kitchen. No smoking inn.

RATES: Spring and fall, $139 to $199, double; summer and winter, $109 to $139, double; includes continental breakfast and afternoon wine and cheese. $10 for each extra adult in suite. Children twelve and under free. Inquire about discounts for singles, long-term stays, and corporate rates.

OPEN: Year-round.

FACILITIES AND ACTIVITIES: Free off-street parking. In heart of waterfront historic district. Nearby: historic sites, restaurants, shuttle transportation to visitor center. Walking distance to antiques shops and downtown Charleston.

Located minutes from business district. Telephone, computer and modem setup, excellent work area in room; fax, copy service available; meeting room.

*L*ike so many Charleston inns, this B&B inn had a different function in its earlier time. It was a three-story stationer's warehouse built about 1900. The building's renovation not only kept the heart-of-pine beams and locally fired red brick, which are typical of the period, but actually emphasized them. The lobby soars three stories high, with skylights; the original huge, rough beams are fully visible, an important part of the decor.

The original plan to use the renovated building as a condo complex didn't work out, which probably was bad news for some investors; but it's great for inn guests now, because the rooms, which are really suites, are huge. At least one wall in each features the exposed old brick. The ceilings are about

20 feet high. Because all the rooms were fit into an existing shell, no two rooms are exactly the same shape or size. Nothing is exactly predictable. The resulting little quirks, nooks, lofts, and alcoves add a lot of interest.

The living rooms are furnished in period reproductions with comfortable chairs and sleeper sofas to accommodate extra people. What's more, you really can cook in the kitchens. If you ask for place settings and basic kitchen utensils when you make your reservations, the kitchen will be ready when you arrive. The inn is just across the road from an excellent Harris Teeter supermarket housed in an old railroad station. I don't think it would be appropriate to whip up corned beef and cabbage or deep-fried chitlins in this environment, but the arrangement is great for preparing light meals—a good way to save your calories and your dollars for some sumptuous dinners in Charleston's excellent restaurants.

Clearly this isn't the kind of place where everyone sits around the breakfast table comparing notes about dinner the night before, but the continental breakfast (with sweetbreads baked at a plantation in Walterboro) and the evening wine and cheese are set up in the lobby so that guests can sit in conversational clusters. If someone on the staff thinks that you may have some-

thing in common with another guest, he or she will take the trouble to intro-
duce you. Indeed, the staff here is personable and helpful—attitudes you
don't always encounter in Charleston hostelries. A visitor from a Scandina-
vian country said that if this is Southern hospitality, he likes it.

HOW TO GET THERE: From I-26 East, take the Meeting Street/Visitor Center
exit. Go 1²⁄10 miles to Hasell Street. Turn left and go through the next traffic
signal. From Route 17 South, take the East Bay Street exit, go 1³⁄10 miles to
Hasell and turn left. From Route 17 North, after crossing the Ashley River,
exit to the right and go through the first traffic signal onto Calhoun Street.
Drive 1⁴⁄10 miles to Easy Bay Street, turn right, and go to the second traffic
signal (Hassell Street) and turn left. The inn is on your right.

The Battery Carriage House Inn
Charleston, South Carolina 29401

INNKEEPER: Katharine Hastie

ADDRESS/TELEPHONE: 20 South Battery; (843) 727-3100 or
(800) 775-5575; fax (843) 727-3130

WEB SITE: www.charleston-inns.com

ROOMS: 11, plus 1 suite; all with private bath, either a steam bath or
whirlpool, robes, private entrance, cable television, and telephone.
Limited wheelchair access. No children under twelve. No smoking inn.

RATES: $109 to $229, single or double; includes continental breakfast,
beverages, and turndown service. Two-night minimum stay on
weekends.

OPEN: Year-round.

FACILITIES AND ACTIVITIES: Nearby: walking distance to restaurants,
houses, museums, and city marina; short drive to shopping on Broad
and King Streets, the Old Exchange Building and Dungeon, and theaters on Queen and Church Streets.

BUSINESS TRAVEL: Located minutes from business district. Direct-dial
telephone with answering machine; concierge service for tours and
restaurants; fax and copy service available.

*F*rom the front door of the Battery Carriage House you see White Point Gardens, the Battery, and Fort Sumter in Charleston Harbor, where the Civil War (or in Southern lingo, the War of Northern Aggression or the "recent unpleasantness") began.

Built in 1843, this landmark antebellum house was home to ancestors of the current owners, Kat and Drayton Hastie. Photographers from all over the world have shot this house, and film directors have used it as the setting for such films as *North and South* and *Queen.*

As a guest here, you stay in the large carriage house behind the main house, where the garden separates you from street noise. Several of the rooms have four-poster canopy beds and are decorated with local artists' watercolor paintings. The suite is particularly peaceful, with a cream carpet over parquet floors and bare brick walls.

In the parlor, a gaming table is outfitted for checkers, chess, and backgammon, and you'll find a separate bridge table. We have trouble imagining who'd come to Charleston and spend the time playing bridge, but you can if you find three other people willing to play.

In the afternoon, this is a nice place to drink wine and discuss dinner plans. Or you can move out into the gardens or the Lady Bankshire Rose Arbor.

Another special place sets this inn apart. On the ground level, underneath the front porch, you can sit in wicker chairs hidden from the street by a wrought-iron fence, pillars, and plantings. From here you see the White Point Gardens and the harbor and catch a cool, steady breeze in the shade.

Speaking of cool breezes, the inn is said to be inhabited by two ghosts. One is a man's torso, the other a friendly (and certainly more useful) full-figured male. They hang around Rooms 8 and 10. No extra charge.

HOW TO GET THERE: From I–26, take the Meeting Street exit where I–26 ends. Follow Meeting to Battery, and make a right. From U.S. 17 North, cross the Ashley River Bridge and bear right onto Lockwood Boulevard. Keep making every possible right until you are on Murray Boulevard. Then make a left on King Street. Turn right onto South Battery. From U.S. Highway 17 south, take East Bay or King Street exit and follow the street to the Battery. The inn is at 20 South Battery.

Elliott House Inn
Charleston, South Carolina 29401

INNKEEPER: Al and Mavis Boerman

ADDRESS/TELEPHONE: 78 Queen Street; (843) 723–1855 or (800) 729–1855; fax (843) 722–1567

WEB SITE: www.elliotthouseinn.com

ROOMS: 26; all with private bath, telephone (some with dataports), and television.

RATES: $125 to $150, single or double; includes continental breakfast, wine and cheese reception, turndown service with chocolates. Inquire about off-season rates.

OPEN: Year-round.

FACILITIES AND ACTIVITIES: Large whirlpool in courtyard, bicycles. Nearby: walking distance to restaurants, historic sites, tourist attractions, and antiques shops.

BUSINESS TRAVEL: Located five minutes from commercial district. Telephone in room, corporate rates.

*B*usiness people who spend a lot of time in Charleston (poor babies!) say this is one of their favorite B&B inns, because the people on staff are "so sweet" and the rooms are so comfortable.
The building is a renovated three-story frame house built about 1865, expanded with a newer section. The rooms are furnished in period reproductions, with such modern amenities as color televisions hidden away in walnut armoires. Oriental rugs cover good wood floors, and Oriental-patterned wallpaper carries through the theme. The rooms are all different, furnished with period reproductions.

If you stand back and inspect the entire building, you'll notice that the second- and third-floor balconies slope noticeably toward the ground. Seems that the earthquake of 1886 knocked things a bit wopperjawed. Everything is structurally sound, but the result of the quake is evident in the slant of those balconies, a touch that appeals to people associated with the place who enjoy its uniqueness.

Elliott House is ideally situated if you're planning to spend some time walking through the historic streets of Charleston. It is in the heart of downtown Charleston, a block from the antiques district in one direction, a block from famous historic sites in the other.

At the end of a day of sight-seeing or business, when it's nice enough to be outside, you'll enjoy the courtyard. Designed around the whirlpool, it includes fountains and shady sitting areas and gleams with flowering plants most of the year. What a place to enjoy a glass of wine!

It would be a mistake to relax with your wine so much that you miss dinner, however, because the inn is right next to 82 Queen, one of Charleston's better restaurants, with an exotic menu.

HOW TO GET THERE: Take the Meeting Street exit from I-26; go south on Meeting to Queen and right onto Queen. The inn is in the first block.

Fulton Lane Inn
Charleston, South Carolina 29401

INNKEEPER: Mary Kay Smith, manager

ADDRESS/TELEPHONE: 202 King Street; (843) 720–2600 or (800) 720–2688; fax (843) 720–2940

WEB SITE: www.charminginns.com

E-MAIL: fli@charminginns.com

ROOMS: 27; all with private bath and television. Two fully equipped wheelchair accessible rooms. No smoking inn.

RATES: $100 to $210, single; $120 to $230, double; $195 to $275, suite; includes continental breakfast and afternoon sherry. $20 each additional person. Children under twelve years old free.

OPEN: Year-round.

FACILITIES AND ACTIVITIES: Located in the heart of the antiques district. Nearby: shopping at the Old City Market and The Shops at Charleston Place, restaurants.

*A*fter Hurricane Hugo in 1989, all the king's horses and all the king's men couldn't put the building at King Street and Fulton Lane back together again. The building's history probably contributed to its demise: The two-story structure is thought to have been built in haste for the World Expo in 1912. The first story was flimsily constructed, barely able to support the second story; but it looked good. The second story was handsomely covered in decorative tin. But 204–206 King Street wasn't up to the storm of the century. Two architects, Will Evans and Joe Schmidt, made a detailed drawing of the building before bulldozers razed it.

What rose from the ashes is a building so sympathetic to its surroundings that it looks just right with its centuries-old neighbors. This was particularly important because two attached buildings, 202 and 208 King Street, were part of the project. In keeping with the King Street tradition of shops on the ground floor and sleeping quarters above, Golden and Associates Antiques and A'Riga IV Antiques, longtime tenants evicted by the storm, have reopened at street level, off of the Fulton Lane Inn lobby. Guest rooms are on the second and third floors of the three buildings.

Evans and Schmidt were brought back to design the shops and the B&B inn. They modeled the new building after the demolished structure, incorporating the lines and even some of the decorative tin salvaged from the old building by The Historic Charleston Foundation. The inn's owner asked for an interior with a cool, but sexy feel. That it is. The sherbet-green halls, with glossy white wainscoting, and the guest rooms, with chenille bedspreads, wicker lampshades, and floor-to-ceiling windows that catch a steady breeze from the nearby harbor, make this quiet, private place special.

The inn provides an Old Charleston atmosphere with all the modern amenities, including stocked refrigerators, kitchens in the suites, and some baths with whirlpools. From many of the rooms you can see the infamous Fulton Alley. Today it's part of the fashionable downtown business district and the location for the elegant Fulton V restaurant and Historic Charleston Foundation offices. But way back when, the very building occupied by the venerable foundation was one of the city's most notorious brothels. Now *that's* what we call "living history."

HOW TO GET THERE: The inn is a half block south of the intersection of King and Market Streets.

<hr />

Indigo Inn
Charleston, South Carolina 29401

INNKEEPER: Brian Limehuse

ADDRESS/TELEPHONE: One Maiden Lane; (843) 577–5900 or (800) 845–7639; fax (843) 577–0378

WEB SITE: www.aesir.com/indigoinn

E-MAIL: IndigoInn@aesir.com

ROOMS: 40 rooms; all with private bath, cable television, telephone with dataport.

RATES: $105 to $185, double occupancy; includes Hunt Breakfast, newspaper, and afternoon hors d'oeuvres.

OPEN: Year-round.

FACILITIES AND ACTIVITIES: Courtyard, elevator, concierge. Nearby: Charleston historic district, museums, casual and fine dining, antiques shopping, nightlife.

BUSINESS TRAVEL: Telephone with dataport; fax and copy service available.

This wonderful inn epitomizes the old saying, "You can't tell a book by its cover." The subdued blue of this plain-Jane three-story stucco inn replicates the hue of indigo, from which the inn takes its name. In the 1700s, indigo, which yields blue dye, was a major cash crop in the Low Country, and its immense profits financed many of the opulent mansions in the historic district. The simple building occupied by this intimate four-diamond B&B inn was built in 1850 as an indigo warehouse. Completely transformed today, its unassuming exterior belies the charming guest rooms, enchanting New Orleans–style courtyard, and two floors of wraparound galleries completely hidden from casual view. Dedicated to upholding Charleston's long-standing tradition of gracious hospitality, the Indigo Inn has been honored by numerous national magazines and newspapers.

Our visit was during perfect spring weather, so we spent every spare minute in the semitropical plant-filled courtyard listening to the tinkling fountain, reading the newspaper, or talking over where we'd been that day and where we wanted to go next. The courtyard's cast-iron tables and chairs made the perfect place to take breakfast and afternoon refreshments. We'd brought our own bottle of wine, so it seemed only natural to drift back out into the courtyard to enjoy a glass later in the twilight before setting off for dinner.

We were grateful that the courtyard is so inviting, because the rooms are a little on the small side. Reminiscent of a bygone era, the charming eighteenth-century bed chambers are quite similar. Furnished primarily with period reproductions, the rooms feature four-poster beds and wallpapers and fabrics appropriate to the last century. Modern conveniences include private bath, telephone, and television.

Our day got off to a good start with the generous Hunt Breakfast that is set out on an antique sideboard in the cozy, wood-paneled lobby each morning. More than a continental breakfast, it includes fruits of the season, juices, hot beverages, a selection of homemade breads, and ham biscuits. Mm-Mm good. Had the weather been bad, we could have enjoyed our meal in the adjacent sitting room or in our own room. When we returned from a hard day of sight-seeing, we found hors d'oeuvres and hot and cold beverages waiting in the sitting room.

One more great thing about the Indigo Inn is its terrific location just a block from the famous Market and near dozens of attractions and restaurants.

HOW TO GET THERE: From I–95 north or south, take I–26 east to the Meeting Street/Visitors Center Exit. Continue 1²⁄₁₀ miles on Meeting Street to Pinkney Street; turn left onto Pinkney then left into the parking lot at the Indigo.

The John Rutledge House Inn
Charleston, South Carolina 29401

INNKEEPER: Linda Bishop; Richard T. Widman, owner

ADDRESS/TELEPHONE: 116 Broad Street; (843) 723–7999 or (800) 476–9741; fax (843) 720–2615

WEB SITE: www.charminginns.com

E-MAIL: jrh@charminginns.com

ROOMS: 19 in the main house and 2 carriage houses; all with private bath, television, telephone, and refrigerator; some with Jacuzzi; some with wheelchair access. No-smoking rooms available.

RATES: $150 to $245, single; $170 to $265, double; $275 to $345, suites; includes continental breakfast. Extra person in room $20. Children under twelve free.

OPEN: Year-round.

FACILITIES AND ACTIVITIES: Full breakfast. Nearby: restaurants, walking distance to historic sites of Historic Charleston; theaters, shops, Charleston's slave market, historic tours.

This B&B inn has taken connoisseurs of inns by storm, not only for its historic value and its elegance, but also for its vitality. In Charleston, some established inns seem to have reached the point of polite indifference. When you talk to people at this one, their pride in the place and their concern for guests are refreshing.

When you meet the innkeeper, Linda Bishop, you get a good idea of what the truly skillful Southern hostess of antebellum times must have been like. Linda translates that graciousness and skill into contemporary situations. She speaks knowledgeably about the city and this inn without ever boring

you and without ever losing sight of the reasons you are visiting. She negotiates stairs, narrow walks, and hallways in a simple, fashionable, long dress effortlessly and looks just right doing it. Most important, she sees to it that whatever should happen does, and she makes it look effortless. She fits perfectly into a building of this elegance and historic importance.

First, the history: John Rutledge, signer of the U.S. Constitution, lived here. The house was built in 1763 and is one of only fifteen homes of signers of the Constitution standing today. Also, much of the history of South Carolina was made during meetings in the ballroom and library.

As for the elegance, original plaster moldings and intricate ironwork have been restored, as have twelve marble mantels carved in Italy. At the risk of sounding disrespectful—when you look around, the phrase "really spiffed up" comes to mind. Bordered parquet floors simply take your breath away, as does the expanse of the ballroom where, from 4:30 to 6:00 P.M., guests are invited to mingle and share complimentary refreshments. If you're wearing your just-you clothes, we honestly can't tell you that you'll feel like a part of the room's history, but it is nice to go there knowing that Pinkneys and Laurens and Rutledges were once in that same space plotting the future of their state and nation.

The guest rooms are furnished in a mixture of antiques and period reproductions, with warm, cheerful colors—rose, peach, deep green, and ivory. Rooms in the carriage house are smaller and simpler than those in the main house, but they are still luxurious.

Breakfast has become an elaborate affair here, with some of the offerings directly related to the history of the house. For instance, the house specialty is biscuits with hot sherried fruit, because John Rutledge loved sherry. If you want a bigger breakfast, you can order from a printed menu that is hung on your doorknob each evening. The choices range from the biscuit with sherried fruit to such Southern favorites as grits or poached eggs with shrimp and hollandaise sauce. Health-conscious choices have also been included. The continental breakfast items are complimentary. The charge for the more elaborate entrees is marked on the menu. You also choose what time you'd like your breakfast to be delivered and where—in your room or in the courtyard.

HOW TO GET THERE: The inn is near the corner of King and Broad Streets. Ask for a map when you make a reservation.

Kings Courtyard Inn
Charleston, South Carolina 29401

INNKEEPER: Reg Smith

ADDRESS/TELEPHONE: 198 King Street; (843) 723-7000 or (800) 845-6119; fax (843) 720-2608

WEB SITE: www.charminginns.com

E-MAIL: kci@charminginns.com

ROOMS: 41, with 4 suites; all with private bath, television, and telephone, some with fireplace; some with wheelchair access.

RATES: $105 to $195, single; $125 to $215, double; includes continental breakfast, complimentary wine and sherry on arrival, evening brandy and chocolates, morning newspaper. Extra person in room $20. Inquire about rates for suites.

OPEN: Year-round.

FACILITIES AND ACTIVITIES: Bar service in courtyards all afternoons but Sunday; whirlpool tub. Nearby: restaurants, historic sites and tours, tourist attractions, antiques shops.

The B&B inn is a three-story 1853 building designed in the Greek Revival style. The building is one of historic King Street's largest and oldest structures and has had many usages in its 130 years of existence: high-quality shops and private residences, and at one time the upper floors were used as an inn catering to plantation owners, travelers with shipping interests, and merchant guests.

We are endlessly fascinated by the old-city way of creating little areas of calm and quiet away from the streets with courtyards. It's done well here, with two brick courtyards filled with tropical plants and geraniums and accented with fountains: One has a large whirlpool tub, and the other provides lots of shady spots for enjoying a cocktail.

The rooms are decorated individually and furnished with period reproductions. Some have canopied beds; some have fireplaces. They feel quiet, cool, and restful after you've been out pounding the Charleston sidewalks for a day.

The same tranquil feeling prevails in the lobby, where the fireplace and Audubon prints could as easily be part of a family living room as an inn. The desk of the concierge is here, too, with some very pleasant people to help with tours, transportation, and advice We were impressed with the friendliness of the staff.

Kings Courtyard has received a nice honor. In 1989 it was one of thirty-two hotels recognized by the National Trust for Historic Preservation's new

"Historic Hotels of America" program. Hotels chosen must be at least fifty years old and recognized as having historic significance.

HOW TO GET THERE: King Street parallels Meeting Street. From King Street, turn left on Market Street or Horlbeck Alley to park in the city parking lot behind the inn.

The Lodge Alley Inn
Charleston, South Carolina 29401

INNKEEPER: Greg Overmier

ADDRESS/TELEPHONE: 195 East Bay Street; in South Carolina, (843) 722-1611 or (800) 845-1004; fax (843) 722-7497

WEB SITE: www.lodgeallyinn.com

E-MAIL: lodgeallyinn@aol.com

ROOMS: 34, plus 60 suites and 1 penthouse apartment; all with private bath, television, and telephone; some with wheelchair access; some suites with whirlpool tub.

RATES: $139 to $310, single or double; breakfast extra.

OPEN: Year-round.

FACILITIES AND ACTIVITIES: Breakfast, lunch, dinner, and lounge open to public and guests. No alcohol served on Sunday. Free parking. Located on a restored alley in the heart of Historic Charleston, within walking distance of most historic sites. Nearby: carriage tours, Waterfront Park.

BUSINESS TRAVEL: Located five minutes from the business district. Telephone in room, good work surface in suites; fax, copy service available; conference facilities; corporate rates.

*T*his is one of those saved-from-the-wrecking-ball stories. The whole alley of old warehouses was supposed to have been wiped out in 1973 to make way for condominiums, but the Save Charleston Foundation and some enterprising developers got into the act, saved the alley, and restored the buildings.

There's a lot of elegance in Charleston's history, which is reflected in the inn. When you arrive, you walk under a canopy, and a uniformed valet comes to park your car—or, in our case, to park Carol's vintage Cadillac. We weren't sure how it would fit in with all that Charleston elegance, but the valet said not to worry, he'd take care of the old girl as if she were his own.

A bellman, also in uniform, helped us get our bags to our room, making sure that we noticed the neatly hidden and well-stocked little refrigerator, the gas-log fireplace, and the eighteenth-century furniture reproductions. We were fascinated by one wall of the room: It still had the original brick and a huge exposed beam left from the old warehouse. The wide floor planks had the kinds of nicks and dark spots you'd expect to find in a warehouse. The floors were finished to a high gloss and partly covered with Oriental rugs. From our window, we could see the steeples of some of Charleston's famous old churches.

The Lodge Alley Inn has gradually been renovating the other old warehouses around it to create an interesting variety of rooms and suites, many especially suited to small groups and business meetings. The rooms in one area have a less formal, Country French decor and are very spacious. Some have a second-level loft for bedroom and bath, with dining, living, and kitchen space below. If you have special requirements, mention them when you call for reservations. Even if you end up with a kitchen, though, you should give the restaurant a try.

At one time the restaurant served with formality, but now the mode is casual courtyard dining, under umbrellas at wrought-iron tables in spring and fall. The restaurant has the only grand rotisserie in town, from which such delicacies as Chateaubriand and rack of lamb are served with potato, pasta, or rice. You often dine to the music of a jazz band if you eat outside in spring or fall. The rest of the time, of course, there's ample seating indoors.

HOW TO GET THERE: I–26 and U.S. 17 are the major routes into Charleston. From either, turn right just before the Cooper River Bridge onto East Bay Street. Go 2 miles. The inn is on the right.

Maison Du Pré
Charleston, South Carolina 29401

INNKEEPERS: Lucille and Bob Mulholland; Mark Mulholland, manager

ADDRESS/TELEPHONE: East Bay at George Street; (843) 723–8691 or (800) 844–INNS

WEB SITE: www.maisondupre.com

ROOMS: 15, including 2 suites; all with private bath, television, and telephone.

RATES: $98 to $200, single or double; includes continental breakfast and afternoon "Low Country tea." Inquire about off-season rates.

OPEN: Year-round.

FACILITIES AND ACTIVITIES: Patios and landscaped gardens, facilities for small meetings, parties, weddings. Located in historic district of Charleston, next to the Gaillard Auditorium. Nearby: restaurants, historic sites and tours, antiques shops.

Maison Du Pré, dating back to 1804, comprises five buildings—three restored single houses and two carriage houses—surrounding a brick courtyard full of flowers, fountains, and an old well. Most innkeepers like to say that each room of their inn is different. When you consider all the nooks and crannies and assorted shapes and sizes inevitable in a collection of five old buildings, you can see that at Maison Du Pré that boast would almost inevitably have to be true.

There's a morning room, an evening room, an upstairs drawing room fitted out with a grand piano, a space for meetings and formal dining, and, of course, the fifteen guest rooms variously furnished with period furniture, antiques, and Oriental rugs. The most memorable is undoubtedly the honeymoon suite, which has an old claw-footed bathtub (and a separate shower in case your love of history does-n't extend to bathing), and a fireplace. You get a chilled bottle of champagne when you rent this suite. The unusually nice courtyard and gardens unify all buildings and rooms and provide a pleasant common area in good weather.

Like so many of Charleston's old buildings, the Maison Du Pré would have been condemned had not the Mulhollands restored it. They've left their personal stamp throughout the buildings by decorating with Lucille's own oil paintings, watercolors, and pastels and her husband Bob's pen-and-ink drawings, as well as a collection of other works by Low Country artists. All the bedrooms are named after the French Impressionist painters.

The sense of Maison Du Pré as a family project seems even stronger to me since Hurricane Hugo devastated Charleston in September 1989. The Mulhollands, like many people in Charleston, fled to safety, waiting out the storm in Spartanburg, South Carolina. When they returned, they found that they couldn't get to their home on Sullivans Island but that Maison Du Pré remained relatively unharmed in the midst of all Charleston's destruction. They opened the inn for business as soon as the power was restored and moved temporarily with their two schnauzers into the little brick carriage house. They've been back in their own home for years now, but the special feeling of family shelter remains.

HOW TO GET THERE: The inn is between George Street and Laurens Street on East Bay.

Meeting Street Inn
Charleston, South Carolina 29401

INNKEEPER: Allen Johnson

ADDRESS/TELEPHONE: 173 Meeting Street; (843) 723–1882 or (800) 842–8022; fax (843) 577–0851

WEB SITE: www.aesir.com/meetingstreet

E-MAIL: meetingstreet@aesir.com

ROOMS: 56 rooms; all with private bath, television, telephone, piazza.

RATES: $89 to $225; includes continental breakfast, afternoon refreshments, turndown service.

OPEN: Year-round.

FACILITIES AND ACTIVITIES: Garden courtyard, oversized Jacuzzi. Located in historic district of Charleston. Nearby: Waterfront Park, museums, historic houses and buildings, restaurants, boutiques, antiques shops.

BUSINESS TRAVEL: Elegant boardroom can accommodate up to twelve.

*T*ypical of Charleston construction, one of the front doors of this B&B inn admitted us not into the interior of the pink three-story stucco structure, but into a lovely brick side courtyard overlooked by two glamorous piazzas (Charleston's grandiose term for verandas or galleries). From the courtyard an extra-wide door, reportedly constructed to accommodate hoop skirts, permitted us entry into the gracious lobby. (If you don't want to take the scenic route, another front door leads directly inside, but, hey, this is Charleston—why not get into a Charleston tradition?)

So perfectly does the 1870s edifice work as an inn, we would never have guessed that it has such a checkered past—serving variously as a saloon, restaurant, wholesale wine and beer dealership, brewing and ice company, club and restaurant, antiques shop, auto parts distributorship, dental equipment sales office, liquor store, and bicycle rentals storefront. The venerable building has been an inn only since 1981. We first saw it during a visit in 1983 and have kept up with its changes and progress nearly every time we visit Charleston. Since 1992 the inn has been under the stewardship of Frances (Franki) Limehouse, whose other inn restorations include the Indigo Inn and Ansonborough Inn, and the Jasmine House and Baker House bed-and-breakfasts.

Despite its history of commercial use, the building is in the style of a Charleston single house and provides distinctive lodging in fifty-six guest rooms that open onto the lush garden courtyard. Each lavishly decorated guest chamber features high ceilings and antique reproduction furnishings, including canopy beds and ornate four-poster rice beds (so called because the carving on the bed posts represents rice plants). Period reproduction wallpapers either compliment or match the bed coverings. Other furnishings and accessories are carefully chosen to create an Old Charleston ambience and a unique personality for each room. Some rooms boast a decorative fireplace and/or whirlpool bath; all make such concessions to the twentieth century as modern private bath, television, and telephone.

Each day begins with a continental breakfast of fresh fruit and juice, bagels, ham biscuits, Danishes, muffins, hot beverages, and a newspaper and ends with a chocolate on your pillow. In between you might want to unwind in the oversized courtyard hot tub, linger over complimentary afternoon refreshments of wine and hors d'oeuvres, or imbibe your favorite libation from the lobby bar. The friendly staff is always ready to help you with sightseeing suggestions or reservations.

Bustling Meeting Street, the heart of the historic district, and the ever-popular City Market are right at your doorstep, as are Charleston's renowned restaurants, boutiques, and antiques shops.

Middleton Inn 🏨
Charleston, South Carolina 29414

INNKEEPERS: Dayle Gray

ADDRESS/TELEPHONE: Ashley River Road; (843) 556-0500 or (800) 543-4774; fax: (843) 556- 0500

WEB SITE: www.middletoninn.com

E-MAIL: middletoninn@mindspring.com

ROOMS: 50 rooms, all with private bath, telephone, television.

RATES: $99 to $129 for standard rooms, $119 to $149 for superior rooms.

OPEN: Year-round.

FACILITIES AND ACTIVITIES: Two restaurants at the inn, one at the plantation; pool, tennis courts, croquet, rental bicycles and boats, gardens. Nearby: historic Charleston, plantations, gardens, beaches.

BUSINESS TRAVEL: Ideal for small meetings and retreats, small meeting rooms; dataport, copy, and fax service available.

"*W*hat were they thinking?" we both gasped in complete shock when we pulled out of the heavy woods into the clearing and saw the starkly ultramodern building that is the Middleton Inn. First of all, we expected just about everything in Charleston to be historic or at least *look* historic. Second, this inn is on the property of Middleton Place, a famous eighteenth-century plantation with world-renowned gardens—the oldest landscaped gardens in America.

Well, our reaction just goes to show how little *we* know. When it was completed in 1987, the design won the highest national honor of the American Institute of Architects. Concrete, walls of glass, and sharp angles distinguish the exterior. The interior and furnishings are also contemporary. If modern design is OK with you, read on; this inn has much to recommend it.

Located on a bluff above the Ashley River just 14 miles from Charleston, the inn offers a wealth of activities. You'll have free daylight access to the famous gardens, the stable yards where artisans often work, and the plantation restaurant and gift shop, and you can tour the museum house for a small fee. Recreational activities include a swimming pool, clay tennis courts, guided horseback rides, kayak tours, and nature hikes.

Middleton Place rose to prominence as a rice plantation in the 1700s. Flooded rice fields that border the river are maintained to attract migrating and resident waterfowl and other wetland inhabitants. Solitary tours or those taken with an experienced naturalist may be rewarded with sightings of otters, wood ducks, deer, egrets, herons, and, fall through spring, a pair of nesting bald eagles. You can explore miles of bicycle and nature trails. During the winter you can propel a flat-bottomed keowee (a kind of kayak) through rice fields and canals. Bicycles, kayaks, and keowees are available to rent.

Decorated with understatement, the interior of the inn displays sleek, clean lines and earth tones. Prodigious use of natural wood paneling provides warmth. Each guest room showcases cypress wall paneling, handcrafted furniture, and floor-to-ceiling windows. A definite plus—every room boasts a wood-burning fireplace. Large European-style bathrooms feature marble floors, oversized tile tubs, and lots of natural light coming through privacy-ensuring glass-block walls.

When it comes to meals, Middleton Inn offers breakfast in the dining room daily. For lunch, try the Middleton Place Restaurant, located in an old outbuilding on the grounds of the plantation. Try the Low Country specialties such as hoppin' John, ham biscuits, okra gumbo, she-crab soup, collard greens, and Hugenot torte. Dinner is available at the inn's cafe on Sunday and Monday or at the Middleton Place Restaurant the remaining evenings, when sophisticated entrees such as pan-fried quail, scallops, beef, or chicken dishes lead the menu. Reservations are recommended for dinner.

Neighbors of the Middleton Inn on the Ashley River Road are Magnolia Plantation and Gardens, Audubon Swamp Gardens, and the National Trust for Historic Preservation's Drayton Hall. Charleston is only minutes away.

HOW TO GET THERE: From I–26, exit at 199A and go through Summerville. Turn left onto SC 165, then left onto the Ashley River Road (SC 61 South). The inn is 5 miles ahead on the left—½ mile past the entrance to Middleton Place.

Planters Inn
Charleston, South Carolina 29401

INNKEEPER: Larry Spelts

ADDRESS/TELEPHONE: 112 North Market Street; (843) 722–2345 or
(800) 845–7082; fax (843) 577–2125

WEB SITE: www.plantersinn.com

E-MAIL: plantersinn@charleston.net

ROOMS: 57, plus 5 suites with separate sitting rooms; all with private
bath, television, and telephone. No-smoking rooms; the inn is handicapped accessible.

RATES: $150 to $275, single or double; $250 to $375, suites; includes
continental breakfast in room, afternoon tea in parlor.

OPEN: Year-round.

FACILITIES AND ACTIVITIES: Restaurant. Located in City Market.
Nearby: tours; walk to historic sites, shopping on King Street and in
the Shops at Charleston Place.

A Charleston native remembers the Old City Market this way.
"It was the kind of place where for less than $10 and in less
than half an hour, you could get a bowl of chili, a tattoo, and
a social disease."

The Market is still the center of action, especially for tourists, but it has
changed. In the past twenty years, the city has put money and muscle into
revitalizing neglected parts of downtown, including the corner of Market
and East Bay Streets, the very intersection where you now find Planters Inn.
Today the Market bulges with arts, crafts, interesting shops, street vendors,
carriage tours, and, of course, tourists.

In the 1840s, the building that is now Planters Inn housed the offices of
Hornik Company, a wholesale dry goods distributor. It became an inn in 1983.

Inside the inn you can't hear the commotion of the busy market. And the
single most distinctive feature about the guest rooms is their sheer size. Even
in fine older homes you don't often see bedrooms this large. These are furnished with Baker reproduction four-poster beds. Armoires hide the televi-

sion and drawers. Settees, chairs, and a coffee table create a separate sitting area in each room.

Prints of horses in the quiet, tan hallways carry the British-born planter's theme from the rooms to the front parlor, where tea is served in the afternoons. You'll notice a number of Audubon prints in this room and the foyer. The artist, who spent much of his time living and working in Charleston, was—and, indeed, still is—much revered in these parts.

The parlor has a pine plank floor muffled by two Oriental rugs and, over the fireplace, an Adams mantel. In the afternoon, the inlaid sideboard is filled with fresh flower arrangements and wine and cheese for guests. They sometimes sit at an antique secretary in a bright corner of this room to write postcards as they sip wine.

The Planters Cafe serves "New World Cuisine," featuring local seafood, gourmet meats, and imaginative uses of herbs and vegetables.

In January 1999 the inn became a member of Relais & Chateaux, which is renowned for wonderful standards of service. Over the years we've watched the property grow and improve from a simply good property to the really fine one it is today.

This is a quiet, well-run inn sheltering you right in the middle of an area that produces all the excitement you can stand—even without the chili, the tattoo, and the disease.

HOW TO GET THERE: From I-26, take the East Bay Street exit downtown, turn left on South Market Street, and take the next left on Church Street. Go left again onto North Market Street. (You must make this U-turn because North and South Market Streets are both one-way.) The inn will be on your right at the Meeting Street intersection. Parking is on a first-come, first-served basis in the lot to the left of the inn.

Two Meeting Street 💚
Charleston, South Carolina 29401

INNKEEPERS: The Spell Family: Pete, Jean, and Karen

ADDRESS/TELEPHONE: 2 Meeting Street; (843) 723-7322

ROOMS: 9; all with private bath, television.

RATES: $155 to $265, single or double; includes continental breakfast. Minimum two-day stay requested on weekends. No credit cards.

OPEN: Year-round.

FACILITIES AND ACTIVITIES: High tea each afternoon. Nearby: restaurants, walk to most historic sites in Charleston.

On a scale of one to ten for elegance, Two Meeting Street is at least a twelve. Incredible. It's a renovated 1892 Queen Anne mansion filled with family antiques, Oriental rugs, lamps, silver, and crystal. The Tiffany stained-glass windows and carved-oak paneling are simply breathtaking.

The guest rooms are in this B&B inn similarly luxurious, with four-poster and canopied beds and period furniture.

The family whose antiques fill the house is the Spell family. David Spell, who was innkeeper for many years, has sold the property to his brother and sister-in-law, Pete and Jean Spell. They and their daughter, Karen, are all involved in managing the inn, while David has moved to a new, smaller inn, the Belvedere.

During a time when many family inns are being gobbled up by corporations and losing the sense of human involvement that made them special, it is a joy to be able to tell you that all continues in the personal tradition in this inn, known for its museum-quality furnishings.

We don't want to give you the impression that the inn feels like a touch-me-not museum. It's livable. There is a small kitchen on each floor, for cooling wine and making coffee and snacks.

And staying at the inn is fun. From the piazzas, you can see everything that goes on in Battery Park. In the early evening, guests often gather on the

porch for sherry or a cocktail and conversation and to watch the action in the park: kids, couples, carriages. Weddings are the best fun. As one guest said, "We sit and gawk."

A favorite story around the inn is about the time a television crew caught a guest playing the banjo as he sat on the piazza. They interviewed and filmed him as though he were a typical Charlestonian passing the time on a warm evening, and they included the piece in a documentary about Charleston life. Never mind that he was actually from Ohio, visiting Charleston for the first time in his life.

Another guest, whose hobby is collecting vintage clothing, dressed in costumes of the period all during her stay.

The exterior of the inn, with its sweeping piazzas and gleaming white paint, is one of the most photographed and sketched and painted buildings in Charleston. You often see artists in Battery Park, facing the inn, deeply absorbed in trying to capture its splendor on paper or film. Not surprisingly, the inn has also been discovered by the television travel programs.

HOW TO GET THERE: From I–26 or U.S. 17, take the Meeting Street exit and stay on it until you come to the Battery, at the end of the street. The inn is at the corner of South Battery and Meeting.

Vendue Inn
Charleston, South Carolina 29401

INNKEEPER: Linda Edmison

ADDRESS/TELEPHONE: 19 Vendue Range; (843) 577-7970 or
(800) 845-7900; fax (843) 577-2913

WEB SITE: www.charleston.net/com/vendueinn

ROOMS: 45; all with private bath, television, and telephone, some
with whirlpool, some with fireplace; some with sitting area.

RATES: $130 to $165, double; $115 to $140, single; $190 to $225, junior
suites; $225 to $250, large suites; includes continental breakfast and
wine and cheese. Rates lowest between July 1 and September 14.

OPEN: Year-round.

FACILITIES AND ACTIVITIES: Dinner for guests and the public by
reservation Monday through Saturday, bar service with dinners in
dining room, cocktails overlooking courtyard and on roof. Nearby:
historic sites and tourist attractions of Charleston, antiques shops.

BUSINESS TRAVEL: Telephone in room, fax and copy machine available.
Concierge and meeting planner on site.

*Y*ears ago, on our first trip to Charleston we stayed at the Vendue,
and we've kept up with its growth and changes ever since. We
walked in about 5:00 P.M. to find guests sipping wine in the sunken
indoor courtyard while a piano player entertained from the main floor overlooking the courtyard and thought we'd gone to heaven. On Saturday
evenings, the music includes a violin and cello. Even with the music, though,
sometimes we'd rather enjoy a cocktail up on the roof garden, from where
you can see Patriot's Point and Fort Sumter and enjoy the coolest breeze
around. Off the porch is a refrigerator that you can use if you'd like to keep
something not offered by the inn.

The inn is in the French merchant district, created in what was once an
old warehouse. At various points throughout the inn, you can still see the old
beams and old pine floors burnished to a rich glow.

The guest rooms vary in size and style. They may have canopied or poster
beds, with Oriental rugs and eighteenth-century reproduction furniture.
Some suites have sitting rooms with fireplaces, whirlpool tubs in the bath-

rooms, and wet bars. In a new addition, junior suites are done in a French style consistent with the inn's location in the French Quarter of Charleston. These have marble baths with whirlpools, marble fireplaces, and luxurious sitting rooms. Many of the rooms have spectacular views of the harbor.

The inn's restaurant, called The Library at Vendue, is decorated in a bright, eclectic style, with lots of leather-bound books tucked into niches around the restaurant. The cuisine is continental with Southern overtones. Not surprisingly for Charleston, the seafood dishes are outstanding. Other specialties include lamb, beef, duck, and Italian entrees. (You can have cocktails and hors d'oeuvres on the rooftop before dinner if you like.)

For intimate dinners or private parties, you may request a separate dining room.

HOW TO GET THERE: From I–26, take Route 17 north at the Mt. Pleasant Junction. Get off and take a right onto East Bay Street for 2 miles (past the old market). Take a left on Vendue Range.

Victoria House Inn
Charleston, South Carolina 29401

INNKEEPERS: Rick Widman, owner; Beth Babcock manager

ADDRESS/TELEPHONE: 208 King Street; (843) 720-2944 or (800) 933-5464; fax (843) 720-2930

WEB SITE: www.charminginns.com

E-MAIL: vhi@charminginns.com

ROOMS: 14, plus 4 suites; all with private bath, television, and telephone; some with whirlpool. No-smoking rooms available. Limited wheelchair access.

RATES: $120 to $175, single; $140 to $195, double; $185 to $245, suite; includes continental breakfast and afternoon wine and sherry;

turndown service. Extra person $20; children under twelve years old free.

OPEN: Year-round.

FACILITIES AND ACTIVITIES: Located in the heart of Charleston. Nearby: walking distance to restaurants, antiques shops, historic sites.

*L*ocation, location, and location. The Victoria House Inn is on King Street, the Rodeo Drive of Charleston for more than 200 years. A friend, who wouldn't live anywhere else, put it this way, "When you wake up on King Street, you're already somewhere." The area has more antiques shops, boutiques, fine restaurants, and music clubs than you could do justice to in a month's time. Staying here provides just the right balance for folks who want to be in the thick of things but also need a little rest and relaxation.

You enter the lobby off this B&B inn off an alley on King Street. In keeping with the building's Romanesque style, popular in the 1880s, the lobby is decorated with antiques and period reproductions such as the late-Victoria sofa and the gold-painted Eastlake mirror. An interior designer complemented the furnishings with sheer lace panels and terracotta and gold tasselled silk damask valances for the floor-to-ceiling windows. The glossy white wainscoting is accentuated by dark green striped wallpaper above—the stripes make the 12-foot-high ceilings seem even higher.

You might fall in love with the suite that has a bay window with a table and armchairs overlooking King Street. From this spot, you can watch the morning get going while you're having your first cup of coffee and enjoying the morning paper. Thick mauve curtains frame these windows. A floral print of gold, mauve, green, and white adds a touch of romance to the tablecloth and bedskirt.

There's a nifty quirk in the inn, too. The handles on the water faucets in the baths turn backwards—by design—from the way American-made handles turn. They give the inn a European flair! Perhaps it was an effort to overcome the inn's inauspicious beginnings. After the earthquake of 1886, the building was leased and renovated as the city's YMCA, which had a gymnasium on the first floor. But don't think you can pass off turning faucet handles back and forth as a workout!

HOW TO GET THERE: The Victoria House is on King Street just south of the Market Street intersection.

Claussen's Inn at Five Points
Columbia, South Carolina 29205

INNKEEPER: Ron Jones

ADDRESS/TELEPHONE: 2003 Greene Street; (803) 765–0440 or (800) 622–3382; fax (803) 799–7924.

ROOMS: 21, plus 8 suites, some bilevel; all with private bath, telephone, clock radio, television, desk; some with kitchen facilities, ceiling fan, and/or private balcony; some wheelchair accessible.

RATES: $105 to $120 for rooms, $120 to $135 for suites; includes continental breakfast, sodas, fruit, and wine, turndown service; Extra person $15; children younger than twelve years old are free in the parents' room.

OPEN: Year-round.

FACILITIES AND ACTIVITIES: Courtyard lobby with skylights, fountain, hot tub. Nearby: University of South Carolina, museums, galleries, shops.

BUSINESS TRAVEL: Desk, telephone with dataport; meeting space can accommodate up to one hundred.

*A*s soon as we learned that this B&B inn was located in a building constructed in 1928 as Claussen's Bakery, we were intrigued and had to check it out. Once we did, we were sorry we couldn't stay longer. Situated on a tree-shaded street in the Five Points district conveniently near the campus of the University of South Carolina, the neighborhood in which the inn is located has a quiet residential feel with sidewalk cafes, small shops, and good restaurants only steps away.

Warm brown-toned bricks concealed the many delights in store once we got inside. A courtyard-like area with lush plantings, terra-cotta tile floors, a fountain, and groupings of indoor/outdoor furniture are all under the cover of a huge skylight, which gave us the impression of being outside. What a treat this must be on days when the weather is less than ideal. A continental breakfast of juice, hot beverages, and muffins and croissants is served here each morning, and a complimentary bar with sodas, wines, brandy, sherry, and fresh fruit is available all day. The courtyard makes an ideal place to relax with one of the inn's magazines or newspapers or to gather with friends or business associates for some quiet conversation. Many other original architectural features have been preserved throughout the building.

Spacious, well-appointed guest rooms are a giant step above cookie-cutter motel/hotel rooms, although they aren't as distinctive and individual as you might find in a great bed-and-breakfast. Traditional furnishings are period reproductions and overstuffed upholstered pieces. Many beds are romantic four-posters or iron and brass. Ample storage and closet space as well as generous amenities contribute to the modern creature comforts. We particularly liked the bilevel suites with a sitting room and bathroom on the first level and a loft bedroom and bath on the second level.

The inn's location near the University of South Carolina makes it an ideal place to stay for parents and those doing business with the college. Tourists to Columbia will find love trendy Five Points. We'd definitely stay here on a future trip to Columbia.

HOW TO GET THERE: Take I-126 into town, where it turns into U.S. 76. Follow U.S. 76 to Harden Street and turn right. Follow Harden to Greene Street and turn right. The inn is in the first block on your right.

Rosemary Hall
and Lookaway Hall 🦋
North Augusta, South Carolina 29841

INNKEEPER: Geneva Robinson

ADDRESS/TELEPHONE: 804 Carolina Avenue; (803) 278–6222 or (800) 531–5578; fax: (803) 278–4877

ROOMS: 23 rooms; all with private bath, robes, hair dryer, cable television, direct-dial telephone with dataport, clock radio; some with sitting room, porch, whirlpool; some wheelchair accessible; not suitable for children.

RATES: $89 to $195 single or double occupancy, includes breakfast, afternoon refreshments, evening hor d'oeuvres at the cocktail hour, turndown service; High Tea served once a month.

OPEN: Year-round

FACILITIES AND ACTIVITIES: Parlors, verandas, beautifully land-scaped grounds, courtyard, sunken garden, twenty-four-hour concierge. Nearby: historic district; across the river from Augusta, Georgia; museums, art galleries, golf courses.

BUSINESS TRAVEL: Telephone with dataport; meeting space for up to 125; fax and copy service available.

Two of the best places to stay in Augusta, Georgia, aren't in Georgia at all but across the river in North Augusta, South Carolina. The epitome of Old South elegance and Old World luxury, these two extraordinary sister Greek Revival mansions located across the street from each other were built at the turn of the century by wealthy brothers James and Walter Jackson high on a hill above the Savannah River where they could gaze across to Augusta, Georgia, without any other structures impeding their view. Today they operate as an exceptional four-diamond B&B inn in the European tradition, and, despite the intervention of a century, we sat in rockers on the majestic many-columned verandas and enjoyed a similar vista.

Inside the towering foyer in Rosemary Hall, we could just imagine a deter-mined Rhett Butler carrying a protesting Scarlett up the breathtaking grand staircase. Framed by two majestic fluted pillars at the bottom and two ornate converted gas lamps, a stained-glass window, and a portrait at the landing, the staircase then splits and continues its course to the second floor. Throughout the houses, extraordinary original curly-pine paneling, wood-work, light fixtures, door fixtures, and tile surrounding the fireplaces reveal the immense wealth these brothers enjoyed. Public parlors and dining rooms are elegantly furnished with original antiques, period reproductions, impressive artwork, and Oriental carpets.

Between the two mansions and a new addition built onto Lookaway Hall are twenty-three spacious guest chambers—eight at Rosemary, five at Lookaway, and ten in the addition. Rooms in the main houses benefit from high ceilings and tall windows. Carefully chosen antiques and reproductions as well as lavish fabrics give each room its own seductions that allow you to escape to another time. Every bed chamber has a private bath and all the modern conveniences; some boast a secluded sitting area, private veranda, and whirlpool tub to promote relaxation.

With the staff's commitment to traditional European service, guests are treated to a complimentary full breakfast, afternoon tea and cookies, and evening hors d'oeuvres. A more extensive, traditional English High Tea is offered once a month, and cocktails are available at a nominal charge.

Recapture the romance and charm of a bygone era by lounging in the elegant parlors or on the verandas or strolling through the well-manicured grounds.

HOW TO GET THERE: From I-20 west, as soon as you cross the Savannah River, take exit 1 and go 2⁶⁄₁₀ miles south on Martintown Road. Just before the third traffic light, turn right onto Carolina Avenue. Rosemary Hall, where you will check in, is ½ mile down the hill on the right.

Sea View Inn
Pawleys Island, South Carolina 29585

INNKEEPER: Page Oberlin

ADDRESS/TELEPHONE: Box 210; (843) 237-4253; fax (803) 237-7909

WEB SITE: www.virtualcity.com

ROOMS: 20; all with private half-bath, showers at ends of halls, some with air-conditioning.

RATES: $95 to $120, single; $70 to $98, per person, double occupancy; three meals a day. Weekly: $650 to $795, single; $460 to $630, per person, double occupancy; three meals a day. Minimum two-night stay. Priority given to stays of a week or longer. Inquire about spring watercolor weeks and fitness weeks. No credit cards.

OPEN: Last week of April through October.

FACILITIES AND ACTIVITIES: Beachfront and umbrellas, crab dock in salt marsh. Nearby: boating, fishing, naturalist's studies in the salt marsh and surrounding area.

*P*awleys Island is a small sea island, 4 miles long and one house wide, where the people are proud to say that nothing changes and nobody hurries. You won't find any commercial activity here, just what Page likes to call "barefoot freedom at its best."

Guest rooms are simple and comfortable. The living room has a brick fireplace, grass mats on the floor, and couches and chairs upholstered in pastel colors. There are good books everywhere.

Many watercolors, mostly beach and water scenes, hang on the walls. They are the work of artists who take the week-long watercolor workshop held at the inn early each spring. Some of the pictures are for sale.

The beach is the kind of soft white sand that seems to beg to be pictured on canvas or watercolor paper.

You can hear and see the ocean from practically every point in the inn, including the dining room. Meals served here emphasize Low Country foods such as gumbos and black-eyed peas with corn bread, and seafood in some form each day. The desserts range from a creamy chocolate pie to a light and fluffy peanut butter pie.

If you're here for the early spring wellness week, when people come to shake off winter lethargy with yoga, daily massage, and exercise, the meals feature vegetarian entrees, seafood, and whole grains. Then in the fall, there's a nature week featuring bird talks, shelling, beach walks, canoe trips, and other outdoor activities.

During the rest of the season, sunning, swimming, and shelling take up guests' time. Toward the end of the day, they sometimes gather on the porch facing the marsh, where they keep their spirits on the shelves and in the refrigerator for an afternoon cocktail. Even if no other people show up, you're not exactly alone on the porch. You can talk to the green parrot in the big white cage. We don't know his name. He wouldn't tell us.

HOW TO GET THERE: From Route 17 northbound, turn at the PAWLEYS ISLAND sign onto the connector road. In less than a mile you must turn left or right. Turn left. The inn will be about four telephone poles south of the chapel.

Liberty Hall Inn
Pendleton, South Carolina 29670

INNKEEPERS: Tom and Susan Jonas

ADDRESS/TELEPHONE: Liberty Hall; (864) 646-7500 or (800) 643-7911; fax (864) 646-7500

WEB SITE: www.bbonline.com/sc/liberty

E-MAIL: libertyhall@carol.net

ROOMS: 10; all with private bath, television, and telephone. No smoking in guest rooms.

RATES: $75 to $79 per room, includes continental-plus breakfast. Cot or additional person in room, $15.

OPEN: Year-round except for major holidays.

FACILITIES AND ACTIVITIES: Dining room open for dinner for guests and the public Monday through Saturday; reservations appreciated; full liquor service. Located in Historic Pendleton, which is on the National Register of Historic Places. Nearby: golf, Lake Hartwell, Clemson University, many historic sites, Pendleton Playhouse.

BUSINESS TRAVEL: Telephone, computer and modem setup, excellent workspace in room; fax available; conference facilities.

*S*ome innkeepers get tired and burn out. Some just keep getting more and more proficient. Tom and Susan Jonas are in that second category. Their inn, which was built around 1840, began life as a five-room summer home, became part of a dairy farm, then served as a boarding school. Operating as an inn since 1985, the rambling structure with the full-

length, wraparound verandas on both floors features spacious, high-ceilinged rooms, heart-pine floors, antiques, local arts and crafts, and charm in abundance.

The inn is comfortably furnished with period antiques and lots of Williamsburg blue, rose, and burgundy in the draperies, bed covers, and linens; the beds are still firm and comfortable. Sue has added to those basics lots of little personal items: books, family pictures, knickknacks, her mother's needlework, and quilts from her own collection. And, being a reader, Sue saw to it that every room has a good lamp on each side of the bed. The overall effect is that you can settle into a room as comfortably as if your own mother had fixed it up for your visit.

But let's talk about food, because the Jonases are such good cooks. The menu changes regularly, but you can expect something like crab cakes or a spectacular beef tenderloin filet marinated in a special sauce, plus chicken entrees and probably some other seafood choices. Tom and Sue say fresh ingredients and inspiration determine what they offer.

Tom continues to refine and expand his wine list while keeping the offerings in a price range that will not require you to take out a second mortgage to buy a bottle of wine. Tom says the list changes often because he is always looking for a good value.

HOW TO GET THERE: From I-85, take exit 19B toward Clemson and follow U.S. 76/28 almost to Pendleton where Business 28 turns to the right. The inn is on the right, shortly after you turn. From U.S. 123, take 76/28 to Pendleton and turn left onto Business 28. Go past the town square. The inn will be on your left.

Woodlands Resort and Inn 💚
Summerville, South Carolina 29483

INNKEEPER: Joe Whitmore

ADDRESS/TELEPHONE: 125 Parsons Road; (843) 875–2600 or
(800) 774–9999; fax (843) 875–2603

WEB SITE: www.woodlandsinn.com

E-MAIL: groupsales@woodlandsinn.com

ROOMS: 19, including 9 executive suites, 4 junior suites, and 6 superior rooms; all with private bath, two telephones, television with VCR,
alarm/radio, in-room safe, and robes; some with fireplace and/or
whirlpool bath and heated towel racks. Three rooms are accessible to
the disabled.

RATES: $295 for superior rooms, $325 for junior suites $350 for exec-
utive suites, all double or single occupancy; includes afternoon tea
upon request, turndown service, valet parking, and leisure activities;
meals and spa services extra. Woodlands' Honeymoon Package ($425)
includes accommodations in an executive suite, Iron Horse Cuvee
Champagne, rose petals on bed, chocolate-covered strawberries, and
candlelight picnic. Available Monday through Thursday, the Five Diamond Package includes a four-course dinner for two for $350 in a
junior suite or $400 in an executive suite. The Golf Package ($375 for
junior suite, $425 for executive suite) includes breakfast for two, a
round of golf per person on a nearby course, and a golf amenity. Special arrangements for limousines, flowers, spa services, and additional
dining can be arranged through concierge.

OPEN: Year-round.

FACILITIES AND ACTIVITIES: Breakfast, lunch, and dinner in dining
room; bar, conservatory, all-natural day spa; two English clay lighted
tennis courts, professional croquet lawn, seasonally heated outdoor
swimming pool with poolside food and beverage service; nature trails,
bicycles. Facilities for weddings and small conferences. Nearby: historic Summerville and Charleston, plantations, many golf courses,
ocean beaches, seasonal theater, antiques shopping, galleries.

BUSINESS TRAVEL: Located 20 miles north of Charleston; executive
conference center can serve 130 for dinner or 225 for a reception;

boardroom for eight; private dining room for twelve; fax; audiovisual equipment; food service.

*I*t was after dark, but we knew we were in for a treat from the moment we wended our way through the towering pines and up the circular driveway to the clearing dominated by an imposing, white-columned neoclassical mansion. Spotlights on the exterior and lights blazing from the windows cast a welcoming glow. Alighting at the foot of the stairs sweeping up to the expansive veranda and turning our car over to valet parking, our royal treatment, based on quintessential Southern hospitality, began.

Built in 1906 and a luxurious private home until 1993, Woodlands was renovated and expanded to become an exquisite inn in 1995. The original house provides space for a delightful formal parlor and sumptuous guest rooms. Wings added to both sides of the main house blend perfectly with the original structure and create room for suites, a restaurant, a lounge, and a conservatory. Elegantly appointed, without succumbing to the decorator look, public rooms and guest rooms reflect the Anglo-Indian and West Indian styles that so influenced the Low Country in past centuries. You feel that you are in a gracious home rather than a hotel.

You'll be thrilled with whichever lavish, spacious guest room or suite you're lucky enough to be assigned. Each has a distinct personality, but all are created with an eye to style and creature comforts with magnificent furnishings, four-poster or canopy king- or queen-size rice beds, upscale amenities, and all the modern conveniences. Some rooms boast sitting areas, gas-log fireplaces, whirlpool baths and separate showers, or heated towel racks. Fresh flowers—usually signature yellow roses—as well as a split of iced Perrier-Jouet champagne await you in each chamber, so kick off your shoes

and relax in a deep chair while you imbibe this extravagant welcome. So enticing are the guest rooms that you may never want to leave yours, but the resort offers many inducements to tempt you out to explore and enjoy.

Created with the purpose of providing a restorative retreat par excellence for the body, mind, and spirit, the resort tempts guests with a variety of activities in the relaxed gentility of the countryside. Sit in a rocker on the veranda with a good book, exercise vigorously on the tennis courts, play a leisurely round of croquet on the professional lawn, swim in the pool, play badminton or pitch horseshoes, or enjoy the forty-two acres of grounds by bicycling or strolling the nature trails. After exercise, perhaps you can pamper yourself with the services of the spa: facials, manicures, pedicures, herbal body wraps or sea salt glows, or massage therapy. Fresh fruit, honey, and cocoa butter are a few of the natural ingredients used to create the delightful treatments, which are performed by candlelight. If your afternoon schedule permits, request afternoon tea in the luxurious Winter Garden, a cheery conservatory furnished with wicker.

Dining is a gastronomic experience at Woodlands and should be savored. You dine while listening to the lilting strains emanating from the grand piano. Chef Ken Vedrinski's innovative, sophisticated, contemporary regional cuisine with an Asian influence has been recognized each year since 1997 with the AAA Five Diamond Award for Culinary Excellence—an award shared by only a few other restaurants in America; Woodlands is the only one so honored in South Carolina. The stunning circular formal dining room seats seventy-five and offers many windowside or tucked-away tables perfect for lovers. Those who want to watch Chef Vedrinski at work may request a seat at the chef's table in the kitchen. Menus change daily, and you may order your dinner in three to five fixed-price courses. Presentation and service are exemplary. You can accompany your feast with a selection from the award-winning wine list. When you return to your bed chamber, you'll find that nightly turndown service includes chocolates or cookies handmade by Woodlands' pastry chef. Sweet dreams are guaranteed.

All this, as well as impeccable service and attention to detail, has earned the one-of-a-kind resort the designation as one of only seventeen AAA Five Diamond Resorts and Restaurants in the country in 1997, 1998, and 1999. It is also a member of the prestigious world-renowned Relais & Chateaux collection of exquisite hotels—one of only four in the Southeast. The estate sanctuary at Woodlands is the perfect place for a honeymoon, anniversary, or other special occasion—or just because you deserve a special getaway.

HOW TO GET THERE: Take exit 199A off I–26 to Summerville (Highway 17A, Main Street). After you cross the railroad tracks, watch for the town square; turn right (north) onto Route 165 (West Richardson Avenue) and follow it to Parsons Road (on left). Turn left; Woodlands is on your left.

Summerville:
Flowertown in the Pines

During the eighteenth and early-nineteenth centuries, the wealthy of the Low Country around Charleston escaped from the oppressive summer heat and humidity and the threat of malaria by retreating 20 miles inland to the higher, drier, cooler, pine forests of the town of Dorchester, now Summerville. This haven was their own closely guarded secret until 1886, when the International Congress of Physicians, meeting in Paris, declared Summerville to have one of the two most healthful climates in the world—especially for those with respiratory problems. Once the secret was out, almost overnight the tiny village became a world-renowned summer and winter retreat for the international elite.

Thus began the Golden Age of Summerville and hotels and inns sprang up as well as grand mansions, which served as seasonal "cottages" for the wealthy. William Howard Taft and Theodore Roosevelt wintered there. Although the hotels and inns are long gone, many of the other architectural gems survive today, and there's no more delightful way to spend an afternoon than to drive up and down the tree-lined streets to admire the mansions and imagine the grandeur of the past. Downtown Summerville is a quaint village surrounding a manicured Town Square with charming gift shops and restaurants. During the springtime Flowertown Festival, more than 200,000 visitors descend on Summerville to admire the flamboyant azaleas and more restrained dogwoods, as well as to inspect the art being sold by local, regional, and national artists.

Select List of
Other South Carolina Inns

Holley Inns
235 Richland Avenue
Aiken, SC 29801
(803) 648-4265

Upscale old hotel/motel; 48 rooms; restaurant, bar, continental breakfast, afternoon tea.

Harbour View Inn
2 Vendue Range
Charleston, SC 29401
(843) 853-8439 or (888) 853-8439

Historic commercial building across from waterfront park; 52 rooms and suites; continental breakfasts, afternoon refreshments.

Rutledge Victorian Inn
114 Rutledge Avenue
Charleston, SC 29401
(843) 722-7551 or (888) 722-7553

1880s Italianate mansion; 10 rooms, 1 suite; 7 baths; some with fireplace; continental-plus breakfast.

Wentworth Mansion
149 Wentworth Street
Charleston, SC 29401
(843) 853-1886 or (888) INN-1886

1880s Second Empire town house—tallest in Charleston; 21 rooms and suites, some with fireplaces; evening wine tasting, restaurant.

A. Cypress Inn

16 Elm Street
Conway, SC 29528
(843) 248–8199 or (800) 575–5307

Located at the water's edge; 12 rooms; some with whirlpool bath and/or fireplace; full breakfast.

Daufuskie Island Club and Resort

1 Seabrook Drive
Daufuskie Island, SC
Mailing address:
P.O. Drawer 23285
Hilton Head Island, SC 29925
(843) 842–2000 or (800) 648–6778

Island accessible only by ferry; 52 rooms, 37 cottages; golf, tennis, pools, equestrian center, three dining facilities.

The Inn on the Square

104 Court Street
Greenwood, SC 29648
(864) 223–4488 or (800) 231–9109

Historic warehouse building converted to an inn; 48 rooms; restaurant, bar, pool; caters to business travelers.

Main Street Inn

2200 Main Street
Hilton Head, SC 29925
(803) 681–3001

Classical hotel built to resemble Old South Carolina inns, 33 rooms; pool, hot tub, spa; continental breakfast and afternoon tea; member of Small Luxury Hotels of the World.

Litchfield Plantation

Litchfield Plantation - River Road
Pawleys Island, SC 29585
(803) 237–9322 or (800) 869–1410

Eighteenth-century rice plantation on 600 acres; 1750 home, carriage house; 32 rooms and suites; restaurant, tennis, golf, pool, beach.

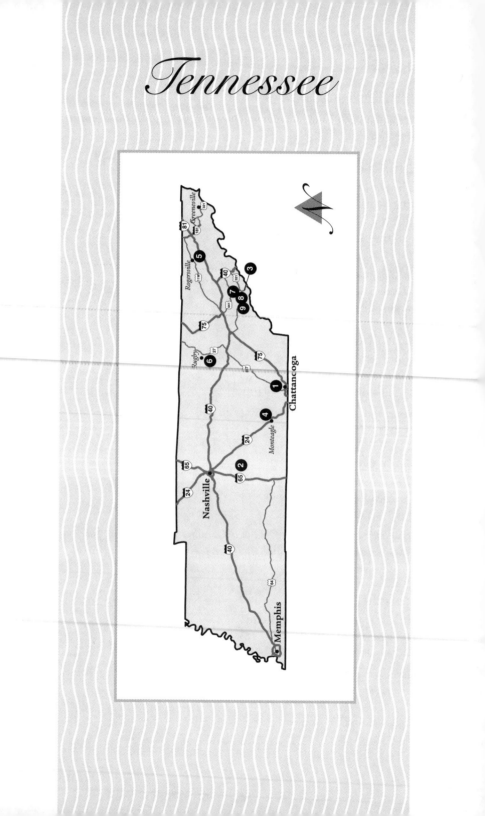

Tennessee

Tennessee

Numbers on map refer to towns numbered below.

* *A Top Pick Inn*

Adams Hilborne Inn
Chattanooga, Tennessee 37403

INNKEEPERS: Wendy and David Adams

ADDRESS/TELEPHONE: 801 Vine Street, (423) 265–5000 or
(888) IIN–JOY; fax (423) 265–5555

WEB SITE: www.innjoy.com

E-MAIL: innjoy@worldnet.att.net

ROOMS: 7, plus 3 suites; all with private bath, telephone, and cable
television; 1 room equipped for handicapped. No smoking inn.

RATES: $100 to $175, rooms; $150 to $250, suites; single or double;
includes continental breakfast. Two-night minimum on weekends.

OPEN: Year-round.

FACILITIES AND ACTIVITIES: Restaurant; gift shop; free, lighted,
off-street parking. Nearby: restaurants, University of Tennessee/
Chattanooga, The Challenger Learning Center, Eggleston Hospital.
Short drive to The Incline, a National Historic Site on Lookout
Mountain, Civil War battle sites, the Hunter Museum of Art, the
Tennessee Aquarium.

BUSINESS TRAVEL: Convenient to downtown and University of Ten-
nessee/Chattanooga. Meeting rooms, modem attachments, fax, good
work space in rooms.

*W*ell, Wendy and David did it again! Their Adams Edgeworth Inn
on the Monteagle Assembly Grounds in Monteagle is a notewor-
thy accomplishment that succeeded immediately. It never crossed
anyone's mind that having opened one inn Wendy and David would want
another, so their anouncement of the Adams Hilborne took us by surprise.

To the Adamses it makes perfect sense. They simply talk about having
"the Country House" and "the City House." Wendy says, "Chattanooga's
only forty-five minutes away."

So, okay, the City House—with that Adams touch. This is a European-
style hotel in an 1889 Victorian building that looks like a castle. The exterior
is built of native mountain stone that makes it look almost fortified against
the storm troopers. Wendy and David found photographs and written
descriptions of a twin house built in New Orleans that guided them in this

renovation. The great oak staircase has been buffed to a soft gleam. There are hand-carved coffered ceilings, arched doorways, and Tiffany glass windows, all looking as splendid as they must have when they were new. The hotel is in the Fort Wood Historic District, a Civil War site, where buildings in a variety of architectural styles sit sedately amid the trees, giving you some sense of having stepped into a very good neighborhood at the turn of the century.

The rooms inside Adams Hilborne Inn have 16-foot-high ceilings and hand-carved moldings. They are furnished with fine antiques and museum-quality art, then completed with such creature comforts as cotton sheets and an abundance of pillows. Some of the rooms have fireplaces adorned with their original mantels. The furnishings honor the history of the building; then, in the names of the rooms, Wendy and David honor the Adams ancestry with not just names but also with the appropriate coats of arms.

In the public areas some of the outstanding features are 11-foot-tall pocket doors, original fixtures, antique chairs that are actually comfortable (Wendy calls them "cushiony"), a splendid stone fireplace, and, to quote Wendy again, "tons of books" everywhere.

The inn's restaurant has gone through several changes over the past few years, but has now stabilized. Dinner is served Monday through Saturday evening in the gorgeous ballroom and on the porch. The cuisine is described as regional American and includes such dishes as baked-seared salmon steaks stuffed with crab meat, crab-filled corn fritters, stuffed lobster tail (our personal favorite), at least one pork dish each day, and a catch of the day.

HOW TO GET THERE: From I-24 take Highway 27 north. Take the Fourth Street exit (1-C) from Highway 27. Go through five traffic lights until you come to the University of Tennessee Round House Arena. Turn right in front of the building, following the street along the campus to a stop sign. Turn right onto Vine Street. The inn is at the corner of Vine and Palmetto.

Bluff View Inn ♥
Chattanooga, Tennessee 37377

INNKEEPERS: Jane Poston and Brian Johnson; Dr. and Mrs. Charles
A. Portera, owners

ADDRESS/TELEPHONE: 412 East Second Street; (423) 265-5033,
ext. 238 or (800) 725-8338; fax (423) 757-0120.

ROOMS: 16 rooms and suites; all with private bath, telephone with
dataport, television, clock radio; some with coffeemaker, sitting area,
canopy bed, balcony, fireplace, and/or whirlpool tub.

RATES: $100 to $185 for rooms; $225 to $250 for suites, double
occupancy, includes full breakfast.

OPEN: Year-round.

FACILITIES AND ACTIVITIES: Restaurants, porches, gardens. Nearby:
Hunter Museum of American Art, River Gallery, Houston Museum of
Decorative Arts, River Gallery Sculpture Garden.

BUSINESS TRAVEL: Renaissance Commons Conference Center offers
meeting and banquet facilities; telephone with dataport.

We've discovered a wonderful little secret in Chattanooga. Yes, the
city is the home of the famous Choo Choo, the Tennessee Aquarium, the historic Tennessee Valley Railroad, numerous important
Civil War sites, Rock City Gardens, and Ruby Falls. But high up on the bluffs
above the Tennessee River is an arts enclave—a delightful neighborhood of
museums, working artist studios, galleries, parks and gardens, restaurants
and cafes, and a great inn. Called the Bluff View Art District, the creative
haven is anchored by the Bluff View Inn.

Such elegant accommodations are offered in each of the three mansions
that together make up the inn, we don't know how you'd choose only one.
Although they are of different styles, each house features high ceilings, large
airy rooms, tall windows, beautiful hardwood floors, elegant fireplaces, and
magnificent furnishings. Check-in for guests is at the English Tudor–style
Maclellan House, so let's begin our tour there, where the dark-green front
door opens into a world of bygone elegance. Built in the late 1800s, the house
has been home to only two families. We first visited a couple of years ago,
when the house was decked out as a Decorator's Show House raising money
for charity. Although some of the decor was pretty far out, we knew it was
only temporary and recognized the fine architectural details that shine today
now that the froufrou has been removed. Many of the furnishings you'll see

Bluff View Art District

Fascinated by the artsy European/New Orleans–style ambience and wonderful old homes in the hilltop neighborhood surrounding the Hunter Museum of American Art, in 1991 Dr. and Mrs. Charles Portera began buying up and restoring homes and commercial buildings in what is now called the Bluff View Art District. They began small, with the building that now houses the River Gallery, but in just eight short years they've created or attracted the Bluff View Scenic Overlook, River Gallery Sculpture Garden, Rembrandt's Coffee House, Tony's Pasta Shop and Trattoria, the Back Inn Cafe, the Renaissance Commons Conference Center, and the Bluff View Inn. Despite all these attractions, the area is a small, quiet 2-block cul-de-sac perfect for walking. You can spend an hour, a day, or a weekend there.

A feast for the eye, the nose, and the palate, Bluff View serves up visual and culinary arts, history, architecture, and landscaping. You might see a chocolatier hand-dipping truffles in the chocolate kitchen window; you'll surely get tantalizing whiffs of fresh bread just out of the oven at the bakery. For lunch or dinner, sample upscale Italian fare and rich desserts at the Back Inn Cafe located in the rear of the Martin House. Located in the carriage house of the Bluff View Inn's Thompson House, Tony's Pasta Shop and Trattoria serves a classic Italian menu specializing in fresh house-made pastas, sauces, and rustic Italian breads. Rembrandt's Coffee House offers breakfast, lunch, and dinner as well as fine coffees, handmade chocolates, and freshly baked pastries. The very swanky Renaissance Commons Conference Center offers downtown's most elegant Sunday brunch.

Looking for art? The Hunter Museum of American Art houses an impressive collection of paintings, sculpture, and other art forms in a traditional building and a postmodern addition overlooking the river. You'll find an astounding array of glassware at the Annie Houston Museum of Decorative Arts. (The museum's array of pitchers is a hoot.) The River Gallery showcases the work of local and regional artisans, and their nearby River Gallery Sculpture Garden contains both permanent pieces of outdoor sculpture and traveling exhibitions.

Street fairs and musical performances keep the district hopping all year long. If for any reason you decide you don't want to spend every second of your visit on the bluffs, the historic neighborhood is conveniently connected to downtown and the North Shore on foot via Tennessee Riverwalk and the Walnut Street pedestrian bridge.

are one-of-a-kind heirlooms original to the house. Luxurious accommodations are found in six rooms and an exclusive penthouse suite. In the midst of all this Old World charm, however, you'll find all the modern comforts and conveniences: private bath, telephone, and cable television. Two rooms and the suite feature whirlpool tubs and Queen Anne–style handcrafted African mahogany vanities. Gardens surround the Maclellan House, and it offers spectacular views of the river and Maclellan Island. There's also a popular new bocce ball court and a pleasant terrace.

Directly across the street is the traditional Colonial Revival–style C. G. Martin House built in 1927. A full-length columned portico creates the quintessential Southern veranda. Double front doors lead into the main foyer, from which you can see the grand staircase and into the warmly paneled library. Upstairs, three spacious guest chambers are furnished with beautiful antiques complemented by carefully chosen traditional and contemporary art. Each of these rooms boasts a fireplace and whirlpool bath as well as cable television and a telephone. This house, too, offers splendid river views, and an addition in the rear houses the Back Inn Cafe, which offers indoor and outdoor dining.

Around on the next block is the 1908 Thompson House, a typical Victorian with a wraparound porch. It was the residence of an early mayor of Chattanooga. Today it offers four guest rooms and two apartment-sized suites. Ideal for a longer stay, the suites offer a living room, bedroom, spacious bath with a whirlpool tub, and a fully equipped kitchen with a breakfast area. What's special about these suites, however, is that they boast gas-log fireplaces in both the living room and the bedroom.

Regardless of where you lay your head, a luscious gourmet breakfast is served in the lovely Audubon Room at the Maclellan House. In good weather the French doors may be thrown open to the herb garden and views. Breakfast choices might include French toast made from inn-baked baguettes topped with strawberry-kiwi glaze or an Italian sausage and portabello mushroom omelette. If you're in a hurry, you could always grab a muffin and a cappuccino at Rembrandt's Coffee House.

HOW TO GET THERE: From I-24 take exit 1C, the Fourth Street exit. Go 7 blocks on Fourth Street and turn left onto High Street. Go 2 blocks to East Second Street and turn right. Check in at the Maclellan House on the left.

Peacock Hill Country Inn
College Grove, TN 37046

INNKEEPERS: Walter and Anita Ogilvie

ADDRESS/TELEPHONE: 6994 Giles Hill Road; (615) 368–7727 or (800) 327–6663; fax (615) 368–7933

WEB SITE: www.bbonline.com/tn/peacock

ROOMS: 7, plus 3 suites; all with king-size beds and private bath; some with whirlpool tub, all-around spray shower, and/or fireplace; some with handicapped access.

RATES: $125 to $145 for Farmhouse Rooms, $145 for McCall House Rooms, $165 for Log Cabin Suite, $185 Grainery Suite, $225 for McCall House Suites; all double or single occupancy; includes full breakfast, beverages, and snacks; $20 additional charge for extra people in room; $15 per night for horse stable, including feed. Fireside Suppers for $20 and box lunches for $10 with forty-eight hour advance notice. No smoking indoors.

OPEN: Year-round.

FACILITIES AND ACTIVITIES: Two parlors, dining room with hospitality bar, sunporch, books, games, television with VC, good selection of videos, fitness equipment, riding and walking trails, stalls for those who bring their own horse, gardens. Fireside dinners or boxed lunches can be arranged. Nearby: Country music and other attractions of Nashville and Williamson County; Civil War sites and antiques shops of Franklin, including the Carter House and Carnton Plantation, Murfreesboro, and Lynchburg-home of the Jack Daniels Old Time Distillery; Natchez Trace parkway; Henry Horton State Resort Park with eighteen hole golf course; Tennessee Walking Horse National Celebration in Shelbyville; Saturn Auto Plant in Spring Hill.

BUSINESS TRAVEL: Less than an hour's drive from Nashville; ideal for small corporate retreats.

*I*t was the end of a very long day in Nashville, and we were snaking our way along country roads through rolling countryside in the heart of Tennessee, on the lookout for our destination. The velvety darkness was pierced only by our headlights, the twinkling stars above, and lights from occasional houses. Suddenly, welcoming beams streaming from the windows and the spotlighted sign of a stylized peacock alerted us that our journey had come to an end. We turned gratefully into the driveway and up the hill. As we alighted from the car, we were greeted enthusiastically by Abby, an English Sheepdog, who made us feel right at home. She led us past floral borders to the full-length, rocker-filled front porch of the one-story 1850s farmhouse that serves as the focal point of the Peacock Hill Country Inn, where we were welcomed by owners Walter and Anita Ogilvie.

We didn't actually see any of the three dozen peacocks, ancestors of which have inhabited the property for generations and which give the B&B inn its name, but we were assured that they were there and could be seen swaggering around the 700-acre working cattle ranch and farm during the day. The original farmhouse comprised only three high-ceilinged rooms connected by the same exposed, hand-hewn, red cedar beam and flanked by two brick fireplaces. Today these handsomely restored and cheerily decorated rooms serve as the inn's entry and two comfortable, inviting parlors. The Ogilvies have added a large wing that houses their kitchen, other public rooms, and five guest rooms. The warm, cozy breakfast room features clapboard walls, a checkerboard floor, and a brick fireplace as well as a hospitality bar where guests can get coffee, soft drinks, and snacks anytime day or night. French doors from the breakfast room

lead onto an enclosed brick-floored sunporch with wicker furniture and ceiling fans. This is one of the most popular spots for relaxing at the inn.

Five spacious guest rooms in the Farmhouse, which are named for the Ogilvies' five grown children, vary in style and theme from country to Victorian to spring garden to Americana, but all sport all the modern amenities, including king-size beds, piped-in music controlled by bedside knobs, and wonderful bathrooms with whirlpool or claw-foot tubs and separate showers.

Although the exterior reveals little more than a rugged old farm building with a wagon port, the adjacent Grainery actually houses a handsome guest suite with a loft living room, a spacious Cottage Toile bedroom with a gas-log fireplace and whitewashed poster bed, and a European limestone bath with a double whirlpool and a separate shower. Other charming features include original poplar floors and painted beams as well as a fully furnished kitchenette. The old wagon port now serves as a private patio with bent-willow furniture. An old smokehouse has been converted to the Log Cabin Suite, where a fireplace dominates the exposed-log living room. There's an iron canopy bed in the loft bedroom, a claw-foot tub and separate shower in the bath, and private porch. Between the main house and the smokehouse, a trellised brick walkway and cottage garden provide another restful retreat.

Located in the hollow just a mile down the road is the McCall House, an antebellum farmhouse that has been completely restored and renovated to the house three luxerious suites with private entrances, two with private screened porches, and one with a private deck. All these suites contain a king-size bed; fireplace; large, luxury private bath with a European all-around spray shower and double or claw-foot tub; TV/VCR; microwave; and small refrigerator. Premier among the suites is the Grand Suite, which gives the illusion of an English manor house, with a spacious log living room and original fireplace built in the mid-nineteenth century. Guests at the McCall House may fix their own breakfast or walk or ride over to the Farmhouse for a morning repast that includes a hot dish accompanied by freshly squeezed juice, fruit, and hot homemade biscuits.

Bourbon Brownies

1 package brownie mix
1 ½ tablespoons almond extract
1 cup chopped peacans
2 cups sifted powdered sugar
⅓ cup bourbon
1 (12-ounce) package chocolate chips
1 stick butter, soft
1 tablespoon shortening

Mix brownie mix according to package directions.

Add nuts. Pour into jellyroll pan. Bake 350 degrees, 25 minutes.

Pour bourbon over hot brownies. Refrigerate.

Cream butter, extract and sugar. Spread on cold brownies.

Melt chocolate chips and shortening.

Spread over top. Let cool and cut into bars.

HOW TO GET THERE: From I-65, take exit 46 Columbia/Chapel Hill and go east on Highway 99 and go 3$\frac{9}{10}$ miles. Turn left on Highway 431 North and go 4$\frac{6}{10}$ miles to Flat Creek Road. Turn right and go 6$\frac{2}{10}$ miles to Giles Hill Road. Turn left and go $\frac{1}{2}$ mile to the inn. From I-24 take exit 78 (Franklin/Murfreesboro). Go west on Highway 96 for 12$\frac{8}{10}$ miles. Turn left onto Highway 31A South. Go 7$\frac{1}{2}$ miles to Arno-Allisona Road. Turn right and go 1$\frac{1}{2}$ miles to Giles Hill Road. Turn left and go 2$\frac{8}{10}$ miles to the inn.

Buckhorn Inn
Gatlinburg, Tennessee 37738

INNKEEPER: Rachael Young

ADDRESS/TELEPHONE: 2140 Tudor Mountain Road; (423) 436–4668; fax (423) 436–5009

WEB SITE: www.buckhorninn.com

E-MAIL: buckhorninn@msn.com

ROOMS: 6, plus 4 cottages, 2 guest houses; all with private bath, cottages and guest house with television, refrigerator or kitchenette, and fireplace.

RATES: $115 to $250, double; includes full breakfast.

OPEN: Year-round, except Christmas.

FACILITIES AND ACTIVITIES: Fixed-price, set-menu dinner for guests by reservation, $25 per person. Ice available. Spring-fed lake stocked with bream and bass. Located on thirty-five acres. Nearby: hiking, swimming, tennis, racquetball, basketball, skiing, golf, shopping, and tourist activities. Close to Gatlinburg and Great Smoky Mountains National Park.

BUSINESS TRAVEL: Small conference facilities.

The Buckhorn Inn sits atop a knoll where a log cabin once stood, overlooking the Smoky Mountains and, especially, Mt. LeConte. The inn was built in 1938 by Douglas Bebb, whose brother Hubert, an architect, designed it. The inn remained in the family for many years, but the estate of the late Mr. Bebb was sold to Robert, Rachael, and Lindsay Young in the mid-1970s.

Everything looks better than ever. And the short drive up the hill from the glitz of Gatlinburg bringing you to the simple white building well settled

into mature landscaping and woods still soothes your jangled nerves, as does the view of the highest peaks of the Smokies.

Inside, the living room and dining room are divided from each other in one big, long room by a large stone fireplace in the middle of the front wall. The chairs and love seats are cool and summery looking in ivy-patterned upholstery.

From here, doors open out onto a narrow porch separated from a well-manicured lawn by a low hedge. From the lawn, stone steps lead to a groomed trail that meanders about the grounds.

Once when we stopped here, we met an elderly woman who had first visited the inn when someone gave a trip here to her and her husband as an anniversary present. She has come back every year since, even though her husband has passed on. We also met a young couple entranced with the grand piano, the rockers, and the generous supply of books. They had come intending to follow a full-steam-ahead schedule of hiking, fishing, and fitness but had been lulled into rocking and reading instead.

The inn has always been known for its good food and that, too, is better than ever. Everything is home cooked daily, from breads to desserts. A professional chef on staff creates sophisticated menus. At breakfast, for instance, your choices, in addition to standards such as country ham and eggs, might include a strawberry or walnut waffle with bacon or Buckhorn's own version of müesli. At dinner they serve up four-course gourmet dinners with entrees ranging from marinated beef tenderloin to salmon Florentine en croute.

HOW TO GET THERE: Take U.S. 441 to Gatlinburg and turn onto U.S. 321 north at Gatlinburg Chamber of Commerce corner. Follow U.S. 321 north about 5 miles. Turn left at Buckhorn Road and go ¾ mile. Turn right at BUCKHORN INN sign. The inn is ¼ mile on the right.

Adams Edgeworth Inn
Monteagle, Tennessee 37356

INNKEEPERS: Wendy and David Adams

ADDRESS/TELEPHONE: Monteagle Assembly; (931) 924–4000 or (878) ELA–XINN; fax (931) 924–3236

WEB SITE: www.innjoy.com

E-MAIL: innjoy@worldnet.all.net

ROOMS: 13, plus 1 suite with kitchenette; all with private bath; some rooms with fireplace or wheelchair access. Smoking on verandas only.

RATES: $75 to $155, single and double; includes full breakfast. Two-night minimum on weekends.

OPEN: Year-round.

FACILITIES AND ACTIVITIES: Five-course candlelight dinner by reservation; gift shop; on grounds of Monteagle Assembly. Nearby: golf, tennis, Tennessee State Park, wilderness and developed hiking trails, Sewanee University of the South, Monteagle Wine Cellars.

Occasionally someone opens an inn that seems destined from the beginning to become a classic. Edgeworth is such an inn. The owners, David and Wendy Adams, put uncountable hours of study, thought, and travel into defining the kind of inn they wanted. Then they put at least that much into finding the right building in the right location. They wanted a good-sized inn, in a rural setting, elegant but not formal. They wanted a full-service inn, serving dinner as well as breakfast.

The three-story Victorian house, nearly one hundred years old, on the grounds of the Monteagle Assembly (sometimes called "the Chautauqua of the South"), is perfect because it was built as an inn. Outside, David and Wendy expanded established perennial gardens to enhance the sense of rural seclusion. It looks like everything has been growing here forever.

Inside, they refurbished and brightened the interior without hiding the wood floors or changing the inn's warm character. They brought a large, eclectic collection of museum-quality art, as well as antiques and interesting mementos they and their grown children have picked up in world travel. Also, they have some wonderful items from the years Wendy's father spent as a United States ambassador, including the gold-edged ambassadorial china upon which Wendy serves dinner. She has even found some of the antiques that were originally in the inn and returned them to their proper places.

Some of the guest rooms have been designed around quilts made by her mother and grandmother that Wendy uses as bedcovers. The library and guest rooms overflow with books. Classical music deepens the feeling of serenity in the sitting areas and floats out onto the shady porches.

If you prefer an active retreat to a sedentary one, the state park and wilderness areas offer more possibilities than you could explore in a lifetime. Because David has family with homes on the Assembly grounds, he knows the area intimately and takes pleasure in sharing. You can, he asserts, even find places to go skinny-dipping. The facilities of the Assembly offer more sedate versions of swimming and walking.

After your daytime exertions, you definitely should plan on a dinner at the inn. Wendy dims the lights in the formal dining room and you dine by candlelight, often to live piano or guitar music. Some of the offerings are chicken Florentine, fresh salmon, and angel-hair pasta with Wendy's secret sauce. Wendy's cuisine includes lots of fresh herbs, lightly cooked and sauced fresh vegetables, fine cheeses, and delicate desserts. Each dish looks as good as it tastes.

HOW TO GET THERE: From I–24 take exit 134 into Monteagle. In the center of the village you will see a steel archway with a MONTEAGLE ASSEMBLY sign. Turn through the arch. Once on the grounds, follow the green-and-white centennial celebration signs to the inn, $^2/_{10}$ mile from gate.

Hale Springs Inn
Rogersville, Tennessee 37857

INNKEEPERS: Capt. and Mrs. Carl Netherland-Brown; owners

ADDRESS/TELEPHONE: 110 West Main Street; (423) 272–5171

ROOMS: 9, including 3 two-bedroom suites; all with private bath and television; 8 with working fireplace.

RATES: $45 to $70, double; includes continental breakfast. Inquire about rates for single.

OPEN: Year-round.

FACILITIES AND ACTIVITIES: Lunch Monday through Friday, dinner Monday through Saturday, for guests and public; brown bagging wine permitted. Restored formal gardens and gazebo. Nearby: walking tour of Historic Rogersville, many historic sites in upper East Tennessee; Smoky Mountains, Cherokee Lake, swimming, tennis, golf.

Hale Springs Inn is just one-half block away from the courthouse. It was Election Day when we were there, and from the dining-room windows we could watch voters come and go while supporters of one candidate or another wandered around waving signs. It seemed right to be observing contemporary political activity from the inn where presidents Andrew Jackson, James K. Polk, and Andrew Johnson all stayed (not together, mind you). The inn was built in 1824, and skilled restoration has kept its historic interest alive without sacrificing comfort.

The rooms are all big and bright, with high ceilings, good plumbing, and cheerful decor. All the rooms but one have a working fireplace. We like the fact that when the rooms are not occupied, their doors are kept open so that you can see how each one is furnished. You can pick up a self-guided—tour brochure and go through the inn one floor at a time, noting such things as an authentic East Tennessee bed, wardrobe, and chest of drawers in the John McKinney Room and a mantel in the Andrew Johnson Room that was brought from Philadelphia by wagon in 1824.

The restaurant in the inn balances history and contemporary tastes equally well. The costumes of the service people, the decor, and the music all reflect the Colonial period. The menu features many chicken dishes as well as such specialties as grilled salmon, shrimp scampi, and fettucine. You dine by candlelight.

HOW TO GET THERE: Rogersville is on Highway 11W about 65 miles east of Knoxville and 30 miles west of Kingsport. Follow the main street into the center of town to the town square and the inn.

Newbury House at Historic Rugby

Rugby, Tennessee 37733

INNKEEPERS: Historic Rugby

ADDRESS/TELEPHONE: Highway 52 (mailing address: P.O. Box 8); (423) 628–2441; fax (423) 628–2266

WEB SITE: www.historicrugby.org

E-MAIL: hritnn@aol.com

ROOMS: 5, 2 cottages and 1 suite; 3 rooms with private bath; both cottages with private bath and 1 with wheelchair access.

RATES: $62 to $85, single or double; $10 for each additional person; includes full breakfast at Harrow Road Cafe. Breakfast not included in cottage rates. Children of any age are welcome in the cottages; children older than twelve in Newbury House. Two-night minimum stay required weekends in October.

OPEN: Year-round.

FACILITIES AND ACTIVITIES: Cafe open for breakfast and lunch daily; for dinner Friday and Saturday; closed Thanksgiving Day, December 24 and 25, January 1; brown bagging wine permitted. Tour of historic buildings, crafts commissary, bookshop, print shop, "gentlemen's" swimming hole (now for ladies, too). Nearby: Village is at Boundary A of the Big South Fork National River and Recreational Area; hiking, rafting, fishing, horseback riding, Blue Heron Coal Mine, Big South Fork Scenic Railway, Tennessee's oldest winery.

*F*or this place to make any sense to you, you need to know that once upon a time in England all the good jobs and positions of power went to the first sons in English families. Second sons didn't get much of anything. Thomas Hughes was a reformer who tried to change that by starting the Rugby colony in the wilderness of Tennessee as a cooperative, class-free agricultural community where second sons could create their own world and still enjoy British ways. Like most utopian attempts, it never quite worked, partly because no one prepared those younger sons for what they were getting into.

Staying here may not have been a lot of fun for those unprepared English sons, but it's great for a tourist today. Facilities are owned and operated by nonprofit Historic Rugby, a museum/preservation organization. The National Trust for Historic Preservation calls Rugby one of the most authentically preserved historic villages in America.

In addition to getting a glimpse into the life of another time, you get the pleasures of a nicely kept inn with good beds, some exposure to the local mountain culture, and access to wonderful crafts.

Authentic historic accommodations are offered in three village buildings. Dormers peek out of the deeply overhanging mansard roof of Newbury House. Built in 1880, it was

Rugby's first boardinghouse. Restored as a bed-and-breakfast inn, it features a large, inviting, book-filled parlor with a fireplace and offers three modest guest rooms with private baths and a two-bedroom suite with a shared bath. Lace curtains grace the windows, and antiques, some of them original to Rugby, give the cottage its charming Victorian character. Guests enjoy the veranda, sunporch, and the pond in the secret garden.

Pioneer Cottage was the first frame building constructed in Rugby, in 1879. It was originally called Asylum House because it was the place young men stayed when they arrived in the colony until they were able to build a house of their own. Founder Thomas Hughes stayed here himself on his first visit. Hand-planed poplar board-and-batten walls give this cottage a more rustic ambience than that of the inn. Rented to families or groups traveling together, the cottage's one downstairs bedroom and two upstairs guest chambers can accommodate up to ten people. Its large parlor, fully equipped kitchen, and screened-in porch make it ideal for family reunions and other small gatherings.

Newly constructed, but historically accurate, Percy Cottage is a picture-book Victorian Gothic with accommodations for three in a charming upstairs two-bedroom suite under the steeply slanting ceilings. Downstairs is a kitchenette/sitting room.

A stay in Newbury House includes hot beverages served in the parlor in the morning, a full breakfast at the Harrow Road Cafe (more about this in a moment), and hot beverages and cookies available all day. Breakfast and other refreshments are not included in stays at either of the cottages.

Although the inn is carefully attended by a resident hostess, this is not the kind of place where you lounge about chatting with the innkeeper. You'll find a letter on your bed telling you about the possibilities of the whole village. Your interaction is with the entire village and its staff, all of whom are educated to answer questions not only about Historic Rugby, but also about the surrounding area. Even breakfast is an interaction with the village, because it is served in the village cafe, where you have a choice of several Southern breakfasts such as buttermilk pancakes with sugar-cured ham or scambled eggs with biscuits and gravy. It's all spelled out for you on a Victorian menu card.

This Victorian theme is echoed in a new, successful Victorian book shop called the Board of Aid, where you can get books about Rugby's history as well as other Victorian-era literature.

The Rugby Commissary, now selling the work of about one hundred area craftspeople, has improved steadily in recent years and is considered by some visitors to be better than any other in the state. Much of the work is done by people who take the workshops Historic Rugby sponsors in weaving, quilting, making white-oak baskets, cornhusk crafts, and the like. Write for a full schedule. You may choose to plan your visit here to correspond with one of the workshops. The Commissary also purveys British Isles food products, old-time Watkins extracts and spices, and much more.

A tour of Historic Rugby begins at the Schoolhouse Visitor Centre, where richly detailed interpretive exhibits chronicle the town's century-plus of history. Notice that both the U.S. and British flags fly outside. Tours include the Bavarian-looking Thomas Hughes Free Public Library, which contains its original 7,000-volume collection of books as well as its original furnishings; Hughes's home, Kingston Lisle, which contains many of his personal furnishings; Christ Episcopal Church, a still active Carpenter Gothic church with original furnishings, organ, and stained-glass windows; and the Laurel Dale Cemetery, where early settlers, including Hughes's mother, are buried.

Lunch is served daily at the Harrow Road Cafe, newly constructed on the site of the original cafe of the same name. The cafe, which conforms to

The Haunting of Rugby

In the historic village of Rugby, current residents say that the past occasionally spills over into the present with otherworldly visits from spirits who cling tenaciously to their old homes. For example, if you stay overnight at Newbury House, you might be sharing your room with an unexpected guest. Some of the furniture in Newbury House was saved from the old Tabard Inn when it burned to the ground in the mid-1880s. The old hotel's manager had killed his wife there, and apparently these pieces of furniture carry some residue of their restless spirits. Guests have reported being awakened in the night to find the image of a man standing over their bed.

Mysterious goings-on keep life interesting at the privately owned Roslyn, which is often open for tours during the annual pilgrimage. In addition to hearing the tread of ghostly footsteps in the hall and seeing the vision of a woman in Victorian dress crying in the hall, it has been reported that the house frequently locked itself if the owner stepped outside. More than once there were the apparitions and sounds of a tally-ho carriage drawn by four horses racing up the driveway and disappearing into the woods where there is no road. Further investigation revealed that the place where the ghostly carriage disappeared was the location of the village's original High Street. Other people have been frightened out of their wits by the specter of a tall man in a black shroud or cloak hovering over the bed and surrounded by a luminous glow.

The town's impressive library was overseen by a fastidious, no-nonsense German named Mr. Bertz, who wouldn't let anyone borrow any of "his" books until they were properly cataloged. The staff often sense a presence in the library and wonder if he is checking to see that the collection is being properly taken care of. Even the founder's house, Kingston Lisle, has its own odd occurrences: The bed covers won't stay straight. Ask about these stories and others when you're on a tour. For the most fun with ghosts, arrange a visit close to Halloween for the Ghostly Gathering.

Rugby's historic architecture, serves meals in two wood-beamed dining rooms. The cuisine is a combination of Cumberland Plateau home cooking and British Isles specialties.

From Rugby, you can explore rugged gorges, trails down to the Clear Fork River, waterfalls, natural arches, and many other attractions.

HOW TO GET THERE: Rugby is on Route 52, between Elgin and Jamestown, Tennessee. From I–75, take State Highway 63 east, then go south on Highway 27 to Highway 52. Go west on 52 about 6 miles. From I–40, go north on Highway 27 or 127 to 52.

Blue Mountain Mist Country Inn 📱
Sevierville, Tennessee 37862

INNKEEPER: Sarah Ball

ADDRESS/TELEPHONE: 1811 Pullen Road; (123) 420–2335 or (800) 497–2335; fax (423) 428–1720

WEB SITE: www.bluemountainmist.com

E-MAIL: blumtnmist@aol.com

ROOMS: 11, plus 1 suite; all with private bath; 2 with Jacuzzi; 4 with wheelchair access; 5 two-person cottages with Jacuzzi and fireplace. No smoking inn.

RATES: $98 to $140, double; $10 less for single; includes full breakfast. Extra person in room, $15.

OPEN: Year-round.

FACILITIES AND ACTIVITIES: Television room, conference room, outdoor Jacuzzi, permanent horseshoe court, volleyball and badminton, walking trail. Nearby: restaurants; short drive to Pigeon Forge, Gatlinburg, and Great Smoky Mountains National Park; Smoky Mountains Craft Community.

BUSINESS TRAVEL: Conference rooms, dataports, full audiovisual, fax, copier; good for small conferences.

*B*lue Mountain Mist is a Victorian-style farmhouse built in 1987 specifically to be used as a small conference center and B&B inn. Consequently, the interior is bright, cheerful, and spacious, escaping the sense of gloom and spaces being forced into unnatural uses that sometimes afflicts old mansions converted to inns.

The inn is in the foothills, where you find lots of rolling farmland and can see in all directions. The Balls have built the inn on a portion of the farm belonging to Sarah's parents, and the family feeling pervades the operation. Quilts and furniture from Sarah's family are part of the inn's decor, and a picture of the inn drawn by Sarah's son, Jason, in 1987 when he was in kindergarten, hangs framed in a position of honor at the foot of the stairs near the front door. Sarah's mother stops in regularly with fresh flowers for the inn, and folks do a lot of visiting.

Visiting is encouraged by cozy upstairs and downstairs sitting areas, each with a fireplace, and by the rocking chairs on the big wraparound porch from which you have a great view of the surrounding countryside as well as the inn's nicely kept grounds.

The guest rooms, furnished with country antiques, are as airy and pleasing as the common areas of the inn. The Rainbow Falls Room, however, stands in a class by itself. It has a huge hot tub set up on a platform behind a stained-glass window in a rainbow falls design created by a local stained-glass artisan. The carpet, drapes, and bedding pick up deep greens and blue-greens from the stained glass, producing a stunning effect.

The Sugarlands Room, usually used as the bridal suite, catches your imagination, too. The hot tub in this room is on a platform in a windowed turret, with a view of the mountains. The room is decorated in white, mauve, and mint green.

The five cottages in the wooded area behind the inn are a new feature. Designed for two people, each cottage has a queen bed, fireplace, kitchenette, two-person Jacuzzi, porch with swing, and a grill and picnic table in the yard.

HOW TO GET THERE: From I–40, take exit 407 onto Highway 66 south, proceeding to Sevierville. Turn left onto Highway 411. At the fourth traffic light, turn right onto Lower Middle Creek Road. Go 3⁹/10 miles and turn left onto Jay Ell Road. The inn is 1½ miles on the left.

Richmont Inn 💟
Townsend, Tennessee 37882

INNKEEPERS: Susan and Jim Hind and Jim, Jr., and Hilda Hind

ADDRESS/TELEPHONE: 220 Winterberry Lane; (423) 448–6751; fax: (423) 448–6480

WEB SITE: www.thesmokies.com/richmont–inn/

E-MAIL: richmontinn@worldnet.att.net

ROOMS: 10 rooms; all with private bath, robes, piped-in music, coffeemaker, hair dryer, refrigerator; most with double-sized whirlpool tub, fireplace, and balcony; one room with wheelchair access.

RATES: $105 to $150 includes full breakfast, afternoon coffee and tea, and evening gourmet desserts.

OPEN: Year-round.

FACILITIES AND ACTIVITIES: Sitting room, dining area, potting shed, greenhouse, chapel. Nearby: Great Smoky Mountains National Park, hiking, biking, fishing, horseback riding, whitewater rafting, golf, swimming, historic tours, antiques and mountain crafts shopping.

BUSINESS TRAVEL: Meeting facilities for up to twenty-five.

*W*e remember driving through deep woods and pulling up in front of what appeared to be an unusual weathered gray barn—not just any barn, but one where the square upper story overhangs the smaller lower story. In fact, the B&B inn is modeled after the Appalachian cantilever barn, which is a hallmark of nearby Cades Cove and indigenous to the mountainous areas of eastern Tennessee and western North Carolina. With its ideal, secluded location facing Laurel Valley and towering Rich Mountain, for which it is named, we knew the inn would make a perfect getaway.

We were warmly greeted by Susan and Jim Hind, who explained the barn's style to us and told us that farmers often chose that design because the overhang provided shelter for animals in bad weather. Asked why they had chosen to model their bed-and-breakfast after these interesting structures, Jim said simply, "I've always loved barns."

Our first impression was that the interior would be as rustic as the exterior, but we were partially wrong. True, the main living/dining area does have mortar-chinked barn-wood walls, the 13-foot-high ceilings are open to the exposed beams, and broad planks and gray slates cover the floors. But the fireplace wall is formally paneled in white and is embellished with fine moldings and a graceful mantel. Antiques, traditional furnishings, comfortable overstuffed sofas and chairs, original sculpture, and French paintings create an upscale total look.

A huge corner window in the dining area permits an unparalleled panorama of the valley and mountains. The stunning view from here is ever-changing, depending on the time of day, the season of the year, and the weather. What a perfect place to enjoy a gourmet breakfast, which might be something scrumptious such as an egg-and-sausage casserole or apple-cinnamon pancakes with fresh fruit and maple syrup. When darkness settles, candles are lit and the room is transformed into a romantic scene for sinful desserts.

Considering that the exterior of the inn gives the impression that there are few windows, you might be surprised to find that each guest room actually has windows that permit an amazing amount of light as well as stunning views. Guest chambers are named for obscure and unselfish men and women who made major contributions to the history and culture of the Great Smoky Mountains: Horace Kephart, author; Robert Mize, dulcimer maker; William Bartram, botanist; Francis Asbury, circuit rider; Lucy Morgan, founder of the Penland School of Crafts; Bascom Lamar Lunsford, "Music Man of the Mountains"; Captain John Stuart, English soldier; and three great Native Americans—Nanye-hi (Nancy Ward), Cherokee chieftaness; Sequoyah, inventor of the Cherokee alphabet; and Attakullakulla, peace chief of the Cherokees. Each of these chambers is decorated in a manner that pays homage to its namesake. Old barn paneling, folk art, canopy beds, a stained-glass window, log walls, and Native American art set each room apart from every other. Each, however, brims with modern comforts and conveniences such as a private bath, a king- or queen-size bed, piped-in music, hair dryer, coffeemaker, and lounging robes. Most boast a wood-burning or gas-log fireplace, double-size spa tub, and private balcony. The Nancy Ward Room, which also features a wet bar and refrigerator, is large enough to double as a conference room or special events room.

The Hinds recognize that many visitors love the property and its surroundings so much that they'd prefer not to leave at all, so they can provide some other meal options at an additional fee. An adjacent building serves from spring through fall as a casual cafe where you can enjoy a fondue dinner. They will also provide dinner baskets so that you can enjoy a private "picnic" in your room This basket might be filled with such delicacies as cold chicken breast, smoked trout, salad, fruit, Brie and bread. They'll prepare similar picnics for you to take on hikes and other outings. Look for more additions and surprises in the future.

HOW TO GET THERE: As you enter Townsend at Mile Marker 26 from Maryville on U.S. 321 North, take the first right onto Old Tuckaleechee Road. Turn right on Laurel Valley, the next paved road, and go ⁸/₁₀ mile through the stone wall entrance. Go to the crest of the hill and turn left.

Blackberry Farm 💙
Walland, Tennessee 37886

INNKEEPERS: Brian Lee; Kreis and Sandy Beall, owners

ADDRESS/TELEPHONE: 1471 West Millers Cove; (423) 984–8166; fax (423) 983–5708

WEB SITE: www.blackberryhotel.com

E-MAIL: blackberry@relaischateau.fr. Or info@blackberryfarm.com

ROOMS: 23 estate rooms and 16 cottage suites; all with private bath, feather bed, television, VCR, and telephone; suites with whirlpool bath and fireplace. Wheelchair accessible.

RATES: $395 to $550 for rooms, $650 for cottage suites; includes all meals, afternoon tea, and recreational equipment and amenities; deduct $100 for single occupancy; deduct $100 during winter months; a two-night minimum is required for all stays; Friday and Saturday may not be split unless reserved one week prior to arrival and space is available; a three-night minimum is required for the month of October on weekends.

OPEN: Year-round.

FACILITIES AND ACTIVITIES: Restaurant, outdoor heated pool, tennis courts, stocked fishing ponds, putting green, hiking and nature trails, bicycles, fully equipped fitness room. Nearby: Great Smoky Mountains National Park, antiques and crafts shops.

BUSINESS TRAVEL: 25 minutes from Knoxville; facilities for small conferences: wood-paneled boardroom, three meeting rooms in Chestnut Cottage, conference equipment.

*A*fter traveling several miles of winding mountain highway, we turned off onto a country road and meandered through a valley, or cove, of neat-as-a-pin farmsteads before we came to the stately Virginia fence and gateway to Blackberry Farm. Our anticipation mounted as we drove up the heavily wooded hill to the stunning frame-and-stone country house perched at the top—the late afternoon sun glinting off its large walls of windows. We were welcomed at the front door of this inn as if we were long-lost relatives returning to a beautiful family home. Our luggage was whisked inside and our car spirited off and we were escorted to our room in the elegant Guest House next door, which blends so perfectly with the restored manor house that you'd swear they were built at the same time. Recently, Holly Glade Cottages of suites have been added, scattered throughout the grounds. In all the resort boasts forty-two luxurious accommodations, including those in the historic main house.

This sophisticated and gracious country inn is the centerpiece of an 1,100-acre estate bordering the Great Smoky Mountains National Park. A stylish ambience reminiscent of great English country houses is achieved in all the public rooms and guest chambers by the lavish use of English and American antiques, period reproductions, floral chintz fabrics, opulent window treatments, and carefully selected art. Sumptuous guest rooms are spacious, comfortable, and lavishly decorated, but the new, knock-your-socks-off Cottage

Suites are even larger and boast king-size feather bed, whirlpool bath, wood-burning fireplace, entertainment center, stocked refrigerator/pantry, and covered porch.

Our favorite activity is simply to pull up a pair of rocking chairs from the ones lined up across the stone patio so that we can gaze out at the vast expanses of forests and rolling lawns. We never get tired of the glorious panorama because it's always changing, depending on the season, weather, and time of day. More likely than not, early morning reveals a heavy mist draped over the peaks, educating you as to why Native Americans called the ridges the Smoky Mountains. Gradually the veils of mist lift, revealing not only the forests but also birds and wildlife. If you've forgotten binoculars, borrow a pair from the collection sitting on the windowsill. On the occasional inclement day or during the winter season, the public lounges are filled with books, magazines, and games to help you enjoy your time of utter relaxation by a blazing fireplace.

Although the attractions of the national park, as well as several small towns filled with antiques and crafts shops, may entice you off the property, you may opt not to leave it at all. A splendid restaurant specializing in creative Southern cuisine allows you to eat all your meals on the property. A pool, tennis courts, fishing ponds, putting green, shuffleboard, and bicycles attract more active guests, as do hiking along secluded mountain trails crossing burbling streams and canoeing. Orvis-certified instructors provide free fly-fishing demonstrations on Saturdays, and all fly rods and flies are provided. Try your hand in the stocked pond or in Hesse Creek, which flows out of the national park. Cooking schools are scheduled periodically throughout the year. Christmas at Blackberry Farm is a never-to-be-forgotten experience.

Associated with the prestigious Relais & Chateaux collection of gemlike hotels, Blackberry Farm, a place of unparalleled accommodations, extraordinary personal service, and exquisite culinary experiences, is guaranteed to lull you into the "Blackberry state of mind" and to create great memories.

HOW TO GET THERE: From I-75, exit onto U.S. 321 east to Walland; just past Walland watch for West Miller Cove Road, turn right and follow the signs to the inn.

Select List of
Other Tennessee Inns

Hachland Hill Inn

1601 Madison Street
Clarksville, TN 37043
(931) 647-4084

1790 house; 6 rooms, 3 cottages; some with fireplaces; restaurant.

Mountain Harbor Inn and Restaurant

1199 Highway 139
Dandridge, TN 37725
(423) 397-3345

Sprawling lakeshore inn on Douglas Lake; 4 rooms and 9 suites; patios and verandas, restaurant.

Whitestone Country Inn

1200 Paint Rock Road
Kingston, TN 37763
(423) 376-0113 or (888) 247-2464

Newly constructed traditional home; 12 rooms; all with fireplace and whirlpool tub; includes country breakfast; lunch and dinner served by reservation at additional charge; borders wildlife refuge, lake.

Maplehurst Inn

800 West Hill Avenue
Knoxville, TN 37902
(800) 451-1562

1918 town house and addition converted to an inn; 15 rooms; breakfast buffet.

The Hermitage Hotel

231 Sixth Avenue North
Nashville, TN 37219
(615) 244-3121 or (800) 251-1908

1910 grand beaux arts hotel; 112 suites; restaurant, two bars.

The Spence Manor
11 Music Square East
Nashville, TN 37203
(615) 259-4400

Favorite with recording professionals; executive level; 45 suites; restaurant, pool.

Union Station Hotel
1001 Broadway
Nashville, TN 37203
(615) 726-1001

1900 Romanesque-influenced railroad station; 111 rooms and 13 suites; two restaurants.

Parish Patch Farm and Inn
625 Cortner Road
Normandy, TN 37360
(931) 857-3017 or (800) 876-3017

Working cattle and grain farm on the Duck River; 15 rooms and suites, some with fireplaces; pool, restaurant in historic flour mill, bar.

Armour's Red Boiling Springs Hotel
321 East Main
Red Boiling Springs, TN 37150
(615) 699-2180

Historic 1924 hotel; 21 rooms; full breakfast.

The Thomas House
520 East Main
Red Boiling Springs, TN 37150
(615) 699-3006

Built in 1890; 30 rooms; full breakfast.

Little Greenbrier Lodge
3685 Lyon Springs Road
Sieverville, TN 37862
(423) 429-2500 or (800) 277-8100

Rustic 1939 mountain lodge; 10 rooms; breakfast.

Pin Oak Lodge

567 Pin Oak Lodge Lane
Wildersville, TN 38388
(901) 968-8176

Rustic lodge; 20 rooms, 18 cottages; some with fireplace or kitchen facilities; pool, tennis, restaurant, lake.

Indexes

Alphabetical Index to Inns

412   Indexes

Inns on the Ocean, Bay, Lake, or River

Inns for Business Travelers

(downtown location*, meeting/convention facilities,
and/or special guest room facilities)

Secluded Inns

Inns in Restored Historic Buildings

(* denotes historic home)

Inns with Provisions for the Disabled

Inns with Restaurants or Where Other Meals Can Be Served by Special Arrangement

indulge in some southern comfort